AT THE CROSSROADS OF MUSIC AND SOCIAL JUSTICE

ACTIVIST ENCOUNTERS IN FOLKLORE AND ETHNOMUSICOLOGY
David A. McDonald, editor

AT THE CROSSROADS OF MUSIC AND SOCIAL JUSTICE

EDITED BY BRENDA M. ROMERO,
SUSAN M. ASAI, DAVID A. MCDONALD,
ANDREW G. SNYDER, AND
KATELYN E. BEST

INDIANA UNIVERSITY PRESS

This book is a publication of

Indiana University Press
Office of Scholarly Publishing
Herman B Wells Library 350
1320 East 10th Street
Bloomington, Indiana 47405 USA

iupress.org

© 2022 by Indiana University Press

All rights reserved
No part of this book may be reproduced or utilized in any form or by any means, electronic or mechanical, including photocopying and recording, or by any information storage and retrieval system, without permission in writing from the publisher. The paper used in this publication meets the minimum requirements of the American National Standard for Information Sciences—Permanence of Paper for Printed Library Materials, ANSI Z39.48-1992.

Manufactured in the United States of America

First Printing 2022

Cataloging information is available from the Library of Congress.

ISBN 978-0-253-06476-9 (hardcover)
ISBN 978-0-253-06477-6 (paperback)
ISBN 978-0-253-06478-3 (e-book)

*In memory of
bell hooks (1952–2021)
and
David Rolfe Graeber (1961–2020)*

CONTENTS

Preface / Andrew G. Snyder and Katelyn E. Best   ix

Acknowledgments   xiii

Introduction: Pathways toward a Justice-Oriented Ethnomusicology / David A. McDonald   1

PART I: *Truth Telling and Listening Lovingly*

1. Diversity on Repeat: The Deceptive Cadence of Social Domination in Ethnomusicology / Kyra D. Gaunt   21
2. Social Justice and My Work as a Music Scholar, Teacher, and Artist / Steven Loza   40
3. Punk and Politics and Transforming Musical Academe / Brenda M. Romero   49
4. Going Forward with Vigilance: American Indian Music Is Always There / Charlotte W. Heth   68
5. Deliver Me from Danger, Èṣù-Elẹgbára! Musical Offerings in Social Justice / Paul Austerlitz   76

PART II: *Radical Inclusivity*

6. Ethnocentrism 2.0: Hearing-Centrism, Inclusivity, and Musical Expression in Deaf Culture / Katelyn E. Best   85
7. Pink Menno Hymn Sings: Queerness, Inclusivity, and the Mennonite Church / Katie J. Graber   105
8. Unsettling Euro-American Conceptions of Race in the Egyptian Independent Music Scene / Darci Sprengel   123

9. Reclaiming *Nanook of the North*, Tanya Tagaq's Sonic and Performative Counterpoints to Inuit Stereotypes / Ho Chak Law   *142*

10. "If I Could Go Back in Time": Rethinking Popular Culture, Social Justice, and the Compassionate Gaze in Palestine / David A. McDonald   *160*

PART III: *Coalition Building*

11. Promoting Social Justice through Irish Traditional Music: A New Model for Applied Research / Alexandria Carrico   *181*

12. The Sonic Politics of Interracial Coalitions / Susan M. Asai   *200*

13. "¡Vamos a Pelear en la Guerra!": Musical Manifestations of Coalition Building in the South Texas Chicano Movement / Erin E. Bauer   *217*

PART IV: *Direct Action*

14. "Music Is Liberation": The Brass Liberation Orchestra and Direct Action / Andrew G. Snyder   *239*

15. Ecological Frictions and Borderless Futures: Art and Activism on a Sailing Ship / Rebekah E. Moore   *259*

16. Raising the Imperative for Direct Action / Susan M. Asai   *277*

17. Circling Back on Direct Action: On Difference and Representation / Brenda M. Romero   *282*

List of Contributors   *291*

Index   *295*

PREFACE

ANDREW G. SNYDER AND KATELYN E. BEST

AT THE CROSSROADS OF MUSIC AND SOCIAL JUSTICE aims to promote a justice-oriented ethnomusicology, one that puts ethics at the forefront of the concerns of researchers, teachers, and practitioners of the world's diverse musical practices. The book seeks to amplify critical perspectives and methods that contribute to conscious engagement with social justice in all aspects of ethnomusicological life. Emerging from the Society for Ethnomusicology's (SEM) Crossroads Section for Difference and Representation, the book's varied chapters offer research at the crossroads of music and social justice, intersecting further with a diversity of social categories—including race, class, ethnicity, gender, sexuality, and disability—in ways that highlight the challenges facing marginalized communities and identities as well as those communities' creative responses. As such, the volume is designed to be a reading source for social justice-oriented curricula and to be an example of research with real-world impact.

The topics featured in *At the Crossroads of Music and Social Justice* portray the music making of myriad individuals, communities, and social movements as tools to transform oppressive social and political conditions, seeking to be inclusive and creative in approaches to research and writing. This book is divided into four sections that represent a sequence of political actions beginning with genuine listening to marginalized perspectives and leading ultimately to political transformation. Further explained in the introduction, these consist of "Truth Telling and Listening Lovingly," "Radical Inclusivity," "Coalition Building," and "Direct Action." The chapters within these sections represent a range of theoretical frameworks meant to interrogate the successes and limitations of music's efficacy in empowering marginalized communities.

This book emerged as the result of the Crossroads Section's inaugural prize for best papers on music and social justice at the 2018 SEM conference in Albuquerque, New Mexico, initiated by Brenda M. Romero and Susan M. Asai. The three prize winners—David A. McDonald, Katelyn E. Best, and Andrew G. Snyder—joined Romero and Asai as editors of this volume, which would feature chapters based on the other presentations submitted for the prizes. McDonald, who won top prize, was also asked to write the introduction, and it deftly provides a conceptual mapping for the organization and stakes of the book. Based on the collaborative work of the editors and authors, the book offers ethnographic chapters focusing on cases from around the world that show musicians and communities critically theorizing the ethical value and possibilities of their artistic work.

In addition to these more traditional ethnographies, the editors invited six established ethnomusicologists, mostly scholars of marginalized communities who have supported the Crossroads Section through leadership and advocacy, to reflect upon their concerns with the intersections of music and social justice throughout their careers. In these autoethnographies—texts connecting autobiographic documentation with larger cultural and political contexts—the scholars narrate their experiences as ethnomusicologists, illuminating challenges and barriers to their professional development, sense of worth, and participation in their home institutions as well as within the SEM body. The personal stories reveal structural racism and expose attitudes and organizational structures that must be reconfigured to establish greater equity and inclusion. These chapters function as a reminder that issues of social justice are not relegated to a space on the "outside," divorced from everyday life and experience. Rather, they are pervasive problems living within every space we inhabit that are often left unnoticed by those unaffected by them. If we fail to reflect critically on our own environments, we effectively Other our own sites of research, positioning them as objects of study, instead of cultural sites for critical engagement and action.

We hope that this mix of genre, format, length, and voice featured in this volume reflect the plurality of experiences and passions of the authors themselves as the volume aims to break down traditional barriers through its design and structure. Indeed, we conceive of these as the book's "diversity of tactics."

Some of the debates that are highlighted in these pages—including the precarious work of marginalized scholars, the racist legacies that continue to structure our field, and the efficacy of socially engaged research—speak specifically to the critical juncture of the field of ethnomusicology at a moment when the world confronts an acute series of crises. We expect that the volume will, therefore, prove particularly interesting to ethnomusicologists, the SEM community, those interested in music and social justice, and teachers of undergraduate courses on those topics. But the challenges ethnomusicology confronts can also be understood as case studies that illuminate much broader issues in the contemporary academy and the broader social and political world in which we live, and we hope that the book will appeal beyond music studies. Indeed, the current upheaval in the Society for Ethnomusicology in which this volume is born was well articulated by Dr. Danielle Brown at the height of the uprisings in the summer of 2020 in her essay titled "Open Letter on Racism in Music Studies, Especially Ethnomusicology and Music Education," which is frequently referenced in the book.

Following Dr. Brown's lead, we believe that, as ethnomusicologists, we should be working to remove the need for the clarifier "justice-oriented" ethnomusicology, as this ethical exigency should already be embedded within our practices, shape the currents of our thoughts, and guide the course of our actions in every aspect of ethnomusicological life. The fact that we need to raise awareness to issues of social justice, and to even classify a category as such, calls attention to the continuing existence of ostensibly apolitical approaches to research and writing that relegate justice-oriented action to specific sites, times, or spaces. The challenge is to reevaluate and reenvision what music in search of justice looks and sounds like and to probe the extent of musicians' roles as agents for political and social change. To this end, it is the sincere hope of all the editors that *At the Crossroads of Music and Social Justice* be a contribution to the ongoing development of justice-oriented curricula and scholarship.

ACKNOWLEDGMENTS

WE WOULD LIKE TO EXPRESS our appreciation to all contributors and participants who gave life to this anthology, sometimes merely by allowing some to be truly heard for the first time, even though we always knew "who" they were.

We thank those who paved the way and those who will forge new directions and an infinite number of new paths at the crossroads of music and social justice in the future.

And to the many friends and colleagues who have been pillars of social justice in their daily lives and in their professional institutions, we express our gratitude.

The Editors
January 1, 2022

AT THE CROSSROADS OF MUSIC AND SOCIAL JUSTICE

INTRODUCTION

Pathways toward a Justice-Oriented Ethnomusicology

DAVID A. MCDONALD

AT THE CROSSROADS

Ethnomusicology stands, once again, at a crossroads. For each generation there is a critical juncture, a point of decision, from which the discipline must be reimagined, redefined, and repurposed. This is ours. Danielle Brown's "An Open Letter on Racism in Music Studies" frames this juncture perfectly: "an organization, whose predominantly white members by and large research people of color, is and can be nothing other than a colonialist and imperialist enterprise." "No matter how hard we try to convince ourselves otherwise, until ethnomusicology as a field is dismantled or significantly restructured, so that epistemic violence against BIPOC (Black, Indigenous, and other People of Color) is not normalized, Black lives do not matter."[1]

While inspired by recent events, this crossroads is nothing new. Ethnomusicology is a field that emerged within, and continues to benefit from, colonial logics that presume (predominantly White) scholars uncritically entitled to understand, consume, and represent the musical lifeways and experiences of Indigenous, Black, colonized, and other historically marginalized peoples. Rooted in liberal modernist thought, early ethnomusicologists were guided by the myths of objectivity, positivism, and an ahistorical and autonomous view of the ethnographic encounter. Many of these early scholars felt a calling to save, preserve, or rescue Indigenous musics from erasure and, in the process, validate non-Western music as a legitimate scholarly pursuit. And while ethnomusicology was proudly imagined by its practitioners as a bulwark against colonialism, its knowledge, presented as dispassionate or objective, foreclosed any ability to critically question how hierarchies of power and privilege emerged under specific and strategic contexts (Gourlay 1978, 1982). Our duty to help masked our scholarly desire to extract, possess, and control.

As ethnomusicologists later adopted postmodern and postcolonial techniques, concerns over the politics of representation resulted in ever increasingly theoretical explorations of legibility, difference, and otherness. And while these moves were heralded as emancipatory, in revealing power/knowledge networks used to constitute the self through the production of the Other (Fanon 1952; Said 1978; Spivak 1988; Gilroy 1993), the retreat into theoretical hermeneutics enacted its own kind of erasure by domesticating and denying Indigenous epistemologies. In imagining ethnomusicology as a voice for the colonized, many scholars refused to recognize the epistemic violence their biased ventriloquism enacted on the (un)speaking subaltern (Spivak 1988; Tuck and Yang 2014a).

More common is the fallacious idea that ethnomusicological interest in the lifeways and experiences of others sufficiently enacts a kind of social justice by raising awareness. And yet attempts to know, understand, and appreciate others, under the ruse of diversity or multiculturalism, could be the discipline's most egregious act of epistemic violence. Though well intentioned, ethnomusicologists have too often conflated the struggles of their interlocutors with their own intellectual work in a move that valorizes researchers while silencing the researched. Such work masks the violence of the status quo, refusing to reflexively consider ethnomusicology's complicity in the production of colonial and imperial relations (Robinson 2020; Tuck and Yang 2012). Indeed, we remain at a crossroads. As Danielle Brown asserts, ethnomusicology remains a colonialist and imperialist enterprise. And it would be wise for all of us to sit with this realization, to reflect on the discomfort it elicits, and to begin the essential work of restructuring (or dismantling) the field.

Danielle Brown's recent provocation nonetheless follows from, and aligns with, a long tradition of scholars working to address issues of social justice, difference, and exclusion in ethnomusicology. The Crossroads Project, later renamed the Crossroads Section for Difference and Representation, founded by Kyra D. Gaunt in 2003, similarly took shape in response to these issues. Its mandate "to mitigate racism, sexism, and other forms of social domination through a radical politics of care; sharing our musical selves, participant-observations, and publications about musical communities and symbolic musicmaking," proposes a justice-oriented approach to ethnomusicology.[2] The Crossroads Section addresses not merely the methods of ethnomusicological research but also the structure of the discipline itself. For example, scholars participating in the Crossroads Section are committed to ending racism, social domination, and violence so as to gain equal rights and respect for people who identify as Black, Indigenous, women, and/or people of color.[3] They challenge heteronormativity, stand for marginalized sexual groups, and are allies on behalf of people with disabilities. As part of this work, the Crossroads Section has worked closely with the SEM board to sponsor roundtable discussions, research panels, and plenary sessions on issues of equity and inclusion. Most recently, this work has involved sharing strategies and pedagogical resources for addressing White supremacy, xenophobia, and heteronormativity in the ethnomusicology classroom.

Without question, the Crossroads Section has catalyzed a much-needed conversation on justice, resulting in a significant increase in justice-oriented papers, roundtable discussions, and plenary sessions. These conversations have subsequently provided institutional support for emerging activist methodologies, creating spaces for justice-oriented approaches to develop and circulate. More than simply rethinking how we practice ethnomusicology, these conversations have sought to address systemic forms of racism, colonialism, and supremacy that threaten the legitimacy of the discipline itself. It would seem that in this moment issues of social justice have assumed a prominent place in ethnomusicology. Perhaps at no other time has the discipline been so open to critical, activist, and justice-oriented approaches to musical thought and behavior.

Seizing on the moment, Crossroads Section cochair (2015–19) Brenda M. Romero proposed assembling this anthology. Together with cochair Susan M. Asai, she aspired to build on and extend current conversations on social justice by amplifying emerging research, supporting early career scholars, and listening to senior scholars who have fought systemic biases throughout their careers. The chapters in this anthology, therefore, represent a cross section of developing research, short autobiographical reflections, and longer position statements focused on advancing social justice approaches. Each of the chapters are thus presented as quick, useful, thought-provoking case studies that push the boundaries of the discipline and invite further conversation.

Likewise, the chapters that compose this anthology collectively gesture toward a justice-oriented sensibility that reflects and amplifies Crossroads Section values: a radical politics of care, participatory listening, and sharing lifeways and experiences through music making. While the topic of social justice may be emerging as a universally acknowledged concern, for it to move beyond a mere passing phase requires critical self-reflection and direct action. One of the objectives of this anthology is to undertake some of this foundational work by exploring specific theoretical, methodological, and thematic concerns in ethnomusicological praxis. This approach takes seriously calls to transform the discipline: first, by recognizing ethnomusicology's colonial and imperial moorings (extraction, consumption, representation, and privilege) and, second, by advancing a justice-oriented restructuring that listens with, rather than speaks for, colonized, excluded, and other historically marginalized peoples.

Situated at a crossroads, the chapters in this anthology collectively gesture toward a new path, one that seeks to identify and eliminate injustice in both its discursive foundations and embodied manifestations. In their accumulation, these chapters argue that addressing injustice requires engaging with the political dynamics of our work, locating ourselves within intersectional fields of position and privilege, and fully coming to terms with (and refusing) the colonial legacies of the ethnographic encounter. Acknowledging the political consequences of bearing witness to the lives of others is a first step (McDonald 2021). Critical exploration of our positionality as scholars and the philosophical assumptions that govern representation is equally essential. And mobilizing our methods toward refusing colonial legacies is crucial (Simpson 2007).

While the authors presented in this anthology take many different roads, each attempts to "listen otherwise" and to redirect their work toward justice-oriented destinations (Robinson 2020, 11). In surveying the diverse array of case studies and testimonials several important themes emerge. For example, each of the authors presented here propose new ways in which ethnomusicologists might explore and dismantle the underlying premises of colonial knowledge production. They collectively demonstrate the difference between interventions that serve to replicate relations of power and those that might lead to dismantling those same relations. And they collectively suggest (and in some ways enact) a new justice-oriented ethnomusicology that embodies the Crossroads Section commitment to diversity, equity, and inclusion.

What I describe here as a justice-oriented ethnomusicology might be productively imagined as the result of four interrelated points of intervention: truth telling, radical inclusivity, coalition building, and direct action. Nested, overlapping, and at times sequential, these four points of intervention provide an orienting framework for this volume while marking specific entry points for discussion and reflection. I envision these four points of intervention to be the foundation of a justice-oriented ethnomusicology. And in the following sections I explain how they each contribute to these goals.

TRUTH TELLING AND LISTENING LOVINGLY

Kyra D. Gaunt writes in her contribution to this anthology, "One cannot effectively address the situation if one does not fully become aware of the wounds of long-term oppression" (22). She continues: "If we fail to unearth our personal stories detailing the harms of marginalization, we may miss the opportunities before us—to offer repair and listen lovingly to those affected by past faults and fissures. In other words, we have an opportunity to emotionally and compassionately, rather than academically or logically, *sense* our way through the social change. We must fully recognize who we keep leaving behind to drown in despair and how" (23).

In these inspiring words, Gaunt reminds us that "to go forward as scholars in SEM from 2020 on, we must first go back and listen with courage, curiosity, and compassion" to the trouble and trauma of our field. "Listening lovingly to those affected by faults and fissures" is an appropriate first step in laying the foundation of a justice-oriented ethnomusicology. bell hooks similarly argues that there can be no social justice without love and no love without justice. "The heart of justice is truth telling," she writes, "seeing ourselves and the world the way it is, rather than the way we want it to be" (2000, 33). And Paulo Freire speaks of love as a vital force in the pursuit of social justice. "In the absence of a profound love for the world and for people.... No matter where the oppressed are found, the act of love is commitment to their cause—the cause of liberation. And this commitment, because it is loving, is dialogical" (1970, 89). Should we decide to listen, Gaunt, hooks, and Freire have eloquently charted us a path toward a new ethnomusicology. It begins with truth telling and listening lovingly to difficult uncomfortable truths for which there are no easy solutions. It requires that we see the world as it is, seeking out the oppressed especially among our ranks. And it demands we commit ourselves to the cause of their liberation.

It is with this inspiration that Professors Romero and Asai solicited autoethnographic reflections by ethnomusicologists whose experiences as scholars, performers, teachers, and mentors foretell an often-neglected history of the field. While by no means representative or comprehensive, these autoethnographic reflections are included to provoke further conversation about our discipline and ourselves. This is part of a larger commitment to "listen lovingly," to better know ourselves, and to enact a larger commitment to recognize and support each other. What emerges in these essays is a fascinating and long overdue retelling of ethnomusicological history, one that reveals a more textured narrative of trouble, trauma, and triumph. In listening to these experiences, we begin to recognize who we keep leaving behind. And with each telling, we move purposefully toward repair and reconciliation.

Throughout these essays there is an overarching theme, an acknowledgment of what might be called "the promise" of ethnomusicology. Perhaps we have all had this experience: a moment in our lives when ethnomusicology promised a new way of thinking about musical thought and behavior. Steve Loza was inspired by ethnomusicology to put performance and scholarly work in the service of larger social justice initiatives. Brenda M. Romero looked to ethnomusicology for support in her passions for research, performance, and composition. Susan M. Asai found in ethnomusicology a means to explore and amplify musical and political coalitions. Charlotte Heth has used ethnomusicology to bring attention to the many injustices ethnomusicologists committed against Native Americans. And Paul Austerlitz was lured to the field by its "revolutionary potential," as a progressive force for human rights and cross-cultural engagement (77).

The promise of ethnomusicology is indeed powerful. We are often drawn to the field with promises of political transformation, cross-cultural engagement, or supportive spaces within which to explore historically excluded or marginalized music and musicians. But for whom are the promises of ethnomusicology fully realized? In each of these essays we are confronted with the reality many BIPOC ethnomusicologists face when the promise of ethnomusicology is too often met with cruel institutional racism, compassionate colonialism (multiculturalism, diversity initiatives), and unchecked White privilege. As ethnomusicologists we must honestly ask ourselves whether we are following through on the promises of our discipline. Steve Loza writes: "In my ethnographic and musical studies of Latinx and African American artists, there is no way to evade the dynamic experiences of racism and sociocultural marginality they have lived.... In studying Mexican and Cuban musical cultures, it struck me how many rich traditions—folk, popular, and chamber/symphonic and their contexts—are simply not included in scholastic surveys of music used in teaching music theory and history. Frankly, this is shameful, ethnocentric, and as much an affront to social justice as the segregated practices of Jim Crow in the South and former president Donald Trump's Mexico-US wall" (44).

Loza continues, "I have consistently reacted to [SEM's] Eurocentric intellectual and cultural frameworks. The overwhelming bias in favor of cultural theories formed outside native contexts and the lack of diverse racial and ethnic voices has frustrated me as a member" (46). In her open letter, Danielle Brown shares how the denial of people of color to "tell and interpret their own stories" led her to resign from a tenure-track position "because of [her] dissatisfaction with academia in general, and ethnomusicology in particular."[4] Brenda M. Romero recalls her many frustrations working to decolonize the music curriculum. Rebekah Moore grapples with "the extractivism of ethnomusicology's past and present, wherein the cultures of Black, Brown, and Indigenous people are so often mined like nonrenewables for settler-scholar's professional gain" (272). And Kyra D. Gaunt brings to light "moments of oppression and social domination" she experienced: "moments that epistemically muzzled marginalized voices limiting our agency within SEM, as well as in our respective workplaces where epistemic violence has also been on repeat" (35). This is us. It's time we own it.

And yet in listening lovingly to these authors, we learn that the promise of ethnomusicology is cause for neither celebration nor shameful retreat. For in each of these essays, we bear witness to ever-more imaginative ways to pursue social justice from within academia's historically exclusionary spaces. As a scholar and performer Steve Loza created essential inroads for Latinx music and musicians at UCLA and in the local community. This work supports "social justice issues as a way to counter the status quo and disrupt the lip service on diversity that persisted in the university system" (42). Susan M. Asai used her academic position to facilitate intercoalitional collaboration among Asian American and African American composers. Shared musical affinity among artists, she writes, "speak to the potential for interracial political coalitions to foster a future that reaches for equality and human dignity for all" (213). Brenda M. Romero has devoted much of her career to institutional transformation, deploying a synergistic research paradigm as a means of amplifying collaboration in SEM and elsewhere and working to remove obstacles for students of color. Kyra D. Gaunt's ongoing work in the Crossroads Section has opened spaces for BIPOC scholars to tell and interpret their own stories, to insist that their work be recognized, and to demand that their authority be acknowledged.[5] This is work that fulfills the promise of ethnomusicology, and it should be recognized and celebrated as such. This is who we need to be.

In his experiences working with Afro Dominican, African American, and Haitian musics, Paul Austerlitz reveals the work every ethnomusicologist must undertake: critically interrogating our investment in White privilege and White supremacy. With humility he asks: "Where do I, as a white man, fit into the world of African-based spirituality? Unlike conventional academic work aiming for unbiased reportage, and unlike 'world music' projects intended solely for personal expression, my involvement with Afro-Dominican, African American, and Haitian cultures is motivated by mystical needs, creative needs, and activism. My hope is that my musical offerings will contribute, in some small way, to the ongoing struggle for social justice from which these musical traditions were born" (79–80).

Austerlitz reminds us of the importance of critical self-reflection at each and every stage of our work. It is simply not enough to listen lovingly to the voices of our friends and colleagues. We must identify and examine unmarked forms of listening privilege in our own lives, and pursue what Dylan Robinson calls a "critical listening positionality" (2020, 10). This involves a "self-reflexive questioning of how race, class, gender, sexuality, ability, and cultural background intersect and influence the way we are able to hear sound, music, and the world around us" (ibid.). As a cisgendered abled White male raised ignorantly on the unceded lands of the Apache, Cheyenne, and Ute peoples, I find these lessons both important and humbling. For no amount of public support for Indigenous rights, Palestinian or otherwise, absolves me of the many benefits of White privilege and White supremacy. Fully accountable to, and questioning of, my positionality, ethnomusicologists like myself must be willing to interrogate our unrecognized complicity in the systemic violence of the field. Or as Stephan Pennington writes, we must be willing to "do the very hard work of undoing white supremacy [from] within—and not avoiding that work through good deeds or wallowing in self-indulgent white guilt. Destroying the university, renaming the discipline, doing ethnography, giving up ethnography, none of this matters if you don't do the consciousness raising within oneself. Confronting the mirror."[6]

While there is great variation in how truth commissions are designed, their missions are largely the same in that they create spaces where past wrongs can be disclosed, examined, and confronted. Participatory listening practices such as these can be extraordinary tools for healing the wounds of systemic oppression: when they include all parties, when they occur at a systemic level, and when they directly address and repair the material and professional losses inflicted. Most important, truth commissions are deployed at a point of political transition (a crossroads). They are used to break with a past record of abuse, to promote reconciliation, and to obtain political legitimacy (Hayner 1994, 604). In these autoethnographic essays, we begin the process of looking for those we have left behind, giving space for listening lovingly, and committing to the very hard work of undoing White supremacy from within. But most important, we seek to rebuild the legitimacy of ethnomusicology as a worthwhile endeavor.

RADICAL INCLUSIVITY

Standing at a crossroads, the authors in this anthology clearly demonstrate that there are many routes toward a justice-oriented ethnomusicology. One of the strengths of this anthology is its great diversity in theoretical orientation, thematic content, and methodological approach. Indeed, this is one of the few volumes for which a standard area studies paradigm proves inappropriate.

Rather, each of the research chapters presented here might best be grouped by specific types of interventions. For some, this involves critically documenting the activism of individual artists or groups (Bauer, Law, McDonald, Moore, Snyder). For others, this involves calling attention to musical communities historically neglected or excluded in ethnomusicological praxis (Best, Carrico, Graber). And for yet others, this involves developing novel justice-oriented research methodologies (Best, Carrico, Moore, Sprengel). These authors collectively demonstrate a diverse range of theoretical, practical, and methodological pathways through which we might restructure the field. They remind us that while there is not one single road we must take, the journey must begin.

In their accumulation the authors presented in this anthology argue that we must: bring attention to mechanisms of knowledge limitation, contest appropriation, and publicly renounce ethnographic knowledge that refuses or limits Indigenous epistemologies. For each of these authors, ethnomusicology may be deployed as a tool to make audible processes of systemic violence, and through ethnographic engagement pursue radical inclusivity in identifying and confronting forms of injustice. This approach to inclusivity, as Dylan Robinson explains, "is not a call for everyone to be included at all times and all places, but instead a call for openness toward including those who are not granted legitimacy or status within the systems of work we participate in" (2020, 238).

Katelyn E. Best makes such a call, arguing for the inclusion of Deaf musicians and audiences in contemporary ethnomusicological praxis. In combatting hearing-centrism, Best argues that: "It is necessary to include alternative narratives of musicking, those that have been ideologically excluded from an assortment of narratives designated as 'the norm,' and incorporate them as an essential and fundamental component to a comprehensive study, knowledge, and understanding of music. Music education, when covertly rooted within a Western system, denies the diversity of practices, manifestations, and constructions of music existing outside of its framework and, consequently, reproduces institutionalized notions of music that are, in turn, imposed and forced on the very practices that have been left out" (98).

In examining hearing-centrism as it impacts Deaf communities, Best seeks to begin "a process of decolonizing systematic structures of oppression that have and continue to disable Deaf people and Deaf perspectives" (ibid.). This is work that not only reveals a community rarely granted legitimacy in ethnomusicology but also brings our attention to the limits of our own knowledge production. Hearing-centrism, presented as its own variant of ethnocentrism, is but another systemic bias that continues to limit ethnomusicology, dominate Deaf communities, and subsequently stifle Deaf expression. Best argues that ethnomusicologists must engage in a "constant critique and reflection of potential hearing-centric biases, practices, and rhetoric" so as to reorient "histories of music and sound to incorporate a Deaf lens" (ibid.).

Alexandria Carrico makes a similar argument in her work with neurodivergent musicians in Limerick, Ireland. In both chapters, the authors approach disability not as defect or disorder but rather as a unique historically excluded minority group. This approach refocuses ethnomusicological inquiry onto the systemic forces that have historically excluded neurodiverse and Deaf musical life from scholarly recognition. In her chapter, Carrico develops a novel methodology that brings neurodiverse and neurotypical musicians together in participatory Irish trad music sessions. Carrico writes that "this experience not only cemented feelings of group solidarity between two previously disparate groups but also recontextualized how many of the neurotypical musicians viewed disability" (190). Within the scope of this project, the trad sessions served as a site of integration, facilitating opportunities for social transformation by creating a radically inclusive musical environment.

Katie Graber explores how LGBTQIA members of the Mennonite Church use singing to radically reimagine and enact new forms of community. For her collaborators, music is a key resource for enacting queer positionalities and creating an inclusive community that holds and accepts intersectional diversity. Graber's chapter complicates conventional notions of diversity, and in the process demonstrates how the ethnomusicological tendency to focus on queer people's nonbelonging and pain inadvertently reinforces their exclusion. She eloquently asks that we tend to the contradictions that emerge in our work without oversimplification, that we push back against the liberation/assimilation binary, and that we pursue a kind of scholarship-activism that builds on moments of unity and allows for individuality to radiate from those present. Graber writes:

> We knew there would be no easy solutions.... All we can do is continue working and being vigilant about small decisions.... Singing together can create moments of inclusion, *but scholars and activists have to continually search out the fine distinctions of who feels that unity and who does not.* Singing allows for (but does not guarantee) singular, embodied experiences in which people have the potential to both hear and not hear all the diversities, to realize that songs already hold queerness and the possibility for singing diversity. Understanding and articulating this possibility is one way to step beyond liberation versus assimilation, but it is a step that we (both scholars and activists) have to keep taking. We cannot sing a song or write an article and be done. (118–19, emphasis added)

Darci Sprengel's exploration of racecraft in Egypt similarly engages with the exclusionary limits of conventional discourse. In her chapter, she documents how the tendency to equate Arab/North African with "Black" in Egyptian contexts enacts its own kind of exclusion and alienation, in effect, furthering the logic of colonial White supremacy. She proposes the need to study Arab anti-Blackness not only as a product of European colonialism but also as a contingent and dynamic historical process in its own right. "Egyptian artistic production and local campaigns for racial equality cannot simply be viewed as local representatives of these larger movements without losing the nuance and complexity through which they also speak back to such movements" (137). Radical inclusivity requires that scholars committed to social justice make space for Indigenous epistemologies without merely importing American correlates. To do otherwise only reinforces colonial logics that further enable epistemic violence.

Both Law and myself (McDonald) chronicle activist artists working to transcend the colonial gaze of international audiences. Law argues that Tanya Tagaq's performance of *Nanook of the North* counteracts extraction and instrumentalization of Indigenous imagery and knowledge through sonic means, reshaping Inuit stereotypes to align with Indigenous epistemologies. He writes: "Tagaq proactively revives Inuit throat singing while deflecting critics from a misguided reception of music and the moving image based on Inuit stereotypes. Her live score for *Nanook* is driven by neither repetition nor resolution but, rather, vitality and empathy. Her onstage presence urges validation of the Inuit as cosmopolitan and communitarian instead of racialized and romanticized.... She elicits deep listening from the audience on her own terms, so that the Inuit can be seen and heard with substantial and almost irresistible attention as vibrant and empowered" (154).

In similar fashion, I explain how Palestinian rapper Tamer Nafar's recent move into acting was widely criticized by international audiences as a kind of "selling out" to pop interests. For Nafar, acting in feature films and singing love songs is an important activist endeavor in that these projects not only expand visibility of Palestinian experience but, more importantly, also diversify how Palestinians might appear in the public imaginary. In feature films and love songs Palestinians are not mere objects of Israeli violence but authors of their own experience. In this way, popular culture can be seen as an act of countervisibility, not only redefining Palestinian representational logics, but also reclaiming a kind of agency to create outside and beyond the compassionate, colonial, and romantic gaze of international audiences.

Graber, Law, and I suggest a fundamental lesson for ethnomusicologists seeking to adopt a justice-oriented stance in their work. The pervasive image of

Indigenous and queer communities as victim is partly the result of misguided scholarly efforts to solicit support for basic human rights. But the effect of this solicitation is rarely positive, as the reiteration of these images serve only to naturalize the condition. Indeed, ethnomusicologists' bias toward explicitly political performance too often forecloses opportunities for humanizing and connecting. The romanticization of pain narratives limits our capacity for ethnographic engagement, disempowers Indigenous communities, and further reinforces colonial domination. As I write with regards to ethnomusicology's fascination with protest songs: "We (ethnomusicologists) 'are boxed in,' so focused on conventional forms of political intervention that we fail to recognize and value the superficial, the mundane, the human ways of being Palestinian. If it were not for the occupation, if it were not for the dire humanitarian crisis, Palestinians would not exist in the ethnomusicological imagination. This form of romanticization limits our capacity for ethnographic engagement, disempowers Palestinians, and further advances colonial logics that valorize White (male) cisgendered voices while maintaining the inferiority of Indigenous communities" (173).

In each of these chapters we are reminded that for a justice-oriented ethnomusicology to thrive we must make the settler colonial metanarrative the object of research (Tuck and Yang 2014). This requires that we continually evaluate the positionality of the researcher and the researched, exposing the complicity of ethnographic research in the production of settler colonial knowledge (Simpson 2007, 69; Tuck and Yang 2014a, 225; Tuck and Yang 2014b, 812; Robinson 2020, 34).[7] We must call attention to, and interrogate, conventional power networks. We must allow Indigenous (and other historically excluded) communities the space to tell their own stories on their own terms (Simpson 2007). And most important, we must leverage the resources of the academy to expand representational practices and opportunities.

COALITION BUILDING

Throughout many of the chapters included in this anthology there is an intellectual focus on the ways through which music and music performance provide essential tools for coalition building and political mobilization. Erin Bauer's rich historical analysis of the Chicano movement in South Texas, challenges conventional "fixed" notions of genre, class, and identity. But more important, Bauer demonstrates how this fluidity of musical style and representation facilitated coalition building within the Chicano movement. Conjunto Aztlán not only confronted issues of social injustice in their music and activist work but did so in a way that transformed lingering stereotypes of *conjunto* as solely representative of working-class culture. Through their revitalization of these genres among upwardly mobile, college educated, middle-class audiences, Conjunto Aztlán contested stereotypical notions of the US-Mexico border as a folkloric Other in favor of a more modern alternative. And in the process, the group redefined what it meant to be *tejano* (Texas Mexican) beyond the limits of old-fashioned musical traits and corresponding perceptions of a fundamentally rural, working-class, and traditional community.

Just as the culturally familiar sounds of conjunto served to mobilize diverse Mexican communities in support of the Chicano movement in the 1970s, so too did music provide pathways for collaboration among Asian American composers and performers seeking to support the Black Lives Matter Movement (BLM). Susan M. Asai notes that for many Asian American musicians support for, and participation in, BLM offers a chance to counter accusations of Whiteness while recognizing the debt owed to Black communities for their civil rights gains. In free jazz, Asian American performers were afforded an alternative and deeply personal field with which to deny Eurocentric parameters and harmonic structures while exploring improvisational ideas gleaned from African American blues and gospel roots. Such forms of improvisation enabled dialogue between musicians, "a space in which artists [could] speak their own language yet communicate with one another" (206). She concludes that "musical exchanges between cultural groups model and plant seeds for intercoalitional cross talk in the broader social and political realm. Inventive musicking builds communal and empathetic consciousness and richly imbues the cultural landscape of the United States with the potential to promote a more inclusive political terrain and, ultimately, a more equitable society" (213).

Just as free jazz improvisation has the capacity to facilitate dialogue and intercultural communication, Alexandra Carrico observes a similar phenomenon in traditional Irish music sessions where participatory music facilitates exchanges across neurotypical-neurodivergent boundaries. Coalitions emerge as neurotypical participants come to rethink and reimagine neurodiverse lifeways. She believes that the infrastructural design of this kind of applied project could be utilized to unite populations through community-based music making. And finally, Andrew G. Snyder notes that in the work of the Brass Liberation Orchestra (BLO), participatory HONK! performances serve to materially transform protest spaces into a kind of liberatory utopia. In what Snyder calls "prefigurative politics," these performances enact new social and political relations temporarily manifesting utopic inclusivity (244). In each of these chapters, we find unique solicitations for dialogue and intercultural communication in the musical encounter. These authors note opportunities to explore the amelioration of difference through sounded thought and behavior. And while many have previously discussed the group forming capacities of musical performance, here we find case studies where such performances further coalition building efforts toward strategic social justice destinations.

DIRECT ACTION

If the pathway toward a justice-oriented ethnomusicology begins with truth telling, creates spaces for radical inclusivity, and attends to coalition building, its final destination must include direct action. This is the subject of Andrew G. Snyder's ethnographic exploration of the Bay Area Brass Liberation Orchestra (BLO). As a means of taking matters into your own hands, direct action is when "'the people directly affected by the problem take action to solve it' in ways that alter power relationships and give them a sense of their own power defined on their own terms" (Bobo 2001, 11, quoted in Snyder, 243). David Graeber writes that direct action is "a way of actively engaging with the world to bring about change, in which the form of the action—or at least the organization of the action—is itself a model for the change one wishes to bring about" (2009, 206, quoted in Snyder, 244). Similarly, this volume was initially conceived as a form of direct action where the editors and contributors each attempt to take matters into their own hands: first, by collectively identifying colonialist and imperialist privilege and, second, by taking direct action against it. This is a volume that imagines a new ethnomusicology through its enactment, using collaborative, participatory, and synergistic approaches. Susan M. Asai reveals this in her autoethnographic reflection. She notes how decolonizing methods were used throughout the editing process for this volume: seeking out diverse voices, encouraging varied writing strategies, mentoring marginalized scholars with limited access to publishing opportunities, and facilitating an ethos of openness, confidence, and accessibility. Indeed, this is an intentionally coalitional publication, a gathering of "scholars from a constellation of backgrounds and orientations that have the potential to expand and enrich research within our discipline" (279). The coalitional and synergistic foundations of this work, Asai and Romero note, serve to heighten the justice-oriented potential of this (or any) publication.

Social justice is not a possible result of unjust methods developed from within unjust institutions. Our path toward a justice-oriented ethnomusicology requires that our work, our methods, our society, our discipline model the changes we wish to bring about. As Snyder explains:

> Direct action is a form of "prefigurative politics," in which the action is a performative manifestation of new social and political relations as well as an

explicit and targeted petitioning of power. The performance of freedom is not only the freedom *to* enact change on one's own terms but also freedom *from* conventional social and political relations that would inhibit such action. Building on Judith Butler's insight (2015) that action is performative and enacts new realities, I consider direct action to be the performative enactment of utopia (Dolan 2001), in which freedom from the state is experienced, if only temporarily, and can thereby be imagined and worked towards more completely. (244, emphasis in original)

"Music is liberation," the Brass Liberation Orchestra (BLO) declares in its mission statement: not merely in structuring the musical interactions of participants, but in performatively soliciting and enacting possible forms of liberatory social and political relations (ibid.). In performing this belief, the BLO pursues creative interventions of instrumental protest that use music to respond to an oppressive society, to sustain political movements, and to enact the world they want to live in. This includes operating as a leaderless, horizontal collective, where decisions are made through a consensus model, where radical inclusivity governs membership, and where hierarchy is avoided. As Snyder concludes, the BLO constitutes both a means to an end and an end in itself. It proves that direct action is an effective means of political engagement that makes change possible. He demonstrates how music and other forms of performance are a crucial means through which change is achievable, not merely as participatory action or presentational spectacle, but as "performative and affective experiences that maintain enthusiasm and combat activist burnout through raucous celebration" (255).

In reading this chapter, I am inspired by the BLO as a model for rethinking ethnomusicology. How might our discipline evolve if it were governed by similar values and practices? As the BLO brings together musicians in the service of direct action initiatives, what if SEM operated similarly, with the explicit intent of "changing policy and as an anarchistic performance of uninhibited freedom not restrained by laws, conventions, and the state" (254)? Instead of "promoting the research, study, and performance of music in all historical periods and cultural contexts,"[8] what if SEM was reimagined as a collective of activist-scholars who use musical thought and behavior as a means through which to imagine and enact liberatory sound and politics? What if the institutions of ethnomusicology were each instruments of direct action?

I pose these questions not merely as provocation but as a sincere inquiry. For ethnomusicology to effectively respond to Danielle Brown's "An Open Letter on Racism in Music Studies," for it to sufficiently respond to contemporary political demands, we must be willing to ask tough questions and take drastic steps. While by no means a comprehensive or authoritative approach to social justice, this anthology nevertheless invites conversation on how we might begin to move forward. Presented in the form of short autoethnographic essays, research-based case studies, and position statements, the chapters assembled in this anthology collectively recognize the need for taking drastic steps. The authors expose the inherent contradictions of conventional ethnomusicological praxis in a move to open new fields of inquiry. It is apparent that traditional ethnomusicological methods have proven to be incomplete. What we might conclude from these chapters is that advancing the cause of social justice isn't so much a function of adhering to a set of rules, as it is adopting a critically self-reflexive posture devoted to eliminating the continually emergent injustices inherent to the ethnographic encounter and interrogating our personal investments in White privilege and supremacy. Here I propose that this work might occur in four interrelated phases: truth telling, radical inclusivity, coalition building, and direct action. But regardless of how this work proceeds, it is essential that we develop the tools necessary to identify systemic forms of injustice and recognize the many ways in which we are implicated in the systems of oppression we strive to eliminate. It is simply not enough to critique systems of oppression without fully divesting from the discourses that support them. We must ask difficult questions of ourselves: how did we come to be in a position of privilege relative to those we study?

While pursuing an open-ended communicative dialogue explicitly aligned with our interlocutors' needs often results in contradictions and inefficient paths toward publication, a humanistic engagement that honors both openness and indifference without the suppression of dissent is an inspiring path that resolves many aspects of the social justice problem (McDonald 2021). A justice-oriented ethnomusicology, conceived here as an ethical process or stance, therefore relies on our capacities for vulnerability, humility, and critical self-reflection as well as a commitment to align ourselves alongside our interlocutors in the pursuit of their needs. This kind of approach carries with it incredible potential for what Maxine Greene has labeled, "wide awakeness," an open-eyed and open-eared engagement with the larger social fabric of our lives, and the diverse ways that individuals reveal themselves through collective work (Greene 1995, 35). Greene has been influential in developing a critical pedagogy of possibility, imagination, and social change, and I cite her work here as a final conceptual tool to help us reimagine the ethnographic encounter (Rautins and Ibrahim 2011, 25). For there is no pursuit of social justice without an open awareness of the inequities that surround us and inform our relations and a pervasive sense of outrage at the epistemic violence that governs our normal, everyday lives. The imperative to critically unpack systemic forms of violence that undergird our world is, therefore, the foundation of a justice-oriented ethnomusicology.

NOTES

1. Danielle Brown. "An Open Letter on Racism and Music Studies," *My People Tell Stories* (blog), June 12, 2020, https://www.mypeopletellstories.com/blog/open-letter/.
2. The Society for Ethnomusicology, "Crossroads Section for Difference and Representation," mission statement, accessed November 25, 2021. https://www.ethnomusicology.org/page/Groups_SectionsCR/.
3. Society for Ethnomusicology, "Crossroads Section."
4. Danielle Brown. "An Open Letter on Racism and Music Studies."
5. Society for Ethnomusicology, "Crossroads Section."
6. Stephan Pennington. 2020. "Decolonizing Ethnomusicology." Facebook comments post, accessed June 15, 2020, used with permission. https://www.facebook.com/groups/161177417731635/search/?q=stephan%20pennington.
7. I use the term *settler colonial knowledge* to refer to research methodologies and resultant knowledge streams that are the product of—and serve to normalize, reinforce, or otherwise render invisible—settler colonial relations. As opposed to Indigenous knowledge, settler colonial knowledge is "inquiry as invasion," the academic codes and practices that "territorialize knowledge as property and researchers as claimstakers" (Tuck and Yang 2014b, 812).
8. The Society for Ethnomusicology, "About SEM," SEM mission statement, accessed November 15, 2021. https://www.ethnomusicology.org/page/About_SEM/.

BIBLIOGRAPHY

Bobo, Kim, ed. 2003. *Organizing for Social Change: Midwest Academy Manual for Activists*. Minneapolis: Seven Locks Press.
Butler, Judith. 2015. *Notes toward a Performative Theory of Assembly*. Cambridge, MA: Harvard University Press.
Dolan, Jill. 2001. "Performance, Utopia, and the 'Utopian Performative.'" *Theatre Journal* 53 (3): 455–79.
Fanon, Frantz. 1952. *Black Skin, White Masks*. New York: Grove Press.
Freire, Paulo. 1970. *Pedagogy of the Oppressed*. New York: Continuum Books.
Gilroy, Paul. 1993. *The Black Atlantic: Modernity and Double Consciousness*. Cambridge, MA: Harvard University Press.
Gourlay, Kenneth A. 1978. "Towards a Reassessment of the Ethnomusicologist's Role in Research." *Ethnomusicology* 22 (1): 1–35.
———. 1982. "Towards a Humanizing Ethnomusicology." *Ethnomusicology* 26 (3): 411–20.
Graeber, David. 2009. *Direct Action: An Ethnography*. Oakland: AK Press.

Greene, Maxine. 1995. *Releasing the Imagination: Essays on Education, the Arts, and Social Change*. San Francisco, CA: Jossey-Bass.
Hayner, Priscilla B. 1994. "Fifteen Truth Commissions—1974 to 1994: A Comparative Study." *Human Rights Quarterly* 16 (3): 597–655.
hooks, bell. 2000. *All about Love: New Visions*. New York: William Morrow.
McDonald, David A. 2021. "Sincerely Outspoken: Toward a Critical Activist Ethnomusicology." In *Transforming Ethnomusicology: Methodologies, Institutional Structures and Policies*, edited by Beverly Diamond and Salwa El-Shawan Castelo-Branco, 73–86. Oxford: Oxford University Press.
Rautins, Cara, and Awad Ibrahim. 2011. "Wide-Awakeness: Toward a Critical Pedagogy of Imagination, Humanism, Agency, and Becoming." *International Journal of Critical Pedagogy* 3 (3): 24–36.
Robinson, Dylan. 2020. *Hungry Listening: Resident Theory for Indigenous Sound Studies*. Minneapolis: University of Minnesota Press.
Said, Edward. 1978. *Orientalism*. New York: Vintage Press.
Simpson, Audra. 2007. "On Ethnographic Refusal: Indigeneity, 'Voice,' and Colonial Citizenship." *Junctures* 9:67–80.
Spivak, Gayatri Chakravorty. 1988. "Can the Subaltern Speak." In *Marxism and the Interpretation of Culture*, edited by Cary Nelson and Lawrence Grossberg, 271–316. Urbana: University of Illinois Press.
Tuck, Eve, and K. Wayne Yang. 2012. "Decolonization Is Not a Metaphor." *Decolonization: Indigeneity, Education & Society* 1 (1): 1–40.
———. 2014a. "R-Words: Refusing Research" In *Humanizing Research: Decolonizing Qualitative Inquiry with Youth and Communities*, edited by Django Paris and Maisha T. Winn, 223–48. Thousand Oaks, CA: Sage Press.
———. 2014b. "Unbecoming Claims: Pedagogies of Refusal in Qualitative Research." *Qualitative Inquiry* 20 (6): 811–18.

PART I

TRUTH TELLING AND LISTENING LOVINGLY

ONE

DIVERSITY ON REPEAT

The Deceptive Cadence of
Social Domination in Ethnomusicology

KYRA D. GAUNT

REPEATING OURSELVES

To contextualize what follows, I composed these thoughts in three intersecting contexts: (1) between the first and second waves of the COVID-19 pandemic in the United States, (2) as demonstrations of the Black Lives Matter movement occurred worldwide following the violent deaths of Ahmaud Arbery, George Floyd, and Breonna Taylor, and (3) as the United States experienced its most contentious presidential election in living memory.[1] We, the members of the Society for Ethnomusicology (hereafter, SEM), reckoned with our own unfulfilled and thwarted expectations around diversity at the same time. This is my testimony of how we got stuck in a loop of denial; deceptively feeling ourselves through performances of "diversity" in a rondo of social domination that kept us rooted, returning to the same old key.

In 2004, on the eve of SEM's fiftieth anniversary, the society's then-president, Timothy Rice, wrote the following in the fall quarterly newsletter under the headline, "How is SEM doing on diversity?": "My sense is that these questions are matters of some urgency for SEM and for many, and perhaps most, of our members ... and the formation of a standing committee [on diversity] testifies to the importance of these questions at this moment in our history" (Rice 2004, 1).

Despite the acknowledgment that questions of diversity *must* be addressed within SEM, systemic change would not be tracked or felt. More than fifteen years later, as Indigenous (Stó:lō) ethnomusicologist Dylan Robinson stated at our 2020 Virtual SEM Conference during the global COVID-19 pandemic, "We are drowning in recommendations, up to our ears in calls to action" (Robinson 2020).

Diversity has felt like lip service in SEM—the repeated deception that fools only those whose privilege is protected by existing systems. Like a deceptive cadence, we repeatedly return to social domination, reliving the same good intentions with little satisfaction or structural change: "Intentionality without habituality is empty; habituality without intentionality is blind [or, to disrupt repeating ableist language, lacking perception, awareness, or discernment]" (Kilpinen 2015, 160).

In music making, as in the repeated efforts of diversity initiatives since 2004, repetition can be transformative when enacted as a *deliberate practice* that transforms the roles and habits of people within an ecology. Habits of vulnerability, disclosure, and trust must be repeated and rewarded. They must be practiced and modelled to prevent the recurrence of social harms to members of vulnerable and marginalized groups. But mere repetition without an intentional outcome is monotonous. It clouds the judgment of those in positions of power and keeps them from noticing the lack of development in their efforts. Roles (and their effects) may remain unchanged no matter who occupies the office. SEM, like other institutions, has been stuck in the repeat(ed) signs of diversity. Diversity cannot be like Pachelbel's Canon in D; an ostinato of strings sacred and endlessly played without question, assumed to be beloved. Perhaps, it could be a *ring shout* resisting the shared subjugation of silence around marginalization.

In 2003, I was appointed by Ellen Koskoff (president, 2001–3) and the SEM Board of Directors to chair a standing committee tasked with responding to the exclusion and inequality within our ranks, leading to the creation of the Crossroads Project on Diversity, Difference, and Under-Representation (renamed the Crossroads Section for Difference and Representation in 2017).[2] The focus on "underrepresentation" rather than "representation" was intentional on my part, given the cultural resistance to talking about race back in the early aughts. To talk about race was considered "racist" and led White colleagues to blame the oppressed for pointing to their own oppression. Envisioned as an emergent and applied project, I wanted to help keep our eye on the hidden harms affecting women, people of color, and members of other marginalized groups in order to unsettle existing structures of domination. It was clear to me, as a woman of African descent in SEM, that we as a society generally tended to be indifferent to the harms experienced by our professional society's most marginalized members. One cannot effectively address a situation if one does not fully become aware of the wounds of long-term oppression.

If we fail to unearth our personal stories detailing the harms of marginalization, we may miss the opportunities before us—to offer repair and listen lovingly to those affected by past faults and fissures. In other words, we have an opportunity to emotionally and compassionately, rather than academically or logically, *sense* our way through the social change. We must fully recognize who we keep leaving behind to drown in despair and how. My aim for the Crossroads Project was to help SEM members fathom how a "politics of care" opens up broken hearts, leading to both justice and joy. As the authors of *Joyful Militancy: Building Thriving Resistance in Toxic Times* remind us, "participating in joy's unfolding means being partially undone and transformed through an open-ended, uncontrollable process" (Montgomery and bergman 2017, 277). What if we created spaces for songs and stories of repair, using listening and singing as a politics of care? The Crossroads Project became that space—a space for restorative emotional justice in SEM.

To go forward as scholars in SEM from 2020 on, we must first go back and listen with courage, curiosity, and compassion. In what follows, I offer personal stories of trouble and trauma that are *signals* of structures of domination, introducing key definitions and thoughts about how forms of domination work.

A RING SHOUT

During a pivotal moment of joy and injustice in Toni Morrison's Pulitzer Prize–winning novel *Beloved*, enslaved elder Baby Suggs delivers a kind of sermon as she stands in a secret hush arbor where fellow Africans in bondage voiced their agentive selves through song and dance. She calls her people together into the clearing, inviting the children to laugh, the men to dance, the women to weep and moan. The "counterclockwise, circular" ritual about which Morrison writes is what musicologist Samuel Floyd and others refer to as the *ring shout* (Floyd, Zeck, and Ramsey 2017, 78). With their right shoulders facing out, freedom seekers shuffled the weight of their bodies to a kaleidoscope of shouts, moans, thuds, hums, and hollers expressed to familiar tunes, folktales, and even satirical jokes to stave off the effects of the daily dehumanizing forced labor.

The work of historian Sterling Stuckey (2013) revealed how the ring shout formation was the ritual through which diverse groups of Africans became "African American." The holy Baby Suggs spoke to her people in seclusion, beyond the constant surveillance that forced African hands and bodies into centuries of unpaid labor: "She did not tell them to clean up their lives or to go and sin no more. She did not tell them they were the blessed of the earth, its inheriting meek or its glorybound pure. She told them that the only grace they could have was the grace they could imagine. That if they could not see it, they would not have it" (Morrison 1987, 103). The antebellum ring shout was a co-constitutive, open-ended space for an improvised and antiphonal practice sought to counter the generational trauma and terrorism of human trafficking.

Within the ring shout led by Baby Suggs, Black women (whose reproductive, sexual, and domestic labor and healing knowledge were systematically exploited), men (whose wisdom around crops, woodcutting, and metallurgy was exploited), and children (whose work as playmates to White children and whose ability to fit into tight, precarious spaces were exploited) all found momentary solace and succor. Through their singing and chanting of rhetorical devices like "juba this and juba that / juba killed the yellow cat / Juba!!," they found their humanity; through moaning and gesticulating, the enslaved African could imagine rejuvenation, escape, and a reinvention of their condition. Under the ecological threat of being *whupped*, raped, *wukked* to death, sold, recaptured after escape, and replaced by another crop of humans after death, freedom seekers learned to make sense of their lives amid their despair. In co-creating a timeline of shuffling and thudding feet, they expressed a momentary justice in the release of participating in the prayerful leisure and play. Freedom seekers embodied musical meaning, sometimes mimicking their work, symbolizing their productivity in artful display.

My enslaved African ancestors arrived in the colonies nine generations before me and probably participated in something like a ring shout. Still, the social forces of domination—schooling, silencing, and segregation—likely prevented the ring shout's transmission down to me. "Modifications" appeared in the rhythmic and melodic patterns. Ideas were "transmigrate[d] to different cultural environs" (Rosenbaum [1998] 2012, 172). New styles of music making emerged, including spirituals, work songs, and field hollers.

The ring shout was a creative and Godly space where Africans could compose a mental map of reality expressed through movement, circular motion, improvisation, and their ethnic difference. Many would survive, resist, escape, and at least critique their condition through music making (Floyd 1991). In and through the immediate release and socially embodied cognition of laughter inside the ring shout, our African ancestors made sense out of no sense, and we—the living, whose lives were made possible by those who survived—can find a semblance of our ethnic heritage intact in our participation in music.

This chapter was written during an unprecedented moment of racial reckoning. In 2020, as the Society for Ethnomusicology and institutions around the world confronted and reckoned with the Black Lives Matter movement and the COVID-19 pandemic, we began to finally grasp how difficult it is to free ourselves of the abstractions of White supremacy's social domination with its diversity initiatives. Perhaps we could do with a contemporary ring shout or two.[3]

BECOMING/SURVIVING AS AN ETHNOMUSICOLOGIST

> I just wanted people to know what real Negro music sounded like.
> ... Was the real voice of my people never to be heard?
> —ZORA NEALE HURSTON, *DUST TRACKS IN THE ROAD*,
> QUOTED IN BROOKS 2010, 617

I became an ethnomusicologist after years of stage fright affected my ability to complete a doctorate in voice. In an effort to compensate for things left out of my public education, I did everything I could during my doctoral studies in both voice and musicology courses to learn more about Black people making music. I tracked over one hundred operas by Black composers on four-by-six note cards after the eighteenth-century opera scholar in the Department of Musicology—a White, male scholar—cautioned, "You won't find much." He never encouraged me to publish those findings. Later, I noticed how the music of Black Americans, not to mention other cultures, was never taught as lessons in embodied knowledge, what I came to call *kinetic orality*—close readings of the embodied scripts of call-and-response, syncopated lessons in gendered linguistic play and musical behavior—which I introduced in my dissertation (1997) and further explicated in my book *The Games Black Girls Play* (2006).

This concept explored how *musical blackness* was socially learned rather than biologically determined (Gaunt 2006, 49). For example, the rhymed chants and embodied musical play of Black girls are *in-body formulas* (Drewal 1992, 7) or *oral-kinetic études* (Gaunt 2006, 2) of musical blackness passed down intergenerationally. Black girls were tastemakers of musical blackness expressed in the chants and embodied percussion of their hand-clapping games, cheers, and double-dutch rope play from rural to urban settings throughout the twentieth century. In girls' hidden musicianship was a habitual demonstration of community (of me and we). Game songs represented an early formation of a Black popular music making. They were a system of musical expression that existed in dialogue with male-dominated music production and distribution in the record industry. Girls' games were much more than child's play or nonsense. Becoming an ethnomusicologist gave me permission to discover my ancestors' musical practices and reintroduce a lost heritage to myself, my readers, and my students. The liberty was mine, but I still felt enslaved to the hegemony of traditional music curricula: "It cannot be repeated too often that nothing is more fertile in prodigies than the art of being free; but there is nothing more arduous than the apprenticeship of liberty" (de Tocqueville [1835] 2002, 274).

My first faculty position involved teaching the music of Black folk in the Music Department at the University of Virginia (UVA), founded by Thomas Jefferson on January 25, 1819. When I joined in 1996, it was the top public university in the nation and 13 percent of the student body was Black. At the beginning of my second semester as a professor, two things happened that left me feeling marginalized as the only Black female faculty member in our department. First, at my annual review, the department chair asked, "How much of the time do you *teach* music?" As ethnomusicologists, we often feel singled out; our approach to music-as-culture defies the logic of contemporary Western art music curricula. Judith Becker, who was my dissertation advisor at the University of Michigan, wrote of this ideological dilemma: "Because we often cannot perceive it, we deny naturalness, great complexity, and meaningfulness to other musical systems. Despite all protestations to the contrary, to deny equivalences in all three pillars of belief—that is, naturalness, complexity, and meaningfulness, to the musical systems of others—is ultimately to imply that they are not as developed as we are. The doctrine of the superiority of Western music is the musicological version of colonialism" (Becker 1986, 342). I expected to feel marginalized as an ethnomusicologist, but additional *stereotype threats* surfaced because I was Black *and* female. A stereotype threat is a feeling that threatens your sense of belonging ("Stereotype threat" n.d.); the identity a music profession granted me was imperiled. My status was also endangered because of the unorthodox way I used embodiment and social learning rather than books as pedagogy to teach musical blackness and hip-hop (see "Stereotype threat" n.d., Steele 1997, Pennington et al. 2016). Hip-hop *as music* had not yet been fully embraced as an academic study in 1996. That same year, discrimination in public schooling came to the Oakland (California) school board, which passed a two-page resolution highlighting the plight of African American students in the district in order to improve their academic success by using African American English spoken by Black students as a second language or pathway to teaching and learning standard classroom English. President Clinton's secretary of education, congressional officials, and even Maya Angelou opposed the resolution in a firestorm of debate over so-called Ebonics in a way not dissimilar to the polarizing and racially charged reactions to critical race theory and the 1619 Project, the historical work that was created for the 400th anniversary of the arrival of the first Africans brought to the former US colonies.

When the department chair asked me how much time I spent teaching music, my amygdala got hijacked. While commiserating with one of my White female colleagues after that incident, she suggested that I should have responded to the question of "How much of the time I teach music" with "100 percent," without hesitation. But my exposure to hundreds of microaggressions of anti-Black racism and sexism didn't grant me the mental space or possibility of thinking that "100 percent" was a plausible answer. Repeated experiences of minimization, and my own novice feelings precluded the possibility of claiming I'd done nothing wrong. Instead of second-guessing myself, I could have stood my ground. Sociologist Ruha Benjamin (2019) reminds us that the structure of racist domination reproduces distorted perceptions of those who are marginalized by social institutions in ourselves and others. "We should acknowledge that most people are forced to live inside someone else's imagination. And one of the things we have to come to grips with is how the nightmares that many people are forced to endure are the underside of elite fantasies about efficiency, profit, and social control."

The second thing that framed my feelings of being marginalized during that first year at UVA was the hate mail I received. The letter shocked everyone in the music department—everyone but me, as the sole person of color within it. Composed on an old hunt-and-peck typewriter, the letter was signed, sealed, and delivered with a postmark from Hampton Roads, Virginia. It began with a racializing salutation followed by a text that unmasked its elite need to control who was hired and why: "Dear Ms. Afro, You will excuse me for not hibernating [hyphenating] the salutation with the word American as it is impossible for me to consider your cursed race as such or even human for that matter."

To be honest, I initially thought the letter was a joke. I imagined some grad school buddy had sent it because they knew I was headed to Virginia, a fully Republican state at the time, with the exception of Charlottesville. Marked by typos and mechanical traces of mechanical overstrikes white-out could never fully erase, the White supremacist logic unfolded the author's anger over the musical miscegenation of my hire, but not that of my White colleague who taught African music:

> I am outraged by your gall in teaching the vulgarity of Afro music to White students at UV. I am equally so in regard to the university administration which is apparently composed of a bunch of mud brain morons to permit this. . . .
> Introducing African music towhite students is just another way to Africanize their minds so they will thinking and act African. . . .
> The stark fact is that theAfrican race has never produced anything of benefit to mankind in spite of the ludicrous assertins of Black History (Fiction) which in it itself is an insilent frauf and thievery of other peoples cultures and accomplishments.

> The world would be blessed, mostly America, if the absence of the vile African race were possible. And maybe some day that will be.
> You conniving little Afro twit, take your African fulth to an Afro university where it belongs.
>
> Yours in Stark Truth,
J.L. Bersovich

I needed a hush arbor to combat the normalized denial of my humanity captured in the letter. Senior colleagues who read it apologized for the personal impact but did nothing to combat the structures of domination that normalized Black disenfranchisement from classrooms, music curricula, and career advancement in systems like tenure. That level of repair could only be a dream often deferred in the name of diversity. What system of dehumanizing logic set Bersovich's anger aflame across generations of White American men's unearned privilege to teach Bach or Ellington? What mental maps of reality inherited as a culture turned a probable UVA alum into a gatekeeper and campaigner for oppression?

HOW STRUCTURES OF DOMINATION WORK

Ruha Benjamin (2019) offers one of the most resourceful definitions of the social constructed-ness of racism: it is a "productive" human endeavor. I quote her extensively to challenge readers to notice how "racism" could be swapped for terms like marginalization, orientalization, colonization, or White supremacist capitalist patriarchy (with a nod to the late Black feminist ancestor, bell hooks). Benjamin's nuanced explanation of the gendered and disabling roles of anti-Black racism and sexism expanded my understanding of these caste systems:

> Racism is productive, and by that, I don't mean that racism is "good," but [rather it has a capacity] to produce things of value to some, even as it wreaks havoc on others. Because we're taught to think of racism as an aberration, a glitch, an accident, an isolated incident, a bad apple, in the backwoods, and outdated; rather than as innovative, systemic, diffuse, an attached incident, the entire orchard, in the Ivory Tower, and forward-looking—productive. In sociology, my field, we like to say race is socially constructed, but we often fail to state the corollary that racism constructs.

Benjamin continues: "Racism, among other axes of domination, helps to produce this fragmented imagination—misery for some, monopoly for others. This means that for those of us who want to construct a different social reality—one grounded in justice and joy—we can't only deal with [or] critique the underside, but we also have to wrestle with the deep investments, the desire even, that many people have for social domination." The monopoly of White, heteronormative privilege and bias is intangible; we do not see it and rarely acknowledge it. Bias shows up in the silent and persistent erasure of indifference to anti-Black racism and sexism in our culture.

I recognize that most non-BIPOC ethnomusicologists might fail to fully grasp how systemic social domination works within SEM or how we've siloed ourselves from the advances in recruitment and retention of Black and Brown students and future faculty practiced by the American Musicological Society (AMS). Beginning in 1995, AMS's Committee on Cultural Diversity instituted what has become the Eileen Southern Travel Fund to expose undergraduates and terminal master's degree candidates of color to various aspects of the field. Too often racism seems to demand attention only when something like hate mail arrives. The harm that's done is soon forgotten. What's more, no one tracks these harms, which affect individual and collective bodies, ambitions, hearts, and minds. Diversity initiatives are like a deceptive cadence that does not end such violence.

When SEM's annual meetings come to a close, the repeat sign of White, patriarchal supremacy kicks in. After the "repeat sign"—after the return to workplace discrimination or microaggressions that circulate in the water cooler conversations of the marginalized—we music scholars go back and play out the same measures of dissatisfaction with diversity, albeit with some slight accent on the original character or tone of diversity. It is a refrain that leads to decay; the theme and variations are always "urgently" promoting diversity. The cast (the actors) change, but the same structure remains, perpetuating harm with its hierarchical habits and socializing scripts. Without operationalizing what *oppression* means—defining its why, how, where, and when—we may never remove the abstractions that hide anti-Black racism's irrational logic and maintenance. We cannot make or monitor habits that resist lasting social change when repeated efforts at diversity "may give momentary pleasure, [but are] of no assistance whatever for dealing with the future" (Phillips [1966] 2013, 36–37). We must begin to justly trans-act (together-and-at-once) with those harmed by the hidden structures of domination and those whose unearned privileges benefit from anti-Black and sexist oppression with a new tune or approach—small habits and communal rituals of listening, remembering, and caring.

What follows are definitions to begin problem-solving issues that have been operating to effectively (re)produce oppressive habits, for if you cannot say what is it we are un-doing, you cannot see what is being undone. Sociologists Susanne Bohmer and Joyce L. Briggs define oppression as "those attitudes, behaviors, and pervasive and systemic social arrangements by which members of one group are exploited and subordinated while members of another group are granted privileges" (1991, 155). If we do not operationalize oppression or social domination, the prevailing ambiguity contributes to our mindlessness. Without definitions we can operationalize we cannot satisfy the kind of work social change demands of us in the field of ethnomusicology.

Here are four core aspects of a larger, interlocking structure of oppression, according to political sociologists Davita Silfen Glasberg and Deric Shannon (2011), to which we must attend:

1. Political economy: [not necessarily neutral] interactions and intersections between the economy and the state that structure (or *construct*) pervasive class inequities within systemic social arrangements by which members of one group are exploited/subordinated, while members of another group are granted privileges
2. Patriarchy: the symbolic and tangible maintenance and justification of male dominance as if it were a natural, inalienable right, which enforces and thereby reproduces inferiority and subordination of womxn, femmes, and effeminate men
3. Racism: the ideology of White superiority and its power structure, mainly expressed as anti-BIPOC oppression and inequality
4. Heteronormativity: advantages accorded to specific groups and not others because of their sexual and gender practices

Ethnomusicologists' initiatives at achieving equity and increasing inclusion will fail without a meeting of the minds, an agreement among us all about these aspects of oppression and how they work and intersect in our discipline and our day-to-day experiences.

MAINTAINING DOMINATION: *FIRST COME, FIRST SERVED*

> The one in front of the herd drinks clear water.
> —AFRICAN PROVERB (UNSUBSTANTIATED)

The bones of the prevailing White supremacist, patriarchal system surfaced at my first meeting as an elected member of the SEM council's nominating committee in 2003. The committee chooses a slate of candidates for elected positions, including president-elect and council members. When I suggested a more inclusive slate by pointing out Black members' exclusion, the idea was immediately resisted by a White male in the meeting. He was responding to my calling attention to race. For him, my critique seemed like an indictment that racism was in the room, where no racists existed. It felt like the messenger was the problem as much as the message, and a reversal of harm was necessary. He shifted attention away from White supremacy and toward and against me as a Black woman with intersecting marginalized identities. *White fragility* as a term had not yet become a thing to call out in the early aughts. I left feeling utterly abandoned, not only for raising the concern for inclusion, but also for merely raising my voice. No one came to my defense or joined my concern. I was on my own.

I met with then-president Ellen Koskoff (2001–3). I offered several tactics that would make inroads toward inclusion, such as giving marginalized scholars the opportunity to chair panels, paper sessions, and committees like the SEM council. I had observed how chairs never questioned the habit and inherited practice of first come, first served in selection processes as an aspect of the structure that maintains domination for a few. The proverb at the opening of this section, "The one in front of the herd drinks clear water," commonly attributed to Africans, speaks to the issue. We who believe in ethnomusicology's value, with its immediate attention on marginalized people and communities making music, need to start questioning the repeated patterns perpetuated in our habits of practice that are White, male, sexist, and heteronormative.

In my first report to the SEM board as Crossroads Project chair in 2004, I boldly imagined that our new habits of listening could "eventually impact individual programs not only relative to recruitment and retention, but also [to] quality of life issues of concern to our committee and to our members at large" (Rice 2004). My aim was to create conversations that make a difference and provide useful and practical outcomes with joy and ease.

As of 2020, the Society for Ethnomusicology, founded in 1955, is a global, interdisciplinary network of over 1,700 members representing over 850 institutional members, primarily based in the United States. Many of us are practicing musicians working with people, consultants, and communities who make music within structures of power. Still, the underlying structures of racism and White supremacy that surface as repeated forms of structural oppression rarely accompany our musical voices at past meetings of the Society for Ethnomusicology. Caste hides even its shadow: "Caste is the infrastructure that we cannot see.... [Caste is] the tool of the underlying infrastructure" (Wilkerson 2020).

Amid the uprisings following the killing of George Floyd, ethnomusicologist Danielle Brown called attention to the repeat signs of diversity in her "Open Letter on Racism in Music Studies": "Until ethnomusicology as a field is dismantled or significantly restructured, so that epistemic violence against BIPOC is not normalized, Black Lives will not matter.... [Music studies] might change individual minds and hearts and make people feel better, but I repeat [our diversity initiatives] will not put a dent in the system. All they will do is redesign the system and create another economy within the system that benefits white people" (Brown 2020). By paying closer attention to the habits that produce patterns of domination, we could begin to elicit comments from those who have not yet been heard at our annual meetings and form digital avenues for maintaining connections between annual meetings. It needs to be more than a one-to-many listserv in an age of many-to-many, socially networked communication in the twenty-first century. We need to create a few hush arbors and learn to dance and sing ourselves into a new kind of society.

Panel chairs could ask the society's newest members to contribute their thoughts or questions first during the Q&As to avoid turning the structure of first come, first served into a straightjacket replicating predictable dominance. In meetings, we could invent and borrow subaltern ways of inviting and including elders or the missed and marginalized voices on a subject to enter the conversation using a circle formation instead of a line. The world shows up not only in the structures we assume to be normal and expected but also in the fundamental set of assumptions about authority and voice that go unquestioned. These hidden assumptions are what produce the epistemic violence of silence. The majority's tyranny is a silencing and leveling mechanism that gets set in motion through repetition. How do we empower the meek to speak up and encourage the loud to give up and share space?

Institutional biases are inherent to the logic of systemic structures that limit our perception and behavior. All of us who function as committee chairs unwittingly perpetuate social dominance patterns when we wield Robert's Rules of parliamentary order as a weapon of influence in unethical ways. We all may use the rules to resist challenges to our comfort in the existing social order. We believe we are being fair even as we each play our individual parts as actors in the intentional oppression and marginalization of others. Law professor Trina Grillo (1948–96) frames this political paradox in her article "Anti-essentialism and Intersectionality: Tools to Dismantle the Master's House": "[S]ometimes the governing paradigms which have structured all of our lives are so powerful that we can think we are doing progressive work, dismantling the structures of racism and other oppressions, when in fact, we are reinforcing the paradigms" (1995, 17). We do all this in the name of following the rules, which maintains more than momentary order. As Benjamin (2019) said, "it wreaks havoc for some, and monopoly for others." We never stop to ask whose order we may be maintaining and how their rules fit for the community we imagine living in right now.

We've sullied inclusion and deterred equity in the name of diversity. We've dismissed and excluded members of marginalized groups who were the last people allowed to enter spaces of academic authority—namely, BIPOC faculty and students. We avoid questioning our most sacred and fundamental assumptions, which are the contexts in which activity arises into consciousness. *First come, first served* has been a default that determines what is possible and what is not, who is out of place and who is welcome in some capacity or role, and whose words matter and whose questions threaten some order.

A PRIZE AND A PROBLEM

Some know I was one of two recipients of the SEM's prestigious Alan Merriam Prize for the most outstanding English-language monograph published between 2005 and 2006. My book *The Games Black Girls Play: Learning the Ropes from Double-Dutch to Hip-Hop* was among thirty-four books nominated.[4] When I received the prize, I was in the midst of a trial to save my job at a senior college in the CUNY system. The day after I returned to New York City from the SEM annual meeting, I had to defend my tenure-track appointment at a hearing before all thirteen department chairs in the College of Arts and Sciences.

Deborah Wong, then-SEM president and Merriam Prize Committee chair, called and invited me to attend the Fifty-Second Annual Meeting at Ohio State University that year to receive the Alan Merriam Prize. After I hung up the phone, I lost my usual composure and began screaming and jumping up and down alone in my office. I had dreamed that my work might receive this kind of recognition, but I'd forgotten my dream in the sea of oppression and depression I suffered. What's more, news of the prize was overshadowed by the precarity of my (third) tenure-track position: depending on the outcome of the hearing, I might have been out of a job despite being awarded the prize. I was experiencing incredible elation *and* one of the most harrowing moments of my career.

The vote was favorable, but the dean of arts and sciences decided to relocate my tenure-line from the Department of Performing Arts to Sociology and Anthropology to avoid retaliation. Even the chair of the Department of Black and Hispanic Studies, a full professor who was the only person of color among the thirteen department heads, insisted the case against me involved racism. I balked at the notion. I blamed myself. Denial is part of the trauma of structural domination for those racism subordinates; denial hides shame. Only in hindsight did I realize I should have trusted his point of view. Suffering in silence is one of the troubles of denial.

Returning to the 2004 SEM newsletter column on diversity, President Tim Rice posed a gender question: "Do female ethnomusicologists run into systemic barriers in their training, job applications, and the tenure process and give up on their ambitions to teach?" Sixteen years later, Danielle Brown (2020) answered a question that continues to wreak havoc for many, especially for Black women in SEM. She shared how the inability of people of color to "tell and interpret their own stories" led her to resign from a tenure-track position "because of my dissatisfaction with academia in general, and ethnomusicology in particular" (Brown 2020). While Danielle, one of my former PhD students, left her tenure-track position, I am still seeking tenure twenty-five years into my career in ethnomusicology.

After so much personal and professional strife, I am more aware of my agency and social power as a scholar and as a Black woman. Still, it saddens me that I can name nine Black women, including Danielle Brown, who gave up their ambition to work as Black women ethnomusicologists in academia over the last twenty years. One left a graduate program before finishing her dissertation, and yet she landed a great and hopefully fulfilling job in the end. Others weren't fortunate enough to receive offers for a tenure-track position, a problem that seems to disproportionately affect BIPOC scholars. The pattern in the lack of retention relative to Black women in the discipline became apparent only as I began writing this chapter. If we mean business about diversity, we cannot know whether we are making a difference without tracking both recruitment and retention for women of color throughout graduate programs in ethnomusicology. I actually left the discipline a few years after winning the Merriam Prize. If I had not returned, I would have become the tenth in the group.

We all have war stories of gatekeepers in our professional lives. I'm not unique, but I have suffered disproportionately as a woman of African descent in the field of music. For more than a decade, I have worked over the wounds of my intersectional oppression. I convinced myself that the only way out was to claw my way back and learn the skills and competencies to overcome those harms. Thus, I have established a robust publishing record since my return to a tenure-track position in 2017. The most challenging aspect of my journey to getting tenure later than expected is watching several former graduate and undergraduate students become associate and full professors, one with hundreds of publications on his CV. I've learned much from all my setbacks. Still, the structural slights could have been avoided had equity initiatives been more holistic and much more operational.

CONCLUSION

In the article, "'Sister, Can You Line It Out?': Zora Neale Hurston and the Sound of Angular Black Womanhood," African American feminist and Yale professor Daphne A. Brooks (2010, 617) foregrounds Hurston's notions about the power of Black music, which are shared by many Black women ethnomusicologists: "For Hurston, singing not only operates as a mode of embodied cultural documentation, but it also upsets the putative boundaries between scholar and cultural informant, individual and community, folk culture and modernity, and gendered spaces of work and play" (2010, 617). Our journeys should be freer of the deceptive cadences of diversity both in the Society for Ethnomusicology and in universities, especially at predominantly White institutions of higher learning. Throughout this chapter, I spotlighted moments of oppression and social domination that I often did not notice or document when they occurred, moments that epistemically muzzled marginalized voices limiting our agency within SEM as well as in our respective workplaces where epistemic violence has also been on repeat. We all equally deserve a politics of care. We all equally deserve a politics of repair. But it must begin with those most affected by past harms. Intersectionality is the path to upending structural violence: "When I am faced with such uncertainty and find myself unable to speak, anti-essentialism and intersectionality are to me like life preservers. They give me a chance to catch my breath as the waves come crashing over me, and they help me sort through my own confusion about what work I should be doing and how I should be doing it" (Grillo 1995, 17).

Music has always been an asset in resolving conflict, easing tension, and reconciling difference. We all know this. It is why we love music and love studying music making as both a beneficial or prosocial process whether or not we are excavating music's potential for harm or violence, as I do in my current research on Black girls' online musical play.

Learning to be inclusive at a structural level is one of the hardest parts of being free in US society. The hard part involves a remapping of our perceived reality that stems from the ways bodies and culture interact: "thinking of bodies as transactional means thinking of bodies and their environments in a permeable, dynamic relationship in which culture does not just affect bodies, but bodies also affect culture" (Sullivan 2001, 3). Each of our bodies is entangled in this matrix as an organism constantly trans-acting with its internal and external environment, including ideologies of domination and subordination. When it comes to undoing White supremacy, norms of ability, and patriarchy, how do we learn to imagine and coordinate undoing structural violence? How do we invent new habits and discover the intentional and affective labor required to maintain a new social order together and at once? It is the lack of maintenance, the hard labor involved in maintaining social habits of inclusion and equity, that often leads to the repeat(ed) signs of diversity.

Lasting change, given the entanglement of bodies, can only emerge from a deliberate practice of small acts in an emergent process. The evolution of diversity initiatives has not emerged from the top-down, meted-out, majority-rule committee work that dominates most SEM-elected leader bodies. It took Danielle Brown, a Black woman who left the field of ethnomusicology, to call us into a reckoning with ourselves. An unorthodox musical pathway could be more desirable.

By slowly moving together, paying attention to the cross flows, missteps, and vulnerabilities that emerge in our communications, allowing harms to air through story and song rather than caveat or committee, we will begin to notice what is required to build *trust and community* organically. As the honorable statesman and civil rights organizer Representative John Lewis (1940–2020) reminded us: "Never, ever be afraid to make some noise and get in good trouble, necessary trouble" while doing one's part to create a "fair, more just society" (Bote 2020). We must stop and listen. We must ponder the doubtful situation we are in to determine *what actually happened* and *what is still happening* relative to marginalization, racialization, sexualization, trauma, and discrimination within SEM. A small, deliberate practice of sharing can leverage and shift the larger axes of structural domination when practiced over a long period of time.

Calling for a politics of care is a feminist project that fuels the mission of the Crossroads Section for Difference and Representation, articulated as "We— the feminist architects of the Crossroads Project in honor of BIPOC members, sexual minorities, visible and invisible persons with disabilities within SEM—deserve respect for the work we have been forging from our mission, our section meetings, and events, and publications [like this anthology]. We deserve professional beneficence, credit for our authority as well as our material and immaterial labor, and we deserve to be acknowledged for that work, cited, cared for, and represented in the Society's history and memory for our coordinated efforts since 2003."

The unprecedented year 2020 has changed everything. The time has finally come to remove the needle from diversity's broken record. Listening together. Circling up, freeing our bodies of harm. Dancing off the burdens we have carried thus far with some percussive hand-clapping, foot-stomping, field-hollering. Or just sharing a simple story of taking part in rituals of music making that have healed us along the way. Even the latency of a ring shout via Zoom would do until we can be face-to-face again once a COVID-19 vaccine is fully distributed. Our liberation and freedom from injustice as a society depends on imagining something beyond the deceptive cadences that have defined calls for diversity until now.

NOTES

1. I dedicate this extended meditation to the ancestors whose legacies in music and dance turn the pages of my mind, including Zora Neale Hurston and Toni Morrison. And to all of the past co-chairs of the Crossroads Project and Section, particularly the editors of this volume, I offer gratitude for keeping our minds and hearts on the prize—musical, social, and emotional justice within SEM and society at large.

2. In 2020, Brenda M. Romero, former cochair of the Crossroads Project, informed me that the section name was changed to increase SEM membership activity and avoid a "damage-centered" appeal (Tuck 2009).

In 2009, Eve Tuck wrote an open letter to educators to interrupt the "long-term impact of 'damage-centered' research—research that intends to document peoples' pain and brokenness to hold those in power accountable for their oppression" (409). While the Crossroads Project has begun to sponsor research, much of the healing work I envisioned in 2003 (not to mention in 2020) is consistent with a model of restorative justice—"to repair the harm after a damaging incident, to repair the damaged relationship between the two parties in conflict and restore the offender back to the community" (Kidder 2007, 4). While we can and should avoid "damage-centered" research, an aim of the Crossroads Project was maintaining focus on those who are underutilized and whose labor and voices often go untapped and unrecognized in professional situations.

3. I recommend readers watch Afro-British singer-songwriter and record producer Michael Kiwanuka's (2016) music video "Black Man in a White World" for an Afro-futurist rendering of the ring shout.

4. In the interest of making hidden labor visible, I want to acknowledge and thank the 2007 SEM Alan Merriam Prize Committee, including Paul Austerlitz, David Borgo, Tina Ramnarine, and Deborah Wong (chair). Our intentions must live in habits so we might avoid glossing over what can often become a habit of exploitation hidden by omission. The 2007 co-winner was Michael Largey's *Vodou Nation: Haitian Art Music and Cultural Nationalism* (University of Chicago Press, 2006).

BIBLIOGRAPHY

Becker, Judith. 1986. "Is Western Art Music Superior?" *Musical Quarterly* 72 (3): 341–59.

Bohmer, Susanne, and Joyce L. Briggs. 1991. "Teaching Privileged Students about Gender, Race, and Class Oppression." *Teaching Sociology* 19 (2): 154–63.

Bote, Joshua. 2020. "'Get in Good Trouble, Necessary Trouble': Rep. John Lewis in His Own Words." *USA Today*, July 18, 2020. https://www.usatoday.com

/story/news/politics/2020/07/18/rep-john-lewis-most-memorable-quotes-get-good-trouble/5464148002/.

Brooks, Daphne A. 2010. "'Sister, Can You Line It Out?': Zora Neale Hurston and the Sound of Angular Black Womanhood." *American Studies* 55 (4): 617–27.

Brown, Danielle. 2020. "An Open Letter on Racism in Music Studies: Especially Ethnomusicology and Music Education." *My People Tell Stories* (blog), June 12, 2020. https://www.mypeopletellstories.com/blog/open-letter/.

De Tocqueville, Alexis. (1835) 2002. *Democracy in America*. Translated by Henry Reeve. 2 vols. Penn State Electronic Classics Series Publication. State College: Pennsylvania State University. http://seas3.elte.hu/coursematerial/LojkoMiklos/Alexis-de-Tocqueville-Democracy-in-America.pdf/.

Drewal, Margaret T. 1992. *Yoruba Ritual: Performers, Play, Agency*. Bloomington: Indiana University Press.

Floyd, Samuel A. 1991. "Ring Shout! Literary Studies, Historical Studies, and Black Music Inquiry." *Black Music Research Journal* 11 (2): 265–87.

Floyd, Samuel A., Melanie Zeck, and Guthrie Ramsey. 2017. *The Transformation of Black Music: The Rhythms, the Songs, and the Ships of the African Diaspora*. New York: Oxford University Press.

Gaunt, Kyra D. 1997. "The Games Black Girls Play: Music, Body, and 'Soul.'" PhD diss., University of Michigan.

———. 2006. *The Games Black Girls Play: Learning the Ropes from Double-Dutch to Hip-Hop*. New York: New York University Press.

Glasberg, Davita Silfen, and Deric Shannon. 2011. *Political Sociology: Oppression, Resistance, and the State*. 2nd ed. Los Angeles: Pine Forge.

Grillo, Trina. 1995. "Anti-Essentialism and Intersectionality: Tools to Dismantle the Master's House." *Berkeley Journal of Gender, Law & Justice* 10 (1): 16–30.

Kidder, Deborah L. 2007. "Restorative Justice: Not 'Rights,' but the Right Way to Heal Relationships at Work." *International Journal of Conflict Management* 18 (1): 4–22.

Kilpinen, Erkki. 2015. "Habit, Action, and Knowledge from the Pragmatist Perspective." In *Action, Belief and Inquiry: Pragmatist Perspectives on Science, Society and Religion*, edited by Ulf Zackariasson, 157–73. Helsinki, Sweden: Nordic Pragmatism Network.

Montgomery, Nick, and carla bergman. 2017. *Joyful Militancy: Building Thriving Resistance in Toxic Times*. Chico, CA: AK Press.

Morrison, Toni. 1987. *Beloved*. New York: Alfred A. Knopf.

Pennington, Charlotte R., Derek Heim, Andrew R. Levy, and Derek T. Larkin. 2016. "Twenty Years of Stereotype Threat Research: A Review of Psychological Mediators." *PLOS ONE* 11 (1). https://doi.org/10.1371/journal.pone.0146487.

Phillips, Trevor J. (1966) 2013. *Transactionalism: An Historical and Interpretive Study*. Edited by Kirkland Tibbels and John Patterson. Ojai, CA: Influence Ecology.

Rice, Timothy. 2004. "SEM Soundbyte: How Is SEM Doing on Diversity?" *SEM Newsletter*. Society for Ethnomusicology. September 2004. https://cdn.ymaws.com/www.ethnomusicology.org/resource/resmgr/newsletters/38_4_sep___2004.pdf/.

Robinson, Dylan. 2020. "Disrupting White Supremacy in Music and Sound Studies." Roundtable at the Annual Meeting of the Society for Ethnomusicology (virtual), October 23, 2020. https://cdn.ymaws.com/www.ethnomusicology.org/resource/resmgr/2020_annual_meeting/program_book_sem_2020_10.28..pdf/.

Rosenbaum, Art. (1998) 2012. *Shout Because You're Free: The African American Ring Shout Tradition in Coastal Georgia*. Athens: University of Georgia Press.

Steele, Claude M. 1997. "A Threat in the Air: How Stereotypes Shape Intellectual Identity and Performance." *American Psychologist* 52 (6): 613–29.

"Stereotype Threat." n.d. Scientific Workforce Diversity at the National Institutes of Health. Accessed June 1, 2022. https://diversity.nih.gov/sociocultural-factors/stereotype-threat.

Stuckey, Sterling. 2013. *Slave Culture: Nationalist Theory and the Foundations of Black America*. New York: Oxford University Press.

Sullivan, Shannon. 2001. *Living Across and Through Skins: Transactional Bodies, Pragmatism, and Feminism*. Bloomington: Indiana University Press.

Tuck, Eve. 2009. "Suspending Damage: A Letter to Communities." *Harvard Educational Review* 79 (3): 409–28.

VIDEOGRAPHY

Benjamin, Ruha (@ruha9). 2019. "'Are Robots Racist?' guest lecture video link, suitable for high school to grad school, book clubs, and other groups. . . ." MP4 file accessed via Twitter, December 11, 2019. https://twitter.com/ruha9/status/1206979028764315649/.

Kiwanuka, Michael. 2016. "Black Man in a White World." *YouTube*. 3:33. March 28, 2016. https://youtu.be/-TYlcVNI2AM/.

Wilkerson, Isabel. 2020. "Caste in America: Isabel Wilkerson with John Dickerson | LIVE from NYPL." *YouTube*. New York Public Library. 1:09:41. August 2020. https://youtu.be/FxpouTYfJKY/.

TWO

SOCIAL JUSTICE AND MY WORK AS A MUSIC SCHOLAR, TEACHER, AND ARTIST

STEVEN LOZA

IN THE PROCESS OF WRITING this piece, I watched the film *Malcom X* for a second time. Some days before, US congressman John Lewis had passed away; it had been almost forty years since he marched with Dr. Martin Luther King on the Edmund Pettus Bridge in Selma, Alabama. Most recently, our country watched in horror as policemen murdered George Floyd on the streets of Minneapolis. In response, the UCLA Herb Alpert School of Music instituted an Anti-Racist Action Committee to increase the numbers of students and faculty of color, revamp the curriculum, and more—changes that should have been in place many years ago. The struggle continues.

I ask myself, "How have I dealt with issues of race and inequality in my vocation as a university professor of ethnomusicology, a musician, composer, and producer of academic and artistic events?" What first comes to mind is how I integrate social justice issues in my musical compositions. To complete my bachelor's degree in music at California State Polytechnic University, I performed a senior recital. The principal piece I composed was a three-movement suite entitled *Emancipation from Strife*; the main theme focused on racism and the hope that we would someday overcome it. Forty-five years later, I periodically listen to the suite, which I issued as a CD recording in 1995. The words and music ring as loudly today, perhaps more loudly, than they did then. The following excerpts are verses taken from the second movement:

> Where is the ghetto,
> I'd like to know.
> Where is the jungle
> Where children grow?
> The Lord doesn't have to worry about me seeing the Light,

What He's got on His hands is a first-rate plight.
Racist, bigot, prejudice, words of the day,
The Lord doesn't care. He'll get His way.

Every step in my early career was affected or caused by political and cultural forces. My doctoral dissertation (UCLA, 1985) documented the musical life of the Mexican/Chicanx people in Los Angeles, and a later version was published as a book entitled *Barrio Rhythm: Mexican American Music in Los Angeles* (1993). Upon finishing the dissertation in 1985, I started teaching in the UCLA Department of Music in a faculty position that has been funded by the UCLA Chicano Studies Research Center to this day.

TEACHING AND THE UNIVERSITY

My goal as a teacher has been to integrate into my courses aspects related to social justice. As a specialist in Latin American and Chicanx/Latinx musical cultures, I not only initiated coursework focused on social justice but also found it necessary to customize studies that would serve students of color, especially Chicanx/Latinx students. In my first year of teaching, I developed an undergraduate course on the musical life of Chicanx/Latinx people in the United States. A Ford grant made it possible for me to design a multicultural curriculum that included an undergraduate course entitled "Musical Aesthetics in Los Angeles." The course directly interfaced with the 1994 volume *Selected Reports in Ethnomusicology*, for which I served as editor. Additionally, I advanced a graduate seminar, examining musical cross-cultural aesthetics and multiculturalism. In general, my courses signified and activated many issues around teaching and publishing related to cultural and intellectual bias in the so-called music canon. During the ravaging Los Angeles Rebellion of 1993 following the Rodney King court trial, I dedicated a full ethnomusicology seminar session to a discussion of the event as we were living it in real time. Two African American graduate students enrolled in the seminar had much to say and teach the other students.

A major social event that has continued to impact me to this day is the 1993 hunger strike at UCLA organized by Chicanx students, faculty, and community members, demanding the development of a Chicanx Studies Department. Nine individuals conducted a hunger strike over a two-week period, risking their health and lives for a cause they deemed urgent and necessary. Invited to serve as one of the faculty negotiators, I participated in a campus march to support the strike. I recall wondering if I should join the strike while in the midst of my tenure evaluation and decided to hell with the fear of being denied.

From 1996 to 1997, I had the honor of teaching at Kanda University of International Studies in Japan. There, I taught the following courses: World Music, Latin American Music, Latin American Philosophy and Culture, and Multiculturalism in the United States. Fortuitously, due to the students' language specializations, I was able to teach in English and Spanish as well as teach courses unrelated specifically to music, an opportunity I have never had at a US university. Also unprecedented was a special lecture I presented on race, culture, and conflict in the United States, which had over five hundred students in attendance.

Another opportunity came my way in 2002 when I accepted a two-year position to serve as professor of music and director of the newly established Arts of the Americas Institute at the University of New Mexico. It was an eye-opening experience to witness the university's overwhelming emphasis on Western classical music as opposed to local and traditional genres of the state's majority population of Native American and New Mexican Chicanx/Hispanic residents.

Returning to UCLA in 2004, I conducted various projects and offered classes supporting social justice issues as a way to counter the status quo and disrupt the lip service on diversity that persisted in the university system. Radical change simply was not possible. An attempt to diversify music theory and history courses in the school of music failed due to a lack of organization and interest among both faculty and students, so it was back to mostly harmony, counterpoint, and "set theory." The Department of Ethnomusicology, nonetheless, continued developing its own separate world music theory and history coursework.

Among the most glaring issues related to jazz programs in the United States are the small number of students of color, especially African Americans, and the persistent Eurocentric mode of teaching. Two years ago, faculty developed a new interdepartmental program in the school of music focused on jazz studies, which previously constituted a part of the ethnomusicology curriculum. The new Global Jazz Studies Program incorporates specific ethnomusicology courses that consider the present and future role of jazz as a cultural form both in the United States and abroad. I currently chair the new Global Jazz Studies program, and one of our major concerns is the unexpectedly low enrollment of African American students in the program and in the School of Music in general. We continue to work fervently on this problem.

SCHOLARSHIP AND RELATED ACTIVITIES

When I began my graduate research during the late 1970s and early 1980s, there were relatively few studies on Chicanx/Latinx music. I felt something had to be done about the paucity of scholarship in this area. I wrote my dissertation on Chicanx musical culture, found in my own backyard, in view of the academic and social need for this study. I became a reflexive ethnographer, which had its advantages, something not very different from many Western scholars studying only Western music. I diverged greatly from that model, however, and today a large part of my research focuses on the intercultural music of Latinx and African American cultures.

Much of my ethnographic work has focused on the musical culture of my own native context, that of being a Mexican American, a Chicano in Los Angeles, my native city. As noted previously, the issue of native ethnography is one that can be assessed in numerous ways. During the 1970s, anthropologists such as Augustus Sordinas and Joseph Aceves and ethnomusicologist Charlotte Heth critiqued such pros and cons, with Sordinas observing that "profound malaise in present anthropological research and reporting is difficult to cure" (1978, 1). He attributed the malaise to a lack of confidence among natives with "alien researchers'" and ethnographers' lack of deep cultural knowledge of and insight into the people being studied. Sordinas concluded "the two syndromes work together to further exacerbate largely illusory claims of 'participant observation.' As a minimum cure the presence of seasoned native ethnographers is suggested" (ibid.). On the other hand, Aceves, noting the care native ethnographers must take in studying their own culture, ascertained that "training in anthropology usually sensitizes one to the nuances of behavior of other people, but may lure the unwary into an assumption that they needn't be as careful in dealing with the behavior of their own people" (1978, 8). Responding to the question of such pros and cons, Heth evaluates the position of the Native American:

> The argument against Indian scholars studying their own music has always been expressed in terms of possible lack of objectivity. Why then is the bulk of the educational system in Europe and America centered around "White Studies," in the guise of humanities, philosophy, world civilization, music history, etc.? If a scholar has a good research design and a well thought-out project, he or she should be able to do a good job. And, subjectivity is not always bad. Indeed, an inside view may help the researcher by providing a set of aesthetic criteria to judge quality in the music and truthfulness in the interviews with performers.
>
> While there are dangers inherent in studying one's own culture, they are not based on the argument of objectivity vs. non-objectivity. Rather, they are contingent on such matters as jealousy, sex and role status, age, closeness to a particular person of power, misunderstanding of motives, initiation

requirements, religious membership, and, occasionally, witchcraft. It is not enough just to be a tribal member by blood or enrollment. (1982, 4)

Much has changed since these views were expressed during the period from 1978 to 1982. The number of Native ethnographers has multiplied in response to the intense social and political lack of representation. Whether or not a level of parity exists in this complex enterprise, it continues to be a valid question and one that should continue to be examined as society continues to evolve.

In my published work, I have not refrained from expressing my social and political views concerning social justice. These viewpoints have revolved around a matrix of race, ethnicity, social and economic class, gender, age, and religion. My research focuses on religion, in particular, because I feel it has been greatly neglected in the field of music. It is as important as the ideological or political dimensions we study in any of the musicology branches. One of the essays I am most proud of is one I read at the 2005 Society for Ethnomusicology meeting and published in *Ethnomusicology* (2006). Entitled "Challenges to the Euroamericentric Ethnomusicological Canon: Alternatives for Graduate Readings, Theory, and Method," the piece critiques issues of intellectual capitalism in academia, and its hegemonic prejudice based on American (US-based) and European standards. My basic question asks, "Where are the intellectual ideas and standards of those of us who are marginalized and who neither conform to or are represented in established biased models?"

In my ethnographic and musical studies of Latinx and African American artists, there is no way to evade the dynamic experiences of racism and sociocultural marginality they have lived. And lived experience, as so eloquently voiced by musical artist, Stevie Wonder, is what music is all about. In studying Mexican and Cuban musical cultures, it struck me how many rich traditions—folk, popular, and chamber/symphonic and their contexts—are simply not included in scholastic surveys of music used in teaching music theory and history. Frankly, this is shameful, ethnocentric, and as much an affront to social justice as the segregated practices of Jim Crow in the South and former president Donald Trump's Mexico-US border wall.

ARTISTRY AND PRODUCTION

As implied previously, my undergraduate days were filled with the idea that I would pursue life as a performer and composer platforms I was already using to fight the realities of racism and discrimination. In deciding to enter a graduate research program, I realized that I would inevitably sacrifice much, if not the majority, of my artistic goals, which in great part were based on my ideals of social justice. I believe that a life dedicated to scholarship and teaching can change the world. I hope it has, and despite the difficulties, I have retained much of my artistry.

Part of the ethnomusicology program I found inspiring was Ki Mantle Hood's bimusical concept that emphasizes being both scholar and musician in our understanding of any form of musical expression in any part of the world. During the 1990s, I reconstituted our mariachi performance class and added an Afro-Cuban music ensemble. I also spearheaded the hiring of internationally acclaimed musicians such as Nati Cano, Jesús Guzman, and Francisco Aguabella to lead these classes. These resident artists filled a need to broaden the musical experiences of not only students of color but all students at UCLA. I taught a Latinx music ensemble for many years, an intercultural improvisation ensemble, and a world jazz ensemble. Also progressive were the public concerts and workshops by the UCLA student mariachi ensemble that I organized. I also recorded and produced four CDs, largely comprising my own jazz/Latin/world music compositions, all with serious messages of social justice. As a performer I have traveled extensively throughout the United States, Mexico, Japan, New Zealand, China, Chile, and Cuba, concertizing with my own and others' ensembles. Performing, studying, and teaching music all represent my social justice goals.

From 1981 through 1996, I was instrumental in producing the Mexican Arts Series at UCLA. The sociocultural philosophy and intent of the series was to compare the artistic encounter of the Chicanx/Latinx experience with that of Mexico in over eighty musical events representing folk, popular, and symphonic/chamber music, art, film, dance, and theater. The series served as an example of academe's outreach to the community, resulting in successfully educating the public about the richness of Mexican arts and culture so often ignored in US society, especially in higher education. I also developed a series of exchange projects between UCLA and the Centro Nacional de las Artes in Mexico City. Twelve UCLA world music ensembles conducted workshops, lectures, and concerts with students and the public in Mexico City. Presently, we are conducting student exchanges between the Global Jazz Studies program and students of the Escuela Superior de Música in Mexico City. The interchanges are transforming the sociocultural outlook of all participating students in both nations.

When I was president of the board at the Latino Museum of History, Art and Culture in Los Angeles from 2007 to 2015, the museum partnered with UCLA and various government and corporate agencies to produce a concert featuring the Mexico City Philharmonic Orchestra. The concert, held at Disney

Fig. 2.1. *America Tropical* by David Alfaro Siqueiros. Color remake posted on-site during the recent reconstruction. Originally painted in 1932 on the façade of Italian Hall in El Pueblo de Los Angeles on Olvera Street.
Photo credit: The City Project. Creative Commons license.

Hall in 2008, included Mariachi Los Camperos de Nati Cano performing various pieces with the orchestra, and the premiere of my own symphonic composition based on the mural *America Tropical*, painted by Mexican muralist David Alfaro Siqueiros (see fig. 2.1). In response to its strong message about US imperialism, the city of Los Angeles whitewashed the mural soon after its 1931 opening on Olvera Street. In another concert, the Mariachi Los Camperos performed pieces with the National Symphonic Orchestra of Cuba. Both productions took place at Casa de las Americas in Havana. To reciprocate, the museum invited a traditional Afro-Cuban ensemble to conduct a two-week residency at UCLA.[1]

Mentioning the previous events is not meant to be boastful. My message is that in all of the productions I have embraced, I have critiqued what so many of us now recognize as the ignorance of and/or implicit bias against non-Western artistic values. Producing events that simultaneously serve teaching, research, and art connects the university with marginalized communities, both domestically and abroad, and models social justice as practice.

MEMBERSHIP IN SEM AND SOCIAL JUSTICE

My experience within the Society for Ethnomusicology has been both positive and negative. I have consistently reacted to its Eurocentric intellectual and cultural frameworks. The overwhelming bias in favor of cultural theories formed outside native contexts and the lack of diverse racial and ethnic voices have frustrated me as a member. One example is vivid. Since its formation in 1955, SEM has primarily elected White board presidents, and mostly male. Only three BIPOC women have been elected president. Two African American women ran for office, and both lost to White men. In all, only five BIPOC individuals have served as president: Robert Garfias (Mexican American), Charlotte Heth (Cherokee), Nazir Jairazhboy (Asian American, originally from India), Deborah Wong (Asian American), and Tomie Hahn (Asian American). Spurred by these issues, I gladly served as chair of the SEM section formerly called Crossroads Project on Diversity, Difference, and Underrepresentation from 2005 to 2008. During my term as co-chair with Lei Ouyang Bryant in 2009, I initiated a conference to explore the theme of diversity, inviting various SEM members to speak. Sponsored by UCLA and the University of Michigan, by way of support from UM associate chancellor Lester Monts, the conference successfully brought together diverse perspectives related to social justice.

CLOSING THOUGHTS

Finally, I would like to report that I am currently developing a proposal to initiate a four-year school in Los Angeles. Its purpose will be to serve high school students coming from underprivileged and low-income families who have no hope of studying music in a major university, often due to their lack of preparation in biased standards such as reading Western music notation and having high grade point averages. The standard for acceptance would be musical ability in any form and a desire to foster social justice in US society. The tentative name of the proposed school is the Black and Brown Conservatory of Music, and it would be open to students of any color and heritage and dedicated to those communities who have suffered from exclusion far too long.

NOTE

1. See also PBS Broadcast (2017).

BIBLIOGRAPHY

Aceves, Joseph B. 1978. "'Competence by Blood': Ethnological Fieldwork in the Ancestral Village." Paper presented at the Annual Meeting of the American Anthropological Association, Los Angeles, California.

Heth, Charlotte. 1982. "Can Ethnohistory Help the Ethnomusicologist?" *American Indian Culture and Research Journal* 6 (1): 63–78.

Loza, Steven. 1985. "The Musical Life of the Mexican/Chicano People in Los Angeles, 1945–1985: A Study in Maintenance, Change, and Adaptation." PhD diss., University of California, Los Angeles.

———. 1993. *Barrio Rhythm: Mexican American Music in Los Angeles*. Urbana: University of Illinois Press.

———, ed. 1994. *Selected Reports in Ethnomusicology: Musical Aesthetics and Multiculturalism in Los Angeles.* Vol. 10. Department of Ethnomusicology, University of California, Los Angeles.

———. 2006. "Challenges to the Euroamericentric Ethnomusicological Canon: Alternatives for Graduate Readings, Theory, and Method." *Ethnomusicology* 50 (2): 360–71.

Sordinas, Augustus. 1978. "Ethnography: In Need of Native Ethnographers." Paper read at the Seventy-Seventh Annual Meeting of the American Anthropological Association, Los Angeles, California.

DISCOGRAPHY

Loza, Steve. 1995. *Emancipation from Strife: Rebel with a Cause; Steve Loza.* Stedman Park, MA: Merrimack Records. MR 10103.

VIDEOGRAPHY

PBS Broadcast. 2017. "David Alfaro Siqueiros' Mural 'America Tropical.'" *Craft in America*, season 9, September 29. Video. Accessed January 6, 2022. https://www.pbs.org/video/david-alfaro-siqueiros-mural-america-tropical-4r7glz/.

THREE

PUNK AND POLITICS AND TRANSFORMING MUSICAL ACADEME

BRENDA M. ROMERO

IN THE LATE 1940S, MALCOLM X began to use the X to protest the names his ancestors had been assigned during slavery.[1] His public activism helped to fuel the Civil Rights Movement. By the 1960s when I was coming of age, the concept of a mainstream public had become fully formed owing to TV shows that dominated the airwaves, no matter where you were in the US. Few channels were available, so we grew up with limited media and prime-time programs that defined what it meant to be "American." This included the *Ed Sullivan Show* and radio shows. As a result, boomers like myself tended to bond over rock and roll.

Having retired from a fraught academic career as the founder of an ethnomusicology program at a majority White university in Boulder, Colorado, I returned to New Mexico to occupy the small acreage of land my family had inherited through the Sebastián Martín Land Grant (in existence since the seventeenth century) that occupies ancestral homelands of the Kiowa-Tanoan peoples. This essay connects my life events to music and social justice, as upon returning, I am learning and relearning more about my history in northern New Mexico, and in new holistic alliances, locally and beyond, I hope to contribute to the well-being of the region.

I am also feeling lingering historical disconnects as evidenced by local conflicts that underlie social tensions caused by drug and alcohol addiction or by misogyny, patriarchy, and colorism.[2] An instance of local colorism that prompts me to recall some of my own personal experiences in contemporary times and as a child with dark(er) skin in northern New Mexico, is evident in a poem, "Adiós Llano de San Juan." Manito anthropologist-composer-lyricist-tradition-bearer David F. García (also my musical duet partner and nonprofit collaborator) found the poem in a literary column, "La Lira Neo-Mexicana" published in *El Nuevo*

Mexicano (in Santa Fe) on September 11, 1930. The poem underscores the poetic learning all students received in their early education in New Mexico and was reinforced in Spanish language newspaper columns featuring the poems of local and regional contributors.

To reiterate, "Adiós Llano de San Juan" is significant in part because it describes an incident of local colorism as nuanced as any contemporary incident of "color-blind" racism.[3] García recites this poem on our recent acoustic recording.[4] Listeners learn in local dialect that the protagonist is *trigueño* (dark skinned) and that Don Elías has told him his truck is broken and can't take him to the bus station where he can catch a bus to Guayuma (Wyoming), where he works as a shepherd.[5] Don Elías's class status is established when he is referred to with the honorific term *don* and because he owns a truck. The poet suggests that Don Elias is prejudiced against him. Northern New Mexico was known for its poverty, rivaling Appalachia, and many Hispanos from New Mexico worked as migrant laborers. Nonetheless, in verse 10, we learn the shepherd had gone "first to Wyoming," then to New Mexico, and then back to Wyoming, scrutinizing folks along the way, implying the shepherd was a Mexican migrant. Verse 11 underscores his noble regard to his dedicated labor as a shepherd and once again reveals his class consciousness: "I send you these verses as a poor man to a rich man." Verse 12 further delineates a local tendency with great accuracy, "Hah! You think because my skin is brown that I am incapable or delinquent in some way, but I am not only capable but responsible in paying my bills. My money is as good as anyone else's!" And in verses 13 and 14 the author uses the term *su merce[d]* (Your Mercy) to call out the errant, supposed "superior," with hopes Don Elias's ears will burn with embarrassment when he sees his behavior bandied about in the poem published in the local newspaper.[6]

As in many of the old southwestern narrative ballads, these verses commemorate local place names and history. This poem reveals a thriving public transit system: the Chile Line, the train line that united northern New Mexico with Colorado between 1880 and 1941, stopped for lunch at the station in El Embudo (which could connect with nearby Mora, Las Vegas, NM, Santa Fe, and north to Denver). Aside from that sixty-one year period of relative prosperity, only in the last twenty-five years or so has a reliable commuter system run along the Santa Fe–Questa corridor in northern New Mexico! It is now more convenient and inexpensive to take a bus to the store or casino, for instance, and elders are not stuck at home because they no longer drive.

Also consistent with the old ballads, the final verse names the composer of the poem or song, in this case José B. Vásquez.[7] García shared with me the final line, in which the protagonist proclaims himself "puritito" chicano in 1930, documenting the term *chicano* as part of the regional vernacular by the 1920s and '30s; in this case, for someone with dark skin who shepherded domesticated animals and perhaps also had experience working the land. The term's origins are contested, but it was used pejoratively in the 1950s and reappropriated by the Chicano movement in the 1960s to valorize the labor of the poor, in particular that of Indigenous peoples and their mixed descendants, who have often been denied colonial property and wealth.

Adiós Llano de San Juan by José B. Vásquez

1
Adiós Llano de San Juan	Goodbye Llano de San Juan
sitio del condao de Taos;	wherein is Taos County;
ya me voy para Guayuma	I am leaving for Guayuma [Wyoming]
a pastorear los ganados.	to herd the animals.

2
El día ocho de julio	On July 8
del mil nueve cientos treinta	of 1930
ya yo estaba alistando	I was already preparing
para salir a la ausencia.	to travel and be absent.

3
Mañana me voy de aquí;	Tomorrow I will leave this place;
voy a buscar un troquero	I am going to look for someone with a truck
que me lleve hasta El Embudo	who will take me as far as El Embudo
a tomar el pasajero.	to catch the passenger train.

4
Para la plaza me fui	I went to the plaza
a buscar a don Elías	to look for Don Elías
que me llevara hasta el dipo	to take me to the depot
en esos meritos días.	on those very days.

5
Don Elías me responde	Don Elías responded
con su voz muy recortada,	in a cutting tone of voice,
yo no le quiero llevar,	I don't want to take you,
está mi troca quebrada.	my truck is broken.

6
Yo por cierto lo creí	I surely did believe him
y ahora me estoy acordando	and now I am remembering
que lo hizo por no llevarme	he did it so he wouldn't have to take me.
y luego anda arebatando [*sic*].	and there he is grabbing what he needs.

7
Otro día que salí
con mi muchila [sic] y maleta
me fui a esperar el correo
que llegara a la estafeta.

The day I departed
with my backpack and suitcase
I went to wait for the mail
to arrive at the post office.

8
En la estafeta de Peñasco
allí sentado estaba
cuando pasó don Elías
con su troquita "quebrada."

At the Peñasco post office
there I was sitting
when Don Elías passed by
in his "broken" truck.

9
Siempre hizo Elías su viaje
el día que yo salí;
lo vi pasar en Peñasco
adelantito de mi.

Elías still made his trip
on the day I left;
I saw him drive by in Peñasco
just ahead of me.

10
Yo me vine para Guayuma
donde había estado primero;
aquí compuse estos versos
como humilde borreguero.

I came to Guayuma [Wyoming]
where I came first;
here I composed these verses
as a humble shepherd.

11
Aquí estoy de borreguero
porque a borreguiar me dedico,
pero le mando estos versos
como de un pobre a un rico.

I am here as a shepherd
because that is my dedicated work,
but I send [Don Elías] these verses
as a poor man to a rich man.

12
Si porque me ve trigueño
creye que no soy formal,
al que le debo le pago
y mi dinero es igual.

If because you see my dark skin
you believe I am not a serious person,
I pay those to whom I owe
and my money is the same [as anyone's].

13
No crea que estoy 'nojado
porque me acuerdo de uste;
es por lo que lo he estimado
y el trato que me dió su
merce [sic].

Don't think I am angry
because I remember this of you;
it is because of how much I valued you
and the treatment Your Mercy showed me.

14
Ya con esta me despido;
voy a mirar mis ovejas.

And so I take my leave;
I am going to care for my sheep.

Creo que será suficiente	I think it will be sufficient
que le ardan las orejas.	that his ears will burn.
15	
Aquí les firmo mi nombre	Here I leave my signature
También con mi propia mano;	also in my own hand;
soy José B. Vasquez	I am José B. Vasquez
y soy puritito chicano.	and am one hundred percent chicano.

(Translation by Brenda M. Romero and David F. García)

The United States has continued to function and maintain fiscal balance that is founded on the backs of this laboring class, a metaphor also exploited in the title of Cherrie Moraga and Gloria Anzaldúa's edited book, *This Bridge Called My Back: Writings by Radical Women of Color* ([1981] 1993). I mention this work also for its call to action and overwhelming influence among Latinas along the US-Mexico borderlands, including myself. The book has been translated into many languages and now enjoys global readership. Women of that movement today include luminaries like Norma E. Cantú (born in Nuevo Laredo, Tamaulipas, Mexico, and raised in Laredo, Texas), president of the American Folklore Society from 2019 to 2021, who has mentored not only me, but many other women of our generation and younger. Her energy is boundless, and in 2017, I had the privilege of conducting collaborative fieldwork with her on the Danza de Matachines (among other names) in Kansas City, Kansas, and Kansas City, Missouri, where Professor Cantú had recently completed four years as professor of Latina/Latino studies at the University of Missouri, Kansas City. There, we documented seven immigrant Matachines danza troupes in December 2017.We also conducted fieldwork among the Pascua Yaqui Tribe in Tucson, Arizona, where ethnomusicologist Janet Sturman helped to orient us to the setting and introduced us to key individuals.

I will add that Mexican colleagues at the Ethnochoreology Department of the Benemérita Universidad Autónoma de Puebla (BUAP) in Puebla, Mexico, among them department founders José Luis Sagredo Castillo and Isabel Galicia López drew inspiration from my fieldwork presentations on Matachines in New Mexico, Mexico, Colombia, and Peru at BUAP's annual Ethnochoreology Colloquium. The two scholars and their colleagues sought to collect more data on this important tradition in Mexico and at the US-Mexico borderlands. The Mexican government funded the BUAP project, and the BUAP sponsored my fieldwork with Professor Cantú in Kansas City and Tucson. Among these scholars and in participation with the BUAP's Annual Ethnochoreology Colloquium, I have found an intellectual home among scholars working with music, movement, folklore, and a wide variety of communities that value music and dance as essential to individual and communal well-being. Something I struggled with as a budding ethnomusicologist was the disconnect between the discipline's emphasis on holistic study while insisting that music be the central element in an event. As I have moved toward more inclusive models, such as my synergy model discussed in the final chapter of this anthology, I have found greater intellectual and spiritual rewards from my work.

FROM WHERE DOES A WORLDVIEW EMERGE?

I was born in Santa Fe, New Mexico, and grew up in a small village farther north, formerly called El Bosque because of the giant cottonwood and willow trees that were ubiquitous in the very narrow landmass between the river and the hillside, where my mother's and father's ancestors had settled. I grew up in Rio Arriba County in northern New Mexico, the seat of Spanish control during the colonial period. On lava boulders all around us we saw petroglyphs as El Bosque occupies ancestral lands of the Kiowa-Tanoan peoples and the Tewa in particular.

I use the term *Manito* with respect to local ethnic-cultural identity because it captures the essence of what drives traditional Hispano cultural beliefs and practices.[8] It derives from Los Hermanos de la Fraternidad Piadosa de Nuestro Padre Jesús Nazareno (The Brothers of the Pious Fraternity of Our Father Jesus the Nazarene), who feel called on to dedicate themselves to Christ-consciousness in visceral ways that intensify during Easter week and sometimes in other contexts, such as a wake for a departed *hermano*, brother. The term *'manito* is formed from the diminutive *hermanito*, little brother or younger brother (Romero 2011), signaling novice status in the Spanish practices of penance and mercy (see Wroth 1991). In deference to the term's general usage among *nuevomexicano* scholars, I have adapted "Manito" without the apostrophe to denote an insider, mixed population generally united by a very particular value system founded on the cultivation of compassion. Nonetheless, the most recent activist scholarship is focused on *"genízaro* consciousness," an acknowledgement of local ethnic hybridity resulting from the enslavement of Native women and girls, in particular.

My mother was very light-skinned. Due to her coveted milky white skin, dark hair, and hazel eyes, she was called *la blanca*. One of her Spanish ancestors, Tomás Miera y Pacheco, came to New Mexico in the late eighteenth century as a cartographer remembered for his maps, today held in museums. My mother's family enjoyed the status of running the community post office and store. She once told me that my father's dark-skinned ancestors were said to have come from Panama, although I always imagined it was said derisively—a colorist slur.

Fig. 3.1. Author's great-grandparents Ignacita and Juan Pedro Romero. Courtesy of author.

Figure 3.1 features two of my paternal ancestors who perhaps reflect my sister's DNA test revealing 1 percent Bantu and Senegalese and 1 percent Middle Eastern ancestries, along with 50 percent of ancestries from the Iberian Peninsula and 43 percent from Indigenous peoples from South to North America.

My maternal uncles performed on violin and guitar for social dances—*bailes*, although this was not as valued in the community as much as laboring in the fields. Thus, my paternal uncles who worked the land held more local authority. Mom was "allowed" to marry my father (and not her light-skinned suitor) as much for Dad's warm nature as for his strong intellect and initiative. They married in the beautiful San Juan Mission in the Pueblo of the same name, in 1936.[9] He later attended one year of college against the odds and eventually became a social worker. Accordingly, my parents identified with *gente decente*—decent folk—who were religious, honest, and self-sacrificing.

My aunt, a Manita and US citizen, and my uncle, of Mexican Huichol ancestry, moved to Mexico in the late 1940s, where my uncle owned a farm. Despite my aunt's citizenship, it took seven years before they were able to return to New Mexico. Because my father assisted with the documents required for my uncle's green card, I learned harsh lessons about governmental exclusionary practices and social injustice. In elementary school, I began to call myself Mexican American rather than "Spanish American," and I gravitated to Mexican trios I heard on the radio in the 1950s. It would be many years before I understood what it means to be a descendant of settler colonization, however.

Dad was a strict authoritarian and talking back resulted in being severely disciplined. Being egalitarian meant he also treated his ten children equally, and one must not stand out. If we got in trouble at school, it was our fault. He suffered from progressive nerve disease—perhaps triggered by his work at "the labs" (the 1940s nuclear labs in Los Alamos, New Mexico). Doctors predicted in 1951 that Dad, then in his mid-thirties, would live only seven more years, but he lived until 1997.[10]

In contrast, my mother tended to favor the lighter-skinned males in the family, who were also the most vulnerable, as I go on to discuss. Like Dad, Mom was also a strict disciplinarian, although Dad meted out any punishment due. As a small child, my mother too had outlived a doctor's dire prediction when he sent her home to die of typhoid fever. Instead, she responded to my grandfather's iced spearmint tea baths and fierce, prayerful determination that she might live. A few years later, federal agents found my mother running the post office at age twelve, and they officially allowed her to continue. She strongly believed in the value of education and regretted attending school only to the fifth grade. Throughout her life, she instilled in her ten children the desire to learn; she lived to be ninety-nine and a half. Our lives changed forever when we lost one of my fourteen-year old twin brothers to an accidental shooting by a fifteen-year old White male associate. Then, when my older sister closest to my age died at thirty-seven of a brain tumor she left three children, including an infant and a middle child who committed suicide at age twenty-nine in 2008. Over time we have lost three brothers (aged forty-nine, fifty-six, and seventy-four) to work- and alcohol-related health problems, stemming in part from culture loss (discussed in the paragraphs that follow).

My father's work took us "far away" to western New Mexico (Gallup), where I attended school from the fifth grade on, alongside Diné, Zuni Pueblo, Mexican American, African American (few), and White students. My older brother Albert (1941–2016) lived for many years with a Diné weaver whose laughter and levity I still recall; only now do I understand how laughter has been a pillar of survival among American Indians. I cannot underestimate how these and the following encounters shaped my life. In elementary school I could already tell there was something wrong, noting my Native schoolmates who rarely spoke up. I was in high school before I began to understand what it might mean to live in the dorms, and only now do I fathom the full horror it must have been for some of my friends. It wasn't until my junior year in high school that I realized I was a product of the public schools that, in general, lined up with a historical trajectory of coloniality of power that many of us now better comprehend. Fortunately, in high school I learned about the Bahá'í faith from a classmate; I subsequently visited Bahá'í homes in Australia, New Mexico, and Ecuador, where I could find myself in the presence of those "different from" myself, a Bahá'í tenet.

In my early childhood in northern New Mexico, Catholicism brought with settler colonialism united some Pueblos and Hispanos in the mission churches and during important Catholic saints' feast days. Water is the force that connects Hispano and Pueblo inhabitants in northern New Mexico today. The most important local Catholic (and public) feast day was and is still the Feast of Saint John, an event in which fifty or so Tewas, Hispanos, and Whites walk together in procession with the bishop of the diocese, priests, and deacons to the Rio Grande, where the bishop blesses the river.[11] Without its water for irrigation, this would be a desert landscape—sandy, sloping beaches of an ancient riverbed. The Annual Seed Blessing Ceremony is performed when the *acequias*, irrigation ditches, are "opening" for the season, a rare inclusive event bringing Native groups and Manitos together. In this ceremony, Dr. David F. García yearly performs the ritual of singing a special "Acequia Song" while rhythmically striking a shovel with a rock.[12] The shovel is a symbol of the communal labor required to clean the acequias prior to letting the water run through for the season, labor García will also contribute with the shovel once the song has invoked a spiritual presence.

Outside of this context, social interaction on a regular basis is rare between Manitos and neighboring Native groups. In order to "give something back," as part of my doctoral fieldwork on the Matachines/Matachina Danza (the only Pueblo ceremonial dance that uses European-rooted instruments), I offered to play violin for the Pueblo of Jemez Matachina between 1988 and 1998. I subsequently taught my youthful Manito successor who plays violin for the Matachina today, as did his grandfather and great-grandfather. It is an honor to be asked to play for the Matachina (the Pueblos' name for the danza), a gesture of friendship that was traditionally bestowed on Manito musicians, who also taught the danza in many cases.

CULTURE LOSS

Turning my attention to contemporary culture loss in New Mexico, I challenge myself to avoid what Eve Tuck calls "damage-centered research," which I discuss further in the final chapter of this anthology.

Many Manitos are the poor descendants of foot soldiers enlisted to fight for the political and religious causes of European imperialism. Sadly, too many young Manitos continue to replicate the violence condoned in colonialism, even inflicting such behaviors on themselves and their families. Manitos are typically descended from the mixing of Spaniards—who counted on receiving stolen Native land in exchange for service to the Spanish court—with Native slaves or captives.[13] Some old *indita* ballads unique to New Mexico testify to mutual cultural practices of taking slaves and the emergence of mixed populations. I often perform inditas like "La cautiva Marcelina" ("Marcelina, the Captive"), which tells of a woman taken to "that place where they are known to eat mare's meat" (Mendoza and Mendoza 1986, 481, author's translation; see also Romero 2002).[14]

As a child in the 1950s, I learned that our next-door neighbor was of mixed Diné (Navajo) and Manito ancestry. We grew up around this family but other than being told at home, I never heard anyone else refer to the interracial mixing. Some families were accepting of captives as family members; ostensibly, they adapted quickly and with affection in most cases. But exploitation was likely rampant and female captives or dark-skinned mestizas risked being prostituted in order to raise money for the household, resulting in children with different fathers growing up as siblings. I remember my mother telling me who was related to whom in a certain matter-of-fact tone of voice. Women did sometimes avail themselves of the legal system; the "Indita de Juliana Ortega" reveals that Juliana is allowed to divorce a cruel husband, but she is subsequently shunned by the community.

Although popular stereotypes of Manitos might choose to emphasize our quixotic natures, the underlying situation has been the rapid loss of culture and the institutions that sustain it, such as the fiesta complex. Until I had experienced the fiestas in Mexico and Colombia, I was unable to piece together what had happened in New Mexico to obscure the contexts of the danza I study. Yet, even as the 1940s began decades in which young New Mexican Latinx from the old Manito culture began and continue to succumb to alcohol and drugs, a thriving music scene has never ceased to actively connect the Manito community and give voice to a depth of feelings.[15] A well-known weaver as much as award-winning performer-songwriter, Steve Chávez is an important community musician and sound engineer in Española who records and produces the albums of local hip-hop, rock, and Christian artists. Chávez's Recording Studio proves to be an archives of Manito lifeways expressed primarily in popular dance songs.

A LIFE WITH MUSIC

As a child I was lucky to experience live music, and not only at Mass. My mother sang when she was working peacefully at home. When I was two, she taught me to sing my first song, an emblematic New Mexican hymn, "Bendito sea dios, los angeles cantan y alaban a Dios" ("Blessed be God, the angels sing and praise God"). My two older brothers were also musical and played the trumpet and trombone in a high school dance band. For my first Holy Communion celebration (partaking of bread in the Catholic Mass), the band performed with amplified bass and rhythm guitars in our home. In my longing for early musical experiences, I gravitated to piano (wherever I could) as a child. When I was twelve, I taught myself piano basics from a child's method book when I babysat for the band teacher after the child I was watching had gone to bed. I sang in choirs from grades six through twelve. Three elementary school girlfriends taught me to play the ukulele when I was thirteen; subsequently, I began to teach myself classical guitar from notation at age fifteen. In high school, I was fortunate enough to study French with a jazz lyricist/social activist whose ideas turned my naïveté on its head, such that I signed up for a philosophy course called "Revolution, Race, and Zen" as an entering freshman at the University of New Mexico. I began formal training on classical guitar with Cuban-born concert artist Héctor García during that time. After my freshman year, however, I left school and hitchhiked in Europe, where I met my future Australian husband, with whom I had two daughters.[16] I attended the University of California at Berkeley for two quarters prior to moving to Australia, where I studied voice and composition at what was then called the Brisbane Conservatory.

Years later, when I began to study music formally at the University of New Mexico, I felt I owed that privilege to Margaret Nickson, who encouraged me to continue my musical studies. I studied voice with her, and composition with her son, John, during the years I lived in Brisbane (1973–76). No music teacher had ever supported me in my musical studies as did Ms. Nickson, an Irish immigrant who was the wife of the music director at the University of Queensland. Back in the US, I returned to the University of New Mexico and spent the 1977 fall semester at the Centro Andino in Quito, Ecuador, with my two young daughters (aged fourteen months and six years). The following spring, I elected to major in music and my lifelong deepest desire to compose music came to fruition a year later. By my last year in the master of music program, eight years later, however, I saw a future in music theory and composition as just more Western intellectualizing that lacked feeling (although this may be changing). In search of "music with heart," I decided to study ethnomusicology at the doctoral level for its potential to open doors for Native, Black, and Latinx students to study music. I was overjoyed to receive a Special Opportunity Fellowship at the University of California, Los Angeles (UCLA), without which I could not have attended. There, I took my last composition class with distinguished new music composer Elaine Barkin, who "was taken by" my woodwind quintet,

Native Winds (remembering the Battle of Wounded Knee in 1890), a commission by the New Mexico Woodwind Quintet for the fiftieth anniversary of the Wheelwright Museum of the American Indian in Santa Fe in 1987. Elaine Barkin might very well be the reason I still want to compose.

As well, my thirst for understanding more about Native culture and music led me to work with Professor Charlotte Heth (Cherokee) at UCLA. She taught me to "give back" to Native cultures in whatever ways I could, and I began to experience and notice synergy in her classes (discussed further in chapter 17 of this anthology).

LIFE IN ACADEMIA

Attending high school in Gallup, New Mexico, I had noticed a few Native students in the music ensembles. However, over the course of the eight years I studied at the University of New Mexico to complete my bachelor and master of music degrees, I met only two Native students in the program. My teaching position at the University of Colorado came about as a result of a potential lawsuit against the university by a Native student, now a prominent ethnomusicology professor. As a gesture of good faith, the late Americanist professor William Kearns was eager to hire an ethnomusicologist and specialist in southwestern Native and Latinx musics and successfully recruited me for the position, which came with the added responsibility of founding an ethnomusicology program. Once there, however, I quickly learned I must not forget my "place."

When I taught punk rock musical culture as ritual in an ethnomusicology "Music and Ritual" doctoral seminar, a senior White female professor told her students I wasn't teaching them what they needed to know (a Mozart Mass) and advised her students not to take my classes. She also told me I needed therapy. The professor—who had never seen me teach—posed her objections when I came up for tenure, causing great distress. I became violently ill every time I entered the building, running to the restroom and doubling over in pain. After numerous medical exams, I learned I was suffering from acute acid reflux. My health necessarily became a central concern; microaggressions from other conservative music faculty never ceased, exacerbating my tendency toward sadness. These are the politics in academia to which the title of this chapter refers. The cost of emotional labor for BIPOC in academia is disproportionate to that of our White counterparts.

With regard to "emotional labor," during the time I studied or taught at a university my value system underwent many essential changes as I struggled to find my balance after having lost five siblings, an adult niece, and both parents.

I now fully realize that other, especially BIPOC, colleagues also experience these things. Compassion is rarely to be found in academia. I learned about the glass ceiling from the example of my father, who, as an assistant director, could never advance to *director* of human resources because of his dark skin. Much later, I also learned of the glass cliff in academia. It is a good thing I have always appreciated a good challenge.

First, I had to shed an internally colonized "dysconscious" belief that I would never be able to study music since I had no formal training from a very young age.[17] Over the years, I gave positive feedback to a number of young Latinx and other students of color who contacted me, but due to various obstacles, they were unable to actually make it into our program. One student of color who entered the program was only two credit hours away from graduating when he petitioned to have his *shamisen* (Japanese string instrument) classes with ethnomusicologist Jay Keister count in lieu of one performance credit. The response from the then-undergraduate dean was "Why don't you study a *real* instrument?" He left in disgust without completing the degree.

I realize I have interpreted an intellectual Western music tradition based on hypervirtuosity and technical advancements as a form of self-alienation. The heart of music often seems to be absent, just as it is missing in the structural, gatekeeping frameworks of racism and implicit bias that have characterized music programs (see Kajikawa 2019). Among the subtler ways that implicit bias plays out in academia was how everyone wanted my brown body on their diversity committee, women's committee, or advocacy committees for Native, Latinx, and first-generation college students, and on and on. I didn't mind, as all of that was obviously urgent, but the mentors I could have had never stepped up to the plate to help me learn how to minimize these demands on my time and energy. In addition, some colleagues were derisive in their attitudes to the program I was hired to create. When I sought to create a faculty exchange with colleagues south of the border, one dean said, "There is no status in going to Mexico, there is status in going to Vienna." My peers set their sights on writing their first book, rarely having to compete with excessive service obligations. Once tenured, my White colleagues refocused on the book they needed for promotion to full professor. It took one such professor nine years; in contrast, it took me twenty-eight years to become a full professor.

The rhetoric around diversity began to ring hollow as colleagues ignored the broadened scope I brought to the program; I found this disheartening. When the "Special Opportunity Hire" ceases to be perceived as "disadvantaged" and "deserving of pity" and instead is regarded as an academic "rival," attitudes change suddenly and some individuals who were (ostensibly) one's supporters

Fig. 3.2. Mami Itasaka and Jay Keister in performance dress, ca. 2015. Courtesy of Mami Itasaka and Jay Keister.

become adversaries. Competition for resources and students is the bane of academia. In the spring of 2020, the director of the Japanese ensemble, Mami Itasaka, staged a protest on Facebook with her eight thousand followers when the College of Music canceled the World Music ensembles I had cofounded as part of the ethnomusicology concentration in the Musicology Department.[18] Thirty-eight of her followers sent letters to the dean and president of the university, resulting in the restoration of the ensembles (see fig. 3.2).

Collegial solidarity largely did not exist. My approaches to teaching, composing, and research seemed hardly valued by many of my White peers, whose understanding of basic ideas taught in ethnic studies was and continues to be questionable. I was shocked when faced with active resistance from colleagues to changing the names of courses that struggle under the weight of institutional racism; for instance, the course named Music History typically focused on canonic Eurocentric classical music. Because funding for graduate students was competitive, I was doubly infuriated when particularly musically talented students of color were prevented from entering the musicology program because their writing samples failed to meet conventional formats. Tests, such as the

GRE, although arguably biased, continue to be used as measures of universal competence but scores are selectively ignored in some cases and closely scrutinized in others. It was particularly maddening when the university's College of Music website regularly exploited images of dancers from one of the world music ensembles, even as the ensemble itself was underfunded and threatened with being canceled. Also shameless is how the few students of color were often featured prominently on the college website.

At many institutions there has been little collaboration among music faculty in general. Rather than collaborate with ethnomusicologists, for example, most music education faculty choose to teach "Multicultural Music Education," losing valuable opportunities to expose students to the world of ethnomusicology in all its vastness—yet another example of disciplinary gatekeeping. The overall numbers of music students at my institution between 1998 and 2018 declined steadily by 20 percent with the largest decline in music education (25 percent).

Lamentably, over time I increasingly experienced similar obstacles as forms of institutional racism and White privilege. To ensure my goals for greater equity would continue when I retired, I endowed an interdisciplinary Dissertation Award in Music and/or Sound Studies and Social Justice. In the award values statement, I quoted Denver attorney Casey Leier: "This is a lesson I have learned: never take for granted the progress that social justice movements have accomplished, because just as quickly as progress is made, it can be taken back."[19] Social justice takes constant vigilance.

The College Music Society (CMS) has actively sought to disseminate new ideas generated by CMS board members, and board and program committee discussions inspired me to create the CMS Summer Institute on the Pedagogies of World Music Theories in collaboration with other ethnomusicologists. I hosted the institute at the University of Colorado–Boulder in 2005, 2007, and 2010 (see Romero 2015). Ethnomusicologists, composers, performers, and music professors worked from a variety of intersecting and ultimately synergistically transformative viewpoints, giving or attending institute symposia and contributing to dynamic informal conversations. As well, helping facilitate the 2002 SEM meeting in Estes Park, Colorado and the 2009 SEM meeting in Mexico City was intended to help decolonize the society but was accomplished at some financial risk to SEM, exposing a conservative undercurrent within the society. Currently, I am contributing to the fabric of the *Analytical Approaches to World Music* (AAWM) journal and the forthcoming 2022 hybrid conference in Sheffield, United Kingdom, with AAWM cofounder Lawrence Shuster, who is also an activist for contingent labor in music.

While a student in a graduate seminar by guest professor Simha Arom at UCLA, I became fascinated with African musicultural temporalities and began to challenge Western terminologies that fail to acknowledge or capture the essence of another musical system. I developed ways of having students tease out "sameness" and "difference," if for no reason than to show the infinite variety of musical ideas and musical cultures. At the same time, I adapted and developed a student-centered dialogic way of teaching and, when Harvard University stopped requiring many final exams in 2018, I applied their approach in the last class I taught before retirement, on Latin American music. Students submitted their own final exam, complete with answers and a long essay. Comparing the exams was very revealing. As a result, I have no doubt that objective testing is largely obsolete. The student-created exams form the data for an article I hope to develop for publication.

My forthcoming monograph on the history and practice of Matachines danzas took me to many different sites and cultures in New Mexico, Mexico, Colombia, and Peru. Social justice issues permeate the study, as the tradition emerged with colonialism and is widespread. I view the music-dance-theater complex as an enhancement of (native) survivance (i.e., always against the odds established in colonialism) (Vizenor 2008).

I have disclosed a great deal of personal information in this chapter, guided by the idea of the personal being the political. This essay seeks to better clarify the complicated interethnic identities in New Mexico, without the sugarcoating typical of tricultural narratives of the harmonious blending of Indigenous, African, and European peoples and ideas. I have tried not to dwell on the damage itself but instead to create awareness of the different ways in which history and coloniality continue to affect lifeways in rural New Mexico, as they do in academia. I have shared how my life experiences led me to increasingly focus on music and social justice, and how exceptional individuals (including the contributors to this anthology) have helped shape my longing for equity and justice. I have come home, in many ways, after traversing unknown places and learning about the vastness of the world's musics and peoples, however limited that understanding might be. Education is a lifelong endeavor.

In closing, I urge diverse scholars in academia to develop trust with at least one mentor, regardless of skin color, and to share misgivings and problem solve, when possible, always striving to leave a place better than you found it. It is not uncommon for BIPOC in academia to eventually suffer a kind of *empacho*—"chronic heartburn"—due to layers of impacted frustration resulting from prolonged exposure to racist biases and practices. This creates a fraught environment. Stay healthy and don't let them—don't let anyone—rob you of your soul.

NOTES

1. I wish to thank William S. Finger, Casey J. Leier, Katelyn E. Best, David A. McDonald, and Andrew G. Snyder for teaching me about social justice, and Susan M. Asai for her insights and grand sense of humanity.

2. For a comprehensive understanding of the biological, survival functions of skin color and the social construction of race, see anthropologist/paleobiologist Nina Jablonski's *Skin, a Natural History* (Berkeley: University of California Press, 2006).

3. The term *color-blind racism* has been around for some time; sociologist Eduardo Bonilla-Silva (2003) used it in his article "'New Racism,' Color-Blind Racism and the Future of Whiteness in America." I was lucky to meet him in Boulder when he gave a talk for the university Department of Ethnic Studies. After that, I became more sensitive to the dynamics of color-blind racism all around me—which didn't make my life any easier but helped me to know what to call something I had perceived since childhood.

4. *Café y atole* ("coffee and atole" [pron. Ah-TOH-leh]), a local porridge or drink made of toasted blue corn flour, featuring the Dueto Brenda y David (Brenda M. Romero and David F. García), is a compilation of old song traditions in New Mexico and some of García's new compositions, with funding from the Northern Rio Grande National Heritage Area and the Instituto de Embudo.

5. Terminology is subject to "floating," such that *trigueño* may have different connotations in different Spanish-speaking populations. See, for instance, Isar P. Godreau, "Trigueño," in Encyclopedia.com, Social Sciences, Applied and Social Sciences Magazines. Accessed February 23, 2022. https://www.encyclopedia.com/social-sciences/applied-and-social-sciences-magazines/trigueno/.

6. To "su merce[d]" I could add "Ma charmante," left over from the French occupation in the nineteenth century, which I heard used, along with "su merced," terms that perpetuate class status in weekly *tianguis* (open markets) in Mexico City when I held a Fulbright scholarship in Mexico in 2000–2001; I have also heard the terms in the northernmost state of Chihuahua.

7. Although the newspaper lyrics named José B. Velasquez as the composer, García's ethnographic research confirms the author as José B. Vasquez (David F. García, personal communications with author, September 2021).

8. The upper geographical spread of Manito culture goes as far north as the oldest continuously inhabited town in Colorado, San Luis (established in 1851), although some might argue it reaches to Pueblo, Colorado, just north of the original (pre-1848) Mexican border on the Arkansas River. Members of the old culture who have out-migrated from New Mexico or southern Colorado to Denver, Colorado, or Pomona, California (for example), have used "Manito" to refer to their New Mexican and, according to the late tradition bearer Rick Manzanares, southern Coloradan kin (personal communications with the author, 1995).

9. Much later, in 2005 a Pueblo referendum replaced the Spanish name, San Juan, to the ancestral "Place of the Strong," or Ohkay Owingeh. Nonetheless, for centuries individuals have crossed over into each other's cultures, in part because both Spaniards and Puebloans eschewed close-cousin relationships or marriages.

10. Much information about the effects of the nuclear development and testing in New Mexico is withheld from the public. A lingering question in my mind is how nuclear testing may be accelerating global warming as a form of heat that will continue to radiate for generations.

11. In 2018, I helped carry the *bulto*, the statue of the saint during that procession, and my absence in 2019 was duly noted: The individual is not invisible in the old ways of simply being.

12. "A capala," as García's father, Floyd, suggests in jest (*pala* is Spanish for shovel). García performs the "Acequia Song" (composed by Roger Montoya) on our forthcoming CD.

13. The European colonizers believed the land was only worth what could be extracted from it, preferably by slaves.

14. To listen to a variety of inditas, see my 2008 CD, *Canciones de mis patrias, Early New Mexico Folksongs*.

15. Although the term *Latinx* was not in use until the 2010s, I use the term in this essay to avoid gender binaries.

16. Men have played important supporting roles in my musical career; however, further discussion is beyond the scope of this essay.

17. In chapter 6 of this anthology, Katelyn E. Best (2022) discusses Tom Humphries's concept of audism, which he based on racism. I extend her use of Joyce King's term *dysconsciousness* as discussed through Genie Gertz's work on "dysconscious audism" to internal racism or internal colonization. The term *dysconsciousness* also describes Darci Sprengel's (2022) descriptions of a globalized internalized colorism in Egypt in chapter 8 of this anthology. In the same vein, African American scholar Michael Eric Dyson (2021) identifies "toxic masculinity" to describe males who have internalized the myth of male supremacy.

18. Mami Itasaka is a Japanese classical and folk dance practitioner licensed with the Bando School of Classical Japanese dance under the name Miko Bando.

19. Casey Leier, personal communications with the author, Evergreen, Colorado, March 19, 2019.

BIBLIOGRAPHY

"Adiós Llano de San Juan." 1930. Poem in column, "La Lira Neo-Mexicana." *El Nuevo Mexicano* (Santa Fe, NM), September 11, 1930.

Best, Katelyn E. 2022. "Ethnocentrism 2.0: Hearing-Centrism, Inclusivity, and Musical Expression in Deaf Culture." In *At the Crossroads of Music and Social Justice*, edited by Brenda M. Romero, Susan M. Asai, David A. McDonald, Andrew G. Snyder, and Katelyn E. Best. Bloomington: Indiana University Press.

Bonilla-Silva, Eduardo. 2003. "'New Racism,' Color-Blind Racism and the Future of Whiteness in America." In *White Out: The Continuing Significance of Racism*, edited by Ashley W. Doane and Eduardo Bonilla-Silva, 271–84. New York: Routledge.

Dyson, Michael Eric. 2021. "Chaos or Community." Public lecture sponsored by the University of Colorado in Denver and Boulder. January 22, 2021. Aired on *Alternative Radio*. David Barsamian, 89.3 FM. February 20, 2021.

Jablonski, Nina G. 2006. *Skin: A Natural History*. Berkeley: University of California Press.

Kajikawa, Loren. 2019. "The Possessive Investment in Classical Music, Confronting Legacies of White Supremacy in U.S. Schools and Departments of Music." In

Seeing Race Again: Countering Colorblindness across the Disciplines, edited by Kimberlé Williams Crenshaw. Berkeley: University of California Press.

Mendoza, Vicente T., and Virginia R. R. de Mendoza. 1986. *Estudio y clasificación de la música tradicional hispánica de Nuevo México*. Mexico City: Universidad Nacional Autónoma de México.

Moraga, Cherrie, and Gloria E. Anzaldúa. (1981) 1993. *This Bridge Called My Back: Writings by Radical Women of Color*. Watertown, MA: Persephone Press; New York: Kitchen Table, Women of Color Press.

Romero, Brenda M. 2002. "*La Indita* of New Mexico: Gender and Cultural Identification." In *Chicana Traditions, Continuity and Change*, edited by Olga Najera-Ramirez and Norma E. Cantú, 56–80. Champaign: University of Illinois Press.

———. 2011. "New Mexico and *'Manitos* at the Borderlands of Popular Music in Greater Mexico." In *Transnational Encounters: Music and Performance at the U.S.-Mexico Border*, edited by Alejandro Madrid, 287–311. New York: Oxford University Press.

———. 2015. "A Theory of Infinite Variation." In *Discourses in African Musicology: J. H. Kwabena Nketia Festschrift*, edited by Kwasi Ampene and Godwin Kwafo Adje, 125–54. Ann Arbor: University of Michigan Maize Books.

———. Forthcoming. *Matachines Transfronterizos: Warriors for Peace at the Borderlands*. Folklore Studies in a Multi-Cultural World Series. Champaign: University of Illinois Press.

Romero, Brenda M., Susan M. Asai, David A. McDonald, Andrew G. Snyder, and Katelyn E. Best, eds. 2022. *At the Crossroads of Music and Social Justice*. Bloomington: University of Indiana Press.

Sprengel, Darci. 2022. "Unsettling Euro-American Conceptions of Race in the Egyptian Independent Music Scene." In *At the Crossroads of Music and Social Justice*, edited by Brenda M. Romero, Susan M. Asai, David A. McDonald, Andrew G. Snyder, and Katelyn E. Best. Bloomington: Indiana University Press.

Vizenor, Gerald Robert. 2008. *Survivance: Narratives of Native Presence*. Lincoln: University of Nebraska Press.

Wroth, William. 1991. *Images of Penance, Images of Mercy: Southwestern Santos in the Late Nineteenth Century*. Norman: University of Oklahoma Press.

DISCOGRAPHY

Dueto Brenda y David. 2022. CD. *café y atole*. Self-produced. Jack Loeffler, sound recording and mastering engineer.

Romero, Brenda M. 2008. CD. *Canciones de mis patrias, Songs of My Homelands; Early New Mexican Folksongs*. Includes enhanced content. Emotional Logic Studios and Records. 1998-2000. Edited by Kevin Harbison and David Grasser.

FOUR

GOING FORWARD WITH VIGILANCE

American Indian Music Is Always There

CHARLOTTE W. HETH

AMERICAN INDIAN MUSIC AND SOCIAL justice have intersected and informed each other from before colonial times to the present. This brief chapter is an overview of a few historical and contemporary intersections of social justice in the practice and development of American Indian music, with a focus on Oklahoma.

I was born and grew up in Oklahoma and had one grandfather who was a Cherokee Indian and one who was a cowboy. Both were born in Indian Territory (now Oklahoma) in 1882 and 1888, respectively. Oklahoma was segregated when I was a child—Black and White, not Indian—and my hometown of Tulsa had one of the worst "race riots," or Black massacres, in 1921, before I was born. At least three hundred people died, eight hundred were injured, and thirty-five city blocks and 1,200 homes were destroyed. Small aircraft firebombed the Greenwood section of North Tulsa, and looters ransacked stores and homes throughout. Yet I never heard anyone talk about this until I was an adult. In 2021 on the one-hundredth anniversary of the Greenwood massacre, local and national television stations aired multiple documentaries, and the city and the community held celebrations of rebirth. Historically, Black Oklahomans saw Greenwood as a jewel of a town where they could shop and interact at will. It was a gathering place for citizens of the more than fifty all-Black towns in twentieth-century Oklahoma (see also Smith 2021, and Smith 2019).

In Tulsa, my interactions with African Americans were mostly through music. We had choir and band exchanges with the Black schools on a regular basis, and I volunteered to play piano in all-Black churches during vacation Bible school. Otherwise, I had no opportunities to know African Americans until college. We were friends with two Mexican American families through my dad's work and with one Chinese American family through church. Lebanese and Syrian immigrants, who were primarily Christian, owned stores and restaurants. I had to go out and look for diversity. From 1962 to 1964, I spent two years in Ethiopia as a Peace Corps volunteer and learned a little about tribes and ethnic groups in that African country. For those who also search for diversity, I offer this brief essay in the hopes that readers will learn something about American Indians and American Indian music and their intersections with social justice. I will begin by talking in general about Native musical practices, with a focus on the Trail of Tears.

COMMON CAUSE

In American Indian, Indigenous, Native American, or First Nations life, we find common cause. First Nations peoples find comparable uses for music based on related worldviews, reactions to outside influences, and everyday observances. In Native popular music, we encounter mainstream Western genres, syntheses, fusions, and instrumental combinations not found in mainstream musics or in countries outside the United States and Canada. Just as in Native art, critics of Native music look for "roots" and are slow to embrace innovation, synthesis, and mainstreaming. On November 5, 2021, the first international Indigenous musical festival—Rock Aak'w—showcased several Native artists. For several artists, this was their first time on the mainstage of a festival. Rock Aak'w brought musicians from around the world in a virtual celebration of music, Indigenous values, and family. It felt like a family reunion as relatives came together to share a range of musical styles like blues, jazz, folk, and more (Crouse 2021).

First Nations start with—are oriented to—the people and the land. American Indian nations structure music to fit their worlds and their differing views of the world in general. We, as Indians, address our music to gods, people, and the natural world. In an ideal world, music functions in all aspects of Native life with all inhabitants of a community sharing in ceremonies, rituals, social events, and lifeways—all connected to the original land.

RESETTLEMENT FAR FROM HOME

In the United States and Canada, government policies have deliberately shrunk aboriginal lands to reservations and allotted lands, and Native populations have been forcibly (and occasionally voluntarily) removed, relocated, and resettled far from home. First came the conquerors looking for treasure, slaves, and adventure; next came the missionaries looking for souls to save or condemn; third, educators appeared looking for amiable pupils to indoctrinate and "mold"; and fourth, and most importantly, came settlers looking for land. The Treaty of New Echota, signed in 1835 by a splinter group of Cherokee leaders with the US government (at the behest of President Andrew Jackson), forced the removal of the entire Cherokee nation from their original homelands. Other southeastern US tribes—the Choctaw, Chickasaw, Muskogee, Yuchi, and Seminole—suffered the same fate. White settlers drew lots for the vacated land.

Before the removal, the Georgia militia and federal troops together forced Cherokee families from their homes into stockades, similar to concentration camps. In Georgia alone, there was one militiaman for every four Cherokees, including children. The Cherokees could not resist the soldiers. The Trail of Tears (1835–39), or "the trail where they cried," was an 850-mile journey, completed mostly on foot by seventeen thousand Cherokees in several cohorts from Tennessee, Georgia, North and South Carolina, and Alabama to Indian Territory, now Oklahoma. Only thirteen thousand arrived in Indian Territory. One-fourth of the Nation died in transit. My mother's Cherokee ancestors were forced to make the journey. They settled in eastern Oklahoma, and many of my cousins still live there today.

In 2021, thirty-nine federally recognized tribes now live in Oklahoma. Only a few tribes, such as the Kiowa, Comanche, Caddo, and Wichita, were indigenous to these lands; a majority of the tribes had also been removed from their homelands in the Northeast, Southwest, Midwest, California, and the Northern Plains.

What happened to the music during all this turmoil in what is now the United States of America? The European invaders suppressed immeasurable numbers of languages and musics alike. Because the missionaries realized that Indian people loved music, however, they began translating hymns into Indian languages and even publishing hymnals. Before Removal, two hundred years ago in 1821, the Cherokee Nation approved the Cherokee syllabary invented by the famous Cherokee polymath Sequoyah. Next, the Nation itself published the first hymnal using the syllabary in 1822. The editors included no printed English translation. The hymnal included words only because the Cherokees already knew the tunes. Even now Christian hymns in Indian languages are staples in Indian churches. It is now two hundred years since Sequoyah, or George Guess, invented the Cherokee syllabary, and the Cherokee Nation, the United Keetoowah Band, and the Eastern Cherokee Band are celebrating the bicentennial all year long.

In the 1830s on "the trail where they cried," a few fiddlers helped raise the morale from time to time. Christian Cherokees sang at least three hymns in the Cherokee language—"Amazing Grace," "One Drop of Blood," and another based on the tune of "Home Sweet Home." The translation of "Amazing Grace" speaks of Christ's second coming and the kind people who live here (Christians). The promise is that they will dwell happily, in peace, free from pain and sorrow. This song was sung on the Trail of Tears and continues to be sung as a reminder today, reinforcing the Cherokee philosophies of hope and endurance.

THE BOARDING SCHOOLS AND MUSICAL ABSENCE

In the nineteenth century, Indian boarding schools popped up all over Canada and the United States, some lasting through the 1960s.[1] While the expressed goal was education, the overarching objectives were to assimilate the children and teach them manual arts and domestic skills. Missionaries, whose role was to proselytize and convert Indigenous peoples, staffed many of the schools. Most of the surviving students spoke of their pain at the suppression and loss of their language(s), the prohibition of Native singing and dancing, and the ban on carrying out Indian traditions and religions. Without delving into the damage-centered conversation that could easily ensue here, suffice it to say that after their indoctrination disguised as education, the students who went home were strangers to their own families. The late author D'Arcy McNickle once told me that when he went home to the Flathead Reservation from boarding school, he was speaking "baby talk" in his Native language.

One success in these schools from the musical point of view was Indian bands. Based on military bands featuring brass and drums, the students learned and enjoyed Western music. For Western music (outside of popular music) Native people had to use Western notation and the piano to accompany musical events. The band in the boarding schools did not require a piano or other large instruments; thus, music making was portable and more accessible. In most Native cultures, instruments are small enough to be carried by a few people and thus move with the dancers and singers or in processionals. Even the "big drum" moves into the arena and can be relocated to serve many purposes. In his book *Indian Blues: American Indians and the Politics of Music 1879–1934*, John W. Troutman explored the many ways that Indian people used music and dance as modes and means of resistance. He emphasized the importance of music in cementing identity and in spreading the Indian message of resistance to the greater US population through concerts and traveling shows.

CONSTANT VIGILANCE: THE SOCIAL DISTANCE POWWOW DURING COVID-19

In the time of COVID-19, many community gatherings have been canceled or greatly modified to fit safety standards. One direct outreach using cyberspace is the Social Distance Powwow. A close reading of the Social Distance Powwow demonstrates how music and dance continue to act as cultural resistance through mutual help and encouragement and especially through living traditions. Too, powwow participants are reminded in point one stated below that the colonizers have used division to sow mistrust in the past. Point two calls implicitly on tranquil and reflective, indeed artistic and performative, actions, as opposed to oppressive tactics against oppressors or colonizers. "Creator made us all" is a statement of inclusion, of which the Powwow could be said to be an American icon, insofar as the Powwow unites American Indian nations with synergistic artistry. I quote the recent official statement of Social Distance Powwow from October 6, 2020:

> We at Social Distance Powwow started this page to bring our people together, to help people through tough times, to encourage our people to share songs, dances, language, art, music, stories, and to provide a platform for our people to share their Indigenous businesses and talents with the world. We built a community that inspired each of us by using our traditional values of respect, generosity, wisdom, courage, fortitude, honesty, etc. We appreciate all of your contributions. With this responsibility, our role is to encourage and help one another and live by our traditions.
>
> 1. With the current political climate, we realize that in the political arena, we get led into the colonization of being divided, power struggles and are more susceptible of being conquered.
> 2. So, with that, we have decided to discontinue and will no longer be allowing the mention of any of the names of any political party presidential candidates (for or against), as this leads to a distraction of our role as Social Distance Powwow. We encourage everyone to share their pride of being Indigenous and embrace how Creator made us. We just don't want to use the oppressive tactics actions back against oppressors or colonizers. We appreciate your understanding in helping us to keep the focus on what makes us strong, beautiful, resilient people! Creator made us all! (Benson 2020)

Through this site, in 2020 and 2021, I have seen social distance powwows, dance contests, drumming and singing contests, Jingle Dress Dancers dancing for healing, prayers, requests for prayers, birthday celebrations, artwork, and regalia. I have seen very small gatherings of singers and dancers (less than ten) from distant places as far away as the Arctic, to Mexico. On October 2, 2020, a tribute to the Cozad family of Oklahoma drew 188,500 viewers of the 210,700 Social Distance Powwow members worldwide. This is the power of music and dance in Indian Country. It has never been vanquished.

"Stompdancers, shellshakers, and stickballers" is a private Native group on Facebook with five thousand members. Again, teaching and reinforcing basic human values, the site requires its followers to refrain from negativity, to practice respect, to share knowledge, and to open their minds to constructive change. The members also share news of upcoming events, crafts, regalia, and songs. If a member breaks the rules by posting negative attacks, political or religious diatribes, personal condemnations, or uses a fake profile name, he or she is warned once and deleted after the second offence.

As evidenced by these popular social media sites, music of all kinds, I believe, still has the power to bring people together in a way that no other activity can. Think of diverse collaborations, rehearsals, performances, and audiences. What other pursuit celebrates old and young people playing, singing, and dancing together; all genders cooperating in a common cause; and multiethnic, multiracial performers uniting for a shared purpose? That purpose is renewal for the community and its members on a regular basis.

On the dark side, during the COVID-19 pandemic in all of Indian country, many tribes have lost large numbers of Native language speakers. In the Cherokee Nation of Oklahoma alone 123 first language Cherokee speakers died of COVID-19 in 2020. This disease that strikes older people disproportionately is causing a huge loss in music and culture throughout the hemisphere. By bringing people together for fellowship through music and dance, we create and reinforce community, and we create a power for healing. Especially today, with the horror of *yet* new variants of COVID-19, people still need healing for body and mind, for themselves, for other persons, and for their communities.

Health workers, scientists, and public health officials have pushed the pandemic back but have not conquered it. Nevertheless, organizers of powwows, hand game tournaments, arts fairs, and church services are scheduling more frequent events. Native healers need special music to practice their ceremonies and create sacred moments. The COVID-19 virus keeps us apart. On Social Distance Powwow, however, each day Jingle Dress Dancers perform to heal us all.

CONCLUDING THOUGHTS

American Indians travel, relocate, or remain with the land. We come into contact with outside agitators and confront their music. We embrace, adapt, or reject outside musics according to our needs. American Indians have extensive histories of regional interaction, whether friendly or antagonistic. Over time, this interaction has enriched and broadened Indian and non-Indian musical lives. Reciprocal participation in collective ceremonies has been a part of life since the gathering together of diverse tribal representatives first chronicled in colonial times. Today, many tribal groups invite non-Natives to ceremonies such as public corn dances and annual feast days.

While protest songs and ancient melodies alike help us continue Indian life, the preservation and continuation of music also supports social justice in ways enumerated throughout this chapter. Additionally, the power of music can reignite lost memories; arouse, soothe, and entrance; elevate the human spirit; heighten our senses; entertain; transcend hard work; bring people together to make or listen to music; get us moving, by either dancing or marching; and honor humans and gods. Music can even invade our dreams. For many of us who are musicians, music chooses us; we do not choose it. And once it has chosen us, music will not let go. As American Indians, we strive to heal nature, individuals, and our country through music and dance.

NOTE

1. See Adam Mazo's and Ben Pender-Cudlip's documentary *Dawnland* (upstanderproject.org) for a moving introduction to the topic of removing Native children to boarding schools and on to foster homes in Maine.

BIBLIOGRAPHY

Benson, Heather. 2020. "Social Distance Powwow." South Dakota Public Broadcasting. April 10, 2020. Accessed October 2 and October 6, 2020. https://www.sdpb.org/blogs/arts/the-social-distance-powwow/.

Crouse, Tripp J. 2021. "For Indigenous Festival Musicians, Identity and Representation Matter." *Native News Online*, November 14, 2021. Accessed on December 28, 2021. https://nativenewsonline.net/currents/for-indigenous-festival-musicians-identity-and-representation-matter/.

Smith, Jessie Christopher. 2021. "Oklahoma's Black Towns Responding to Tourism Interest after Withstanding Pandemic." *Tulsa World*, October 24, 2021.

Smith, Michael. 2019. "All-Black Town of Boley the Latest Example of Forgotten Oklahoma History to Become Pop-Culture Entertainment." *Tulsa World*, November 11, 2019.

Troutman, John W. 2012. *Indian Blues: American Indians and the Politics of Music 1879–1934*. Norman: University of Oklahoma Press.

VIDEOGRAPHY

Mazo, Adam, and Ben Pender-Cudlip. 2018. *Dawnland*. upstanderproject.org. Video.

FIVE

DELIVER ME FROM DANGER, ÈṢÙ-ELẸGBÁRA! MUSICAL OFFERINGS IN SOCIAL JUSTICE

Paul Austerlitz

THIS SHORT OFFERING ADMONISHES ETHNOMUSICOLOGISTS to interrogate our commitment to socially engaged scholarship and to fathoming the power of music as lived experience. Among the Yorùbá and their descendants in the Americas, crossroads are ruled by the trickster *orisa* Èṣù-Elẹgbára, a master of the auspicious, vital, and dangerous intersections of change; one song befittingly entreats him to "carefully deliver me from danger" (in Mason 1992, 80). As a longtime Society for Ethnomusicology (SEM) member and a lover of ethnomusicology as a discipline, I believe that Èṣù's bamboozling stance of critical and fearless thinking, his insistence on playing the devil's advocate, is crucial to the health of our field.

In graduate school, I was fortunate to study with David MacAllester, who once said that while he had "started out as a scholar of Navajo culture," he "ended up as an *advocate* for the Navajo people."[1] In silhouette with his rigorous background in conventional Boasian anthropology, MacAllester was committed to what we call *engaged scholarship* today. He was also interested in the *efficacy of music as lived experience*, writing the following in a remarkable and provocatively entitled article, "The Astonished Ethno-muse" (1979, 179): "Music is the art, par excellence, that brings transcendence into the lives of humankind. And we [ethnomusicologists] are among the most informed and expert of the purveyors, technicians, and theoreticians of that transcendence!" The twin avatars of engaged scholarship on one hand and high reverence for musical transcendence on the other are crucial to my own ethno-muse. Growing up in the 1960s, I was inspired by the social movements of the times. Focusing on what we call *positionality* today, Amiri Baraka used the term *stance* in his *Blues People* book to focus on jazz musicians' racial and socioeconomic postures

(1963). Ever since reading Baraka while studying with Milford Graves and Bill Dixon in Bennington College's Black Music Division as an undergraduate, I have endeavored to interrogate my own stance as a White, middle-class, North American cisgender male musician, scholar, and spiritual seeker. I am honored to have learned from musicians and ritual adepts in the Dominican Republic and Haiti. I am also fortunate to have been a member of the Society for Ethnomusicology (SEM) since 1985. Coming from an academic family, I am aware of my privileges; my father, an anthropological linguist, had once been an SEM member, and I grew up learning about ethnomusicology at home.

When starting graduate school, I perceived revolutionary potential in SEM, which seemed to meld academic rigor with vibrant currents of transnational creativity. At that time, the concept that *all* global music could be studied academically seemed revelatory. Just listening to music from around the world was propitious: I felt lucky every time I got my hands on a Nonesuch Explorer Series LP. Inspired by the leftist views of seminal figures in the field, I saw SEM as a progressive force. I was also aware, when I joined the society as a graduate student, that it was still primarily a White men's club but remember predicting that things would soon change. By the turn of the century, SEM had exerted its influence and had become mainstream: "world music" classes were required in many colleges and universities, and changing technology made it easy to listen to music from around the world. At the same time, I worried about the field's increasing professionalization as well as the conventionalization of our scholarly paradigms. It seemed to me that many of our dominant scholarly paradigms grew from SEM members' desires for career advancement rather than from the desire to grapple with the difficult issues confronting us. I wondered if SEM was perhaps a victim of its own success: while diverse music repertoires were better known, the field's politically engaged vision seemed less apparent to me. Had the society lost its revolutionary potential? Malcolm X famously opined that the most insidious racism is that practiced in the northern states, where an avowed commitment to human rights is combined with brutal structural inequity. The auspicious intersections of change promised during the earlier phases of SEM had failed to manifest.

I remember being moved by the first Crossroads Project panel, with its spirited discussion, led by Kyra K. Gaunt, about bringing Black and Brown voices to the fore in SEM. Invited to join the Africana Studies program at my institution, I was stimulated by the socially engaged stance prevailing there. Thus inspired, I wrote *Jazz Consciousness: Music, Race, and Humanity* (2007), which considers questions of unequal power relations from a socially engaged, reflexive perspective. I was surprised when my locus of tenure, the Music Department at Brown University, failed to recognize the value of this type of scholarship and denied me tenure.

But Èṣù's lessons began to manifest. I became active in SEM's Crossroads Section and received mentorship from Portia Maultsby as well as from Africana Studies colleagues, who gave me a home at Gettysburg College. I joined KOSANBA, a scholarly society dedicated to the study of Haitian Vodou. Rather than writing another ethnomusicological monograph, I decided to forge an alternative agenda: tying my scholarship to mystical experience, musical performance, the struggle for social justice, and engaged pedagogy.

I embarked on an education in Afro-Caribbean spirituality in the Dominican Republic and Haiti, attending dozens of ritual celebrations in several regions of both countries and undergoing a *kanzo* ritual ceremony under the guidance of the late, great Haitian *houngan* (Vodou priest) Max Beauvoir. My experiences in Haitian ritual settings brought home David MacAllester's lessons about musical transcendence that had inspired me so much in graduate school. We all know that music profoundly affects us: it makes us cry and dance; it is used in war and as an instrument of peace; it inspires patriotism and religious transcendence. Music's power, however, seems indescribable. Maybe this is why scholarship often fails to pay attention to the ways music affects us experientially. The seeming ineffability, however, of a subject should not deter scholarly attention to it. One of the most spectacular manifestations of music's power is its association with altered states of consciousness: when music takes us into a different psychic space, it manifests the apex of its transformative power. Rudolf Otto's 1917 religious studies classic, *The Idea of the Holy*, argues that "non-rational" experience, which seems "ineffable" is not, in fact, beyond the realm of scholarly discourse. Otto invites the reader "to direct his mind to deep religious experience. If he has never felt this, he should read no more" ([1923] 1958, 8). Otto insists that we attend to our *own* encounters with what he calls the *mysterium tremendum*, which "can come as a gentle tide or as intoxicated frenzy, to transport one to ecstasy.... [It] has wild and demonic forms, can be grisly and shuddering" (12).

Later trends in consciousness studies heeded Otto's call. In addition to conducting replicable scientific experiments in the psychology of everyday lived experience, scholars such as Francisco Varela (Varela and Shear 1999, 21–27) rigorously attend to their own practice of Buddhist "mindfulness meditation" as a kind of "experimentation that makes discoveries about the nature and behavior of the mind" (31). Inspired by these approaches and by Becker's seminal work (2004), I embarked on the ethnomusicological study of the efficacy of music in Afro-Caribbean ritual. In addition to standard ethnographic approaches, this project attends to my ritual life in Haiti and the Dominican Republic, recounting and interrogating my own experiences with altered states of consciousness (2013, forthcoming).

At Gettysburg College, I instigated a yearly student trip to the Dominican Republic, focusing on "Music and Ritual as Modes of Afro-Dominican Empowerment." Students attended Afro-Dominican ceremonies and worked with activists struggling for the rights of Dominicans of Haitian descent. I was fortunate to work, also during a sabbatical, as a Distinguished Visiting Research Scholar at the City University of New York Dominican Studies Institute, a remarkable organization dedicated to enlisting scholarly research in the service of the grassroots Dominican community. Allying with social movements promoting the rich African-based traditions of the Dominican Republic, I started the Ensemble Dominicano (ED), which featured my compositions blending jazz with merengue and Afro-Dominican and Haitian ritual music, performing in the Dominican Republic several times a year. Melding cosmopolitan musical currents with marginalized Afro-Dominican traditions, ED's audiences brought upper-middle-class Dominican academics together with working-class Afro-Dominicans. One ED event, for example, sponsored by the Autonomous University of Santo Domingo (UASD) and dubbed "Visitando Altares" (Visiting Altars), brought the top levels of the UASD administration to Villa Mella, a traditional locus of Afro-Dominican ritual activity, for a festival presenting ED along with local Villa Mella musicians. With the support of the United States Embassy to the Dominican Republic, ED also completed two "Jazz sin Fronteras / Jazz beyond Borders" tours, playing for underserved communities in several regions of the Dominican Republic.

In 2008, I released a trilogy of recordings called *Marasa Twa*. In the spiritual traditions of Haiti and the Dominican Republic, the *marasa twa* are magical triplets who manifest divine mysteries. The three albums—*Dr. Merengue*, *The Vodou Horn*, and *Water Prayers for Bass Clarinet*—were recorded in the Dominican Republic, Haiti, and New York, respectively (Austerlitz 2018a, 2018b, and 2018c). Liner notes state,

> I am privileged to have spent my life studying world music cultures. At the same time, I have plunged the depths as a musician and as a seeker of life's meanings. Wedding my artistic and spiritual paths with scholarly research, these albums are the fruit of my sojourn as a musician-scholar....
> Considering that these traditions developed as responses to the vicissitudes of slavery, colonialism, and neo-colonialism, my involvement in them has necessitated prodigious soul-searching. Where do I, as a white man, fit into the world of African-based spirituality? Unlike conventional academic work

aiming for unbiased reportage, and unlike "world music" projects intended solely for personal expression, my involvement with Afro-Dominican, African-American, and Haitian cultures is motivated by mystical needs, creative needs, and activism. My hope is that my musical offerings will contribute, in some small way, to the ongoing struggle for social justice from which these musical traditions were born.

Marasa Twa presents Haitian and Dominican music melded with jazz. My spiritual godfather, Houngan (priest) Max Beauvoir taught me *Lapriyè Djò* (Prayer for the primal wind), a corpus of prayers intoned in a half-spoken, half-sung manner to begin Vodou ceremonies. As Beauvoir teaches, the prayers provide equilibrium among spirits, psyche, thoughts, and our bodies (Beauvoir n.d.) and represents "a tribute of the immaterial patrimony of Haitian oral literature" (2008, 15). The aural texts of Vodou present wisdom, constituting a bible of spiritual teachings. With Papa Max's permission (and vociferous encouragement), I arranged the prayers in a jazz style and, with much help, ventured a translation for CD liner notes. One well-known prayer poignantly appeals to the mystical power of water, ancestral royalty, and the revolutionary power of change.

Anonse, Ozany nan dlo o	We summon the angelic spirits of water,
Oba Kosou miwa, Lawe, Lawe.	And the mirror King of Africa; lawe!
Nan la vil o Kan e	In the mystical town of Okan,
Kriyòl mande chanjan.	Creole people demand justice.

(Austerlitz 2018c)

First, it summons angelic water spirits and then salutes the old monarchs of Africa. Finally, it honors the common folk who rise up to insist on freedom.

Let us end with another song, from the *Vodou Horn*, honoring Èṣù-Elẹgbára's Haitian cousin, the *lwa* (or spirit) Papa Legba. The song, in Haitian Creole, is impossible to translate into English because it consists of ritual phrases derived from African languages whose meanings are equivocal, contested, and guarded by ritual tradition. Its gist, however is this: Papa Legba walks slowly, with a cane. He might seem to be lacking in energy, but Papa Legba is the gatekeeper: he stands at the crossroads and will open auspicious paths for the ethnomusicological future.

Paren Legba ki mache a lada,
Vodou Legba ki mache kó inde,
Paren Legba ki mache a lada lada,
Vodou Legba ki mache ounde me.

NOTE

1. If he were living today, MacAllester would no doubt be using the term Diné rather than the colonized appellation, "Navajo."

BIBLIOGRAPHY

Austerlitz, Paul. 2007. *Jazz Consciousness: Music, Race, and Humanity.* Middletown, CT: Wesleyan University Press.

———. 2013. "La música y estados alterados de conciencia como manifestaciones de la sabiduría afrocaribeña" ["Music and Altered States of Consciousness as Manifestations of Afro-Caribbean Wisdom"]. In *La música y el baile folklorico en la epoca de globalización,* edited by Darío Tejeda and Rafael Emilio Yunén. Santiago, Dominican Republic: INEC and Centro León.

———. Forthcoming. "Music, Mystery, and Ecstasy: The Entranced Ethnomusicologist."

Baraka, Amiri. 1963. *Blues People: Negro Music in White America.* New York: W. Morrow.

Becker, Judith. 2004. *Deep Listeners.* Bloomington: Indiana University Press.

MacAllester, David. 1979. "The Astonished Ethno-muse." *Ethnomusicology* 23 (2): 179–89.

Mason, John. 1992. *Orin Orisa: Songs for Selected Heads.* New York: Yoruba Theological Archministry.

Otto, Rudolf. (1923) 1958. *The Idea of the Holy: An Inquiry into the Non-Rational Factor in the Idea of the Divine and Its Relation to the Rational.* London: Oxford University Press.

Varela, Francisco, and Jonathan Shear, eds. 1999. *The View from Within: First-Person Approaches to the Study of Consciousness.* Bowling Green, OH: Imprint Academic.

DISCOGRAPHY

Austerlitz, Paul. 2018a. *Dr. Merengue.* Oakland, CA: Round Whirled Records. RW0085.

———. 2018b. *The Vodou Horn.* Oakland, CA: Round Whirled Records. RW0084.

———. 2018c. *Water Prayers for Bass Clarinet.* Oakland, CA: Round Whirled Records. RW0083.

Beauvoir, Max. 2008. *Lapriyè Ginen.* Port-au-Prince: Edisyon Près Nasyonal d'Ayiti.

———. n.d. *Lapriyè Djò* ("Prayer for the Primal Wind"). Unpublished audio recording.

PART II

RADICAL INCLUSIVITY

SIX

ETHNOCENTRISM 2.0

Hearing-Centrism, Inclusivity, and Musical Expression in Deaf Culture

KATELYN E. BEST

AT THE 2013 BONNAROO MUSIC and Arts Festival, hip-hop artist Killer Mike spontaneously began freestyling with Holly Maniatty, an American sign language interpreter who was serving as a performance interpreter for the event.[1] While Killer Mike pushed the limits of real-time translation, Maniatty never missed a beat. In an American Public Media podcast interview, Maniatty commented on this experience, remarking, "Killer Mike, when I was doing his show, came down onto the platform ... and he just started spewing every swear that he could possibly think of. I think he was just trying to have a little tête-à-tête with me to see if I could keep up with him, and I did" (Maniatty 2013). While Killer Mike's engagement with Maniatty called attention to her translation of his music, his movement from the stage to the interpreter's platform and subsequent interaction blurred the lines between performance interpreter and performer. Even still, despite the creative translation and performance executed by Maniatty, the delineation between musician and interpreter was never questioned.

Conversely, when Deaf hip-hop artist Signmark first performed in public and employed a hearing vocalist to interpret his lyrics, distinctions between musician and interpreter were misconstrued, and he was initially perceived as a sign language interpreter for his vocalist.[2] While Signmark shared the stage with his vocalist, notions of roles were distorted not by performance location alone but also by hegemonic assumptions that did not take into account a Deaf construction of music, one that decentralizes an aural sensory focus.[3] Since then, Signmark has garnered international attention for his music in addition to his role as a Deaf activist, yet his initial public reception demonstrates challenges faced by Deaf musicians as a result of hearing-centrism. In order to examine the impact of hearing-centrism on musical expression in Deaf culture, this chapter frames hearing-centrism as a form of ethnocentrism and investigates cultural mechanisms and institutions that perpetuate a hearing-centric ideology of music.[4]

THE CONCEPT OF HEARING-CENTRISM

The term *hearing-centric*, while not a standard dictionary entry, can be found throughout scholarly literature, although predominantly within deaf studies.[5] Appearing in use from at least the 1990s onward and increasing in popularity in the 2010s, the first development and written implementation of the term is, as far as I can determine, unclear, which suggests that any kind of broader conceptual application is a byproduct of its function as a descriptor. While this term is to some extent inherently self-explanatory, it has been applied in different ways. Some scholars have used this word to identify a focus or priority based on a hearing point of view, often appearing in conjunction with the term *Deaf-centric* (Rosen 2007; Fleischer et al. 2015; Bath 2016). Others have used it to describe a process of catering to hearing bodies, particularly in regards to communication practices (Roberts and Mugavin 2007; Purdy 2016; Batamula and Pudans-Smith 2017). Some instances, primarily in literature unrelated to deaf studies, employed this term to refer to an aural sensory focus (Folio 1992; Simmonds and Brown 2011; Carney 2020). Still more have applied it as a sociocultural bias (Singleton and Tittle 2000; Holcomb 2010; Maler 2015; Gertz 2016; Silvestri, Ehrenberg, Dick, and Shim 2018). The application of this word within scholarly literature informs the concept of hearing-centrism, yet, without a codified definition, the term has often been conflated with other concepts, such as audiocentrism and aural-centrism.

In order to differentiate among these terms, it is useful to take into account the concept of audism, which often results from these centric perspectives. Applying the Latin word "to hear"—*audire*—to the framework of racism, in 1975 Deaf scholar Tom Humphries coined the term "audism," which is "the notion that one is superior based on one's ability to hear or behave in the manner of one who hears" (Bauman 2004, 240). Audism, like racism, consists of discriminatory behavior and prejudices but is based on hearing ability.[6] The term *hearing-centrism*, unlike the words *audiocentrism* and *aural-centrism*, employs the word *hearing* instead of a variant of *audire*, evoking a sociocultural perspective informed by a shared sensory experience of the world based on a reliance on hearing. If considered within the framework of ethnocentrism, hearing-centrism, as I propose within this chapter, could be defined as a cultural bias based on a hearing perspective. Within this context, hearing-centrism describes the act of imposing hearing cultural standards onto Deaf culture and evaluating Deaf cultural output based on those etic standards. This biased perspective, in turn, supports audism and contributes to audist behavior. Unlike hearing-centrism, audiocentrism and aural-centrism do not inherently evoke a cultural component but rather reference a sensory bias. In this regard, these terms do not function as a form of ethnocentrism, differentiating them from the concept of hearing-centrism. When applied to music, hearing-centrism is, as I define it, manifested as a musicultural bias based on a hearing perspective that is shaped by an aural-centric experience of sound (Bakan 2007, 10). While this concept's application is not limited to Deaf culture, it has significantly distorted perceptions of Deaf musicking and subjugated Deaf individuals to an audist ideology that continues to Other them.

POSITIONALITY AND BACKGROUND

Given the focus of this chapter, it is important to address my own background and positionality as a researcher. I am what you could refer to as a NERDA (Not Even Related to a Deaf Adult), an acronym I first came across when interviewing DJ Nicar Bocalan, a musician and hearing ally to deaf artists.[7] As a hearing person, I have been immersed in solely hearing environments and, as a music researcher and performer, musically trained within hearing-centric systems. Just as hearing-centric undertones have been naturalized within society and cultural institutions, so too have they been embedded within my own experiences and perspectives of music throughout much of my life. In conducting ethnographic fieldwork by means of documentation, including, but not limited to, artist interviews, written observations, and audio/visual recordings of performances at Deaf festivals, residential schools, and concerts, this perspective of music has been made noticeable, albeit impossible to entirely uproot.

I first began researching Deaf music in 2011 while pursuing my doctoral degree in ethnomusicology at Florida State University, and in 2012, I began conducting fieldwork on tracing the development of "dip hop" in the United States, a style of hip-hop also referred to as sign language rap (Best 2015/2016, 73). I became involved in this area of study because I was interested in learning more about this musical style and the work of its contributors as well as tracing its historical development and the ways it has been used as a platform for Deaf activism. But even more importantly, I saw a gap within ethnomusicology that needed to be addressed—a systemic problem with the way music has been more broadly discussed and constructed from a hearing perspective, one that runs the risk of delegitimizing musical expression in Deaf culture and, by extension, the cultural output of Deaf individuals. In addition to this, much of the preexisting literature on Deaf music that I came across at the time was dominated by music therapy and education. While this literature has contributed toward more inclusive pedagogies and therapies, much of this research employed absolute notions of music that restrict musical experience to hearing standards.[8] In order to deconstruct this discourse, along with my own hearing-centric biases, I wanted to investigate culturally relative constructions of music in Deaf culture. So I employed ethnomusicological modes of inquiry in order to explore what music is and can be from a Deaf perspective.[9]

HEARING-CENTRISM AS A FORM OF ETHNOCENTRISM

While aurality has taken a front seat within Western listening practices, a relative construction of music in Deaf culture is shaped by a shared sensory orientation and cultural perspective molded by language that decentralizes auditory attention in relation to other senses. As art historian Amanda Cachia (2016, 339) notes, "the ear is not the only receptacle for channeling sound, speech, and language." Although variations in hearing range are considerable within both hearing and deaf communities, Deaf people do not rely on audition to navigate the world around them (Bahan 2014). This disposition coupled with cultural practices that engage other sensory modalities cultivates a culturally specific arrangement of sensory input. Within this physically and culturally rooted position, sound is realized intersensorially instead of limited to the ear. As Summer Loeffler notes, "From this exploration [of Deaf musicality], we can see a paradigm shift of music from an auditory-based phenomenon to an experience involving a wider spectrum of senses" (Loeffler 2014, 451). While both deaf and hearing people experience auditory and nonauditory characteristics of sound, nonauditory reception has been ideologically situated as secondary to audition within hearing practice, whereas Deaf people are more attuned to these sonic components based on culturally situated sensory priorities (Sirvage 2016, 294).

Shaped by Deaf aesthetics, Deaf music incorporates multisensory elements that expand the scope of listening practices. Within this context, aural components, if incorporated, share a more equitable, if not lesser, role in relation to other musical aspects. As Deaf studies scholars Jody Cripps, Anita Small, Ely Rosenblum, Samuel Supalla, Aimee Whyte, and Joanne Cripps explain, "Deaf people do not require access to audible sound in order to appreciate music as is expected in auditory culture" (forthcoming, 1–2). While acts of listening have been situated in the ear, sound studies research, according to anthropologist Tom Rice, contextualizes listening within the sociocultural environments in which it occurs. Drawing from Bourdieu's theory of habitus, he argues, "Rather than being a universal set of sensory aptitudes, ways of listening are an aspect of 'habitus,' a set of culturally informed bodily and sensory dispositions" (Rice 2015, 101). As a linguistic minority, Deaf culture is significantly shaped by language, and experiences of listening, in turn, are influenced by social interactions structured by signed language. Within visual-manual communication, "listening" applies to visual reception, and "speaking" is manifested through movement. In her chapter "Imagined Hearing: Music-Making in Deaf Culture," Jeannette DiBernardo Jones points out how culturally informed constructions of listening are demonstrated through American Sign Language (ASL), noting that the sign LISTEN in ASL is placed by the ears to denote auditory listening yet is also placed by the eyes to represent visual listening (Jones 2015, 58).[10] As Deaf educator and former ASL instructor Shannon Marsh explains, "[In] the past decade [the] ASL community has tried to differentiate between hearing and seeing. So, before we'd sign 'listen' by cupping a hand behind the ear or use the '3' handshape and twitch fingers by the ear. But now I myself use that three handshape and twitch finger by the eye."[11] This practice of signing LISTEN by the eyes raises awareness to culturally embodied ways of listening that are not otherwise included within mainstream contexts.

Listening practices within Deaf culture, then, are not confined to audition but also conducted through visual means. Voice, in turn, becomes visible, decolonizing it from auditory constructs. Within this context, voice can be "heard" over sonic noise, across distance, and through transparent physical barriers (Best 2021, 240). Drawing from Rosemarie Garland-Thomson's use of "visual listening" as applied to signed languages, the act of communicating through visual motion can be conceptualized as "visual sounding." I use the term *visual sounding* to refer to "the production of visual stimuli that are processed as rhythmic and spatial patterns and, in essence, metaphorically 'sound'" (Best 2021, 241–42). Within this context, visual components within Deaf music effectively "sound" through motion. A representation of this can be observed in figure 6.1, which includes the phrase "see the music" coupled with images of hands that are illustrated as moving as indicated by the double-contour lines surrounding them. The word *see*, which is used in reference to music, is emphasized through the use of a different font color. The visual and grammatical structure of this phrase in conjunction with its relation to the image of moving hands evokes both notions of visual listening and visual sounding that are manifested within Deaf performance.

Fig. 6.1. Kentucky DeaFestival 2014. Photograph by author. Louisville, Kentucky, August 30, 2014.

Given its cultural primacy and visual nature, signed language plays a significant role in contributing to constructions of music in Deaf culture; however, it is important to emphasize that visual elements are not limited to lyrics (Best 2021, 242). Within Deaf musical expression, nonlinguistic movements can also contribute to shaping dynamics and defining rhythmic and melodic contours; the term *melodic* is applied here to denote a succession of visible "soundings" or, in effect, visual motion.[12]

In conjunction with visual aspects, Deaf music also incorporates tactile elements. Felt by the body, vibrations experienced haptically contribute to musical structure as well. While, as Michelle Friedner and Stefan Helmreich point out, these experiences are not identical, they are shared (2012, 77). Stereo equipment or vibrotactile stimuli can be used in order to enhance the acuteness of this reception. Some artists have incorporated the use of subwoofers, vibrating floors, or other forms of vibrotactile technology, in order to experiment with ways to amplify vibrational articulation.[13] Other times, materials that serve as conductors, such as balloons, can be found in performance settings, as shown in figure 6.2, which is an image from a Signmark performance in Lake Mary, Florida. The sign labeled "Reserved d/Deaf only" marking a reserved area also

Fig. 6.2. Balloons at Signmark's Performance in Lake Mary, Florida. Photograph by author. Lake Mary, Florida, April 24, 2012.

illustrates how performance spaces are structured and are oriented toward specific sensory priorities.

Although music in Deaf culture is shaped by a culturally relative perspective and sensory orientation, a hearing-centric view limits Deaf musical art forms by restricting music to aurality, subsequently, denying the very elements that contribute to this construction. When viewed through this musicultural bias, Deaf music is constricted to an aural-centric experience of sound, which evaluates it based on hearing standards. As a result, Deaf musical expression is characterized as an incomplete or partial experience of music and framed in terms of loss. As music theorist Anabel Maler points out, "In this hearing-centric view of music, deaf people live in a world of silence, cut off both from musical expression and from receiving pleasure from musical works" (Maler 2015, 73). Within this context, music becomes impeded by the condition of being deaf and hegemonically viewed as an impaired experience, locating the source of limitation within the body, which subsequently pathologizes deafness. This etic valuation of Deaf cultural output has not only led to a lack of Deaf musical recognition, but also the exclusion and audist discrimination of Deaf musical practices.

ETHNOCENTRISM 2.0

While ethnomusicology provides an effective platform in which to explore a relative construction of music in Deaf culture, it is necessary to consider cultural mechanisms and institutions that have and continue to perpetuate hearing-centrism in order to deconstruct the power a hegemonic ideology has maintained over musical expression in Deaf culture. Within this context, hearing-centrism is made invisible and naturalized within language, cultural materials, and institutional structures and subsequently viewed as an advanced form of ethnocentrism, an "Ethnocentrism 2.0," so to speak.

While language organizes thoughts and facilitates communication, it also constrains and "limits our horizons" (Kramer 2004, 69). The way the word *music* is employed within language embeds it with fixed notions of what music is, can be, and should be. Feminist scholar Chris Weedon discusses these notions in terms of "common-sense," explaining, "Common-sense consists of a number of social meanings . . . these meanings which inevitably favor the interests of particular social groups become fixed and widely accepted as true, irrespective of sectional interest" (Weedon 1987, 76).

Due to commonsense notions of music, "natural" or "obvious" aesthetics produced by a hearing-centric perspective alienate Deaf culture from musical inclusion. As a result, music has been hegemonically constructed as a cultural product of hearing people and realized as a form of expression that can be accessed by deaf people but never fully experienced by them. For instance, the terms *audience* and *auditorium*, which stem from the word *audire*, linguistically evoke notions of musical reception that are confined to the ear. The word *music*, itself, has also been dominated by aural-centric rhetoric with idioms such as being "tone-deaf," "having an ear for music," and "being able to play by ear" contributing to a reality in which deafness is realized as detrimental to musical development and experience (Best 2018, 1). This, in turn, leads to audist stereotypes of music and deafness that oppress deaf bodies. As Darius "Prinz-D the First Deaf Rapper" McCall explains, "a lot of people think that deaf people can't talk or hear, so how are they able to rap? I get that question a lot, like: 'OK, so if you're deaf, then how are you able to hear the music and stay on beat?'"[14] Prinz-D echoes this sentiment in his song "This Can't Be Life," when he raps, "Heard this same question a million and one times / You can't hear, why you trying to rhyme?" (Prinz-D 2014).

In addition to the power of linguistic discourse in shaping music in society, music has also been marketed, packaged, and sold through mediums that cater to a hearing-centric perspective. For example, headphones are designed to transmit music exclusively through the ear, restricting musical reception to one part of the body.[15] Music recording processes also employ aural-centric structures and tools that determine performance and production quality based on hearing-centric frameworks. As anthropologist Roshanak Kheshti notes, "In the case of the music industry, listening with the ear was developed as a critical focal point for an emerging commodity of sound" (Kheshti 2011, 718–19). She continues, "The ear is central to how the record company imagines the listener, and the ear functions for listeners as a synecdoche for the whole of the listening body" (722). While music may incorporate visual components, without auditory elements it is not conventionally considered music. This realization of music permeates the music industry and has, for example, affected access to artist royalties for Signmark. Musicologist Taru Leppänen remarks, "Gramex has paid Signmark royalties when he has been the producer, but he would like to also be recognized as an artist. Signmark (Kotimaa24) clarifies that according to Gramex, singing in sign language is not singing, because in their opinion recording consists solely of sounds. The reason for denying the royalties according to Gramex was that Signmark does not produce sound in the recordings" (Leppänen 2017, 42). In this example, Signmark's very work as an artist is delegitimized by hearing-centric constructions of sound and structures of "music" production that ideologically limit his musical participation and inclusion within the music industry.

Mass media also promotes and naturalizes hearing-centric representations of music within popular culture. From movies like *Pitch Perfect* to televised singing competitions like *The Voice*, musicianship is determined by aural-centric assessments of musical talent, which manufacture hearing-centric qualifications for mainstream musical acceptance (Best 2018, 2). While media embeds music and performance with qualifications that determine values and places it even further within a hearing-centric discourse, media also distorts constructions of Deaf culture and the role of music in it. In their article "Music and Deaf Culture: Images from the Media and Their Interpretations by Deaf and Hearing Students," music therapist Ann Darrow and Deaf education scholar Diane Loomis explain, "Writers, like most hearing individuals, seem to be intrigued by the notion of a world without music; hence, the topic frequently appears in films with deaf characters. The media have incredible power to influence our perception of others, particularly those with whom we have little contact. It would seem wise then to examine their interpretation of the role music plays in deaf culture" (1999, 91). By portraying deaf individuals as living in a world without music, the media maintains a hearing-centric view of music that centers its corporeal existence in the ear and, in doing so, expels any other conceptions of the term. It further demonstrates a disregard for Deaf experiences of the world. Moreover, if a hearing person has never met a Deaf person, then their only exposure remains framed through the dramatization of actors playing deaf characters in film and television or through a hearing person's perspective as communicated in the news or other media. This limits a mainstream understanding of Deaf people and music in Deaf culture to etic perspectives and interpretations.

Through positivistic misrepresentations of deafness, media reinforces an audist ideology based on a hearing-centric perspective. Weedon writes, "Like the press, the visual and aural media also employ journalistic forms of discourse with their claims to represent truth, objectivity and decent moral standards" (1987, 98). Since Deaf culture is fairly small compared to the rest of the hearing world, media exposure to deafness is significantly more common than face-to-face interactions between hearing and Deaf individuals. Darrow and Loomis point out: "This biased view presented by the media is seldom challenged by direct contact with members of the deaf community. Few hearing people ever meet a person who is deaf; and when they do, language barriers usually obstruct any meaningful communication" (Darrow and Loomis 1999, 93). As a result, Deaf culture is often distorted by an etic perspective, allowing hearing-centric perceptions to more easily dominate Deaf forms of musical expression.

Academic institutions also define and determine realizations of music through curriculum structures, implemented assessments, and music research. Aural exams are used to measure musical perception, musicianship is evaluated based predominantly on aural production, and listening exams assess music comprehension and identification. While these are just a few examples, this aural-centric experience of music both taught and assessed in the classroom produces a hearing-centric reality that is reified through curriculum design and musical classification. Although music education has not traditionally incorporated musical styles created and/or informed by a Deaf perspective, the way music is presented and assessed runs the risk of producing absolute constructions of music. Furthermore, when referring to "music" in general terms, scholarship does not always take into account the varied manifestations of different musics and runs the risk of positioning all music within a hearing-centric framework.

IMPACT OF HEARING-CENTRISM

Aural-centric classifications and manifestations of music not only distort Deaf musical expression but also colonize Deaf constructions of music by limiting what music is and can be, effectively delegitimizing culturally informed components in the process. When a hearing-centric perspective frames music in Deaf culture, the music is reconstituted; elements that are interpellated as hearing characteristics are brought to attention, while those that are not are disregarded or devalued. Within this subjugated reconfiguration, Deaf musical expression is ideologically forced into a state of liminality that does not encapsulate either Deaf or hearing aesthetics (Best 2018, 2). When a hearing-centric mindset is imposed on Deaf music, this process denies the recognition not only of Deaf language and culture but also Deaf values, sensory experiences, and expressions thereof.

Music produced by and for Deaf people has been documented since the early 1900s (Cripps et al. 2017; Loeffler 2014; Bauman 2014), yet Deaf cultural constructions of music have historically been marginalized and entangled with hearing-centric regimes that dominate music discourse and veil audist behavior under the guise of inclusion. As Deaf studies scholar Hilde Haualand points out, "attempts to 'include' Deaf people and make Deaf people *hear same* too often results in oppression of the Deaf embodied ways of perceiving, mapping, and learning about the world" (2008, 120). By "hear same," Haualand is referring to shared ways of hearing that are culturally and linguistically informed, which influence community inclusion based on shared reception.[16] Endeavors to "help" deaf people access "music" not only deny Deaf musical output but also ideologically disable Deaf experiences and deaf bodies.

The impact of hearing-centrism on Deaf culture has led to what social scientist Genie Gertz (2008) labels "dysconscious audism." Drawing from education scholar Joyce King's concept of dysconscious racism and applying it to audism, Gertz defines dysconscious audism as "the acceptance of dominant hearing norms, privileges and cultural values by Deaf individuals, and the subsequent perception of hearing society as being more appropriate than Deaf society" (2016, 329). The term *dysconscious*, as Gertz explains, identifies a partial awareness. When linguistically paired with a discriminatory ideology such as audism or racism, this term signifies an awareness of thought but an ignorance regarding the oppressive nature of that thought (Gertz 2008, 223).[17] This concept, as it relates to music, represents an acceptance of a hearing-centric perspective and the resulting view that hearing people are more attuned to music than Deaf people. This accounts for why music has historically been considered to be a product of hearing culture for many Deaf people. Within this context, music is represented as something that can be appreciated by deaf people but defined by hearing people. This view effectively denies a culturally relative construction of music in Deaf culture and limits what music is and can be to hearing-centric views that cater to hearing bodies. In doing so, it devalues Deaf experiences and reinforces audism. As Gertz argues, "by internalizing dysconscious audism, deaf people disempower themselves and contribute to a continued perception that being deaf and promoting the values and norms of Deaf culture is an obstacle to success. They may believe the only way to succeed is to become 'like hearing'" (2016, 331). Hearing-centrism, based on this dysconscious view, fosters the idea that Deaf people cannot successfully express music without the help or assistance of a hearing person.

Hearing-centrism undermines a Deaf experience of the world, disabling it and devaluing it through audist ideologies. As a result of hearing-centrism, music has been constructed as a form of expression that Deaf people can experience but never have complete access to. This ideology reinforces discrimination of Deaf musical expression that subjugates Deaf ways of life to an audist ideology. A hearing-centric view of deafness as a world without sound not only denies the rich and comprehensive intersensorial experience of sound and motion that shapes music in Deaf culture but also limits deaf expression, stereotypes deaf bodies, and delegitimizes Deaf voices based on a phonocentric perspective of language. As a result, Deaf musicians have faced discrimination and been denied recognition and financial compensation for their work based on music production structures that cater to hearing bodies and listeners.

Hearing-centric views of music also excuse a lack of inclusive platforms for music performance and education. With a concentration on assimilation instead of acculturation, efforts are placed on making Deaf experiences and bodies more like hearing ones. This, in turn, debilitates Deaf people while reinforcing audism. Within this context, Deaf people are forced to work within systems and structures that suppress Deaf ways of being and impair development and growth through a lack of appropriate resources and linguistic access. As Thomas K. Holcomb notes, "deaf education practice has reverted to hearing-centric approaches in which the core of Deaf cultural values has been de-emphasized or devalued" (2010, 474). Within the context of these practices, deafness is situated as an obstacle to musical access, and remediation is justified in the face of cultural genocide.

BREAKING DOWN THE IDEOLOGICAL DIVIDE

The impact of hearing-centrism on musical expression in Deaf culture has prompted music scholars to develop theoretical frameworks that function to counter hearing-centric rhetoric and promote d/Deaf perspectives within music studies. Leppänen calls for "critical studies of Hearing" in order to "enhance non-audist methodologies of music and sound studies and to grasp the ethical and political issues in studying Deaf cultures" (2017, 36). Within this context, Leppänen proposes the concept of "becoming Deaf," which, as she explains, "denotes moving away from audism, moving away from discrimination on the basis of ability to hear and from the conventional ways of experiencing music in terms of non-Deaf people" (46).

Similarly, Jones has proposed the notion of "hearing deafly," which she identifies as "a way of making and listening to music that is specifically Deaf, celebrating deafness in a way that situates the Deaf as a cultural minority within a hearing world" (2015, 55–56). This position allows hearing people to think beyond the frameworks and systems engrained within hearing communities, particularly those tied to hearing. As Cachia points out, "It is the majority of those who have the capacity to hear that must learn to hear in ways that challenge the frameworks in which we have been trained to listen" (2016, 326). "Hearing Deafly" not only broadens the scope of listening practices but also theoretically supports and contributes to processes of "Becoming Deaf." Musicologist Jessica Holmes decolonizes musical expertise from hearing processes through her discussion of "expert listening." As she explains, "d/Deaf listeners challenge the primacy of aurality relative to the other senses, and ultimately reveal that hearing need not be a prerequisite for or the basis of listening expertise" (Holmes 2017, 173). These theoretical considerations, while by no means limited to the ones provided, present critical frameworks with which to decolonize musical hearing-centrism.

While this literature contributes to decolonizing Deaf music from hearing-centric biases and evaluation, challenges still remain when writing from an etic perspective to make visible the hearing-centric tendencies that have become naturalized and made invisible within discourse. For example, while Leppänen calls for critical studies of Hearing, she unintentionally applies a hearing-centric perspective when describing Signmark's album, commenting, "Signmark's albums include a DVD that makes music visual and more accessible for d/Deaf audiences" (Leppänen 2017, 38). Likewise, Jones (2015, 57) remarks that "Signmark (2010) and Sean Forbes (2012) rap in ASL and have created DVDs of music videos to accompany their albums." Given that signed language is a fundamental component of dip hop, the CD is in actuality an accessory to the DVD and only includes partial components of the music (Best 2015, 74). Referring to the audio format, the component that does not encompass Signmark's or Sean Forbe's complete musical expression and artistry, as primary and the audio/visual format as a supplement to it, reaffirms hearing-centric structures that promote audist hierarchies. In discussions with dip hop artists, I found that one of the fundamental components that was consistently considered integral to this music was the use of sign language (Best 2015/2016, 74). If a song within this style of music does not incorporate sign language, it is not considered dip hop. Given this, while audio recordings provide elements of an artist's musical work, it remains supplementary to video recordings and live performances that feature sign language. Recorded audio has and continues to be reinforced as the tangible product of music due to the structure of the music industry, the design of platforms through which to disseminate music, and the cost difference between producing audio versus video recordings. Yet this structure systemically suppresses Deaf music by valuing auditory components over others. With this in mind, the statements should read "Signmark's albums include a CD component in order to market to wider hearing audiences" and "Signmark (2010) and Sean Forbes (2012) rap in ASL and have created CDs to accompany their albums." This analysis in no way criticizes the work of Jones or Leppänen as their scholarship significantly contributes to the field of Deaf and music studies. It is rather an attempt to keep moving toward understanding the inherent power of hearing-centrism and raise awareness to its hidden nature in order to remove this iteration of ethnocentrism.

CONCLUSION

Examining hearing-centrism, its sites of production, its varied forms and manifestations, and its impact on Deaf culture begins a process of decolonizing systematic structures of oppression that have and continue to disable Deaf people and Deaf perspectives. In addition to applying theoretical frameworks that promote the ideological liberation of Deaf culture from hegemonic domination, we must endeavor to dismantle the structures and systems that continue to uphold hearing biases and, subsequently, stifle Deaf expression. This involves a constant critique and reflection of potential hearing-centric biases, practices, and rhetoric. It also involves reorienting histories of music and sound to incorporate a Deaf lens.

In order to combat hearing-centrism within the study of music, it is necessary to include alternative narratives of musicking, those that have been ideologically excluded from an assortment of narratives designated as "the norm," and incorporate them as an essential and fundamental component to a comprehensive study, knowledge, and understanding of music. Music education, when covertly rooted within a Western system, denies the diversity of practices, manifestations, and constructions of music existing outside of its framework and, consequently, reproduces institutionalized notions of music that are, in turn, imposed and forced on the very practices that have been left out. As Haualand warns, "If a community is confused with a group of people who *hear same*, this will limit the possible fields of anthropology and deteriorate the full picture of how human communities are constructed" (2008, 121). The inclusion of Deaf music within music education is not only important for a greater representation of the diversity of musical practices but also integral for disrupting hearing-centric systems of oppression.

In framing hearing-centrism as a form of ethnocentrism, cultural mechanisms that have oppressed Deaf cultural output can be unmasked and made more noticeable. In doing so, narratives of music and Deaf culture can be redetermined based on the culturally relative perspective that is revealed, and Deaf bodies can be decolonized from debilitating rhetoric that Others their way of life and experiences. When liberated from hearing-centric perspectives, Deaf people are free to express music and represent it on their own terms. Loeffler notes, "understanding Deaf music, through its unique elements comprising visual language and tactile rhythm within the worlds of sound and silence, contributes to the wider understanding of the nature of music itself" (2014, 436). A relative understanding and recognition of music as defined within Deaf culture contribute to Deaf-centered forms of musical expression that illustrate the fullness of musical expression in Deaf culture while facilitating a broader understanding of listening practices and experiences of sound and metaphorical "soundings" that have been ideologically silenced.

NOTES

1. I would like to first acknowledge the many artists I have had the privilege of interviewing and their work, which continues to break down barriers within the music industry. I would also like to thank Heather Paudler for her constant valuable edits and insights as well as Frank Gunderson and Michael Bakan for their research guidance and support.

2. Warren Snipe, Skype interview by author, August 22, 2013.

3. Distinctions between the condition of being deaf and Deaf culture, a linguistic minority defined by the use of signed language, are made through the use of lower case and capitalized forms of the letter *d*.

4. When referring to Deaf music in this chapter, I am referring to Deaf music in all of its forms, which encompasses a diversity of performance practices (see Loeffler 2014 and Cripps 2018). I do not group these distinctly different styles together to disregard the many variances between them but rather as a way to discuss and reveal the mechanisms that have restricted these forms of expression to hearing-centric frameworks.

5. A search on Google Scholar in July 2020 returned one hundred unique documents that include the precise term *hearing-centric*. Of these results, forty-three were journal publications, twenty-one were dissertations, fourteen were books or anthology contributions, twelve were master's theses, seven were reports or proceedings, and three were not accessible to the author and did not have a clear source of publication.

6. As Deaf scholar H-Dirksen L. Bauman notes in an article titled "Audism: Exploring the Metaphysics of Oppression," which further builds on this concept, "Humphrie's definition of audism would be roughly analogous to the notion of 'individual racism,' in which an individual holds beliefs and exhibits racist behaviors ranging from jokes to hate crimes to low expectations in the classroom" (Bauman 2004, 240). As further highlighted within Bauman's work, this term takes on different forms from individual and systemic to ideological.

7. Nicar Bocalan, email correspondence with author, November 30, 2014.

8. Since this time, music scholars including, but not limited to, music theorists Joseph Straus (2011) and Anabel Maler (2013), interdisciplinary music scholars Zeynep Bulut (2014) and Ely Lyonblum (Cripps and Lyonblum 2017), and music education scholar Warren Churchill (2015) as well as musicologists Jeannette DiBernardo Jones (2015) and Jessica A. Holmes (2016) have published pioneering research from their respective fields on Deaf music.

9. These early ethnomusicological investigations provided the foundation for my dissertation, "That's So Def: Redefining Music through Dip Hop, the Deaf Hip Hop Movement in the United States" (PhD diss., Florida State University, 2015).

10. *Listen* is capitalized here to denote the ASL sign LISTEN in English. This is a form of glossing used when translating sign language in written form.

11. Shannon Dean Marsh, personal communications with author, February 3, 2020.

12. Darius McCall, M4a audio correspondence with author, April 6, 2020.

13. See Troi "DJ Chinaman" Lee (Deaf Rave), "It about the @subpac ... FEELTHE BASS at out events! Thanks for sponsoring us Mr Snook! 🎧🎵🎵🎵 Thanks once again @ allpointseastuk and @towerhamlets for giving us this wonderful opportunity 🙏." Facebook photo, May 29, 2019. https://www.facebook.com/DeafRave1/photos/a.1698965966858728/2238816586206994/?type=3%2F and Warren "Wawa" Snipe (WAWAa's World), "Check this out! It was amazing! 🎧🎵📻 Thanks to Not Impossible for allowing to be a part of this! DOPE! We had a blast!!! Right, Mandy Harvey Amber Galloway Shaheem Jade Bryan Kelly Kurdi" Facebook post, December 20, 2018, https://www.facebook.com/wawasworld/posts/1882901981838220?__tn__=-R%2F.

14. Darius McCall, M4a audio correspondence with author, April 6, 2020.

15. Rice (2015, 102) points out that sound studies research has examined how developments in audio technology has led to "new bodies of audible sound as well as related listening techniques." This research addresses ways the development of audio technology has shaped listening practices and advances a more comprehensive understanding of how these practices have contributed to and reinforced aural-centric views; this literature has yet to engage with and make visible the hearing-centric tendencies that are produced and affirmed within the history of such practices.

16. She also refers to this as "hear (the) same or hear together" (Haualand 2008, 115).

17. This also functions as a form of internalized colonization, a connection Brenda M. Romero discusses in note 16 of her autoethnographic exploration in chapter 17 of this anthology.

BIBLIOGRAPHY

Bahan, Benjamin. 2014. "Senses and Culture: Exploring Sensory Orientations." In *Deaf Gain: Raising the Stakes for Human Diversity*, edited by H-Dirksen L. Bauman and Joseph J. Murray, 436–52. Minneapolis: University of Minnesota Press.

Bakan, Michael. 2007. *World Music: Traditions and Transformations.* New York: McGraw-Hill.
Batamula, Christi, and Kimberly Pudans-Smith. 2017. "Examining Language and Access for Deaf in Central Tanzania." *International Journal of Education and Social Science* 4 (9): 20–28.
Bath, Paula. 2016. "Deconstructing Phonocentrism: A New Genre in Deaf Arts." In *Mobilizing Metaphor: Art Culture, and Disability Activism in Canada*, edited by Christine Kelly and Michael Orsini, 181–97. Toronto, UBC Press.
Bauman, H-Dirksen L. 2004. "Audism: Exploring the Metaphysics of Oppression." *Journal of Deaf Studies and Deaf Education* 9 (2): 239–46.
Berdayes, Vincent, Luigi Esposito, and John W. Murphy, eds. 2004. *The Body in Human Inquiry: Interdisciplinary Explorations of Embodiment.* Cresskill, NJ: Hampton Press.
Best, Katelyn E. 2015. "That's So Def: Redefining Music through Dip Hop, the Deaf Hip Hop Movement in the United States." PhD diss., Florida State University.
———. 2015/2016. "'We Still Have a Dream:' The Deaf Hip Hop Movement and the Struggle Against the Socio-Cultural Marginalization of Deaf People." *Lied und Populäre Kultur/Song and Popular Culture* 60 (61): 61–86.
———. 2018. "Musical Belonging in a Hearing-Centric Society: Adapting and Contesting Dominant Cultural Norms through Deaf Hip Hop." Translated by Carla Shird. *Journal of American Sign Languages and Literatures*, 1–7. http://journalofasl.com/special-issue-music/.
———. 2021. "Expanding Musical Inclusivity: Representing and Re-presenting Musicking in Deaf Culture through Hip Hop." In *Music and Democracy: Participatory Approaches*, edited by Marko Kölbl and Fritz Trümpi, 235–65. Vienna: mdw Press.
Bulut, Zeynep. 2014. "Silence and Speech in Lecture on Nothing and Phonophie." *Postmodern Culture: An Electronic Journal of Interdisciplinary Criticism* 24 (3): 1–31.
Cachia, Amanda. 2016. "Loud Silence: Turning Up the Volume on Deaf Voice." *Senses & Society* 10 (3): 321–40.
Carney, Terry. 2020. "Automation in Social Security: Implications for Merits Review?" *Australian Journal of Social Issues* 55 (3): 260–74.
Churchill, Warren N. 2015. "Deaf and Hard-of-Hearing Musicians: Crafting a Narrative Strategy." *Research Studies in Music Education* 37 (1): 21–36.
Cripps, Jody H. 2018. "Ethnomusicology & Signed Music: A Breakthrough." *Journal of American Sign Languages and Literatures*, 1–6. https://journalofasl.com/special-issue-music/.
Cripps, Jody H., and Ely Lyonblum. 2017. "Understanding the Use of Signed Language for Making Music." *Society for American Sign Language Journal* 1 (1): 78–95.

Cripps, Jody H., Ely Rosenblum, Anita Small, and Samuel J. Supalla. 2017. "A Case Study on Signed Music: The Emergence of an Interperformance Art." *Liminalities: A Journal of Performance Studies* 13 (2): 1–24.

Cripps, Jody H., Anita Small, Ely Rosenblum, Samuel J. Supalla, Aimee K. Whyte, and Joanne S. Cripps. Forthcoming. "Signed Music and the Deaf Community." In *Culture, Deafness, and Music: Disability Studies and a Path to Social Justice*, edited by A. Cruz. Rotterdam, Netherlands: Sense Publishers.

Darrow, Alice-Ann, and Diane Loomis. 1999. "Music and Deaf Culture: Images from the Media and Their Interpretation by Deaf and Hearing Students." *Journal of Music* 36 (2): 88–109.

Fleischer, Flavia, Will Garrow, and Rachel Friedman Narr. 2015. "Developing Deaf Education." In *What Really Works in Secondary Education*, edited by Wendy W. Murawski and Kathy Lynn Scott, 289–305. Thousand Oaks, CA: Corwin Sage Company.

Folio, Cynthia. 1992. Review of *Ear Training for Twentieth-Century Music*, by Michael L. Friedmann. *Journal of Music Theory* 36 (2): 383–89.

Friedner, Michele, and Stefan Helmreich. 2012. "Sound Studies Meets Deaf Studies." *Senses & Society* 7 (1): 72–86.

Gertz, Genie. 2008. "Dysconscious Audism: A Theoretical Proposition." In *Open Your Eyes Deaf Studies Talking*, edited by H-Dirksen L. Bauman, 219–34. Minneapolis: University of Minnesota Press.

———. 2016. "Dysconscious Audism." In *The SAGE Deaf Studies Encyclopedia*, edited by Genie Gertz and Patrick Boudreault. Newbury Park, CA: Sage Publications.

Haualand, Hilde. 2008. "Sound and Belonging: What Is a Community?" In *Open Your Eyes Deaf Studies Talking*, edited by H-Dirksen L. Bauman, 111–23. Minneapolis: University of Minnesota Press.

Holcomb, Thomas K. 2010. "Deaf Epistemology: The Deaf Way of Knowing." *American Annals of the Deaf* 154 (5): 471–78.

Holmes, Jessica A. 2016. "Singing beyond Hearing." *Journal of the American Musicological Society* 69 (2): 542–47.

———. 2017. "Expert Listening beyond the Limits of Hearing: Music and Deafness." *Journal of the American Musicological Society* 70 (1): 171–220.

Jones, Jeannette DiBernardo. 2015. "Imagined Hearing: Music-Making in Deaf Culture." In *The Oxford Handbook of Music and Disability Studies*, edited by Blake Howe, Stephanie Jensen-Moulton, Neil William Lerner, and Joseph Nathan Straus, 54–72. New York: Oxford University Press.

Kheshti, Roshanak. 2011. "Touching Listening: The Aural Imaginary in the World Music Culture Industry." *American Quarterly* 63 (3): 711–31.

Kramer, Eric Mark. 2004. "The Body in Communication." In *The Body in Human Inquiry: Interdisciplinary Explorations of Embodiment*, edited by Vincent Berdayes, Luigi Esposito, and John W. Murphy, 51–86. NJ: Hampton Press.

Leppänen, Taru. 2017. "Unfolding Non-Audist Methodologies in Music Research: Signing Hip Hop Artist Signmark and Becoming Deaf with Music." In *Musical Encounters with Deleuze and Guattari*, edited by Pirkko Moisala, Taru Leppänen, Milla Tiainen, and Hanna Väätäinen, 33–49. New York: Bloomsbury Publishing.

Loeffler, Summer. 2014. "Deaf Music: Embodying Language and Rhythm." In *Deaf Gain: Raising the Stakes for Human Diversity*, edited by H-Dirksen L. Bauman and Joseph J. Murray, 436–52. Minneapolis: University of Minnesota Press.

Maler, Anabel. 2013. "Songs for Hands: Analyzing Interactions of Sign Language and Music." *Music Theory Online* 19 (1): 1–15. https://mtosmt.org/issues/mto.13.19.1/mto.13.19.1.maler.html.

———. 2015. "Musical Expression among Deaf and Hearing Song Signers." In *The Oxford Handbook of Music and Disability Studies*, edited by Blake Howe, Stephanie Jensen-Moulton, Neil William Lerner, and Joseph Nathan Straus, 73–91. New York: Oxford University Press.

Maniatty, Holly. 2013. "How to Rap with Your Hands." Interview by Sean Cole. *The Story*, June 28.

Purdy, Elizabeth Rholetter. 2016. "Technology, Assistive." In *The SAGE Deaf Studies Encyclopedia*, edited by Genie Gertz and Patrick Boudreault, 950–53. Newbury Park, CA: Sage Publications.

Rice, Tom. 2015."Listening." In *Keywords in Sound*, edited by David Novak and Matt Sakakeeny, 99–111. Durham, NC: Duke University Press.

Roberts, Bridget, and Janette Mugavin. 2007. *Alcohol and Other Drug Use in the Australian Deaf Community: A Needs Assessment*. Fitzroy, Victoria: Turning Point Alcohol and Drug Centre.

Rosen, Russell S. 2007. "Representations of Sound in American Deaf Literature." *Journal of Deaf Studies and Deaf Education* 12 (4): 552–65.

Silvestri, Julia, Hannah Ehrenberg, Lauren Dick, and Paul Shim. 2018. "Universal Design for Music: Exploring the Intersection of Deaf Education and Music Education." *Journal of American Sign Languages and Literatures*, 1–11. https://journalofasl.com/special-issue-music/.

Simmonds, Mark Peter, and Vicki C. Brown. 2011. "Is There Conflict between Cetacean Conservation and Marine Renewable-Energy Developments?" *Wildlife Research* 37 (8): 688–94.

Singleton, Jenny L., and Matthew D. Tittle. 2000. "Deaf Parents and Their Hearing Children." *Journal of Deaf Studies and Deaf Education* 5 (3): 221–36.

Sirvage, Robert T. 2016. "DeafSpace." In *The SAGE Deaf Studies Encyclopedia*, edited by Genie Gertz and Patrick Boudreault. Newbury, CA: Sage Publications.

Straus, Joseph N. 2011. *Extraordinary Measures: Disability in Music*. New York: Oxford University Press.

Weedon, Chris. 1987. *Feminist Practice and Postculturalist Theory*. Oxford: Blackwell Publishing.

DISCOGRAPHY

Prinz-D. 2014. "This Can't Be Life." In *Deaf and Loud Underground: Vol. 1*. Produced by DJ Nicar. CD. Detroit, MI: Jeff Bass Music, LLC.

SEVEN

PINK MENNO HYMN SINGS

Queerness, Inclusivity, and the Mennonite Church

KATIE J. GRABER

IN 2015, *THE ATLANTIC* RAN a headline, "Gay and Mennonite," over a brilliant rainbow background with a black-and-white photo of a woman wearing a bonnet-like head covering (Green 2015).[1] The story described a vote in a Mennonite Church USA regional conference concerning the official status of a congregation that allowed LGBTQ membership. The misleading cover photo does not represent the Mennonite Church USA denomination, since very few members (and only those of older generations) wear coverings like the one in the picture. My family has been part of this denomination and its precursors—the (Old) Mennonite Church and General Conference Mennonite Church—for generations, and I have never worn a plain dress or bonnet. My grandmother (born in 1912) wore a smaller head covering all her life, and my mother stopped wearing hers when I was a small child. She quit when it was no longer a meaningful symbol and was, in her words, just another thing to get ready when three children already made her life hectic.[2] Smaller denominations with "Mennonite" in their title do have members who wear plain dress and coverings, but Mennonite Church USA members are generally not distinguishable by visual characteristics, which points to change and growing diversity in the community over many decades.

Mennonite Church USA's (hereafter, MCUSA) biennial national conventions, which have produced conflicting church-wide statements and resolutions about LGBTQ membership, are also the events where the LGBTQ activist and ally group Pink Menno has been most active since its founding in 2009. Pink Menno engages in a variety of direct actions at these events: selling pink T-shirts with inclusive slogans, disrupting delegate sessions, meeting with denominational leaders, and providing off-site activities and educational opportunities for youth and adults. In 2019, for example, the latter included a "Trans 101" seminar and a documentary about a woman who was terminated from her position at a Mennonite agency after marrying her wife.

Pink Menno's most visible and audible actions are hymn sings in the halls of these convention centers: circles of people (many wearing pink) calling out song requests and singing from photocopied Pink Menno songbooks. The booklets with bright pink covers, compiled by each year's organizer and song leader, assert Mennonite identity by reproducing the sights and sounds of official denominational hymnals. The song circles are a tangible way for LGBTQ people to enact inclusion within the Mennonite community. At once, they are proclaiming their presence, assuring young queer people from nonwelcoming communities that there is a larger context of inclusion, and demanding that denominational structures become more officially inclusive.

This chapter will explore the ways Pink Menno uses singing to claim a place in Mennonite communities and structures, how they navigate racial diversity in a denomination often portrayed as White, and how structural and denominational responses might be inclusive without subsuming them. After outlining some context around Mennonites and Mennonite music, I describe how denominational structures relate to the intersection of queer and Mennonite identities. Next, I analyze how hymn sings and musical diversity complicate notions of inclusion and exclusion. Finally, I argue that the rest of the denomination can use musical practices to understand and include queerness without assimilating it.

These inquiries into how music intentionally and unintentionally includes and excludes are significant to other studies of music and social justice. Calling for scholars and practitioners to be vigilant about exclusion may be a truism, but slipping into comfortable routines is a seductive danger. Routines produce situations in which regular participants feel at ease, sometimes not realizing that newcomers struggle to learn their practices or subtle customs. Routines may also assimilate an in-crowd in a way that is antithetical to groups seeking liberation from normativity. On the other hand, queer theorists question whether movements must be either assimilationist or liberationist (either conforming to a mainstream or creating alternatives) (Sullivan 2003). Pink Menno is similarly doing something more complicated than trying to assimilate to, or become liberated from, the Mennonite Church. It is working to create a new situation—not a new church, but a more complicated church in which more diversity is recognized and honored. Music is key to understanding how Pink Menno might enact this way of being in the world that can hold diversity without absorbing it.

MENNONITE MUSICAL CONTEXT

MCUSA is a denomination of sixteen area conferences, about 530 congregations, and sixty-two thousand people that defines itself through beliefs such as nonviolence and adult baptism (Mennonite Church USA n.d.). A dominant narrative connects present-day Mennonites to the Radical Reformation in sixteenth-century Germany and Switzerland, when Anabaptist reformers rejected violence and embraced communal discernment over centralized hierarchies. Today, Anabaptist and Mennonite groups include over two million people worldwide (Mennonite World Conference n.d.). Connections to foundational beliefs since the sixteenth century remain important; however, US scholars have recently critiqued persistent Eurocentrism in understandings of MCUSA and related groups (Hinojosa 2014; Miller Sherer 2010).

Although Mennonites are often portrayed as extremely traditional in the news and popular culture, they are diverse and include many progressive individuals and communities. MCUSA on the whole has become more progressive since tens of thousands of individuals, including entire congregations and area conferences, have severed ties because of shifts toward inclusion of queer people in recent decades. Still, beliefs and practices around inclusion are inconsistent, with distributed authority allowing regional conferences and local congregations to make rules. While some area conferences will ordain queer people, others will revoke ordination for a straight person who performs a same-sex wedding. Some congregations have queer pastors, and others refuse to allow queer members.

My understanding of Pink Menno and MCUSA relies on my involvement in the Mennonite church. On the local level, I am one of several volunteer song leaders at Columbus Mennonite Church, a community that includes many Pink Menno supporters and one of only a few ordained queer pastors in MCUSA. Since 2016, I have been part of a committee that is compiling and editing a new hymnal for MCUSA and Mennonite Church Canada, a process and personal network that has been indispensable to research on Mennonite musical, racial, and ethnic diversity (Graber 2019). I began interviewing Pink Menno song leaders and participants and studying their song booklets in this context, after reading news and following the group on social media for several years.

My first time singing with Pink Menno was in Kansas City in 2019. I was one of several straight allies who helped plan Pink Menno events for this convention, and I helped lead singing there as well. Although their first appearance at the 2009 convention was only miles from my house in Columbus, Ohio, the cost and five-day time commitment was prohibitive at a time when I had an infant and toddler. Conventions in the next odd years were farther away, in Pittsburgh, Phoenix, Kansas City, and Orlando. Only a few thousand people go to national conventions; local congregations often raise money to send a youth group, and they may budget funds to send delegates to vote on resolutions (I was also a delegate for Columbus Mennonite Church in 2019).

To many Mennonites and outsiders speculating about Mennonites, singing is a significant aspect of the performance of community and of being Mennonite. Notably, even the news story in *The Atlantic* mentioned at the outset of this chapter highlights Mennonite singing—the online article includes audio examples, and the subtitle uses a metaphor of music: "They vote on everything. They're committed to peace. Can a church that defines itself by harmony survive dissonance over homosexuality?" (Green 2015). In the meeting described in the article, which was a business meeting rather than a worship service, singing together was still an act of solidarity or cohesiveness as individuals made votes they knew would bind them to some neighbors and separate them from others.

Of course, building community through singing does not "just happen"; it is a historically and geographically contextualized process that needs to be continually rearticulated and enacted. Austin McCabe Juhnke has analyzed how singing was used to establish both cultural cohesion and exclusion in Mennonite denominations throughout the twentieth century (McCabe Juhnke 2019a, 2019b). He describes the publication of *The Mennonite Hymnal* in 1969 as a project that consolidated a conception of White ethnic Mennonite identity in part by emphasizing four-part singing and its connection to the European and Euro-American past. He notes three types of songs that helped do this work: German chorales, nineteenth-century Shape Note songs (many from Mennonite Joseph Funk's 1832 *Harmonia Sacra*), and songs from the *Ausbund* (a collection of Anabaptist martyr hymns in German from 1583) (McCabe Juhnke 2019a, 68–70). He contrasts the reception of *The Mennonite Hymnal* to relative silence about Latino and African American Mennonite choirs in the 1970s that performed at other Mennonite churches and made recordings of songs influenced by popular and gospel styles.

The racial, cultural, and linguistic diversity of Mennonite Church USA has grown since 1969; the denomination now uses both Spanish and English for many official publications and events, and there are six recognized constituency groups based on race that send representatives to denominational meetings.[3] Mennonite denominational hymnals have changed as well; *Hymnal: A Worship Book* (1992) and two smaller supplemental collections, *Sing the Journey* (2005) and *Sing the Story* (2007) contain traditional hymns along with selections of contemporary music and songs from around the world. The newest hymnal, *Voices Together* (2020), includes more than two dozen languages used by congregations in MCUSA and Mennonite Church Canada, along with many more languages and musical styles from around the world. However, the bulk of these hymnals are Western traditional and contemporary songs, and they are most commonly used in predominantly White English-speaking MCUSA churches. In the midst of diversity, there is still a White English-speaking majority and a contested yet still prevalent hymnal culture. Pink Menno must navigate these multiple diversities in its hymn sings that are meant to produce inclusivity.

MCUSA STRUCTURES AND LGBTQ ACTIVISM

Pink Menno is part of a longer history of activism for LGBTQ inclusion in what is now Mennonite Church USA. Stephanie Krehbiel describes the history since the 1970s in her recent dissertation, a forceful critique of the way power is officially and unofficially wielded in MCUSA (2015). The activist group BMC[4] formed in 1976 and worked on interpersonal, congregational, and denominational levels into the 1990s and beyond, when LGBTQ inclusion was an ongoing discussion around the merging of General Conference Mennonite Church and (Old) Mennonite Church into Mennonite Church USA (Krehbiel 2015, 34–44, 50). During that time, BMC responded in writing and in meetings, and they formed the Supportive Congregations Network that now includes over 100 congregations (46, 51–2). The merger that created MCUSA occurred in 2002 and conflicts about queer inclusion have continued. In 2007 the Inclusive Mennonite Pastors formed, defining itself as "a growing, ever-evolving community, not a formal organization" (Inclusive Mennonite Pastors n.d.). Among these groups, Krehbiel characterizes Pink Menno, which began in 2009, as a "loose, mostly web-maintained network of queer- and ally-identified Mennonites" (2015, 66). There is no official membership, and during the time between national conventions, the geographically dispersed group primarily operates through social media (the Pink Menno Facebook page in 2020 has over four thousand followers) and through its relationships to other organizations. Krehbiel summarizes that they work with "the financial and organizational help of" BMC and are "not a discrete organization so much as . . . the public face of current LGBTQ Mennonite activism" (66).

Pink Menno's public face of activism has meant that their leaders and participants have borne the brunt of public backlash. Krehbiel's premise in her dissertation is that "LGBTQ Mennonites often experience church as violent and abusive"; she quotes a friend describing leaving the church like leaving an abusive spouse (4). The adversity Pink Menno has faced prompts some people to ask why participants stay in a church that mistreats them. In fact, there have been quite a few Pink Menno leaders and members who have understandably left in anger and fatigue—a grave loss of passion and talent for MCUSA.[5] At the same time, the assumption that queer people *should* want to leave is equivalent to an assumption that they don't belong. Queer theorist Mary Gray studies a similar framework, investigating representations of rural communities as hostile environments, along with the narrative of LGBTQ youth "escaping" to urban areas. Gray could be describing Mennonite people when she refers to the ways LGBTQ-identifying youth "stand their ground to name their desires and flesh out their local meaning . . . [and] create belonging and visibility in communities where they are not only a distinct minority but also popularly represented as out of place" (2009, 3–4). Focusing on queer people's nonbelonging and pain can inadvertently reinforce exclusion; scholars must understand how music can create belonging and visibility within both explicit and implicit narratives of marginalization.

Many Pink Menno participants claim belonging and visibility by asserting their queer and Mennonite identities as equally important. Addie Liechty is a Pink Menno leader who has written about their life in ways that highlight what it is like to feel these tensions. Here they describe deep feelings of belonging to the Mennonite church:

> I was six years old when I first began to understand my identity as a Mennonite. It was 1990, and Operation Desert Storm had just begun. "Tomorrow there is going to be a Support the Troops rally at your school," my mother had told me. "But we are Mennonites, and we don't believe in war. Part of being Mennonite is choosing not to fight in wars or support fighting in wars. It's up to you if you want to go to the rally or not—I want you to make that choice for yourself." For me, it was a no-brainer. Church was the place where I felt safe and held, where I had a strong sense of identity. I was a Mennonite, above all else—the only one in my class at school. (Liechty 2018)

Liechty also describes a time when they left the Mennonite church, the tensions of losing that context, and, finally, finding an affirming Mennonite community:

> I was learning what it meant to be queer and thrive—something I never saw in Mennonite environments. In Mennonite environments, I was always hiding or pining for acceptance and tolerance. . . . [Now,] I cut my hair short and felt attractive, rather than weird. I embraced myself. However, there was something missing. My amazing queer and queer allied community did not understand the part of me that was Mennonite. As good as I felt about my gender and sexuality, I still felt somewhat fractured. Perhaps this is why

I nearly burst into tears every time a queer identity is celebrated at First Mennonite Church of San Francisco. (Liechty 2015)

In a news article about a public discussion among religious leaders, Liechty was quoted saying, "I know I should stay in this community, but I don't know if I should stay in the larger Mennonite community" (Cassell 2018). That is, their San Francisco Mennonite community is affirming but conflicts in the larger denomination are exhausting and harmful. This layer of church structures is one that is not analogous to queer people dealing with rural stereotypes, since the nationwide denomination *officially* varies widely in thought and practice.

Pink Menno audibility at national conventions has held a microphone to both unity and disunity in these many layers of MCUSA. On one hand, the ever-growing circle of singers joining together in song has demonstrated support and solidarity. On the other hand, individuals associated with Pink Menno have been scolded, maligned, and questioned, as antagonists have responded through resolutions, votes, writing in denominational publications, and leaving the church. Many congregations have left MCUSA explicitly because of LGBTQ inclusion, while others have made more veiled references to biblical interpretation or not wanting to be "distracted" from more important church business by conflict. Without discounting the importance of LGBTQ inclusion in denominational demographics, it is also worth noting that Mennonite churches (indeed, most denominations in North America) have been declining in membership for decades. Conrad L. Kanagy published a member survey of MCUSA in 2005 and credits decreases to an aging population, smaller family size, and lower engagement of younger adults (2007, 55–57, 63).

The congregations and individuals leaving the denomination have also certainly changed the atmosphere at national conventions—in 2009, Pink Menno hymn sings started out with ten to fifteen people, while now they can include hundreds of singers. There is a steady stream of opinion articles on LGBTQ inclusion or exclusion in denominational publications, and some people have written recently about being in the minority because they believe in a "traditional definition of Christian marriage" (e.g., Shedden 2020). While acceptance has grown, there are still many individuals and congregations that encounter Pink Menno's claim of belonging with reticence or hostility.

PINK MENNO, UNITY, AND EXCLUSION

Along with changing numbers, Pink Menno has navigated changes in MCUSA's diversity of language, race, ethnicity, and music in recent decades. Although MCUSA is small relative to many US Protestant denominations, it is large enough that it is difficult to make generalizations about musical practices. In the process of compiling and editing *Voices Together* from 2016 to 2020, I worked with a thirteen-member committee to understand Mennonite music in the United States and Canada today. We conducted a variety of surveys and church visits, observing a broad range of musical practices: the four-part singing tradition celebrated in the mid-twentieth century is still present, sometimes a capella and sometimes with instrumental accompaniment. Organs and pianos are common, as well as other instrumental accompaniment inspired by or embracing a range of styles: jazz, gospel, folk, and contemporary worship. Many communities that use languages other than English sing a combination of traditional Western hymns in translation and contemporary music in translation or originally written in their languages. Some have songwriters in their communities, and some sing older songs from their cultures of origin.

Pink Menno, as its group members sing community and perform gender and queerness, has tried to navigate racial and musical diversity as well. It explicitly engages justice intersectionally; in 2015, Pink Menno seminars included one called "Standing in Resistance to White Supremacy," and that year the group's T-shirts said both "Queer Lives Matter" and "Black Lives Matter." In 2019, Pink Menno and BMC had a presence in the exhibition hall (the first time they had been granted an official space by convention planners), part of a larger display on justice along with the Dismantling the Doctrine of Discovery Coalition and the Mennonite Palestine Israel Network. In recent years, they have also tried to include more diverse music in their songbooks, an issue I will return to in the paragraphs that follow.

In its beginning in 2009, Pink Menno hymn sing events intentionally tapped into the common (though, again, not universal) claim that a capella four-part singing is an important Mennonite tradition. Luke Miller, one of the founding members of Pink Menno, described how he chose songs for the first Pink Menno songbook: "[It was] a subversive way of claiming our Mennonite identity— since Mennonite identity is also wrapped up in singing. So I was specifically looking for hymns that were in . . . traditional four-part harmony but also ones that supported a queer-inclusive worldview. And some were literally just some favorite ones I wanted to bust out."[6]

In that first year, Pink Menno did not request official space or to be listed on the official schedule, knowing it would be denied. Instead, the group just sang. Luke said that although "the hymn sings have become less subversive through the years as more people are familiar with them, in the beginning we had no idea how people would respond. Maybe they'd kick us out of the convention hall, maybe no one would join us, maybe we'd be heckled."[7] Krehbiel described those first singing events: "Fear, discomfort, disgust and curiosity are all palpable in the area around the circle"; and she quotes founder Jay Yoder describing how Pink Menno "brought out the fury" (Krehbiel 2015, 66, 78). In the early years Pink Menno received hostile verbal and written responses, and this is still a potential now. People interrupted the singing to read accusing Bible passages, and some congregations declared they would not return to conventions if Pink Menno would be there.

In the midst of that fear and animosity, singing together had a powerful unifying effect. Luke said, "Your emotions and your senses are heightened through the sense of potential danger. It heightens the sense of connectedness, camaraderie, power that you're creating with the people around you... so that intense connection with the other people that join the circle can make it a much more deeply spiritual or emotionally powerful experience. And there's a lot of fear and tension in your body that can get worked through... I feel like the singing transforms some of the emotions from fear into elation."[8]

Participants describe creating a new reality through singing together: Abbie Miller (sister-in-law to Luke) said, "I think that taking a song that everybody takes for granted, like 'Come, let us all unite to sing God is love'—by taking that and using it as a protest song almost, it's taking something really familiar and turning it on its head. Making it a resistance... singing things into reality."[9] Luke agreed that it was "about just creating and being the actual spiritual community that we were searching for... and maybe that would become part of the institutional church at some point but it's not like we're knocking on the door asking, please let us in so we can do this thing inside of there."[10] Instead, they were performing and creating the reality they desired.

Pink Menno participants are also cognizant that this feeling of creating community can be dangerous; for example, they are very aware of the larger Mennonite denomination's discussions of "community" or "unity" that are actually exclusive. Pax Ressler, who compiled the Pink Menno songbook and led hymn sings in 2013, said, "lots of queer Mennonites and Pink Menno folks were very wary of the word 'unity' as it was used to talk about the church staying together, ... that being the main goal over and above queer folks being affirmed and welcomed in the church."[11] Mark Rupp, pastor at Columbus Mennonite Church, compared singing in inclusive settings to his experience singing in the services officially planned by the denomination: "Singing a song about 'unity in Christ' in those two spaces is going to feel really different.... Singing that in a place where my *presence* is seen as disunity feels coercive, feels inauthentic."[12] Ethnomusicological research has also focused on the dangers of this kind of cohesion; just one example is Herrera's (2018) article about how Argentinian soccer fans enact a potentially violent masculinity by moving and sounding together through homophobic and racist chants. This is a notable contrast, as Pink Menno hymn sings are made up of queer people and allies singing songs intentionally chosen for inclusivity rather than an oppressing group chanting insults.

However, it is impossible to enact a community without also continually constructing new borders. Pink Menno members and planners have recognized that focusing on a capella singing and traditional hymnody is a problematic way to claim Mennonite-ness because it excludes anyone who did not grow up singing those songs or those styles. Current North American Mennonite hymnals are primarily resources for English-speaking congregations, while Mennonite speakers of other languages typically use other hymnals or projected songs. These practices may contain overlapping repertoire, but it would not be entirely shared. Furthermore, many Mennonites (both White and non-White, speakers of English and other languages) sing more contemporary songs that are often oriented toward melodies and instrumental accompaniments. Claiming four-part a capella singing *as* Mennonite, then, can imply that a large swath of Mennonites are not singing Mennonite music. In conversations among White people and people of color in recent years, Pink Menno participants began questioning these assumptions set forth by their performance practices. Luke said that the "White European ethno-Mennonites [came] to realize that what seems like reclaiming an identity and performing music together, as a way of liberating ourselves to be both Mennonite and queer at the same time, might be for a queer person of color another way of feeling like they don't belong."[13] This is an ongoing question—work that will never be resolved or completed; the next section comes back to this issue after a discussion of some ways music can encompass diversity.

HEARING THE NONNORMATIVE

Questions of enacting community and its boundaries are so acute because many Pink Menno participants are aware that performance of identity *is* the process of identification. Performance is a central concept in queer theory (Butler 2004; Sedgwick 2003), along with approaches that seek to understand the irreducible experience of being a person in the world amid larger structures that want to subsume complexities into categories and systems. In queer theory, there are debates about how queerness ought to exist in relationship to those larger structures of normativity (Sheldon 2019; Halley and Parker 2011). When an aspect of queerness is accepted by society, it is no longer queer. Pink Menno evoked this concept in 2017 when they sold red caps that proclaimed, "Make Anabaptism Queer Again." In the case of Pink Menno hymn sings, Stephanie Krehbiel described song leader Pax Ressler's feeling in 2013 that "people were getting 'comfortable' with the Pink Menno presence. They were predictable: they sang nice hymns, and then they dispersed.... They weren't shaking things up anymore" (2015, 109). How can Mennonite structures resist this assimilating force while still being open to queerness, and how can Pink Menno be open to performing many kinds of Mennonite-ness without losing specificity?

The first way to do this would be for Mennonites to recognize that queer people are already part of MCUSA's diversity. Pink Menno's hymn sings are a way to name and enact this very mundane fact; as Pax explained it, they are "inviting people to see queer Mennonites as part of the tradition as opposed to a new thing"[14]—or, more bluntly: "We're here, we're queer, we're Mennonite" (Ressler 2018). In order to accept this reality, Mennonites ought to be able to identify other queerness already present in being Mennonite. In the 1990s, Kay Stoner wrote an article called "How the Peace Church Helped Make a Lesbian Out of Me" in which she describes the similarity in social contexts of (a certain type of) Mennonite church and her lesbian friends: potlucks, birkenstocks, and being comfortable with people staring at her—essentially, being Mennonite taught her to be different from mainstream society (Stoner 1994). Mennonites have a long history of challenging normativity, including explicitly countercultural gender norms such as women's plain dress and men's refusal to participate in war. Many Mennonite women of my mother's generation have never worn makeup or had their ears pierced; this is not specifically queer, but it is certainly not typically feminine in North America today.

In singing, even more, Mennonites accept a range of gendered vocal expression. Luke said, "I think there can be something queer about singing in four parts; the parts are set up on a spectrum that can be mapped onto binary gender, but you can play with this spectrum really easily. It's anybody's option to cross a line and sing a part that is supposedly assigned to a different gender. So even though it appears to be set up on a binary, there are lots of ways to play with parts in the four-part singing tradition that feel very queer."[15] Several interviewees also pointed out that many cisgender people have voices that do not fit the gendered categories of female soprano/alto and male tenor/bass. Young boys typically sing soprano, and many adult women sing tenor. Pax summarized, "There seems to be something inherently queer about that, that in our tradition you maybe start by singing the melody, or start by learning about a particular line, and for some folks, if their voice changes or if over time—I guess this could happen to anyone—to sing a different line or to learn something different."[16]

Many Mennonites think nothing of this ambiguity in their personal history of learning to sing harmony at church, and yet, this is a key moment when they have the potential to recognize their capacity for accepting queerness. Pax described learning soprano, alto, and tenor from their mom, and bass from their dad. A book about Mennonite singing published in 2001 described a variety of learning experiences: a woman said, "My dad would put me on his lap and hold my face and say, 'Sing like I do,' and that's how I learned to sing alto," and "a man remembered that his father didn't sing very much, so he sat beside his mother in church to 'absorb her alto' and learn to sing parts" (Kropf and Nafziger 2001, 58). These stories were not at all meant to be questioning gender performance; they were in a list of heartwarming ("normal") stories about learning to sing. I have not heard people acknowledge this vocal gender bending as a possibility for queer acceptance outside of my questions in interviews. Pax and Luke had ready stories and analyses when I asked, but it is not a typical narrative. As a straight Mennonite ally, I recognize this as part of the work I need to do, to notice and proclaim that we're already in a position to be open to accepting queerness and queer people. Of course, this sentiment could be extended to non-Mennonite contexts as well, always with the caveat of the fine balance between the aspirational "we're all in a place to accept queerness" and the subsuming "we're all queer."

The physical Pink Menno songbooks also make this claim that Mennonite singing has the potential to accept queerness. They include songs from Mennonite hymnals that are implicitly supportive of queer inclusion rather than the many hymns and choral songs that explicitly name queer inclusion. Even recently written texts on inclusion by Mennonite authors are overlooked in favor of songs from denominational hymnals. Instead of singing "Quirky, queer and wonderful, distinct, unique and odd—all of our humanity reveals the face of God" by Mennonite writer Adam Tice, Pink Menno participants sing songs that could be sung in most Mennonite congregations in a weekly service.[17] Such an orientation is significant, demonstrating the importance of already existing Mennonite hymnals to the Pink Menno project. There is only one song in the 2017 Pink Menno songbook from outside these collections: "It Gets Better, Keep on Walking," a text by Randall Spaulding (Pink Menno song leader in 2019) sung to the tune of "Joyful, joyful, we adore thee." Though the phrase "it gets better" alludes to antibullying campaigns, the text is not overtly about queer inclusion. The 2019 songbook (compiled by Randall Spaulding and me) included "It Gets Better, Keep on Walking," and a few others beyond those slated to be in *Voices Together* or the previous denominational collections. Aside from these outliers, Pink Menno songs are familiar to many (especially White, English-speaking) Mennonites, with themes such as proclaiming God's love ("The love of God . . . so measureless and strong") or calls to action ("Wade in the water, God's going to trouble the water").

Not only the content, but also the physical Pink Menno songbook itself stakes a claim on Mennonite hymnal identity. Figure 7.1 shows the front cover

Fig. 7.1. Pink Menno songbook. Photograph by author.

and an inside spread of the 2019 Pink Menno song book, including "Bwana Awabariki (May God Grant You a Blessing)" photocopied directly from *Hymnal: A Worship Book* (including the hymn number 422) and "Calm Me, Lord" copied from *Sing the Story* (without its number 45). The 2017 songbook is structured and styled after these hymnals even more closely: "What Is This Place" is placed at number 1, just as it is in *Hymnal: A Worship Book*. It and the rest of the songs are copied from Mennonite hymnals and given new hymn numbers and headings at the top of the page in the hymnals' fonts. These are small details, but they are significant. *Hymnal: A Worship Book*, *Sing the Journey*, and *Sing the Story* all have the same visual elements, and the people who use those hymnals each week would *feel* the Pink Menno songbooks to be familiar. They likely feel it so deeply that they don't even think about the similarity. For a Mennonite who holds these books in their hands on a regular basis, these Pink Menno pages are saying: you think you're seeing, hearing, and singing a familiar song, but the cover of this songbook is pink; there's queerness embedded in it. But—if a singer thinks back to the hymnal they use in church—there's queerness already there too, in the contents, in the people, and in the singing practices.

However, this brings us back to the question of racial and musical diversity: this heavy reliance on Mennonite hymnals is inclusive to a particular type of Mennonite singer. Some selections in the Pink Menno songbooks clearly signal White Mennonite identity. For example, "We Are People of God's Peace" is based on writings by Menno Simons, the sixteenth-century priest who left the Catholic Church and eventually had the religious movement named after him. Another song, "Praise God from Whom," is a fairly challenging choral piece that many White Anglo Mennonites humbly take pride in being able to sing by memory (see McCabe Juhnke 2019b for an extended analysis). Singing this song in a Pink Menno circle is a clear statement of belonging for those who are able to join in. While Pink Menno song leaders have intentionally included non-English and non-Western songs, those are also from Mennonite hymnals and often in three or four parts (for example, African parallel harmonies are well loved by many hymnal-using Mennonites). When I helped plan in 2019, we added songs we expected to be new to most people and that would be simple to teach. These songs were in Spanish (such as "Me ha mostrado" by the Maranatha! Latin music group) or more explicitly associated with activism (such as "Rich Man's House" by Anne Feeney). We also diversified the song leader role by calling in several different people of different racial/ethnic backgrounds to take turns leading.

Unsurprisingly, we did not solve White supremacy and create a happy diversity. Often, the gathered singers requested favorite songs from denominational hymnals, reinforcing that conception and experience of Mennonite music. Our attempts to add sonic diversity with guitar and drums were hampered by acoustics of high ceilings and carpeted halls. We knew there would be no easy solutions—we cannot create nuanced diversity of gender, sexuality, race, ethnicity, and language by singing the correct song or creating the correct songbook. All we can do is continue working and being vigilant about small decisions (Donna Haraway [2016] calls this "staying with the trouble"). We have to intentionally participate in the process of rearticulating and performing community; scholars often strive to do this whether they are deliberately joining in activism or not. Singing together can create moments of inclusion, but scholars and activists have to continually search out the fine distinctions of who feels that unity and who does not. Singing allows for (but does not guarantee) singular, embodied experiences in which people have the potential to both hear and not hear all the diversities, to realize that songs already hold queerness and the possibility for singing diversity. Understanding and articulating this possibility is one way to step beyond liberation versus assimilation, but it is a step that we (both scholars and activists) have to keep taking. We cannot sing a song or write an article and be done.

FINDING THE COMPLICATIONS

In a blog post about a painful vote that reaffirmed exclusionist policies at a national convention, Luke described the spontaneous hymn sing that followed:

> We sang with such beauty and power and dignity and joy and pain and peace and anger and despair, all wrapped up together as one, uniting us, uniting our voices and uniting our spirits into one great Spirit.... I looked around that wide ever-expanding circle, and my eyes took in the light from the face of one of our queer kids. One of your queer kids... I didn't cry for the church.... But I did weep for how much beauty could radiate from the face of one safe, loved queer kid. (Miller 2017)

This description encompasses many of the contradictions of Pink Menno hymn sings—the simultaneous conflicting emotions, the "our" and "your" that are the same and yet separate, and the loved queer kid who may face hate as soon as they step out of the circle. It demonstrates how the structures of MCUSA and Pink Menno can be both inclusive and exclusive at the same, with layers of insiders and outsiders that potentially shift with each song. This example pushes against the liberation/assimilation dichotomy with a glimpse of a moment of unity that still allows individuality to radiate from the faces of those present. The singing and the reference to Spirit demonstrates how the movement uses tradition to fuel resistance (and how resistance could revitalize a tradition).

Our job as scholars is to seek out these contradictions and tend to them without oversimplifying. Music can be a place where that complexity is analyzed, from repertoires and canons to individual songs and particular performance contexts. Interrogating structures and their inherent internal contradictions is not new, of course. Studying music as it is used to build a better world is also not new, but perhaps seeking to build a more complicated world through scholarship or activism is a fresh focus.

NOTES

1. I am grateful to Pink Menno planners and participants for the time they gave to interviews and feedback on this project, and to the Voices Together committee for countless hours of research and discussions about Mennonite music. I also want to thank Jacob Kopcienski for directing me to the rural queer studies literature, which helped me think through explicit and implicit narratives of belonging.

2. Holly Scott (2018) heard similar responses in her more extensive interviews on this subject. See "Change without a Bang."

3. The constituency groups are the African American Mennonite Association; African, Belizean, Caribbean Mennonite Mission Association; Asian Mennonite Ministries; Iglesia Menonita Hispana; Indonesian Mennonite Association; and Native American Ministries. Two other groups not based on race are Mennonite Women and Mennonite Men. In 2020, the Mennonite Inclusive Pastors group is working on a resolution that includes a call for a new LGBTQIA constituency group (Inclusive Mennonite Pastors 2020).

4. First called Brethren Mennonite Council on Gay and Lesbian Concerns; now called Brethren Mennonite Council for Lesbian, Gay, Bisexual and Transgender Interests.

5. I will not dwell on this pain, but I will note two eloquent and furious essays: Pink Menno cofounder Jay Yoder's (2016) "We Are Dying" and Rae Halder's (2015) "Lament for the Institutionalized Church: Trauma, Rage, and Hope from Kansas City".

6. Luke Miller, interview by author, Columbus, Ohio, May 27, 2018.

7. Ibid.

8. Ibid.

9. Abbie Miller, interview by author, Columbus, Ohio, May 27, 2018.

10. Luke Miller, interview by author, Columbus, Ohio, May 27, 2018.

11. Pax Ressler, Skype interview by author, July 24, 2018.

12. Mark Rupp, interview by author, Columbus, Ohio, January 31, 2017.

13. Luke Miller, interview by author, Columbus, Ohio, May 27, 2018.

14. Pax Ressler, Skype interview by author, July 24, 2018.

15. Luke Miller, interview by author, Columbus, Ohio, May 27, 2018.

16. Pax Ressler, Skype interview by author, July 24, 2018.

17. This text is set to the tune of "For the Beauty of the Earth." There are five stanzas with themes such as Jesus overturning received religion or biblical stories of God challenging cleanliness rules.

BIBLIOGRAPHY

Butler, Judith. 2004. *Undoing Gender.* New York: Routledge.

Cassell, Heather. 2018. "Queer Faith Leaders Issue Call to Take Back Religion." *Bay Area Reporter*, July 18, 2018. Accessed July 18, 2020. https://www.ebar.com/news/news//262830/.

Graber, Katie. 2019. "Mennonite Voices." *American Religious Sounds Project.* Lauren Pond, Producer. Accessed May 23, 2022. http://arspgallery.com/mennonite-voices-exhibit/.

Gray, Mary. 2009. *Out in the Country: Youth, Media, and Queer Visibility in Rural America.* New York: New York University Press.

Green, Emma. 2015. "Gay and Mennonite." *The Atlantic.* Accessed March 18, 2020. https://www.theatlantic.com/national/archive/2015/03/gay-and-mennonite/388060/.

Halder, Rae. 2015. "Lament for the Institutionalized Church: Trauma, Rage, and Hope from Kansas City." *Our Stories Untold.* Accessed September 20, 2020.

http://www.ourstoriesuntold.com/lament-institutionalized-churchtrauma-rage-grief-kansas-city/.

Halley, Janet, and Andrew Parker, eds. 2011. *After Sex? On Writing since Queer Theory*. Durham, NC: Duke University Press.

Haraway, Donna. 2016. *Staying with the Trouble: Making Kin in the Chthuluscene*. Durham, NC: Duke University Press.

Herrera, Eduardo. 2018. "Masculinity, Violence, and Deindividuation in Argentine Soccer Chants: The Sonic Potentials of Participatory Sounding-in-Synchrony" *Ethnomusicology* 62 (3): 470–99.

Hinojosa, Felipe. 2014. *Latino Mennonites: Civil Rights, Faith, and Evangelical Culture*. Baltimore: Johns Hopkins University Press.

Inclusive Mennonite Pastors. 2020. "A Resolution for Repentance and Transformation." Accessed September 20, 2020. https://inclusivepastors.wordpress.com/resolution/.

———. n.d. "Who We Are." Accessed September 20, 2020. https://inclusivepastors.wordpress.com/.

Kanagy, Conrad L. 2007. *Road Signs for the Journey: A Profile of Mennonite Church USA*. Scottdale, PA: Herald Press.

Krehbiel, Stephanie. 2015. "Pacifist Battlegrounds: Violence, Community, and the Struggle for LGBTQ Justice in the Mennonite Church USA." PhD diss., University of Kansas.

Kropf, Marlene, and Kenneth Nafziger. 2001. *Singing: A Mennonite Voice*. Harrisonburg, VA: Herald Press.

Liechty, Addie. 2015. "The Children Are Listening." *The Mennonite*, July 6, 2015. Accessed September 20, 2020. https://anabaptistworld.org/the-children-are-listening/.

———. 2018. "Finding My Place in Ritual and Love as a Queer Mennonite." *Catapult*, December 10, 2018. Accessed September 20, 2020. https://catapult.co/stories/finding-my-place-in-ritual-and-love-as-a-queer-mennonite/.

McCabe Juhnke, Austin. 2019a. "The Lawndale Choir: Singing Mennonite from the City." *Mennonite Quarterly Review* 3 (92): 309–33.

———. 2019b. "Music and the Mennonite Ethnic Imagination." PhD diss., Ohio State University.

Mennonite Church USA. n.d. "Who Are the Mennonites." Accessed September 18, 2020. https://www.mennoniteusa.org/.

Mennonite World Conference. n.d. "World Map and Statistics." Accessed September 20, 2020. https://mwc-cmm.org/world-map-and-statistics/.

Miller, Luke. 2017. "A Love Letter to the Scattered Pink Siblings, from Orlando." *Pink Menno Press*, July 10, 2017. Accessed October 19, 2020. http://www.pinkmenno.org/2017/07/love-letter-scattered-pink-siblings-orlando/.

Miller Sherer, Tobin. 2010. *Daily Demonstrators: The Civil Rights Movement in Mennonite Homes and Sanctuaries*. Baltimore: Johns Hopkins University Press.

Scott, Holly. 2018. "Change without a Bang." *Anabaptist Historians*, August 30, 2018. Accessed September 18, 2020. https://anabaptisthistorians.org/2018/08/30/change-without-a-bang/.

Sedgwick, Eve Kosofsky. 2003. *Touching Feeling: Affect, Pedagogy, Performativity*. Durham, NC: Duke University Press.

Shedden, Matthew. 2020. "The New Orthodoxy of Inclusion." *The Mennonite* 23 (3): 33.

Sheldon, Rebekah. 2019. "Reading for Transgression." In *After Queer Studies: Literature, Theory and Sexuality in the 21st Century*, edited by Tyler Bradway and E. L. McCallum, 171–87. Cambridge: Cambridge University Press.

Stoner, Kay. 1994. "How the Peace Church Helped Make a Lesbian Out of Me." *Mennonot* (3): 10–12.

Sullivan, Nikki. 2003. "Assimilation or Liberation, Sexuality or Gender?" In *A Critical Introduction to Queer Theory*, 22–36. New York: New York University Press.

Yoder, Jay. 2016. "We Are Dying." *The Mennonite*, July 13, 2016. Accessed September 20, 2020. https://anabaptistworld.org/we-are-dying/.

VIDEOGRAPHY

Ressler, Pax. 2018. "Love Activism (First Person Arts)." Directed by Jose Aviles. WHYY. June 17. Video.

HYMNALS

Ausbund das ist: Etliche schöne Christliche Lieder. (1583) 2013. 55th ed. Lancaster, PA: Verlag von den Amischen Gemeinden in Lancaster County.

Harmonia Sacra: A Compilation of Genuine Church Music. 1832. 25th ed. Intercourse, PA: Good Books.

Hymnal: A Worship Book. 1992. Scottdale, PA: Mennonite Publishing House; Elgin, IL: Brethren Press; Newton, KS: Faith and Life Press.

The Mennonite Hymnal. 1969. Scottdale, PA: Herald Press; Newton, KS: Faith and Life Press.

Sing the Journey. 2005. Scottdale, PA: Faith and Life Resources, a division of Mennonite Publishing Network.

Sing the Story. 2007. Scottdale, PA: Faith and Life Resources, a division of Mennonite Publishing Network.

Voices Together. 2020. Harrisonburg, VA: MennoMedia.

EIGHT

UNSETTLING EURO-AMERICAN CONCEPTIONS OF RACE IN THE EGYPTIAN INDEPENDENT MUSIC SCENE

DARCI SPRENGEL

SCHOLARS HAVE HESITATED TO USE a concept of race to understand contemporary social life within Egypt. Anthropologist Farha Ghannam, for instance, refers to "colorism" but cautions against using "American racial categories and histories" to understand the preference for lighter skin (2013, 8–9). Although recognizing that discussions of skin color often index class and regional differences, she contends that the color of the skin is just one factor, among others, that people use to judge and evaluate others. She concludes that "race in Egypt is not the same structuring historical force that we see in other countries, especially the United States," privileging instead the intersection between gender and class as more meaningful in cultivating desires, disciplining bodies, and constructing identities (8–9). One of the most compelling reasons race is rarely discussed in scholarship is that many in the region do not regularly discuss race, considering other social justice issues as more pressing.[1]

This chapter questions the usefulness of a category of race in Egypt by exploring how the contemporary independent music scene acts as a site of racialized processes and practices. I argue that while Egyptian conceptions of difference remain distinct from Euro-American notions of race, they necessarily interact with, and are entangled in, racialized global structures of power. One of the limitations of dominant critical race theory, however, is that it often privileges skin color as a primary marker of racial difference and revolves around a dichotomy of Whiteness/Blackness.[2] Egyptians, by contrast, distinguish a variety of different shades, including *abīyaḍ* (white), *fātiḥ* (pale or light), *qamhāwī* (wheat-colored, light brown), *khamrī* (tawny brown), *asmar* (dark skin), and *iswid* (black) (9).[3] Yet despite the plethora of terms, skin color is not always a primary marker of social difference, and even seemingly common phenotypical terms here, such as "black" and "white," are not fixed, universal categories. Instead, their meanings are socially and historically contingent and therefore should not be taken to be coterminous with Euro-American conceptions (Alcoff 2015, 8). This chapter thus explores how local discourses and practices index racialized relations in dialogue with global racialized configurations of power while maintaining a critical tension between Euro-American analytic categories and local ideas/practices (Deeb and Winegar 2012, 549).

The academic silence around race in Egypt, and in the Southwest Asia and North Africa (SWANA) region more broadly, stems in part from the often unacknowledged, yet racialized, intellectual divisions between diaspora and homeland as well as between North and sub-Saharan Africa. Commenting on the pushback she received toward her study of race in contemporary Ghana, anthropologist Jemima Pierre argues that there is an underlying assumption that race is of concern only in Western and multiracial societies with particular histories of racial conflict, which indicates the extent to which race is seldom treated as global in scope and is assumed instead to be an export of the West and the United States in particular (Pierre 2013a, xi). As a result, she found that Africa stands in as *the* site of racial Otherness yet, paradoxically, "race does not exist in Africa" (xi–xiii). She further argues that the uninterrogated basis of the division between North and sub-Saharan Africa leaves unexamined the global racial projects that have produced and maintained this separation, amounting to a failure to acknowledge "the racial logic underpinning our own research endeavors" (2013b, 548–49).[4] She concludes, then, that one can only be surprised by (or resistant to) the idea of race in Africa "if one does not acknowledge the contemporary legacy and impact of European empire making and 'racecraft,' the design and enactment, practice, and politics of race making" (2013a, xii).

I build from Pierre's assertion that a postcolonial space is invariably a racialized one. But I also maintain that contemporary racecraft in Egypt has a complicated relationship to Euro-American conceptions of race, which have a tendency to equate Egypt, and North Africa generally, to distinctly American notions of "Blackness" and "Africanness."[5] This presumed equivalence erases the distinct racial logics that underlie Egypt's colonization of the Sudan (1821–84) and fails to account for the ways that light-skinned Egyptians enjoy privileged standing within their home society but without access to many of the advantages embodied in Euro-American White privilege. Thus, whereas Pierre's work traces contemporary processes of racecraft primarily to European colonial legacies, the case of Egypt powerfully illustrates that racial categories and hierarchies are not only imports of European colonialism. They are, instead, also indigenous to North Africa (Hunwick 2005; Seikaly 2019; Tayeb

2021).⁶ Rather than existing in isolation from global ideas about race, however, racialized notions of difference also inform social relationships in Egypt in ways that are entangled with European colonial and, more recently, globalized American racial logics. Although scholars have explored historical colonial racialized relations in Egypt, there has been little work on the present. This chapter investigates, then, how we can grapple with the continued presence of White power and privilege and to the correspondingly unequal treatment of sub-Saharan Africans and those with dark skin in *contemporary* Egypt by considering them in relation to—and at times in tension with—more global frameworks (see also Pierre 2013b, 549).

Contemporary independent music in Egypt is a particularly fruitful site to explore racecraft as multilayered because, at once local and international, it is entangled in local and global racial logics. Referred to as *al-mazīkā al-mustaqilla*, independent music as it is understood in Egypt today has been around in its current form since at least the 1970s, when Egypt underwent a period of economic liberalization and "opening" to the West (*al-infitāḥ*). It generally refers to do-it-yourself musicking that occurs without sustained state patronage or support from the multinational music industry. It includes a variety of musical styles; most prominent among them are elements of rock, electronic, hip-hop, and reggae mixed with local and regional aesthetics, including Nubian, *zar*, Gnawa, *rai*, and Arabic pop.

I examine independent music as a site of racecraft by focusing on three concepts that I suggest are inherently racialized: security, *al-agnabī* (foreign/foreigner), and *asmar/samra* (dark or brown skinned). I contend that the first two concepts suggest or afford, each in their own ways, a certain proximity (or distance) to global White privilege. Building from Pierre's use of Charles W. Mills's concept, I use the term global White privilege, or global White supremacy, to refer to the ways White people from powerful nations are positioned as exceptional citizens, bestowed with privileges inherited, in part, from the structural outcomes of colonialism that are maintained today by contemporary American imperialism and the global military-industrial complex (Pierre 2013a, xv). Rather than only existing in relation to global White supremacy, however, I likewise demonstrate that there is a growing awareness in Egypt, among a younger generation especially, that racism, *al-ʿunṣūrriyya*, is a distinctly local social justice issue and a useful concept in combating biases against those with darker skin. The larger stakes of this investigation are thus in questioning how dominant American notions of racial justice accommodate (or not) these emerging Egyptian conceptions and serve the needs of those marginalized in Egypt and in its diaspora. A conception of racial justice that considers the intersections and tensions between these local and global facets is key to understanding some of the challenges for internationalized calls for racial justice and the emergence of global political movements.

Although recognizing that it is absolutely crucial to go beyond a Black/White dichotomy, my limited focus on perceptions of Whiteness and Blackness (or lightness and darkness) here stems from the preliminary nature of this study and from my own positionality as a White American woman. This positionality overexposed me to discussions of White Euro-American foreignness and left me less privy to the experiences and discourses surrounding other types of foreigners (Asian, South American, Black American), among other limitations. Rather than offer conclusions, then, this essay is an initial step toward addressing some larger stakes within social justice–oriented scholarship. Ethnomusicologists, for instance, have largely examined post-1970s Egyptian music in relation to debates about identity and cultural "loss" but, by focusing primarily on notions of "Westernization," they have deracialized the global power dynamics at play. Additionally, imaginaries of ancient Egypt as a Black civilization have long held a special place in African American music and the Black radical tradition in the United States, which raises questions about how contemporary Egyptians, and their own ideals of racial justice, have been included (or not) in these imaginaries.[7] Laying some groundwork toward deeper explorations of these issues, this essay questions the power dynamics that come into play when some calls for racial justice become globalized, while others do not.

CONNECTING HOMELAND AND DIASPORA: RACIALIZING LOCAL AND GLOBAL LOGICS OF "SECURITY"

One of my close friends, whom I will call Mohamed, is in his early thirties and has sung in a number of successful English-language cover bands and bands that compose Arabic originals. In his efforts to build a successful music career among both an Egyptian and regional Arabic-speaking audience, he is required to travel frequently. Unfortunately, his birth name is exactly the same as a man wanted for "terrorism." Whenever we get together in Cairo, he recounts his latest ordeals in traveling. At airports he is often interrogated for hours, sometimes missing his flight. He continually has problems getting visas. The constant harassment he endures occurs not only on flights to North America and Europe but also when he travels to Amman, Beirut, and Dubai. In early 2018, upon returning from a gig abroad, the guitarist in his band was detained on arrival at the Cairo airport and imprisoned for one year without charge.

Mohamed also started a production company in 2015 that sought to use his expertise as a musician to grow the independent music scene across the region. Dozens of concerts that the company organized in Egypt have been canceled at the last minute by state authorities, often due to "security" concerns. When this happens, he loses all the money invested in the event. Other times, his artists' visas are delayed or denied. Although he got into the business to promote fledgling independent musicians in the region, the majority of his company's work has not been on Arabic music due to the aforementioned structures of security that render independent music too precarious to be profitable. Musicians describe visa denial, as well as the application process itself, as humiliating and dehumanizing, causing some to refuse even to apply. Visitors to Egypt with European or American passports, in contrast, are granted visas upon arrival at the Egyptian airport. The power of some nationalities over others, and the extreme devaluing of Egyptian nationality at home and abroad, is such common knowledge that it is a running joke within Egyptian popular culture.[8]

It is well-documented that the policing of Egyptians in Egypt has reached unprecedented levels since the military returned to power in 2013, and, as scholars of migration have argued, borders and visas are violent political tools used to discriminate against specific ethnic, religious, and/or linguistic groups (see Alijla 2020).[9] But the connection between this policing at home and abroad is rarely made in scholarship. There maintains a separation between diaspora and homeland studies, one concerned with race and racialization, the other not (Pierre 2013a, xiv). I suggest that treating the concept of "security" as inherently racialized is one way to connect the experiences of Egyptians in homeland and diaspora (see also Amar 2013). In its privileging of certain bodies over others, it reveals common ideas about the global nature of race. Whereas Euro-American conceptions of race often revolve around, though are by no means limited to, particular phenotypical characteristics, such as skin color, racecraft here emerges in relation to a variety of additional intersecting materialities, including passports and names written on identity cards.

Scholars in a variety of disciplines have documented and analyzed the policing of Black, Brown, and Muslim bodies in the West. In the United States, the program of Special Registration, in place from September 2002 until December 2016, for instance, was a system of state-mandated racial profiling of adult males from twenty-four Muslim-majority countries. It led to approximately fourteen thousand deportation proceedings and the detention of three thousand (Bayoumi 2010). This policing is often treated as entirely separate from authoritarian repression in Egypt. But it is no coincidence that the Egyptian military that carries out its own surveillance on the Egyptian population is the second-largest recipient of US aid (after Israel), receiving $1.3 billion in military aid every year since 1987 (Clingan 2018). To be clear, I am not arguing that authoritarian governance in Egypt is *only* an extension/result of the global war on terror; it certainly existed before 2001 and has its own unique history. However, it is today a part of a globalized military industry that depends on racial ideologies. Understanding the way authoritarianism in Egypt has taken shape in the last decade, who it represses, and who it does not, requires an approach that connects global and local elements. One of the ways to make this connection is through racializing the concept of security in ways that intersect with nationality, religion, and language.

The racialized nature of local Egyptian state policing became perhaps most obvious with the 2016 murder of Giulio Regini, an Italian PhD student at the University of Cambridge. His body was found dumped on the side of a highway with classic signs of the torture inflicted by Egyptian police.[10] Regini's death resulted in an international uproar. Many English-language headlines expressed a sense of shock and bewilderment at how something like this could happen. Egyptian NGOs, however, have documented that forced disappearance, known as *al-ikhtifāʾ al-qasrī* in Arabic, have long been a reality in Egypt. They estimate that three to four Egyptians are disappeared every day (Egyptian Commission for Rights and Freedoms 2015). Most are tortured. Some are returned after days or months, and others are never seen alive again. The Egyptian state has enacted these policies all under the guise of "security" and combatting its own war on terror. Given their difficulties traveling and the policing they endure at home, some of my Egyptian friends have begun to describe Egypt as an "open-air prison."

Crucially, there is rarely, if ever, any international attention given to these disappeared, tortured, and imprisoned Egyptians. The shock at Regini's death demonstrates what Pierre likewise identified in postcolonial Ghana and generally in North Africa: White people—and those from powerful countries especially—enjoy rights, advantages, and special treatment derived from membership in a particular minority "race" (Pierre 2013a, 96–97). The special treatment of certain foreigners in Egypt cannot be explained by nationality alone. Americans in Egypt with dual Egyptian citizenship or those with Muslim or Arabic names are sometimes more likely to be monitored and harassed by authorities on suspicions of "spying." A few days after Regini's body was found, writer Yasmin El-Rifae wrote:

> Waves of people have disappeared, been killed, too many to count, too many to mourn properly. But Giulio's death makes us confront the effect of this

violence, of witnessing it, on our understanding of the world. Even as we
fight this reality, it is with a knowledge that yes, deaths like this will happen
today, and tomorrow—we expect them to. But Giulio is not from this world,
not really. He is a visitor, and in his world, in his family's world, people do not
get killed, jailed, disappeared in the hundreds, month by month. His death
shows us an outrage with a freshness which we have long forgotten, just as it
stuns us with the realization of how we have changed. (El-Rifae 2016)

Here it is Giulio's foreignness—and I argue specifically his non-Arab White, European foreignness—that makes his death most startling. El-Rifae astutely points out that these foreigners live in an entirely different world, with different horizons of possibility not only abroad but also within Egypt. Regini was the exception that helped see more clearly the rule: Egyptian state policing is racialized. It targets Egyptians while securing the relative uninhibited movement of certain "foreigners." Though the Egyptian military's policing is not reducible to global structures of power that secure the privilege of (especially White) people from powerful nations, it is also inextricable from it. Put differently, President al-Sisi's regime is part of a larger, global security apparatus that operates through distinctly racialized logics.

CONSTRUCTING AL-AGNABĪ (FOREIGNER) AS A RACIALIZED CONCEPT

The relative lack of policing of certain foreigners from powerful nations contributes to the special privileged status that these foreigners and their art enjoy in Egypt. The term *al-agnabī*, foreigner, in this context takes on certain racialized undertones associated with this exceptional privilege and status. The word is generally not used, for instance, to refer to African im/migrants or refugees—who are described as *afrīqī/a* (African) or *lāgi'/a* (refugee), respectively—or to describe Arabic speakers from other SWANA (Southwest Asian and North African) countries, who are referred to by nationality (*maghribī/a, libnānī/a,* and so on). The term seems to suggest—though is not reducible to—a proximity to global White privilege. It does not refer only to a particular skin tone but instead encompasses an advantaged social and global standing that affords easy mobility and access to resources, advantages that the White body from powerful nations is the primary, though not sole, inheritor. Scholars have examined how those in the SWANA diaspora (in the West) have an unstable and contingent relationship to Whiteness (see Tayeb 2021); however (and again revealing the divide between homeland

and diaspora), little has been written on how this complex and contingent relationship to White privilege engages Egyptians at home. Significantly, foreign privilege in Egypt does not *only* pertain to relationships with those from outside Egypt. It also informs how Egyptians view their local artistic work and other Egyptians at home, depending on where one is positioned in different proximity to this privilege.

Similar to independent musicians, managers of independent arts spaces in Egypt are routinely harassed and their spaces closed when they are unable to pay police and syndicate officials exorbitant taxes and/or bribes. With dozens of venues having closed in the last few years alone, Cairo now only has about six spaces for independent artists to perform. In repressing its own grassroots arts scene, the Egyptian state opens a market for foreign entities to showcase foreigners as "experts." The foreign nations that securitize Egyptian bodies in the international arena are often the same that provide "aid" in the form of expertise and development in the artistic scenes. Especially in the years immediately following the 2011 Egyptian revolution, the American, French, British, and German embassies were highly active in bringing artists and curators from abroad to give performances, talks, and workshops with their "aspiring" counterparts in Egypt. Recounting his participation in one of these workshops, one Egyptian friend who cofounded and manages an art space in downtown Cairo, told me, "What [the American presenter] had to say wasn't very useful because none of it really applied to our situation in Egypt." The majority of these foreign "experts" are White. Demonstrating the subtle association between al-agnabī and White privilege, when foreign experts are not White, their "foreigner" status, and by extension their expertise, must be proven and performed.[11] Black American agānib (plural of agnabī) in Egypt, for instance, report that they are initially assumed *not* to embody expertise even when in positions of authority (Primo 2015).[12] Whereas the privileged class standing of White foreigners is read immediately in its literal embodiment in White skin, the foreignness of those with Black or Brown skin must be proven, by, for instance, language competency and/or disclosing one's nationality. I return to anti–dark skin racism in the next section.

Extending a technopolitics reminiscent of the colonial era, shortcomings in the cultural sector in Egypt are often consequently framed in terms of a lack in local "expertise"—not in terms of state and global policing that actively prevents the development of sustainable artistic infrastructures for Egyptian artists in Egypt (see Mitchell 2002). This rhetoric is sometimes perpetuated by Egyptians themselves. As my friend Ahmed, an independent filmmaker in his late twenties, told me, "The film scene needs experts from outside to grow it."

The assumption of foreign expertise is similarly demonstrated in the preference among some independent musicians who, for those who can afford it, send their tracks to be mixed abroad in Europe or North America. As a member of one of the most famous independent bands in Egypt told me, "they know what they are doing," implying that Egyptian sound engineers and music producers do not. Foreigners, particularly foreigners from the West, were often assumed to be more professional, educated, and knowledgeable.[13] This privilege extends historic colonial relationships in which the modernization of Egypt throughout the nineteenth and twentieth centuries depended on certain White foreign expertise (see Mitchell 2002). Aspects of this relationship are still actively maintained today by the Egyptian military's practices of "security" as well as Western military and economic dominance that maintain the privileged position of especially White Western foreigners.

For most Egyptians in Egypt, these realities have little to do with race. They pertain instead to unequal access to resources and opportunities amid conditions of global inequality. Sending tracks to be mixed abroad, for example, results in part from a lack of access to the highest-quality production equipment and to music production training programs in Egypt. But in the way that these and other necessary resources are concentrated in particular geographic locations that a global militarized security apparatus renders unequally accessible, they amount to structures of power that index racialized relations and exist in dialogue with global racial identity politics. They help structurally position White bodies from powerful nations as most able to move and embody expertise, among other privileges.

Foreign privilege likewise informs local relationships. Egyptian musicians who spend significant time abroad, for instance, are often treated by peers in Egypt as more successful, upwardly mobile, and thus more knowledgeable of music and the industry. One music group I know decided to add a particular instrumentalist to their band solely because the performer had connections in Europe. This is, in some ways, an expected reaction from musicians who are excluded from lucrative Euro-American markets. Coupled with the state-mandated dearth of opportunities in Egypt, however, it manifests in such a way that upward mobility becomes almost contingent on the approval of, or association with, certain foreigners. As Pierre similarly found in her study, global White supremacy supports an economy of fundamental dependence—on White expertise and White interest (Pierre 2013a, 69–100).

The association of foreignness with class standing and expertise likewise often translates into the "non-political" nature of foreign art, which is much more likely to enjoy a bourgeois "art-for-art's-sake" status. One small arts space located in downtown Cairo hosts multiple concerts of independent music each week as well as other cultural events, including workshops, film screenings, and karaoke in a space that holds about seventy-five people. Although the venue is under constant harassment by police, it explores potentially problematic themes by showcasing foreign art. For example, its weekly film and discussion series explored the theme of "Fear" in the spring of 2016 but solely through foreign films, including Alfred Hitchock's *The Birds*, *8 1/2* by Federico Fellini, *Annie Hall* by Woodie Allen, and *Offret* by Andrie Tarkovsky. The founder and manager told me quite bluntly, "We explore controversial topics like dictatorship but through foreign films and locations such as in Italy, Chile. The authorities do not see this as a threat." This approach further perpetuates the dominance of foreign art and perspectives; but, rather than indicating an uncritical adherence to foreign class standing and expertise, some Egyptians showcase foreign art as a smoke screen to skirt the limitations of the state's policing. This is perhaps the power of global White supremacy; it can be perpetuated even by those who do not adhere to its underlying racial logics.

Similar to Pierre's observation that Whiteness in Ghana meant access to power and privilege, foreignness in this context works as a particular racialized form of privilege that acts as a certain class standing. For Egyptians in Egypt, one's proximity to certain foreigners, especially those who are White and from powerful nations in Europe and North America, can afford certain opportunities and exposure that would otherwise be difficult to access. Significantly, these examples indicate that the structures that maintain global White supremacy also inform how Egyptians relate to each other on a local level—it can inform who they see as able to embody expertise and upward mobility. To say that ideas about social status are solely local or limited to gender and class does not capture the whole story. Instead, it is in part the targeted global *and local* policing of Egyptian citizens, and by extension Arabs and Muslims, that opens a space of special privileges for non-Arab and Muslim foreigners and for foreign art in Egypt. This can produce the false sense that foreign artists and works are somehow better, or exemplary, because they are showcased more often.

ANTI-ASMAR/SAMRA (DARK-SKINNED) PREJUDICE AND GRASSROOTS CAMPAIGNS FOR JUSTICE

The privileging of certain foreigners is also entangled in local biases against those with dark skin, described in Arabic as asmar/samra (dark skin) or iswid/sūdā (Black). Asmar/samra prejudice intersects with global anti-Blackness but is not coterminous with it. In Egypt, ideas about dark skin emerge in part in relation to Egypt's own history as a colonizer of Sudan, calling into question what "Whiteness" and "Blackness" mean in this context and how these terms relate (or not) to more globalized movements for racial justice.

In recent years, there have been a number of cases of anti–dark skin sentiment, including portrayals of Blackface in the Egyptian media and discrimination against African im/migrants. In one instance, a samra woman was refused service by a pharmacist who told her, "I don't take anything from people who are not White" (*Strange and the Marvelous* 2013; see also Eltigani 2019). Many recent incidences of such prejudice reported in the media have been against women, suggesting that gender plays a particularly salient role in social perceptions of darkness and Blackness.[14] When prejudices against those with dark skin intersect with nationality and/or ethnicity, outright violence can occur. In 2005, the Egyptian state used rhetoric of "contagion" and "disease" as justification to violently remove Sudanese refugee protestors, killing at least twenty asylum seekers in what became known as the Mustapha Mahmoud Park Massacre. Scholars and journalists have demonstrated that there is widespread stereotyping in Egypt that links Africans with "disease" (especially HIV/AIDs), crime, and promiscuity or prostitution (Giri 2007; Khalid 2011; Sharif 2015). Abdel Rahman Sherif, founder of the *Black in Egypt* (*al-ʿunṣūrriyya ḍid al-sūd fī maṣr wa al-ʿālam al-ʿarabī*) blog, argues that "there is a staggering contempt of everything that is African. . . . Egyptians even get offended if you refer to them as African" (*New Arab* 2015).

Historian Eve Troutt Powell (2003) demonstrates that Egyptian imaginaries of the Sudan as "property" and the object of their own "civilizing mission" was fundamental to the development of modern Egyptian nationalism in the nineteenth century. She details what she calls "the perspective of the colonized colonizer" in which Egypt's regional power and emancipation from the control of the British were envisioned through Egypt's colonization and unique claim to mastery over the Sudan. Many Sudanese and Nubians were enslaved as domestic servants and soldiers in Egypt throughout the nineteenth and twentieth centuries (Troutt Powell 2012). Even after the colonial period, Egyptian leaders chose the historic land of al-Nuba (Nubia), the site of a powerful African empire that once ran from present-day southern Egypt into the Libyan desert and northern Sudan, for the building of the Aswan Dam. The dam flooded at least forty-four Nubian villages, displacing over 180,000 people and destroying local heritage sites (Ahmed 2017).[15]

For Troutt Powell, twentieth-century depictions of Blackface in this context are not the same as that in the United States. She argues that stereotypical representations of Black Sudanese and Nubian men as servants, slaves, and buffoons were projections of cultural intimacy and connection. The Sudanese were not an Other but a depiction of a preindependence Egyptian self that was "not quite grown up, not yet evolved" (1995, 29). However, the humor in Blackface depends on a sort of anti–dark skin prejudice that elevates light-skinned Arabic speakers (Tayeb 2021). Blackface "humor" thus indexes the extent to which light-skinned Egyptians enjoy privileged status through a certain proximity to Whiteness. But given even light-skinned Egyptians' own slippery relationship to global White privilege, what exactly is Whiteness in this context? Performance studies scholar Leila Tayeb argues that it must be viewed both as a colonial remnant, taking valences of "Europeanness," *and* as operative on another register distinct from Euro-American conceptions (Tayeb 2021).

Among a new generation in Egypt, there is growing awareness that light-skinned privilege amounts to a form of "racism" (al-'unṣūrrīyya) that is not only a foreign import.[16] Formed in 2012, the Alexandrian independent band High Dam, for example, performs what one band member, bassist Ahmed "Remo," calls "African pop music," which includes traditional and contemporary Nubian, Sudanese, and West African songs. Comprised mostly of third-generation (born in Alexandria) Nubians with one elder Juba musician from South Sudan, they chose the name High Dam as a means of "reclaiming the symbol, not as a thing of destruction but as something that can spread the culture." The band performs upbeat songs, their own originals as well as traditional and contemporary Nubian and African ones that they have rearranged with instruments such as keyboard and electric and bass guitars. They have a huge following among (though not exclusive to) the Nubian and African migrant community. The band's image is partially based on wearing bright prints from various African countries, what Remo calls "African clothes." The band is thus not only about Nubian culture, specifically, but instead aims to (re)claim a more generalized "African" identity as indigenous to Egypt (see fig. 8.1). Their track "Ana Nuby" ("I am Nubian"), written by vocalist Hassan Fares "Jamaica," for instance, discusses issues of identity and celebrates the rich heritage of Nubian and African cultures in the following excerpt:[17]

> Chorus
> I am Nubian, Egyptian, African, Arab, I truly love you, al-Nuba, with all of my heart
> I am Nubian, Egyptian, African, Arab, I truly love you, al-Nuba, I will not hide it
> Verse 1
> I am Nubian, Egyptian, dark-skinned (asmar), I come from the south

Fig. 8.1. High Dam band in their signature "African clothing," featuring vocalist Hassan Jamaica, keyboardist and vocalist Karim Mostafa, Mr. Booney on lead guitar, Ahmed Remo on bass guitar, Ahmed Khairy and Mohamed Gomaa on percussion, Mohamed Gomaa and Karem Mahmoud on the drums.
Photo credit: Mahmoud Tag, TaGo Photography. Reprinted with permission.

> I adore my country, my people, my land in al-Nuba deeply
> A civilization, a culture, a heritage, narrated in stories

In addition to lyrically celebrating the mutuality of Egyptian and African identity, many of the band's songs valorize the beauty of dark skin (especially their original song "Ya Gamil Ya Asmar" ["Oh beautiful dark-skinned one"]). The musicians explore these topics because, living in Alexandria, they felt distant from their African heritage. The African and asmar/samra identity that they reclaim, however, do not exist in dichotomous relation to Euro-American conceptions of Whiteness. It emerges, rather, in relation to dominant Egyptian conceptions of self as neither strictly Black nor White, positioning Egyptian and African identities as simultaneous and mutually inclusive.[18]

As another example, twenty-three-year-old media studies graduate Maha Hamada, also Nubian and born in Alexandria, started a 2018 campaign called "No Color" as part of her senior graduation project. The project encompasses

Fig. 8.2. Image from No Color Campaign, featuring Hadir Nashed, Maha Hamada, Salma Yehia, Alaa Gasser, Raneem Hesham, Mariam Hesham, and Fayza Haraby. Photo credit: Adel Essam and Henar Sherif, O Art Studio. Used with permission.

a video, photographs, and a hashtag on social media that encouraged asmar/samra Egyptians to share their experiences of racism. She got interested in the topic because she noticed that "especially on social media if a dark woman marries someone lighter, people will make disparaging comments, and especially if a samra woman marries a foreigner (agnabī), they will say how could he marry this woman? How could he love her? I found that this was really a pervasive problem, but when I would talk about it with my [light skinned] friends, they wouldn't believe me that it was that pervasive. No one would believe that we had racism (al-'unṣūrrīyya) here." It is telling that Mohamed uses the word *agnabī* to refer to someone with fair skin. Within a few days of launching the campaign online, it garnered thirty thousand views on Facebook and thousands used the hashtag to share their experiences of discrimination (see fig. 8.2).

Both Hamada and Remo told me that Egyptian anti-asmar/samra and anti-African racism are not the same as anti-Black racism in the United States or Europe. Mohamed, for instance, was reluctant to compare racism in Egypt to other places. She insisted that anti-samra racism for women in Egypt was largely related to beauty standards and intersected with other aspects of a person's life (see Ghannam 2013, 8–9). Likewise, Remo insisted that racism in Egypt was not the same as that abroad—being asmar/samra, for instance, would not lessen one's chances of employment or increase one's exposure to police surveillance in Egypt.

Thinking through racial ideologies and campaigns for racial justice within Egypt thus presents challenges regarding how these local conceptions of race engage larger, more global movements for racial equality. Dominant understandings of race in Western, English-language academia often emerge from critical race theory grounded in African American history and experience. This discourse can have a problematic tendency to equate Arab/North African with "Black" in a Black/White dichotomy, which some in Egypt experience as alien to their lived experience (Elmeligy 2018).[19] The racialization of Arabs and Muslims as "Black" in the United States can actually work to further the logics of White supremacy and neoliberal capitalism. When Western audiences are invited to understand social justice movements in the SWANA region through the lens of Black American struggle in the United States, the discourse comes to revolve around celebratory narratives of African American progress and victory over injustice, depoliticizing and whitewashing contemporary racial oppression (El Zein 2016). This points to some of the tensions toward, and limitations of, dominant understandings of race in the United States. They can marginalize other, alternative conceptions of racial justice that emerge from and within the global South.

But we also cannot view race and colorism in Egypt as completely isolated from these more global realities. When local prejudices against dark skin and the privileging of certain foreigners intersect not only with gender and class but also nationality and ethnicity (Africans, Europeans, and so on), we must consider how Egyptian conceptions of "race" engage internationally circulating ones. Although an imaginary of Egypt as a Black civilization has long held an important place in the Black radical tradition, for instance, racecraft in contemporary Egyptian artistic production and local campaigns for racial equality cannot simply be viewed as local representatives of these larger movements without losing the nuance and complexity through which they also speak back to such movements. More research is needed to tease out exactly how these campaigns enact distinct conceptions of Whiteness and Blackness as well as other racialized conceptions of difference that exist beside these dominant categories.

NOTES

1. These include addressing increasing economic disparity caused by neoliberal reforms, gender inequality, and human and civil rights, among other issues.

2. I capitalize the word *White* to emphasize the ways Whiteness is a racial construct that occurs through historical processes in which individuals *become* White. See Appiah 2020.

3. Transliteration of Arabic words follows the system used by the *International Journal of Middle Eastern Studies*, except for colloquial Egyptian names, texts, and phrases, which I have adapted using the Hinds and Badawi dictionary of Egyptian Arabic. Transliterations are meant to remain legible to the reader while preserving aspects of dialect, accent, and pronunciation. In instances where names, titles, or organizations have readily adopted an English transliteration, I have maintained their transliteration throughout.

4. This separation was formerly perpetuated by explicitly racist scholarship linking levels of civilization to skin color. In this logic, North Africa was a more advanced civilization because of its proximity to Europe (Pierre 2013b, 548).

5. For example, Pierre claims that the "Arab Spring" is more aptly called the "African Spring" (2013b, 548).

6. Africanist John Hunwick (2005) argues that Arabs "discovered" and "invented" the African continent long before the Europeans.

7. It has been reported that Sun Ra, for instance, was disappointed when he first arrived in Egypt because, "Many of the modern Egyptians did not appear to be *his* people" (Szwed 1997, 292).

8. For example, in the film *'Asal Iswid* (Black honey) the Egyptian American protagonist threatens an Egyptian police officer saying, "My American passport protects me, and no one can touch me." In another scene, a snarling police dog cowers just at the sight of his American passport.

9. The Egyptian state also enacts this violence on others, notably African migrants and Palestinians in Gaza (Alijla 2020).

10. Injuries included cigarette burns, broken bones, and signs of electrocution, torture commonly found among Egyptians detained and/or imprisoned by Egyptian police.

11. Pierre (2013a: 85–95) similarly found in Ghana that the privilege of expertise is literally embodied in White skin whereas black and brown wealth and status must be *performed*.

12. A black female American teacher in Cairo reports that people often assume her assistant is in charge, and she overheard colleagues refer to her as *'abīd*, "slave." She likewise found that people treated her negatively when they assumed that she was African but would subsequently change their behavior after she revealed her American identity (Primo 2015).

13. Pierre (2013a, 85) calls this "the common sense of White merit (and therefore power)."

14. I leave a fuller examination of this issue to another essay.

15. This displacement occurred over two phases in 1902 and in the 1960s.

16. More research is needed to understand the origin of the Arabic term in popular usage.

17. The track is available for streaming at https://www.youtube.com/watch?v=u8B2FfcYwDU. Translation by the author.

18. Its promotion of African heritage links to others in the independent music scene, including Yara Mekawi's Radio Submarine, the Nile Project, and Cairo-based Sudanese musician Asia Madani.

19. Nehal Elmeligy (2018), Egyptian graduate student at the University of Illinois, recently wrote of her frustration at being forced in the United States to adopt a Black and African identity that felt alien to her.

BIBLIOGRAPHY

Ahmed, Mona. 2017. "Nubia's Bittersweet Memories behind High Dam." *Egypt Today*, November 27, 2017. Accessed August 28, 2020. https://www.egypttoday.com/Article/6/34353/Nubia%E2%80%99s-bittersweet-memories-behind-High-Dam#:~:text=The%20establishment%20of%20the%20Dam,now%20as%20%E2%80%9Cold%20Nubia.%E2%80%9D/.

Alcoff, Linda. 2015. *The Future of Whiteness*. Cambridge: Polity Press.

Alijla, Abdelhadi. 2020. "Palestine and the Habeas Viscus: An Autoethnography of Travel, Visa Violence, and Borders." *Borders in Globalization Review* 1 (2): 1–15.

Amar, Paul. 2013. *The Security Archipelago: Human-Security States, Sexuality Politics, and the End of Neoliberalism*. Durham, NC: Duke University Press.

Appiah, Kwame Anthony. 2020. "The Case for Capitalizing the B in Black." *The Atlantic*, June 18, 2020. Accessed October 14, 2020. https://www.theatlantic.com/ideas/archive/2020/06/time-to-capitalize-blackand-white/613159/.

Bayoumi, Moustafa. 2010. "The Race Is On: Muslims and Arabs in the American Imagination." Middle East Research and Information Project, March 10, 2010. Accessed October 14, 2018. https://www.merip.org/mero/interventions/race/.

Clingan, Bruce. 2018. "Commentary: The U.S. Is Right to Restore Aid to Egypt." *Reuters*, July 30, 2018. Accessed October 28, 2018. https://www.reuters.com/article/us-clingan-egypt-commentary/commentary-the-u-s-is-right-to-restore-aid-to-egypt-idUSKBN1KK1YE/.

Deeb, Lara, and Jessica Winegar. 2012. "Anthropologies of Arab-Majority Societies." *Annual Review of Anthropology* 41 (1): 537–58.

Egyptian Commission for Rights and Freedoms. 2015. "Al-mukhtafūn qasran ... fī intiẓār inṣāf al-ʿadāla" ("The forced disappeared ... waiting for justice"). Accessed May 27, 2022. https://drive.google.com/file/d/0B5rfCEjP5e6YenltcFk2VnZlQ2c/view?resourcekey=0-UMe9YCDnG7bJYE32GnG3Hw.

Elmeligy, Nehal. 2018. "American Is Grey-Blind: When I'm Here, I'm Black." *Egyptian Streets*, May 21, 2018. Accessed October 28, 2018. https://egyptianstreets.com/2018/05/21/america-is-grey-blind-when-im-here-im-black/.

El-Rifae, Yasmin. 2016. "Blog: That Metallic Sound That Hits Us." *Mada Masr*, February 6, 2016. Accessed November 5, 2018. https://www.madamasr.com/en/2016/02/06/opinion/u/blog-that-metallic-sound-that-hits-us/.

Eltigani, Nour. 2019. "The Battle of the Races: Egypt's Media Syndicate Finally Took a Stand against Racism." *Egyptian Streets*, May 29, 2019. Accessed September 16, 2020. https://egyptianstreets.com/2019/05/29/the-battle-of-the-races-egypts-media-syndicate-finally-took-a-stance-against-racism/.

El Zein, Rayya. 2016. "From 'Hip Hop Revolutionaries' to 'Terrorist-Thugs': 'Blackwashing' between the Arab Spring and the War on Terror." *Lateral* 5 (1). Accessed July 23, 2018. http://csalateral.org/issue/5-1/hip-hop-blackwashing-el-zein/.

Ghannam, Farha. 2013. *Live and Die Like a Man: Gender Dynamics in Urban Egypt.* Stanford: Stanford University Press.

Giri, Minal. 2007. "On Contagion: Sudanese Refugees, HIV/AIDS and the Social Order in Egypt." *Égypte/Monde arabe* 4:179–98.

Hunwick, John O. 2005. "A Region of the Mind: Medieval Arab Views of African Geography and Ethnography and Their Legacy." *Sudanic Africa* 16:103–36.

Khalid, Sunni M. 2011. "Egypt's Race Problem." *The Root*, February 3, 2011. Accessed January 4, 2020. https://www.theroot.com/egypts-race-problem-1790862617/.

Mitchell, Timothy. 2002. *Rule of Experts: Egypt, Techno-Politics, Modernity.* Berkeley: University of California Press.

New Arab. 2015. "Being Black in Egypt." July 23, 2015. Accessed August 25, 2020. https://english.alaraby.co.uk/english/features/2015/7/23/being-black-in-egypt/.

Pierre, Jemima. 2013a. *The Predicament of Blackness: Postcolonial Ghana and the Politics of Race.* Chicago: University of Chicago Press.

———. 2013b. "Race in Africa Today: A Commentary." *Cultural Anthropology* 28 (3): 547–51.

Primo, Valentina. 2015. "The Reality of Racism in Egypt." *Cairo Scene.* August 5, 2015. Accessed October 2, 2020. https://cairoscene.com/LifeStyle/The-Reality-of-Racism-in-Egypt/.

Seikaly, Sherene. 2019. "Productive Discomforts: Black-Palestine Solidarity." Talk given at the UC Consortium for Black Studies, UCLA, January 24.

Sharif, Raman. 2015. "Jarīdat al-yīūm al-sābʿa tanshur taḥqīqan ʿunṣurrīyyan b-ʿanwān Niggers" [*The Seventh Day* newspaper publishes racist report under the title "niggers"]. *Al-ʿunṣurriyya ḍid al-sūd fī miṣr wa al-ʿālam al-ʿarabī* [anti-Black racism in Egypt and the Arab world] (blog), January 16, 2015. Accessed January 4, 2020. https://blackinegypt.wordpress.com/2015/01/16/جريدة-اليوم-السابع-تنشر-تحقيقا-عنصريا/.

Strange and the Marvelous (blog). 2013. "The Nada Zatouna Incident: The Strange Case of the Racist Egyptian Pharmacist That Came Out of Nowhere!!" April 28, 2013. Accessed September 16, 2020. https://thedomainofthestrange.wordpress.com/2013/04/28/the-nada-zatouna-incident-the-strange-case-of-the-racist-egyptian-pharmacist-that-came-out-of-nowhere/.

Szwed, John. 1997. *Space Is the Place: The Lives and Times of Sun Ra.* Durham, NC: Duke University Press.

Tayeb, Leila. 2021. "What Is Whiteness in North Africa?" *Lateral* 10 (1). Accessed October 18, 2021. https://csalateral.org/forum/cultural-constructions-race

-racism-middle-east-north-africa-southwest-asia-mena-swana/whiteness-in-north-africa-tayeb/.

Troutt Powell, Eve. 1995. "Egyptians in Blackface: Nationalism and the Representation of the Sudan in Egypt, 1919." *Harvard Middle Eastern and Islamic Review* 2 (2): 27–45.

———. 2003. *A Different Shade of Colonialism: Egypt, Great Britain, and the Mastery of the Sudan.* Berkeley: University of California Press.

———. 2012. *Tell This in My Memory: Stories of Enslavement from Egypt, Sudan, and the Ottoman Empire.* Stanford: Stanford University Press.

DISCOGRAPHY

High Dam Band. 2019. "Ana Nuby" (I am Nubian). YouTube.com, December 3, 2019. Posted by Axeer. https://www.youtube.com/watch?v=u8B2FfcYwDU/.

NINE

RECLAIMING *NANOOK OF THE NORTH*, TANYA TAGAQ'S SONIC AND PERFORMATIVE COUNTERPOINTS TO INUIT STEREOTYPES

HO CHAK LAW

> "Suppose we go," said I in conclusion, "do you know that you and your men may have to give up making a kill, if it interferes with my film? Will you remember that it is the picture of you hunting the iviuk that I want, not their meat?"
>
> —ROBERT J. FLAHERTY, *MY ESKIMO FRIENDS*

INTRODUCTION

In the quasi-naturalistic *Nanook of the North* (hereafter, *Nanook* 1922), Robert J. Flaherty staged an infamous scene in which Nanook, an Inuit hunter, bites a phonograph record three times.[1] Nanook looks perplexingly amused by the novelty of the gramophone, although he may as well be intrigued by his aural exposure to Italian opera and Tin Pan Alley hits in this representation of the Inuit's exposure to modern technology (Rotha 1980, 43).

On the evening of February 2, 2016, I attended a screening of *Nanook* in Ann Arbor that featured Tanya Tagaq, one of the most well-known Inuit musicians today. I witnessed how she expressively reanimated the Inuit on screen with a live score blending Inuit throat singing (*katajjaq*), with field recordings from Nunavut (our land) as well as elements of electronic music and popular music genres such as punk rock and heavy metal. Wearing a headband and a short-sleeve T-shirt, she first walked barefoot onto the stage in the Lydia Mendelssohn Theater as the lead singer. She then talked to the audience before the film began. Speaking gently, she tried to establish a good rapport with them by expressing how she appreciated the film with a critical eye. She explained the film's relationship to her ancestors and the natural environment of Nunavut while acknowledging that many scenes were staged by Flaherty. Nevertheless, she denied the necessity of prior knowledge for understanding the film before proclaiming her will to perform her live score in whatever way she wanted.

In this chapter, I will examine how Tagaq has engaged with *Nanook* since the Toronto International Film Festival (TIFF) commissioned her to create and perform a live score on National Aboriginal Day (now known as National Indigenous Peoples Day) in 2012, for the opening night of *First Peoples Cinema: 1500 Nations, One Tradition*.[2] Evolving from musical material of her live album *Anuraaqtuq* (2011), the commission was a notable success for a film series that addressed onscreen representation of the First Peoples by non-Indigenous filmmakers and screenwriters (DeMara 2012). It led to numerous reruns in North America, Western Europe, and Australia. It also inspired the making of *Animism* (2014), a studio album that won Tagaq the Polaris Music Prize and the Juno Award for Indigenous Music Album of the Year. Noting that Tagaq has developed the original commission into a statement of her persistent feeling about a certain haughtiness and aggressiveness associated with cultural misunderstandings of the Inuit, I will discuss how, through her singing voice and stage demeanor on top of her audiovisual realignment by means of film scoring, she engaged actively and critically with both the cinematic apparatus and the imperial gaze. I posit that she counteracted extraction and instrumentalization of Indigenous images and knowledge sonically and performatively, thereby intervening in Inuit stereotypes that "present an image of time statically held together in a singular form" (Thain 2019).

This chapter begins with reflections on my experience of Tagaq's live score for *Nanook*. I then introduce the cultural and creative context of the score as a TIFF commission with a revisionist agenda, before inquiring into how Tagaq has been inspired to "reclaim the film" (Gordon 2014). I will associate the moving image of *Nanook* with a "taxidermic display" (Rony 1996, 100) of premodern Inuit culture that catered to the imperial gaze, before demonstrating two important aspects of Tagaq's film scoring. First, I will compare Tagaq's exemplification of conflicts between aural and visual experiences with a dialectic approach to film form that characterizes Soviet montage theory (Deleuze 1997, 180). Second, I will look into comments from critics who connect her music or performance to expressions of sexuality, spirituality, or primary emotions. I suggest that those comments bespeak Tagaq's ability to transform her audience into deep listeners who are, according to Judith Becker, "profoundly moved, perhaps even to tears, by simply listening to a piece of music" (2004, 2). I contend that such an invocation "of secular trancing, divorced from religious practice but often carrying religious sentiments such as feelings of transcendence or a sense of communion with a power beyond oneself" (ibid.) could deflect the audience from what Dylan Robinson regards as hungry listening, a mode of colonial perception that "consumes without awareness of how the consumption acts in relationship with those people, the lands, the waters who provide sustenance" (2020, 53). In other words, by "reclaiming the film" with her live score, Tagaq disrupts Inuit stereotypes with an expressive assertion of Indigenous people's cultural rights (see also Wiessner 2011).

NANOOK BEFORE, DURING, AND AFTER THE TORONTO INTERNATIONAL FILM FESTIVAL COMMISSION

Only a few years after the emergence of cinematography had the Inuit already become a popular subject on film, mostly for either putting the native village on display or enhancing lectures on expeditions of Arctic peoples. Edwin S. Porter and James H. White shot *The Esquimaux Village* (1901) in Buffalo, New York, during the Pan American Exposition to showcase what they claimed as "scenes [that] are enacted just as they take place in the far away frozen North." *A Dash to the North Pole* (1909) included footage of encounters with the Inuit during the Ziegler North Pole expedition between 1903 and 1905, while William N. Selig, the owner of Selig Polyscope Company who pioneered commercial filmmaking in the United States, produced *The Way of the Eskimo* (1911) and *Lost in the Arctic* (1911) as the first fiction films with an exclusive Inuit cast.

Nanook has been far more well-known than the aforementioned movies because of its status as the first documentary/ethnographic film in history as well as its more extensive exposure of the Inuit to film audiences worldwide. Driven by the belief that "a good film depicting the Eskimo and his fight for existence in the dramatically barren North might be well worth while" (Flaherty 1999), Flaherty deployed cinematography to create portrayals that were "not really lifelike but by convention and repetition ha[d] been made to appear so" (Williams 1983, 261). He presented in *Nanook* a story that was more a dramatization than a documentation of first contact (Calder-Marshall 1963, 97), although in North America many high school and university courses in anthropology and ethnography adopted the film as standard study material (Rony 1996, 99). *Nanook* also gave rise to "Nanookmania," a craze of the 1920s and 1930s that, together with Inuit performers as spectacles in zoos, fairs, museums, and exhibitions in North America and Western Europe during the late nineteenth and early twentieth centuries, "contributed substantially to the elaboration and diffusion of the [Eskimo] stereotype" (Balikci 1996, 44).

Such a history of *Nanook* has involved the film in the politics of primitivist representation that is complicated by evidence of the Inuit's unacknowledged contributions as technicians, camera operators, film developers, and production consultants in the filming process (Ginsberg 2002, 39). One should be aware that the Inuit had instructed Flaherty to take their views of social and cultural interaction into account (Raheja 2010, 195). That does not mean there exists any doubt about Flaherty being affected by the ethnocentric biases and racism of his contemporaries. Charles Nayoumealuk—whose father knew Allakariallak (the actor who portrayed Nanook) personally—has indeed revealed that *Nanook* was aimed at White audiences such that Inuit customs alone were to be shown while the tools of White men were forbidden to be seen (Rony 1996, 123).

In conjunction with various colonial conditions prescribed by the Indian Act, Flaherty's concealment of the Inuit's contribution to *Nanook* had rendered the film almost unknown to the Inuit for half a century. This state of affairs is reflective of the statement Inuit Tapiriit Kanatami made in 2004 that "most of the research on our culture and history has been done by individuals who come from outside our culture" (2). It criticized the fact that "the information that these individuals collected was seldom made available to us" and "the image held by much of the outside world about who we are is usually someone else's creation, not ours" (2). When Tagaq watched *Nanook* for the first time as a child living in Iqaluktuuttiaq (aka Cambridge Bay), she and her schoolmates were still "forbidden from speaking their [native] language or exercising their [native] culture in any way whatsoever" (Wertheim 2019). She recalled that she was "kind of laughing and feeling embarrassed and feeling sad" (Werb 2014). This memory, along with "a million terrible horror stories" (Kurchak 2014) from her exposure to the Indian Residential School system in Canada (see also Government of Canada 2019 and Robinson 2020, 150), seems to have haunted her from time to time. She has mentioned on different occasions how the film's imagery made her feel uneasy or even annoyed (Everett-Green 2014; Gordon 2014). Such lasting feelings might have aroused her indignation when Jesse Wente, an Ojibwe writer and broadcaster who was the Head of TIFF Cinematheque, commissioned her to create and perform a live score for *Nanook* along with title cards (aka intertitles, i.e., subtitles in silent film) translated into Inuktitut, for the opening night of *First Peoples Cinema* on National Aboriginal Day in 2012: "It's really the idea of reclaiming these images for the community.

Here you have a modern-day artist, from the people that this movie is about, re-translating it into a new concept.... You can begin to see the relationship and understand the different points of view that are being expressed" (DeMara 2012). One could thus conceive of her live score as a statement on Indigenous politics:

> Growing up in Nunavut and just the harshness of the environment itself, the ability for people to be able to survive with no vegetation, and just the harshest of environments, it's just incredible to me. I'm very proud of my ancestors. So that's one facet of [*Nanook*], but I'm a natural presenter, like I went to arts school, so I watched it and I was just like, "They put a bunch of bullshit happy Eskimo stereotypes, you know what I mean?" So, I can respond to that as well, with finding some hardcore punk, kind of that feel, kind of put that sound all over it to make it clear. It's really nice because I can take my frustrations of stereotypes all over the world and take that energy and put it in sonically. I reclaim the film. Even though I have no doubt in my mind that Robert Flaherty had a definite love for Inuit and the land, it's through 1922 goggles. It's just nice to be a modern woman, well modern Inuk woman, taking it back. (Gordon 2014)

On another occasion, she said: "I'll be exploring the space between the stereotype of an Eskimo in 1922 and the stereotype of an Inuk woman in 2014. And hopefully erasing all the stereotypes through a thoughtful connection.... One of the stereotypes that I hate is 'happy Eskimo.' 'Happy Eskimo' is nice but not simple, happy Eskimo. The technology today still can't beat the traditional clothing that people wore up there. It wasn't simple" (Walker 2014).

By the time Tagaq brought her live score to Ann Arbor, her expressive intervention in Inuit stereotypes had already left its footprint in Austin, Banff, Calgary, Minneapolis, Portland, Vancouver, Washington, DC, and several other cities in North America and Western Europe. In contrast to the long take (i.e., lengthy shot) and minimal camera movement that have rendered the moving image in *Nanook* static, Tagaq's performing body was vibrant whenever her live score was heard (see also Gordon 2014). She improvised to instrumental support provided by violinist Jean Martin and percussionist Jesse Zubot in addition to a backing track that remixed some field recordings collected at Mittimatalik (aka Pond Inlet) and some "melodies and stuff like that" (Walker 2014). She recorded her music after watching the film four times (Galloway 2020, 109). She committed herself to adapting Inuit throat singing as well as other modes of vocal production, uttering unknown vocables and imitating various sounds of nature, animals, and humans, to address the moving image

Fig. 9.1. Tagaq at the Luminato festival in Toronto on June 10, 2014. Photo credit: Taku Kumabe. Used with permission.

(Stévance and Lacasse 2019, 88). She also made a lot of hand gestures and other body movements along with the moving image, especially when the music was fast, loud, upbeat, and grooving (see fig. 9.1).

In Ann Arbor, I found Tagaq mimicking the emergence of wildness during a scene that depicts a dogfight. Within an artificial soundscape consisting of low pitches, frequent bass drum strikes, and an extreme, heavy-metal loudness, she roared while rigidly shaking her body as if she had gone into a trance. In another scene when Nanook was building an igloo for his family, Tagaq improvised against a violin ostinato while the percussionist was playing a hornlike instrument. There was an increase in tempo when the screen showed a title card that read "complete within the hour," but the music slowed down with her Inuit throat singing juxtaposing the moving image of Nanook digging ice. She returned to her natural voice to sing very high pitches as the audience saw an ice block becoming the window of an igloo, and her imitation of an infantile voice coincided with the succeeding title card: "time for work and time for play."

As I elaborate in the next section, Tagaq confronted the audience with the obstinacy of Inuit stereotypes in *Nanook* by foregrounding the incommensurability between the taxidermic display of the Inuit on screen and the performing body of the Inuit on stage. She brought an embodied subaltern voice of the Inuit to the forefront, exemplifying not only the Inuit's unwillingness to be confined to the past by their history but also their attempt to recover a culture without division between the past and the present (Inuit Tapiriit Kanatami 2004, 4). She was cognizant of how her live score—which she described as "the same thing but . . . also different every time because of improvising with my band"—might bother or even irritate the audience due to its highly dissonant, unmelodic, and nonlinguistic qualities (Gordon 2014). Notwithstanding, as her more recent renderings of the score have demonstrated, she continues to take more and more liberty from conventions of music accompaniment for silent film (see also Kalinak 1992, 40–65; Altman 2004, 231–388); she has made herself more aurally and visually palpable during the screening.

PERFORMING AGAINST THE IMPERIAL GAZE

Grounded in forms of visuality, temporality, and relations between the looking subject and the object being looked at, *Nanook* was meant to be released on the theatrical screen in the United States during a time when exotic display, as in *The Queen of Sheba* (1921) and *The Young Rajah* (1922), was translated as a key element of box-office success. This expectation may explain why, in *Nanook*, an Inuit hunter looks perplexingly amused in the infamous scene that follows a title card stating, "the trader entertains and attempts to explain the principle of the gramophone." The contradiction between this depicted amusement and the fact that European explorers first introduced new materials and technologies to the Inuit in the late sixteenth century (Inuit Tapiriit Kanatami 2004, 11) simply elicits an air of imperialist condescension on the part of Flaherty.

Subsequently, through interviews and other venues, Tagaq expressed her thoughts and feelings about *Nanook* and its reception over time. On the one hand, she identified the Inuit and their land as the main subjects of the film, telling how the moving image provided a glimpse into what Nunavut is and how the Inuit survive on it (Przybylski 2016). On the other hand, she took issue with Flaherty's intention to reenact premodern Inuit culture with "an explorer's mind and a process of discovery" (*Flaherty and Film* 1999), targeting how he reinforced Inuit stereotypes by investing the moving image with a sense of nostalgia or timelessness (Everett-Green 2014; Gordon 2014; Kerr 2015).

The dramatized narrative in *Nanook* has indeed aroused many debates on its cultural, historical, and artistic values for almost a century. It has been both criticized for and defended against issues of distortion, objectification, infantilization, animalization, and romanticization. One could attribute such a contention to how film narration situates the spectator in a position of agency and how race, class, and sexual relations influence the subjecthood of the spectator (Diawara 1990, 33). Accordingly, one might want to consider the relationship between *Nanook* and Tagaq from perspectives of representation, spectatorship, and coloniality of power. Fatimah Tobing Rony's assessment of *Nanook* "as the product of a hunt for images" (1996, 100) and E. Ann Kaplan's scrutiny of how the imperial gaze "reflects the assumption that the [W]hite [W]estern subject is central" (1997, 78) are particularly relevant in this regard.

Aside from the presence of a White trader in one of its early scenes, *Nanook* demonstrates almost no sign of contact with non-Inuit. The cinematic mise-en-scène, which signifies Flaherty's control over what appears in the film frame (see also Bordwell and Thompson 2008, 112), is barely noticeable from the moving image in which "actions and expressions are clearly directed toward the camera and, by extension, the viewer" (Grimshaw 2014, 428). Flaherty preferred the camera to be consistently static across all different shots, offering "a single point of view" (431) that demonstrates how White authorities (such as explorers, merchants, colonial agents, scientists, etc.) treated the camera as a device for capturing and mastering Indigenous cultures.[3] His imperialist depiction of Indigenous people dying, if not already dead, also contributed to the search for truthfulness in *Nanook* as part of "a system of knowledge and power reproducing and maintaining white supremacy" that bell hooks explicated in the context of Black female spectatorship (1992, 117). The Inuit were typecast as "a people without technology, without a culture, lacking intelligence, living in igloos, and at best, a sort of simplistic 'native boy' type of subhuman arctic being" (Senungetuk 1971, 25). They became "the coeval other [that] is done to death by being filmed as a primitive, as though already dead" (Lim 2009, 88). Such a taxidermic display invites the audience to be both the participant (seeing with the eyes of Nanook) and the observer (viewing Nanook with an omnipotent eye), offering risk-free, uninterrupted contact and communion with the depicted people and environment, as if "the literal blood and guts of taxidermy are removed from the scene and safely hidden from view" (Groo 2019, 195). Anxieties about uncertainties or threats that arise from alterities are suppressed (Kaplan 1997, 62) as the film identifies the audience as an active and agentive gazing subject that aims the eye at the Inuit as objectified.

Moreover, in *Nanook*, the display of animal death in scenes of fur trade, walrus hunt, sealskin sewing, and (raw) seal meat eating draws the Inuit into an expression of evolutionary order, situating the Inuit in a man-against-nature narrative as opposed to a respectful relationship with the land (see also Takano

2005, 475–78). Deliberate or not, this deployment of the moving image insinuates racist jokes through "comic" comparisons between "primitive" humans and nonhuman animals (Groo 2019, 194, 198), confining portrayals of the Inuit to the natural world and the "primitive" stage of human development. In fact, *Nanook* set an example for images of non-Western people in Hollywood and British films along with those early film adaptations of *Cleopatra* and *Tarzan of the Apes*. It inspired Paramount Pictures to assign the then codirectors of *King Kong* (1933) to work together on *Grass* (1925) and *Chang* (1927) with original screenplays, exotic filming locations, and native people as actors, even though cinematography and salvage ethnography distinguished *Nanook* from early Hollywood productions as such and influenced the emergence of documentary filmmaking (Lim 2009, 87–88).

By the time Tagaq performed her live score for *Nanook* in Ann Arbor, she was sensitive not only to the obstinacy of Inuit stereotypes but also to "the mimetic and sensuous possibilities now offered the human sensorium by cinema" (Taussig 1993, 200). She responded to these issues through her live score by means of montage, remixing, and improvisation. She reanimated the Inuit on screen with her onstage vitality while countering the removal of the Inuit from modern temporality and contemporary consciousness. She treated each performance of her live score as a unique opportunity to engage the audience with *Nanook* dynamically and interactively, to "play on lived archives of moving image memory across sites of expropriation, exclusion, and contested history" (Thain 2019).

THE POTENTIAL FOR RECLAIMING NANOOK THROUGH AUDIOVISUAL REALIGNMENT

In *Film Form: Essays in Film Theory*, Sergei Eisenstein discussed how, by forgoing the "purely illustrative function" of melodious musical accompaniment while experimenting with nonsynchronization between music and the moving image, one could establish film as an art form that "live[s] in a unity of fused musical and visual images" (1977, 177). He was anxious about how "talking films" would provide the audience a naturalistic illusion of talking people and audible objects (258). He insisted that "sound film" should be a contrapuntal combination of visual and aural images (24) as well as a product grounded in conflicts between optical and acoustical experiences (54–55). These thoughts on the role of film sound were exemplified in his *Battleship Potemkin* (1925), which demonstrated how music could be a montage element capable of unsettling a certain presumed stability and autonomy of meanings arising from the moving image itself and its syntactic logic. For Eisenstein, conflicts are always embodied in film as an art form. A filmmaker must therefore confront the conflict "between natural existence and creative tendency" and "between organic inertia and purposeful initiative" intrinsic to filmmaking. A filmmaker also needs to take responsibility "to make manifest the contradictions of Beings[,] [t]o form equitable views by stirring up contradictions within the spectator's mind, and to forge accurate intellectual concepts from the dynamic clash of opposing passions" (46).

Arguably, Tagaq created and performed a live score that transformed *Nanook* from a silent film of taxidermic display into a "sound film" as Eisenstein envisioned. Not only did she choose not to literally accompany the moving image with easily recognizable motifs or melodies, but her live score also associated her singing voice with the moving image in a way that "foreground[ed] the phonic aspect of utterance and its perlocutionary effect" (Taylor-Neu 2018, 120; see also Jadrnak 2016). Her unmelodic and nonlinguistic singing voice negated the film's explanatory undertone, while the restless shift of stylistic traits (pop, electronic, experimental, punk rock, and heavy metal) in her live score underlay the tension between her cosmopolitan sensibility and the sense of primitivism evoked by the moving image (Galloway 2020, 111). She noted that her intuitive feeling was "more along the lines of where the singing c[a]me from" and she was "trying to get down to where before people were messing around with too many words" (Brown 2009). Unlike Flaherty's deliberate erasure of the Inuit's contribution to their own screen representation, Tagaq openly displayed her physical and affective labor by deploying different modes of vocal production with high intensity and long duration (see also Couture 2019, 166; Stévance and Lacasse 2019, 88). The backing track of her live score allowed her to let the music take her away as she wanted to, with no need to care what the screen illustrated during the performance (Przybylski 2016). She could thus be fully frontal onstage, as opposed to the Inuit captured in the moving image by a "camera hunter." Without being a preacher or an informant who would reveal "mysteries" from the moving image, she expressed musically what she felt and thought about the moving image as an Inuit "being on the land": "The more you remove yourself from nature, the more you think that the Earth belongs to you, and not that you belong to the Earth. I wanted to have a voice for what the Earth is trying to say to us. We're doing terrible, parasitic things to it" (Everett-Green 2014).

While Tagaq did not necessarily comply with the way Eisenstein essentialized conflicts in his aestheticization and politicization of filmmaking, she openly identified *Nanook* with conflicts regarding the historical representation of the Inuit (Nelles 2015), the politics of seal hunting (Kurchak 2014), and the ongoing marginality and vulnerability of Canadian Indigenous women (Frank 2016). She once admitted that Inuit throat singing was a way for her to "express the pain caused by racism, sexism, sexual violence and the horrors that took place, with impunity, in residential schools" (Stévance and Lacasse 2019, 93). It is therefore noteworthy how, along with her effort to "reclaim the film," her live score reframed *Nanook* in a way that gave life to the dictum "art is always conflict according to its social mission, its nature, and its methodology" (Eisenstein 1977, 46).

THE INVOCATION OF DEEP LISTENING AS A FORM OF REDRESS

Tagaq, her collaborators, and her commentators often characterized her music or onstage performances as primal, sexual, physical, and emotional as well as cathartic, channelizing, transformative, and intense. Her relationship with the audience is remarkable in this sense. On the one hand, she recognizes that her music "[is] not palatable to everyone" (Gordon 2014). She is aware of people talking about her performances being sexual and her music sounding like sex, and she finds this fact amusing because she identifies sex as the last thing on her mind (Prasad 2010; Nelles 2015). On the other hand, she refers to herself as a conduit that could "feel the reaction in the room" (Brown 2009). She perceives the audience as "another band member without them even realizing, [who] contribute to the energy in the room [as if] they're driving the music as well" (Przybylski 2016). She feels celebratory in her communication "with every single person at a concert by the mere fact that we're all breathing" (Everett-Green 2014). She also "love[s] the idea of everyone having the same kind of emotion" (Brown 2009). In short, as Jesse Zubot, one of her frequent collaborators, observed: "It's a very primal thing Tanya does, and it's never going to become that confined. What she does is about the moment, and about channeling a place. Most people may not understand where that place is, but they feel it" (Everett-Green 2014).

Tagaq's live score for *Nanook* is a laborious and profound effort to pull the audience away from Inuit stereotypes. One could attribute the effectiveness of this effort not only to her artistic sensitivity and her critical engagement with Indigenous politics but also to how, musically and somatically, she encourages the audience to sense the specific materialities of image, affect, and fantasy so as to resist a certain fetishization of identity manifested in the temptation to equate lifelike imagery with the lives and histories of a "real" cultural group (Chow 2007, 12). The nonrepresentational ineffability of this undertaking compels the audience to look into how primary emotions and the corresponding physiological responses could afford a substantial experience of transcendence (Robinson 2020, 217). It also prompts the audience to ask themselves why, especially in Euro-American cultures, vision has ideologically been far more privileged than other sensory modalities of no less importance to human beings and social life (Taussig 1993, 26).

Inuit throat singing used to be a means for women to have fun and enjoy themselves while attracting animals to be hunted or influencing natural elements (air, wind, and waves) to behave in favor of men who had gone hunting or fishing (Nattiez 1999, 405). According to Sylvia Cloutier, it was a kind of survival music for female members of an animistic society to address themselves to deities of nature and animals, until missionaries began to exert cultural and religious influences on them: "Missionaries came up and banned many things in our culture, and our spirituality was sort of [pause] crushed in many ways, and throat singing was part of that. My mother's generation didn't learn how to do that because people stopped having pride in throat singing in those days, so they didn't pass that on [to] their kids" (*Four Seasons Mosaic* 2005). Some critics have thus accused Tagaq of adapting Inuit throat singing in a way that is contextually and aesthetically distant from itself as part of a musical game between two women on the occasion of spring equinox, summer solstice, and winter solstice (Gordon 2014). Tagaq is unconcerned, however, with such accusations apropos of surface-level authenticity (Rayner 2017). She is instead committed to guarding Inuit throat singing against appropriation by non-Inuit musicians (Rogers 2019) while diversifying styles and social functions of Inuit throat singing in Inuit communities (Galloway 2020, 97). Furthermore, her live score for *Nanook* has retained much of the vitalism and animistic qualities from traditional practice, as she has shown both Inuit and non-Inuit musicians and audiences how she "wanted to have a voice for what the Earth is trying to say to us" (Everett-Green 2014) while using Inuit throat singing to "bring [her] back to a life before colonialism" (Stévance and Lacasse 2019, 93).

Characteristic of Inuit throat singing, Tagaq's use of throat and breathing sounds and her imitation of natural and animal sounds are conducive to arousing primary emotions (fear, anger, surprise, and disgust) most crucial to the survival of the organism (Nattiez 1999, 402, 404; Becker 2004, 45). Her taxing showcase of stamina and virtuosity and her embodiment of rhythm through a pulsating voice on top of dance and hand gestures also facilitate an arousal that could activate certain neural pathways to basic physiological responses (tears, chills/shivers, goosebumps, and perspiration) consequent to experiences of emotions that have plausibly evolved as a survival strategy (Nattiez 1999, 403,

413). Such an arousal perhaps shares with sexual arousal what Judith Becker might identify as "underlying neurochemical similarities," especially when the music tends to be "rhythmically vibrant and somewhat loud, or at least with a piercing tone quality" (2004, 52, 66). In effect, Tagaq's live score for *Nanook* might have elicited "deep listening" (2) from some critics who appeared able "to respond with strong emotional arousal to musical stimulation" (54), as they revealed from their reviews "a joy in the pure bodily experience of strong arousal, a life-affirming quality of feeling truly alive" (67). Neurologically speaking, they were "held within the relative constancy of the continual activation of a particular complex of neuronal groupings" (Becker 1994, 46), during which they might have experienced a selective mental shutdown so that they would respond more readily to new kinds of perceptual and cognitive inputs (47). Their corresponding perception and cognition could also subject them to a certain rhythmic entrainment that would "involve not only acoustic and sensory motor areas of the brain, but areas in many other cortical and sub-cortical areas" (49). Consequently, the moving image of *Nanook* could no longer be a mere matter of documentation or representation for them, as it became part of their experiential exchanges between the past and the present and between the corporeal and the transcendental, regardless of cultural conditioning.

One could assume that through such a physical and affective labor, Tagaq proactively revives Inuit throat singing while deflecting critics from a misguided reception of music and the moving image based on Inuit stereotypes. Her live score for *Nanook* is driven by neither repetition nor resolution but, rather, vitality and empathy. Her onstage presence urges validation of the Inuit as cosmopolitan and communitarian instead of racialized and romanticized (see also Gombay 2010, 237–50, and Rice 2016, 220–42). She elicits deep listening from the audience on her own terms so that the Inuit can be seen and heard with substantial and almost irresistible attention as vibrant and empowered.

CONCLUDING REMARKS

Tagaq altered neither the plot nor the moving image of *Nanook*, but she created a refreshing sonic environment while performing in a way that drew the audience attention no less to her than to the screen. From her stage attire and bodily expressions to her preferences regarding timbre, loudness, and nonharmonic texture, she maneuvered a range of sensory vehicles that refrained the audience from acting like a group of voyeurs in darkness and silence. This is how she actively engaged with the politics of primitivist representation while stirring up the audience through various modes of stimulation. With little talking or explanation onstage but a notable political presence offstage, she deployed her performing body to defy elements that constitute and reinforce Inuit stereotypes in *Nanook* and beyond.

NOTES

1. Two shorter versions of this chapter were presented at the conference Exoticism in Contemporary Transnational Cinema: Music and Spectacle in June 2017 and the Sixty-Second Annual Meeting of the Society for Ethnomusicology in October 2017; I received valuable comments from the audience for expanding the scope of my initial inquiry. Giorgio Biancorosso, Casper Chan, Caryl Flinn, Camilo Mendez, and the editors of this volume kindly read and commented on different drafts of this chapter; their help was crucial to bringing this chapter to completion.

2. In *Proclamation Declaring June 21 of Each Year as National Aboriginal Day (SI/96-55)*, registered by the Government of Canada on July 10, 1996, it declares June 21 of each year as the National Aboriginal Day to mark and celebrate the valuable contributions the Aboriginal peoples of Canada have made and continue to make to the Canadian society and to recognize the different cultures of the Aboriginal peoples of Canada. The Aboriginal peoples of Canada include "the Indian, Inuit and Métis peoples of Canada."

3. Flaherty's "camera-hunter" mentality is best exemplified in one of the title cards from the beginning of *Nanook*: "At last, in 1920, I thought *I had shot enough scenes to make the film and prepared to go home.* Poor old Nanook hung around my cabin, talking over films we still could make if I would only stay on for another year. *He never understood why I should have gone to all the fuss and bother of making the 'big aggie' of him*" (emphasis added).

BIBLIOGRAPHY

Altman, Rick. 2004. *Silent Film Sound*. New York: Columbia University Press.
Balikci, Asen. 1996. "Anthropologists and Ethnographic Filmmaking." In *Anthropological Filmmaking: Anthropological Perspectives on the Production of Film and Video for General Public Audiences*, edited by Jack R. Rollwagen, 31–45. Amsterdam: Harwood Academic Publishers.
Becker, Judith. 1994. "Music and Trance." *Leonardo Music Journal* 4: 41–51.
———. 2004. *Deep Listeners: Music, Emotion, and Trancing*. Bloomington: Indiana University Press.
Bordwell, David, and Kristin Thompson. 2008. *Film Art: An Introduction*. New York: McGraw-Hill.
Brown, Laurie. 2009. "Interview: Tanya Tagaq." September 9, 2009. Improvisation, Community, and Social Practice. Accessed July 16, 2020. http://www.improvcommunity.ca/research/interview-tanya-tagaq/.
Calder-Marshall, Arthur. 1963. *The Innocent Eye of the Life of Robert J. Flaherty*. London: W. H. Allen.

Chow, Rey. 2007. *Sentimental Fabulations: Contemporary Chinese Films.* New York: Columbia University Press.

Couture, Selena. 2019. *Against the Current and into the Light: Performing History and Land in Coast Salish Territories and Vancouver's Stanley Park.* Montréal: McGill-Queen's University Press.

Deleuze, Gilles. 1997. *Cinema 1: The Movement Image.* Translated by Hugh Tomlinson and Barbara Habberjam. Minneapolis: University of Minnesota Press.

DeMara, Bruce. 2012. "TIFF Series Connects Indigenous Cultures Worldwide." *Toronto Star*, June 20, 2012. Accessed July 16, 2020. https://www.thestar.com/entertainment/2012/06/20/tiff_series_connects_indigenous_cultures_worldwide.html/.

Diawara, Manthia. 1990. "Black British Cinema: Spectatorship and Identity Formation in Territories." *Public Culture* 3 (1): 33–48.

Eisenstein, Sergei. 1977. *Film Form: Essays in Film Theory.* Edited and translated by Jay Leyda. New York: Harcourt Brace Jovanovich.

Everett-Green, Robert. 2014. "Primal Scream: Inuk Throat Singer Tanya Tagaq Is Like No One You've Ever Heard, Anywhere." *The Globe and Mail*, May 30, 2014. Accessed July 16, 2020. https://www.theglobeandmail.com/arts/music/primal-scream-inuk-throat-singer-tanya-tagaq-is-like-no-one-youve-ever-heard-anywhere/article18923190/.

Flaherty, Robert J. 1924. *My Eskimo Friends: "Nanook of the North."* Garden City: Doubleday.

———. 1999. "How I Filmed 'Nanook of the North'." *Documentary Magazine.* Accessed July 16, 2020. https://www.documentary.org/feature/how-i-filmed-nanook-north/.

Frank, Priscilla. 2016. "The Inuit Punk Throat Singer Fighting to Protest Indigenous Women: How Björk Collaborator Tanya Tagaq Turned an Inuit Tradition into a Feminist Battle Cry." *Huffington Post*, November 2, 2016. Accessed July 16, 2020. http://www.huffingtonpost.com/entry/tanya-tagaq-throat-singer-inuit_us_58177a00e4b0390e69d190a7/.

Galloway, Kate. 2020. "Experimental and Improvised Norths: The Sonic Geographies of Tanya Tagaq's Collaborations with Derek Charke and the Kronos Quartet." In *Playing for Keeps: Improvisation in the Aftermath*, edited by Daniel Fischlin and Eric Porter, 94–120. Durham, NC: Duke University Press.

Ginsberg, Faye D. 2002. "Screen Memories: Resignifying the Traditional in Indigenous Media." In *Media Worlds: Anthropology on New Terrain*, edited by Faye D. Ginsburg, Lila Abu-Lughod, and Brian Larkin, 39–57. Berkeley: University of California Press.

Gombay, Nicole. 2010. "Community, Obligation, and Food: Lessons from the Moral Geography of Inuit." *Geografiska Annaler*, series B, *Human Geography* 92 (3): 237–50.

Gordon, Holly. 2014. "Inuk Throat Singer Tanya Tagaq on Reclaiming *Nanook of the North.*" CBC News, January 25, 2014. Accessed July 16, 2020. http://www.cbc.ca/news/indigenous/inuk-throat-singer-tanya-tagaq-on-reclaiming-nanook-of-the-north-1.2508581/.

Government of Canada. 2021. "Indian Residential Schools Settlement Agreement." Crown-Indigenous Relations and Northern Affairs Canada, June 9, 2021. Accessed May 19, 2022. https://www.rcaanc-cirnac.gc.ca/eng/1100100015576/1571581687074/.

Grimshaw, Anna. 2014. "Who Has the Last Laugh? *Nanook of the North* and Some New Thoughts on an Old Classic." *Visual Anthropology* 27 (5): 421–35.

Groo, Katherine. 2019. *Bad Film Histories: Ethnography and the Early Archive*. Minneapolis: University of Minnesota Press.

hooks, bell. 1992. *Black Looks: Race and Representation*. Boston: South End Press.

Inuit Tapiriit Kanatami. 2004. *5000 Years of Inuit History and Heritage*. Accessed July 16, 2020. https://www.itk.ca/5000-years-inuit-history-heritage/.

Jadrnak, Jackie. 2016. "Arctic Throat-Singer to Bring 'Nanook of the North' Film Classic to Life." *Albuquerque Journal*, August 26, 2016. Access July 16, 2020. https://www.abqjournal.com/833625/arctic-throat-singer-to-bring-nanook-film-classic-to-life.html/.

Kalinak, Kathryn. 1992. *Setting the Score: Music and the Classical Hollywood Film*. Madison: University of Wisconsin Press.

Kaplan, E. Ann. 1997. *Looking for the Other: Feminism, Film, and the Imperial Gaze*. New York: Routledge.

Kerr, Euan. 2015. "Inuit Throat Singer Makes 'Nanook' Her Own." *Minnesota Public Radio News*, November 18, 2015. Accessed July 16, 2020. https://www.mprnews.org/story/2015/11/18/inuit-throat-singer-makes-nanook-her-own/.

Kurchak, Sarah. 2014. "Tanya Tagaq: Being an Aboriginal Woman is Like Being Scared at a Horror Movie, All the Time." *Huffington Post Canada*, October 8, 2014. Accessed July 16, 2020. https://www.huffingtonpost.ca/2014/10/08/tanya-tagaq-interview_n_5952126.html/.

Lim, Bliss Cua. 2009. *Translating Time: Cinema, the Fantastic, and Temporal Critique*. Durham, NC: Duke University Press.

Nattiez, Jean-Jacques. 1999. "Inuit Throat-Games and Siberian Throat Singing: A Comparative, Historical, and Semiological Approach." *Ethnomusicology* 43 (3): 399–418.

Nelles, Drew. 2015. "The Rise of Tanya Tagaq: Her Music Is Like Nothing Else in the World." *Walrus*, January 15, 2015. Accessed July 16, 2020. https://thewalrus.ca/howl/.

Prasad, Anil. 2010. "Tanya Tagaq: Instinctual Invocations." Innerviews. Accessed July 16, 2020. https://www.innerviews.org/inner/tagaq.html/.

Przybylski, Liz. 2016. "Throat Singer Tanya Tagaq Loudly Combats Indigenous Stereotypes." linkTV, September 8, 2016. Accessed July 16, 2020. https://www.linktv.org/shows/artbound/tanya-tagaq-nanook-of-the-north-throat-singer/.

Raheja, Michelle H. 2010. *Reservation Reelism: Redfacing, Visual Sovereignty, and Representations of Native Americans in Film.* Lincoln: University of Nebraska Press.

Rayner, Ben. 2017. "Tanya Tagaq Addresses Her Art, and Her Critics, at Nunavut Music Week." *Star*, September 29, 2017. Accessed July 16, 2020. https://www.thestar.com/entertainment/music/2017/09/29/tanya-tagaq-addresses-her-art-and-her-critics-at-nunavut-music-week.html/.

Rice, Roberta. 2016. "How to Decolonize Democracy: Indivgenous Governance Innovation in Bolivia and Nunavut, Canada." *Bolivian Studies Journal* 22: 220–42.

Robinson, Dylan. 2020. *Hungry Listening: Resonant Theory for Indigenous Sound Studies.* Minneapolis: University of Minnesota Press.

Rogers, Sarah. 2019. "Should Non-Inuit Performers Be Allowed to Throat Sing?" Nunatsiaq News, April 3, 2019. Accessed July 16, 2020. https://nunatsiaq.com/stories/article/should-non-inuit-performers-be-allowed-to-throat-sing/.

Rony, Fatimah Tobing. 1996. *The Third Eye: Race, Cinema, and Ethnographic Spectacle.* Durham, NC: Duke University Press.

Rotha, Paul. 1980. "Nanook of the North." *Studies in Visual Communication* 6 (2): 33–60.

Senungetuk, Joseph E. 1971. *Give or Take a Century: An Eskimo Chronicle.* San Francisco: Indian Historian Press.

Stévance, Sophie, and Serge Lacasse. 2019. "La musique de Tanya Tagaq comme engagement cosmopolite: Le case de «Fracking»." *MUSICultures* 46 (2): 85–108.

Takano, Takako. 2005. "Connections with the Land: Land-Skills Courses in Igloolik, Nunavut." *Ethnography* 6 (4): 463–86.

Taussig, Michael. 1993. *Mimesis and Alterity: A Particular History of the Senses.* New York: Routledge.

Taylor-Neu, Robyn. 2018. "'All There Is': The Reconciliatory Poetics of a Singing Voice." *American Anthropologist* 120 (1): 113–25.

Thain, Alanna. 2019. "Anarchival Images: The Labor of Chronic Collage." *Intermediality: History and Theory of the Arts, Literature and Technologies* 33. https://doi.org/10.7202/1065014ar.

Walker, Connie. 2014. "Tanya Tagaq Takes on Cyberbullies and Stereotypes." CBC News, June 10, 2014. Accessed July 16, 2020. https://www.cbc.ca/news/indigenous/tanya-tagaq-takes-on-cyberbullies-and-stereotypes-1.2669892/.

Werb, Jessica. 2014. "PuSh Festival: Tanya Tagaq Wrestles with Feelings about Nanook of the North." *Georgia Straight*, January 15, 2014. Accessed July 16, 2020. https://www.straight.com/arts/566076/push-festival-tanya-tagaq-wrestles-feelings-about-nanook-north/.

Wertheim, Jon. 2019. "The Sounds of Inuit Throat Singer Tanya Tagaq." *60 Minutes*, May 5, 2019. Accessed July 16, 2020. https://www.cbsnews.com/news/the-sounds-of-inuit-throat-singer-tanya-tagaq-60-minutes-2019-05-05/.

Wiessner, Siegfried. 2011. "The Cultural Rights of Indigenous Peoples: Achievements and Continuing Challenges." *European Journal of International Law* 22 (1): 121–40. https://doi.org/10.1093/ejil/chr007.

Williams, Raymond. 1983. *Keywords: A Vocabulary of Culture and Society*. New York: Oxford University Press.

DISCOGRAPHY

Tagaq, Tanya. 2011. *Anuraaqtuq*. Victoriaville: Les Disques VICTO CD121. CD.

———. 2014. *Animism*. Toronto: Six Shooter Records SIX086. CD.

VIDEOGRAPHY

Flaherty and Film. 1999. Presented by National Educational Television (1975). New York: Criterion Collection. DVD.

The Four Seasons Mosaic. 2005. Toronto: Media Headquarters Film and Television. DVD.

TEN

"IF I COULD GO BACK IN TIME"

Rethinking Popular Culture, Social Justice, and the Compassionate Gaze in Palestine

DAVID A. MCDONALD

WITHOUT QUESTION PALESTINIAN ISRAELI HIP-HOP group DAM has established itself as the foremost hip-hop collective in the Arab Middle East (McDonald 2013b).[1] Building from their independently released singles; a successful studio album, *Dedication* (2006); and two highly acclaimed documentaries, *Channels of Rage* (dir. Anat Halachmi, 2003) and *Slingshot Hip-Hop* (dir. Jackie Salloum, 2009), DAM now dominates the field of Palestinian music. Each of these projects drew international praise for their explicit activism, documenting Palestinian experiences of racial oppression and foreign occupation during the Al-Aqsa Intifada (2002–6). As the Intifada faded from public view, however, DAM began to take on new issues and new techniques of narration. Their second studio album, *Dabke on the Moon* (2012), demonstrates this transformation. In a departure from their signature diatribes against Israeli oppression, in this album DAM engages issues interior to Palestinian life: religious patriarchy, domestic violence, intersectarian relationships, drug abuse, and mass incarceration. Commenting on this change in approach DAM member Mahmoud Jrere explained, "*Dedication* (2006) was an album where we told the facts, *Dabke on the Moon* (2012) is more like a feature film where we tell stories. Musically and lyrically each album reflects a different age" (Anderson 2012).[2]

And yet despite DAM's success and notoriety, *Dabke on the Moon* was nevertheless strongly criticized by international critics for not being political enough and by local audiences for being too "pop" (i.e., cosmopolitan), missing key Palestinian and Arab musical markers and aesthetics (Nesheiwat 2012). Esteemed scholars Lila Abu-Lughod and Maya Mikdashi went so far as to accuse the group of abandoning its politics and succumbing (i.e., selling out) to international influence. At issue was the group's 2012 music video "If I Could Go Back in Time," codirected by Jackie Salloum and her husband, former DAM member Suhell Nafar. The video presents the tragic story of a young woman murdered by her brother and father for attempting to escape an arranged marriage. Told in reverse chronological order, the video graphically depicts the intrafamily femicide while the artists move through the scenes, angrily lashing out at an intractable religious patriarchy. The video was produced with funding from the UN women's rights organization United Nations Entity for Gender Equality and the Empowerment of Women, and its release coincided with their international media campaign. While this wasn't the first time DAM had taken on violence against women in their work (see their single "al-ḥurīyya unta"), it was the first time they approached the subject with funding provided by an international aid agency.[3]

Abu-Lughod and Mikdashi's strong critique of the video censured the rappers for myriad offenses, most notably for decontextualizing, romanticizing, and, by extension, disempowering women. At the heart of this critique was the claim that by taking on so-called honor crimes, DAM fell into an orientalist trap, reproducing a political logic that situates Palestinian women as "victims of their culture, to be championed by young men with enlightened views, and by foreign intervention in international aid" (Abu-Lughod and Mikdashi 2012).[4] The video, they claimed, failed to provide adequate cultural, political, and historical context, leaving the impression that "honor crimes" are symptomatic of a "barbaric culture and enduring [Palestinian] tradition." Without providing adequate "thickness" of Palestinian lives, they argued, DAM inadvertently reinforced, and perhaps justified, "the conviction that it is Palestinians' backwardness and lack of civilization that should be blamed for violence against women in the community." Rather, the group would have been better served to remind audiences of "the structural violence that is usually front and center in their songs," that is, the occupation. "Honor crimes," they claimed, require a more nuanced discussion, one that acknowledges how the practice is too often co-opted by international organizations as a tool to justify racial hatred. Hence, rapping about "honor crimes" to an international audience invites orientalist thinking, increasing the precarity of Palestinians while unraveling sincere efforts to make gendered violence visible globally.

This episode of public engagement between internationally known hip-hop artists and the academics that study them presents several fascinating lines of inquiry for thinking about the relational dynamics of popular culture, activism, and vulnerability in Palestine (Stein and Swedenburg 2005, 11). For example, in times of crisis, how does popular culture serve to influence, both positively and negatively, the potential impact of, and audience for, activist intervention? Must engaged artists, and in particular Palestinian artists, remain obedient to the demands of their political allies? What effect might radical self-critique have on the larger project of Palestinian self-determination? And finally, how might ethnomusicologists better learn from these gestures to decolonize their work and adopt a more justice-oriented stance toward Indigenous communities?

Since their debut in 2002, DAM has emerged as the most influential and widely recognized Palestinian artists in the world. As pseudo-representatives of the state, conscripted activists, and at times unwilling advocates, DAM faces immense pressure to advance the nationalist causes of diverse constituencies. Balancing the needs and expectations of local, national, and international audiences has proven increasingly difficult, if not impossible. Rooted in local experience, evolving as creative artists, and yet dependent on international patronage, DAM often struggles to negotiate the contested terrain of Palestinian activism, leaving audiences wanting (expecting) more.[5] Since 2002, I have worked closely with DAM in the context of ongoing ethnographic fieldwork among Palestinian artists and activists. In that time, I have watched the group build an audience and market for Palestinian hip-hop, emerging as the most important Palestinian musicians of the twenty-first century (McDonald 2010, 2013a, and 2013b). Here, I argue that while shouldering this incredible responsibility, DAM has nevertheless persisted in developing a new, and potentially more effective, form of activism rooted in creative self-expression, local experience, self-critique, and collective vulnerability. By tracing DAM's long history of political engagement, I examine the discourses that determine "acceptable" forms of activism among competing audiences, and further demonstrate how the field of popular culture serves to shape the potential impact of, and audience for, activist intervention. Finally, I conclude this chapter by highlighting how DAM front man, Tamer Nafar, has attempted to disrupt the compassionate gaze of international audiences, respond to colonial logics of elimination, and carve out autonomous spaces for self-reflection and radical vulnerability.

"CULTURALIZING" VIOLENCE AGAINST WOMEN

Abu-Lughod and Mikdashi drew much of their critique from the ongoing movement among international policy brokers to reframe gendered violence using simplistic and essentialized understandings of "tradition" and "culture." In her work on transnational advocacy networks Celeste Montoya notes that since 2004 international policy has dramatically shifted from global action against gendered violence toward more narrow terms focused on "cultural" forms of violence such as "honor killings" and "female genital mutilation." According to Montoya, this reframing is "rooted in and reinforces xenophobic and racist discourses" (Montoya 2017). The "culturalization" of violence, she argues, serves only to justify the marginalization of vulnerable groups, by situating third-world women as perennial victims of "barbaric others."

Montoya's 2013 book further demonstrates that international policy makers' efforts to "culturalize" violence have dangerous consequences for the communities they claim to protect. According to her research, international efforts to address so-called honor crimes do not result in increased safety of women. Rather, such efforts serve only to reinforce colonialist assumptions that gendered violence is a kind of third-world cultural pathology. When the violence of the other is pathologized, Montoya writes, we justify their othering while excusing and normalizing gendered violence in the West. If international aid agencies are sincerely interested in addressing gendered violence in a meaningful way, Montoya argues, then their efforts should focus on the myriad ways in which gendered violence is experienced globally in concert with other forms of oppression. To focus on a single axis of gender oppression leaves the movement vulnerable to co-optation and further undermines the potential solidarity work necessary to establish and sustain a strong international movement (Montoya 2013).

Approximately one month after Abu Lughod and Mikdashi published their critique, DAM responded. Pushing back against the insinuation that they were politically and intellectually naive, the rappers explained: "This song is one chapter of many in a compilation. Each piece offers a portion of what DAM addresses. We should not have to mention the occupation in every song to prove our political legitimacy" (Nafar, Nafar, and Jrery 2012). This issue is key. Since its formation DAM has skillfully negotiated a political terrain that demands Palestinian artists only speak in relation to Israeli state violence. As such, their early work focused on documenting the experiences of Palestinians living under occupation and as a targeted minority population in Israel. Speaking out against other forces of oppression seemingly betrayed the demands of international audiences singularly focused on ending the occupation. Abu-Lughod and Mikdashi's expectation—that the group focus its efforts solely on "structural violence" (i.e., Israeli oppression)—is problematic in several ways. First, it presumes that gendered violence is not structural. Second, it reveals the conflicted and paradoxical terrain Palestinian artists must navigate as they seek international performance opportunities (Kanaaneh 2013, 4–8). And third, it essentializes Palestinians as the suffering objects of Israeli oppression and international intervention (Faulkner 2014).

But for DAM this song was about matters of local concern. Their infamous hometown, Lyd/Ramleh, claims one of the highest rates of murdered women in the Middle East.[6] DAM continues:

> "If I Could Go Back in Time" is a testimony to the women whose families murdered them over the last few years in Lyd, *where we live*. These deaths do not include the countless women who are subject to abuse and depression in their homes. This issue is not confined to Israeli occupation. We see Arab women being killed over the so-called "honor of the family" in Jordan, Morocco, Egypt, and many other places. There are no Israeli tanks over there. Domestic violence against women happens in all societies and we, as Arab men and women, are fighting against it in our own way....
>
> There is nothing politically problematic with a 3½ minute track that focuses on violence against women *in our community*. In fact, we believe this focus to be a crucial part of our broader political project. Fighting the occupation and fighting sexism and patriarchy is, for DAM, one fight....
>
> We have a strategy that we are implementing. We see the risks in singing about Arab social and political issues. DAM is addressing an Arab audience in Arabic. We can speak to *our own communities* without being worried about how others will abuse it. (Nafar, Nafar, and Jrery 2012, emphasis added)

These comments pose several important questions: To whom are DAM responsible in their activist work? And in times of crisis, what are the aesthetic, political, and cultural lines that delineate "acceptable" forms of activism among various stakeholders? For while Abu-Lughod and Mikdashi were rightfully concerned about the optics of this song among international audiences, they nevertheless failed to take into account its potential impact within and among the communities for whom it was intended. Rapping about "honor crimes," DAM attempts to make a critical intervention into the politicized landscape of *Palestinian* life. Bringing such a profoundly sensitive topic to light inevitably risks international co-optation and stigma, but, and perhaps more importantly, for its intended audiences it creates essential spaces for intimate dialogue. Abu-Lughod and Mikdashi's critique seemingly emerges from their (privileged) position as international scholars working for Palestinian self-determination. In this instance, it appears they wrongly assumed that DAM would be performing in the service of their interests alone.

Citing the 2011–12 revolutions taking place throughout the Arab world, DAM continues:

> This is precisely the moment when we should dispense with concerns over how we may be read (particularly by the West). Propaganda will exploit any issue it deems fit, this does not mean we should turn a blind eye. Arabs are

standing up and demanding a change from within. We see, "If I Could Go Back in Time," as one effort of many in these momentous times....

We are part of a new artistic movement in Palestine that is secure enough to take on the occupation and domestic violence, racism and sexism. We will not shy away from engaging our society's taboos. We believe we can, and we must, tackle these issues with openness, bravery, and honesty. (Nafar, Nafar, and Jrery 2012)

With "If I Could Go Back in Time" DAM seeks to join a post-2011 artistic movement founded on a new kind of antioppression politics: one in which the violence of the occupation is but one of many sites of potential intervention. This is an artistic movement secure enough in its message to look inward, to confront social taboos regardless of potential consequence. On another level, this episode has inadvertently revealed the contested (and highly problematic) terrain of Palestinian activism and the compassionate gaze of international scholars. Inasmuch as Abu-Lughod and Mikdashi criticized DAM for not adhering to the implicit demands of antioccupation rhetoric, with "If I Could Go Back in Time" DAM may have stumbled on a new (and perhaps more effective) form of political activism based in self-critique and collective vulnerability. DAM's refusal to conform to conventional models of antioccupation protest songs has hence created spaces for radical self-representation. This move reimagines popular culture as an infrastructural means to develop new solidarities and new pathways for connection within and beyond the nation-state and further disrupts the compassionate gaze of international scholars and audiences (Karkabi 2013).

JUNCTION 48

With the recent release of the award-winning feature film *Junction 48* (dir. Udi Aloni, 2016), DAM front man, Tamer Nafar, has revived the discussion of gendered violence, popular culture, and Palestinian activism. Working with Israeli Jewish director Udi Aloni, Nafar cowrote (with Oren Moverman) and starred in this semiautobiographical film, telling the story of Kareem (Tamer Nafar), an aspiring Palestinian rap artist trying desperately to break into the Tel Aviv hip-hop scene. Through a coming-of-age romance between Kareem and Manar (Samar Qupti), the film depicts the struggles of a new generation caught between multiple worlds: Palestinian citizens of Israel negotiating the colonial politics of erasure as well as the demands of Arab nationalism and Islamic patriarchy. As Kareem attempts to navigate the political obstacles of the Israeli music scene, he is confronted with a series of crises. His friends are targeted by street violence and police harassment. His girlfriend's cousins have forbidden her to date. His friend's family home is targeted for demolition. And after a family tragedy, his mother begins working as an Indigenous healer. Each of these moments presents Kareem with an existential crisis, wherein he must redefine himself in relation to his surroundings. In the process Kareem undergoes a profound transformation.

As the title of the film suggests, Kareem and his cohort live at the junction of competing social, political, and cultural discourses. Kareem's struggles to balance his career ambitions with his loyalty to his Palestinian community, and to reconcile his secular cosmopolitan lifestyle with Indigenous customs and beliefs, reflect many of the themes Nafar has been rapping about for years. However, inasmuch as the film focuses on the structural violence of the state, it also addresses forces of oppression *within* Palestinian society as well. Much like "If I Could Go Back in Time," *Junction 48* explores intersectional experiences of oppression endemic to Palestinian life.

While the primary conflict pivots on the protagonists' efforts to challenge the impending demolition of a friend's family home, the majority of character development occurs in the story of Kareem and Manar's budding relationship. Coming from two different cultural and economic backgrounds, Kareem and Manar find common ground in music. As their relationship develops, it becomes increasingly difficult to hide their love from Manar's family, who have forbidden her from dating. When news of an upcoming hip-hop concert leaks, Manar's male relatives threaten violence if she performs publicly on stage. Fearing femicide, Kareem forbids Manar from performing with him. In the aftermath Kareem realizes that his response, while well intentioned, exhibits a similar form of patriarchy, denying Manar the agency to decide for herself how to proceed. Ultimately, Kareem yields, welcoming Manar to perform with him on stage. The choice is hers. The film then ends without resolution: Manar, dressed for the performance, staring out her bedroom window deciding whether to risk going out, while her cousins remain staked-out in front of her family home.

THE FEMININE *NAKBA*

As if responding to Abu-Lughod and Mikdashi's initial charge of superficial engagement with intrafamily femicide, Nafar delves more deeply into the dynamics of religious patriarchy and gendered violence in the screenplay. The storyline is more nuanced, presenting multiple subject positions and experiences. While certainly manipulated for dramatic effect, perhaps to the point of cliché, the threat of femicide presents opportunities for character development, dialogue, and engagement. Once the initial threats are made, we witness the responses of various characters: male and female, religious and secular, old and young. These responses are complex, eschewing simplistic interpretations of good and bad, right and wrong. And in its final resolution, the viewer is left with a more textured understanding of how, and under what circumstances, femicide might occur as well as the various means through which individuals might collaborate in response. Reflecting on his motivations for writing the script Tamer Nafar stated: "The film was an abstract way of showing that there is also a feminine *nakba* [catastrophe].[7] Because other than us being oppressed, me, as a man. I am an oppressor as well. . . . It was me trying to show, to take responsibility for the things that I do wrong as a man" (Barrows-Freidman 2017). During one of our interviews I asked Tamer Nafar to clarify this point:

> So, in a way it is criticizing my own self. My own living. It is about feminism in a way. But because somehow we think that chauvinism lies only in religious people, like it is an Arabic [*sic*] thing. And it is not. I really wanted to make it clear that it is a *male thing. It's not an Arab thing*. Don't tell me that it is an Arab thing. *It is a man thing*. Like yes, we kill on the honor of the family, and in Egypt they almost raped women in the square [Tahrir]. In India they rape women. In the US they have pornography. In eastern Europe they have women trafficking. So, don't lay it on me. *It's not bad Arabs. It is bad men*[8] [emphasis added].

Kareem's relationship with Manar presents several opportunities to confront the toxic masculinity alluded to in these comments. As the threat of femicide compels each of the main characters to confront their positionality to gendered violence, in its resolution, the film, eschews culturalizing such violence as merely the result of tradition. Palestinians are represented on all sides of the discussion, each with their own motivations, biases, blind spots, and worldviews. And while no solution is offered, the audience nevertheless bears witness to an intimate encounter of immediate and local concern: families, friends, and loved ones each trying to understand one another under threat of violence.

"IF ONLY"

Kareem's ongoing transformation occurs most poignantly in the performance of the film's signature track, "If Only" [*ya rait*]. Reflecting on the violence of his upbringing, the pressures and obligations of Palestinian resistance, and the conventional masculine imperatives of hip-hop, Kareem pens a love song to Manar, documenting his ultimate desire for a new way of being in the world.

> If only I could write you a song full of clichés, but it's the one thing I can't do. I want to imagine us kissing in the rain, but I hate the rain. It reminds me of our leaking roof.
> I hide my love songs in the drawer, I'll return to them after my problems are solved. Now I'm soaking wet at your doorstep, pull me out of these streets. Cover me with your clothes, I'm afraid to be weak in front of you.
> Exorcise the demon of poverty out of me; the demon of oppression; the feeling that there is no tomorrow. Exorcise my demon of drugs; the loans to the banks. And hug me like there is no tomorrow.
> I write against the siege on Gaza, against those who brought us darkness. I write for the camps, and meanwhile the love song is a refugee in my drawer. I am a refugee on your doorstep. Remind me that oppression is a border, not a need. Take off my clothes, I am ready to stand naked and weak in front of you.
> Create the demon of wisdom in me; the demon of trust. So I won't fear you, nor for you. Create the demon of passion in me; the demon of revolution. I will fight for both freedom and love.

"If Only" stands in stark departure from the hypermasculine songs previously presented in the film. Melodic, slow, deliberate, tender, Kareem's transformation occurs musically. Rather than spitting rhymes for angry effect, Kareem sings his desire to be free from Palestinian resistance. He seeks to be free from politics, from poverty, from drugs, from conventional masculine imperatives. He seeks the privilege of being nonpolitical, to sing a love song full of clichés. But ultimately, Kareem seeks the *privilege of vulnerability*, to stand naked, without fear of, or for, his beloved.

In one of our interviews Tamer Nafar explained his approach to cowriting this song:

> I am in love with this melody. Because the character in the movie is all about rap, sound, effects, but this last song [is] because of the emotion, because the character breaks a lot of inside borders in his spirit. He transforms. He breaks borders and becomes something else. Even musically he is different. Musically he is something more.
>   That's what the song is basically saying. I wish I could write you love songs full of clichés . . . I want to demolish one wall [the Israeli "Separation Wall"], but at the same time, I have built a wall between us. This is the whole point of the song. In my generation. Because sometimes we can do demonstrations against the "Separation Wall," and we can live separated. Man alone and women alone. I wish I could write you a love song full of clichés, but somehow, *I can't write anything but politics*. Somehow, I am very good at

describing the political situation, but when it comes to a love song I find my own borders. I create my own borders.⁹

It was at this point in the conversation that Tamer pivoted toward reimagining masculinity, hip-hop, and the obligations he feels as a Palestinian activist:

> That is why I am writing against honor that was written by men. Because men, we define honor. I am writing against the siege over Gaza, and against those who are stealing the lights and electricity. I'm writing for refugees, and I'm writing against the dictators living in their big castles. Remind me that politics is something that we need to fight, but it is not something that we need to write. I need to fight it, I don't need to write it.
>   This is just an example of the process he [Kareem] is going through. And for me [Tamer] . . . as a rapper to say that I'm willing to stand and be weak in front of you, I think there is an emotional process that I [Tamer] have been through. And that is why I am in love with this song. Because above politics, above society, [for men] *it is still a weakness to show weakness.*
>   And [this] is something that hip-hop has been pushing against for a long time. How do we maintain this masculinity without all of the bad things that come along with it? In this song I am trying to step outside of that [hypermasculine] tradition, and develop a new kind of hip-hop.¹⁰

It is this profound transformation of conventional understandings of hip-hop, masculinity, and Palestinian activism that I seek to amplify. Tamer Nafar's desire for freedom is not only directed against a pervasive colonial enterprise but also against a discourse that envisions resistance as inherently masculine (Butler 2016). So, under what conditions might we imagine Tamer Nafar's call for radical self-critique and vulnerability, his "willingness to stand and be weak in front of you," as an effective mobilizing force in the drive for Palestinian self-determination? In what ways might vulnerability advance emancipatory goals? And how might such a move compel a new, and much-needed, decoupling of masculinity and resistance in Palestine?

ETHNOMUSICOLOGY, SOCIAL JUSTICE, AND THE COMPASSIONATE GAZE

Tamer Nafar's attempts to humanize Palestinian experiences, to inhabit new (non)political spaces, and to rewrite the codes of normative masculinity each occur within an environment wherein Palestinian lifeways are strategically erased from public view. To wit, Patrick Wolfe has effectively argued that the Israeli state (as a settler-colony) is founded on a "logic of elimination," whereby

Indigenous bodies/histories/presence must be eliminated in the act of constructing a new colonial society (Wolfe 2006, 389). In *Junction 48*'s climactic scene where a friend's family home is demolished to build a National Museum of Co-Existence, we witness Wolfe's "logic of elimination" in practice. The Israeli narrative of progressive "coexistence" is ironically premised on the erasure of the Indigenous bodies with whom it claims to coexist. Homes are demolished because, according to state discourse (maps, laws, permits), they were never *really* there in the first place. Their inhabitants' resulting displacement similarly goes unseen in that their erasure only confirms and sustains the "logic of elimination" of which the demolition is an example.

As an act of countervisibility, *Junction 48* facilitates seeing and hearing Palestinians beyond the "logic of elimination." Insofar as Kareem and his cohort hold a very public music performance on top of his friend's demolished home to raise awareness of Israeli state violence, the film itself seeks to mobilize Palestinians as visible, legible, knowable subjects. In each of these acts of intervention the artists seek to bridge the visible and the invisible, the familiar and the unfamiliar. Not unlike the long history of Palestinian national cinema, *Junction 48* deploys counternarrative and countervisibility in the service of emancipatory goals (Dabashi 2006; Gertz and Khleifi 2008).

Junction 48 tells the story of contemporary Israeli life from the perspective of its unintelligible Others. As a corrective to the "logics of elimination," *Junction 48* thus presents significant opportunities for intervention into the regimes of power that foreclose appearance. Narrative from within, telling the story of the dominant from the perspective of the precarious, compels a reassessment of normative codes of difference and the resulting experience of precarity. Tamer Nafar hints at this approach when discussing *Junction 48*'s binational cast and crew. "Collaboration in *Junction 48* can be a vehicle for reconciliation. Our movie is a solution. The solution is when the strong side, the privileged side, will be part of the storytelling of the oppressed side. When Jews and Palestinians work together to tell the story of the oppressed, that's where hope begins" (Mitnick 2017). These interventions create a possible world where the privileged are solicited to see the colonized in a new light, and through that interaction, become what Wendy Hesford describes as "ethical witnesses" (2011, 192).

DAM's rise to international acclaim can be attributed to several factors, most notably, their unique ability to document Palestinian hardship in a format (hip-hop) familiar to, and compatible with, cosmopolitan aesthetics (McDonald 2013b). Drawing from an established musical lexicon of racial dispossession and urban empowerment, hip-hop proved to be a powerful means to engage international audiences and gain acknowledgment of their calls for self-determination. Not only was their music compatible with cosmopolitan tastes, but their documentarian approach conformed to standard representational logics that position Palestinian suffering as an object for international consumption.

The representational logic of documentary media is premised on presenting a suffering victim before the "compassionate gaze" of outside audiences. Suffering is required, demanded, not only to legitimize the effort, but also to reinforce and sustain the privilege of the audience. Not unlike the culturalization of violence discussed previously, the compassionate gaze works alongside the colonial project by essentializing Palestinians as victims, disempowering their political agency, and absolving the first world of its responsibility to address structural violence in the colonial encounter. Playing to the compassionate gaze of international audiences proved incredibly lucrative for DAM in its early years, supporting the group with tour dates abroad when local performance opportunities had disappeared. But at the same time, DAM's documentarian approach created an expectation, a demand, that they conform to standard perceptions of Palestinian identity: as angry victims, as the effects of Israeli state violence, and as the objects of humanitarian intervention.

DAM's shift to storytelling in their second studio album proved controversial for international audiences in that it actively disrupted this documentarian imperative. No longer was the group reporting on Israeli state violence. Rather, DAM began to *create* new scenarios, new characters, and new worlds of interaction and engagement drawn from local Palestinian experience. For those expecting DAM's familiar diatribes against the occupation, *Dabke on the Moon* was a betrayal of sorts, a kind of "selling out" for pop star acclaim. But for the group, it was a strategic tactic to evolve, to develop, and to reclaim the agency to define themselves.

While some criticized Tamer Nafar's move to acting as "selling out," he sees this move as part of a larger activist agenda, a "politics by other means."[11] For Nafar, acting in feature films, writing screenplays, and singing love songs are a means of political engagement in that these projects not only expand visibility, but, more importantly, diversify representational logics. As fiction, *Junction 48* adds an additional element of creativity and playfulness, such that Palestinians are not mere objects of Israeli violence but authors of their own experiences. These works are acts of countervisibility, to be sure, but more important, they serve to redefine the logics of Palestinian representation by reclaiming the agency to create (Faulkner 2014, 160). Tamer Nafar reiterates this point during one of our interviews:

> Author: It seems like you are being boxed in, like you have to [sing] every song about the occupation. And you are not allowed to tell stories, to develop yourself as an artist.

Nafar: No. Somehow "the West" is boxed in. If you look at my albums, my songs, my last song that reached 2 million views is about a car. It is about having fun in a car. Getting drunk and driving around in a car. That is the most popular song in Palestine. Would you cover that? No. You would go for "Who's the Terrorist?" Palestinians get drunk and enjoy it. But when you come from the outside, I mean, "the West," journalists [and academics]. Somehow, they want to *romanticize* us in a way. We are the beautiful ones, those handsome ones that fight the occupation. Like a *Palestinian Chuck Norris*. . . . And excuse me, we get drunk, we get jiggy, some of us pray, some of us are extremists, some of us are not. . . . That is what I am doing in my songs. I am playing my generation. So, it is *you guys* [international audiences, scholars] that come in search of protest songs. If protest songs don't exist, that means we don't exist. *If the occupation doesn't exist, that means we don't exist.* That is romanticizing. And as an artist I don't like that.

After the demonstrations we [Palestinians] go home, we pay bills. There is life. What the Israeli occupation is trying to do is *dehumanize us and disconnect us from the world*. It is important for me to stand up and say, "Fuck the occupation. I want to be part of the world." That is why it is important for me to show that we also die from car accidents. We also die from cancer. We find love. . . . I cannot run away from the spices of my culture, and the politics in my society[12] [emphasis added].

There is a fundamental lesson here that needs to be learned by ethnomusicologists seeking to adopt a justice-oriented stance in their work. The pervasive image of the Palestinian victim is partly the result of efforts to solicit international support for basic human rights. But the effect of this solicitation is not necessarily effective as the reiteration of these images naturalizes the condition. Even for those who are empathetic toward Palestinian self-determination, the perception of Palestinians (or Israelis) as victims does not encourage seeing (hearing) them as equals. Rather, they come to be defined by an absence, not only of basic human rights, but also of political agency (Faulkner 2014).

Because ethnomusicologists have effectively demonstrated the importance of expressive cultural practices in fashioning and sustaining political solidarities, they too often foreclose opportunities for humanizing and connecting in their bias toward explicitly political performance practices. We (ethnomusicologists) "are boxed in," so focused on conventional forms of political intervention that we fail to recognize and value the superficial, the mundane, the human ways of being Palestinian. If it were not for the occupation, if it were not for the dire humanitarian crisis, Palestinians would not exist in the ethnomusicological imagination. This form of romanticization limits our capacity for ethnographic engagement, disempowers Palestinians, and further advances colonial logics that valorize White (male) cisgendered voices while maintaining the inferiority of Indigenous communities.

If the "logic of elimination" is premised on foreclosing Palestinian appearance, then ethnomusicologists must seek opportunities to connect, document, and humanize Palestinians, as neither "freedom fighters" nor "helpless victims." We must seek out opportunities to see, hear, and know Indigenous communities beyond the colonial encounter. We must follow them home from the demonstrations, allow them the privilege of being nonpolitical, the privilege of vulnerability, and the space to be seen and heard on their own terms. Over the years in our many interviews and interactions, Tamer Nafar has challenged me to develop listening practices that extend beyond the compassionate gaze of international solidarity activists. His challenge requires adopting what Dylan Robinson terms "decolonial listening practices" while simultaneously attending to the intersectional positionalities inherent to scholarly research (2020, 37). For me, this work entails ceding control of the listening encounter, relinquishing the biased imperative to center my own scholarly agenda, and fully attending to the transformative politics of Palestinian sensory logics. The goal is to recognize, identify, and abandon the listening fixations of international audiences, and instead adopt a stance that remains "flexible, agile, and responsive to the intersectional layering of [Indigenous and settler] positionality" (Robinson 2020, 38). And finally, this challenge requires that we ask the difficult questions of ourselves: how did we come to be in a position of privilege relative to those being studied? It is simply not enough to critique the legal, economic, and social systems of oppression without engaging our complicity with the discourses that support them. My activist stance in support of Palestinian self-determination, for example, does not absolve me from fully recognizing and decentering my inherent privilege as the beneficiary of a centuries-long project of North American settler colonialism and White supremacy.

These acts are not mutually exclusive. By integrating Palestinians into the world, by humanizing mundane experiences, by revealing the intersectional ways of being Palestinian, and by acknowledging our participation in the colonial project, we implicitly stand against the occupation of Palestinian lives and the colonization of Palestinian lands. This is a different kind of activism, one in which political intervention is made through humanization, mutual recognition, radical self-critique, and collective vulnerability.

I argue that "If I Could Go Back in Time" and *Junction 48* pursue a different (and perhaps more effective) form of activism, fighting the occupation by humanizing Palestinian *difference*, revealing the troublesome messy intimacies of Palestinian life, and laying bare a politics of vulnerability that exposes Palestinians as neither righteous victims nor savage zealots. And while such efforts may be susceptible to co-optation, it is worth considering how such diverse representational strategies increase potential points of contact, countervisibility, and empathy among and between disparate audiences. If, as Tamer Nafar suggests, the Israeli occupation depends on dehumanizing and disconnecting Palestinians from the world, an effective response might be to humanize Palestinian lifeways through shared points of connection. Pop songs and feature films that honestly and sincerely document the intersectionality of Palestinian life would seemingly provide affective spaces for condemning the structural violence of the occupation by first connecting Palestinians to the world through mutual vulnerability, as people who "go home from the demonstrations," "who fall in love," "who die of cancer," "who get drunk." In both "If I Could Go Back in Time" and *Junction 48*, gendered violence against women becomes a means of connecting Palestinians to the global experience of religious patriarchy and toxic masculinity through situated experience, providing counternarrative and countervisibility to Palestinian difference and "the spices of Palestinian culture." Moreover, in reimagining conventional masculine imperatives (of hip-hop and resistance), "If I Could Go Back in Time" and *Junction 48* compel empathetic engagement across diverse ontological fields. These kinds of solicitations should not be dismissed as weakness but, rather, amplified as opportunities for building new solidarities outside and beyond the Israeli-Palestinian crisis. For Palestinians to exist (ontologically) outside of this crisis requires that they first be seen and heard as intelligible, familiar, fallible, complex subjects. Engaging in radical self-critique and tackling society's taboos with "openness, bravery, and honesty" would seem to be powerful means of accomplishing this task.

NOTES

1. Portions of this chapter have appeared previously in the *Journal of Popular Music Studies* 32 (1): 26–43.

2. Janne Louise Anderson. "Palestinian Rappers Spark Debate with New Album." *Al-Monitor*, April 23, 2013.

3. The song "al-ḥurīyya unta" [Freedom for my sister] was one of DAM's first to explicitly engage with the theme of violence against women.

4. The term *honor crime* is quoted directly from Abu-Lughod and Mikdashi's essay. The more accepted terms, *intrafamily femicide* or simply *femicide*, is used throughout this chapter following Shalhoub-Kevorkian and Daher-Nashif (2012).

5. Tamer Nafar, interview by author, Champaign, IL, March 9, 2017.

6. Shlomi Eldar, "How Activists Are Confronting Contract Killings of Israeli Arab Women," *Al-Monitor*, September 28, 2016; Yaniv Kubovich, "One Family Clan, 10 Murdered Women, and Only Two Convictions," *Haaretz*, October 28, 2014.

7. The term *nakba* refers to the "catastrophe" of 1948 that resulted in the expulsion of approximately one million Palestinians from their homes during the clashes that led to the establishment of the Israeli state.

8. Tamer Nafar, interview by author, Champaign, IL, March 9, 2017.

9. Tamer Nafar, interview by author, Champaign, IL, March 10, 2017.

10. Ibid.

11. Ibid.

12. Tamer Nafar, interview by author, Champaign, IL, March 9, 2017.

BIBLIOGRAPHY

Abu-Lughod, Lila, and Maya Mikdashi. 2012. "Tradition and the Anti-Politics Machine: DAM Seduced by the 'Honor Crime.'" *Al-Jadaliyya*, November 23, 2012.

Anderson, Janne Louise. 2013. "Palestinian Rappers Spark Debate with New Album." *Al-Monitor*, April 23, 2013.

Barrows-Friedman, Nora. 2017. "Rapping amid Palestine's Ruins." *The Electronic Intifada*, March 31, 2017.

Butler, Judith. 2016. "Rethinking Vulnerability and Resistance." In *Vulnerability in Resistance*, edited by Judith Butler, Zeynep Gambetti, and Leticia Sabsay, 1–35. Durham, NC: Duke University Press.

Dabashi, Hamid. 2006. *Dreams of a Nation: On Palestinian Cinema*. New York: Verso Press.

Faulkner, Simon. 2014. "On Israel/Palestine and the Politics of Visibility." In *Immigrant Protest: Politics, Aesthetics, and Everyday Dissent*, edited by Katarzyna Marciniak and Imogen Tyler, 147–68. New York: State University of New York Press.

Gertz, Nurith, and George Khleifi. 2008. *Palestinian Cinema: Landscape, Trauma and Memory*. Edinburgh: Edinburgh University Press.

Hesford, Wendy. 2011. *Spectacular Rhetorics: Human Rights Visions, Recognitions, Feminisms*. Durham, NC: Duke University Press.

Kanaaneh, Moslih. 2013. "Introduction: Do Palestinian Musicians Play Music of Politics?" In *Palestinian Music and Song: Expression and Resistance since 1900*, edited by Moslih Kanaaneh, Stig-Magnus Thorsen, Heather Bursheh, and David A. McDonald, 1–14. Bloomington: Indiana University Press.

Karkabi, Nadeem. 2013. "Staging Particular Difference: Politics of Space in the Palestinian Alternative Music Scene." *Middle East Journal of Culture and Communication* 6: 308–28.

———. 2017. "Electro-Dabke: Performing Cosmopolitan Nationalism and Borderless Humanity." *Public Culture* 30 (3): 173–96.

McDonald, David A. 2010. "Carrying Words Like Weapons: Hip Hop and the Poetics of Palestinian Identities in Israel." *Min-Ad: Israel Studies in Musicology* 7 (2): 116–30.

———. 2013a. "Imaginaries of Exile and Emergence in Israeli Jewish and Palestinian Hip-Hop." *Drama Review* 57 (3): 69–87.

———. 2013b. *My Voice Is My Weapon: Music, Nationalism, and the Poetics of Palestinian Resistance.* Durham, NC: Duke University Press.

Mitnick, Joshua. 2017. "Meet the Palestinian Hip-Hop Artist at the Center of Israel's Culture Wars." *Los Angeles Times,* January 11, 2017.

Montoya, Celeste. 2013. *From Global to Grassroots: The European Union, Transnational Advocacy, and Combating Violence against Women.* Oxford: Oxford University Press.

———. 2017. "Combating Gendered Violence in the Face of Right-Wing Populism." *OUPblog,* March 28, 2017.

Nafar, Tamer. 2017. "Interview with Tamer Nafar." Interview by Nora Barrows-Friedman. *Electronic Intifada Podcast,* March 31, 2017.

Nafar, Tamer, Suhell Nafar, and Mahmood Jrery. 2012. "DAM Responds: On Tradition and the Anti-Politics of the Machine." *Al-Jadaliyya,* December 26, 2012.

Nesheiwat, Christina. 2012. "DAM Explores the Unmapped in Their New Album 'Dabke on the Moon.'" *Al-Jadaliyya,* December 19, 2012.

Robinson, Dylan. 2020. *Hungry Listening: Resonant Theory for Indigenous Sound Studies.* Minneapolis: University of Minnesota Press.

Shalhoub-Kevorkian, Nadera. 2010. "Palestinian Women and the Politics of Invisibility: Towards a Feminist Methodology." *Peace Prints: South Asian Journal of Peace Building* 3 (1): 1–21.

Shalhoub-Kevorkian, Nadera, and Suhad Daher-Nashif. 2012. "The Politics of Killing Women in Colonized Contexts." *Al-Jadaliyya,* December 17, 2012.

Stein, Rebecca L., and Ted Swedenburg, eds. 2005. *Palestine, Israel, and the Politics of Popular Culture.* Durham, NC: Duke University Press.

Wolfe, Patrick. 2006. "Settler Colonialism and the Elimination of the Native." *Journal of Genocide Research* 8 (4): 387–409.

DISCOGRAPHY

DAM. 2006. *Ihda' [Dedication].* Red Circle Music (RCM). CD. Lyd, Israel.

———. 2012. *Dabke on the Moon.* Cooking Vinyl Limited. COOKCD 676. CD. Lyd, Israel.

VIDEOGRAPHY

Aloni, Udi, dir. 2016. *Junction 48*. Tel Aviv, Israel: Metro Communications. 95 min. DVD.

Halachmi, Anat, dir. 2003. *Channels of Rage*. Tel Aviv, Israel: Anat Halachmi Productions. 72 min. DVD.

Salloum, Jackie Reem, dir. 2009. *Slingshot Hip-hop*. Ramallah, Palestine: Fresh Booza Productions. 80 min. DVD.

PART III

COALITION BUILDING

ELEVEN

PROMOTING SOCIAL JUSTICE THROUGH IRISH TRADITIONAL MUSIC

A New Model for Applied Research

ALEXANDRIA CARRICO

INTRODUCTION

"That was brilliant, Gráinne!" I exclaimed.

Though she often stayed after our Thursday morning Irish traditional music (trad) workshops to play additional songs, this was the first time Gráinne Joyce had offered to sing, a departure from preferring to play bongo accompaniment while I sang.

"Thanks. I do love that song, 'Katie.' It's one of my favorite Mary Black songs," she said with a smile.

"You did a great job. Will you sing it for the rest of the group?" I inquired.

Since our ninth workshop, the members of the self-named Roselawn Rovers Return had taken to interspersing group songs with individual performances.

"I don't know about that now. I might if you sang it with me, like we did at the pub," she responded.

It was one week since our first community trad session at the Hurler's pub in Castletroy, and I noticed a marked change in all of the Rovers but particularly in Joyce. She had a new sense of confidence that seemed to be a direct result of performing in a community setting.

"So what did you think about the session?" I segued.

"It was brilliant," she responded. She paused before continuing, "And I kind of said, this kind of music is really good. I kind of feel this would actually bring my life back. . . . What I love, really love doing, is the music. And trying to get people to listen to me about things I want to do and sometimes I don't like being told what to do."

"Did you feel like people were listening to you at the session?" I asked.

"Yes, they were definitely listening to me," she replied.

Joyce's reflection provides important insight into the role that participatory genres such as Irish traditional music can play in not only affirming one's musical and social agency but also in establishing a sense of belonging within a community. The other musicians in the session were listening to Joyce, just as she was listening to them; together they were making music and creating social bonds. Such musical and social cohesion is a well-established attribute of Irish traditional music, a genre that is "first and foremost, a participatory and social practice" (Bernini 2016, 39). However, this feeling of belonging and self-actualization is especially important for Joyce and the other Rovers, all of whom are neurodivergent. Individuals like Joyce have brains that "function in ways that diverge significantly from the dominant societal standards of 'normal'" (Walker 2022), and thus are often marginalized within dominant neurotypical society. However, as demonstrated by Joyce's narrative, inclusive community gatherings such as trad sessions provide spaces to challenge and overturn negative stigma about people with disabilities.

While trad sessions can be performative and competitive spaces, most sessions are characterized by an inclusive ethos of group music making in which all people, regardless of age, musical background, or skill, are welcome to participate (Hast and Scott 2004). It was this community-based and participatory value system that gave rise to my hypothesis that trad sessions might be particularly suited to facilitating musical and social exchange between neurodivergent and neurotypical individuals. I found the session's seeming inclusiveness wanting, however. Though the community-based ethos of the session was conducive to neurodivergent musical engagement, few included these musicians. This absence of neurodivergent participation led to the creation of this project, which attempted to break down negative stereotypes about intellectual disability by bringing neurodivergent and neurotypical musicians together through Irish traditional music sessions in Limerick, Ireland.

To my knowledge, this project was the first of its kind to provide an opportunity for neurodivergent adults (specifically people with intellectual disabilities) to engage with musicians from the community through Irish traditional music in Ireland. This research united my background as a professional trad singer and *bodhrán* (Irish frame drum) player with my research on neurodiversity. This work is guided by the neurodiversity paradigm, an approach that views neurodiversity as "a natural and valuable form of human diversity" (Walker 2022). Neurodivergent individuals fall outside the neurotypical majority, making them part of a minority identity category similar to that of race, ethnicity, gender, and sexuality. Such understanding of neurodiversity as a minority identity was central to this project and provided a lens for viewing neurodiversity as an important expression of humanity, as in the social model of disability, rather than through medicalized notions of deficit and disorder (Garland-Thomson 1997, 5; Shakespeare 2013, 215). In addition to drawing on theoretical frameworks and methodologies from Irish traditional music studies and disability studies, this newly created, activist-oriented project is centered in the field of applied ethnomusicology.

According to applied ethnomusicologist Svanibor Pettan, applied projects are "guided by principles of social responsibility, which extends the usual academic goal of broadening and deepening knowledge and understanding toward solving concrete problems and toward working both inside and beyond typical academic contexts" (Pettan, quoted in Harrison 2012, 507). This reflects the changing landscape of the field, in which ethnomusicologists have increasingly begun to engage in on-the-ground musical interventions. These shifts necessitate the creation of new models for conducting ethnomusicological fieldwork that allow scholars to address the needs of our research communities. In this chapter, I propose that this newly created project functions as a model for uniting disability activism with applied research.

The project took place over the course of twenty-two weeks and was divided into two phases. I begin by describing the first phase, which involved facilitating weekly Irish traditional music workshops governed by the principles of informal learning for the Roselawn Rovers Return, a group of twelve neurodivergent adults between the ages of twenty-two and thirty-five. These workshops paralleled my involvement in Cruinniú, a preexisting group of approximately forty seemingly neurotypical trad musicians from the Limerick community. I then examine the second phase of the project, during which I utilized my membership in these groups to bring the two together in the context of the session. Through ethnographic interviews with my collaborators, I share their perceptions of the successes and limitations of this program. Finally, I analyze the ways in which this activist-oriented project both conforms to and expands the boundaries of applied ethnomusicology by placing the researcher at the locus of social change in order to connect two disparate communities.

PHASE I: WORKSHOPS WITH THE ROVERS

For phase one of the project, I collaborated with Ireland's largest nonprofit organization dedicated to serving people with intellectual disabilities, known as the Brothers of Charity, in order to design trad workshops for the neurodivergent participants. The primary purpose of these workshops was, first, to learn pieces to perform at the sessions and, second, to create a musical space in which my collaborators could express their neurodivergent identities without pressure to conform to neurotypical expectations of musical excellence, form a community based on shared music practices, and exercise their agency through musical and social decision-making. Above all, these workshops were designed to provide a safe and welcoming space for the participants to musically and socially express themselves. The Rovers consisted of twelve members who consistently attended weekly workshops: Annie Conway, Diarmuid Cowhey, Jane Hartley, Gráinne Joyce, Stephen Kennedy, Emma McMahon, David McMan, Fiona O'Connor, Isobel O'Sullivan, Eliza Pentony, Emily Redden, and Ríona Ryan. All the participants were neurodivergent and each had multifaceted strengths and challenges, unique personalities, and distinctive musical preferences that contributed to the overall group dynamic. Of these participants, only a few had formal musical training, and none of the Rovers read music. Thus, it was necessary to implement accommodations to make the workshops fun and accessible. We accomplished this by implementing informal learning (IL) practices.

According to Thomas Johnston, Irish traditional musician and trad pedagogy specialist, informal learning occurs outside of traditional educational environments and is characterized by a focus on learning by ear; student autonomy; peer-to-peer learning rather a "teacher-student" dynamic; and the integration of improvisation, listening, and composing with personal creativity (2013, 66). In addition to meeting the practical needs of our group, the IL model reflected many goals of the disability rights movement and thus fulfilled the philosophical aspirations of this project—namely, furthering social justice through community music making. Logistically, these informal practices emerged through a series of accommodations, which ensured the success of my collaborators and provided a space for them to exercise their agency. The first accommodation related to aural knowledge acquisition. We always began by listening to a recording or live demonstration (which I performed). I often provided lyric sheets for the Rovers, which we reviewed line-by-line when initially learning a song. We then employed a call-and-response pattern, during which I sang a line that the group repeated back to me. Though adaptive by Western classical standards, this aural learning was consistent with Irish traditional music pedagogy and thus fit the ethos of the genre as well as the needs of the participants.

The second accommodation involved modifying our definition of what constitutes Irish traditional music. In the context of sessions, trad is most often associated with tunes played on melody instruments, such as whistle, accordion, and fiddle, all of which require years of practice to gain proficiency. However, voice and percussion are essential facets of the genre and are more accessible in terms of teaching, learning, and affordability. Rather than attempting to teach twelve people to play melody instruments, I chose to make the workshops voice and percussion-based. This not only aligned with my own area of expertise as a vocalist and bodhrán player but also provided the group with immediate access to successful participation in the workshops. This accommodation also allowed us to challenge traditional standards of what constitutes musical excellence. The Roselawn Day Center had a small collection of auxiliary percussion instruments housed in a large orange bucket that included triangles, maracas, hand drums, tambourines, and bongos. Between songs, the participants would switch instruments and explore various sounds, which at times resulted in unique timbral creations through unorthodox playing techniques.

Perhaps the most notable instance of this experimentation occurred during one workshop when, after handing out all the instruments, Jane Hartley was left with just the bucket and a spare triangle beater. Hartley served as the "quiet organizer" of the group by passing out instruments, tidying up after sessions, and reminding people of upcoming events. Though she had developed a liking for the bongos, she knew that Fiona O'Connor, who was nonspeaking by choice and generally refrained from outward participation in the workshops, was particularly drawn to them. Thus, Hartley decided to play the bucket instead. However, it was the manner in which she played that caught my attention. When we started singing "Tell Me Ma," Hartley placed the bucket on the table and began playing the bottom with her hand. She continued to experiment with the timbral palate of the bucket through myriad playing techniques. At times it functioned like a *djembe* (West African drum) as she played it upright with open palms. In other instances, she held it like a bodhrán, turning it sideways and sticking her hand inside while striking the outside with the triangle beater. For Hartley, this was a way to express her musical creativity and inquisitive personality while contributing to the multilayered musical texture of the group.

In addition to instrumental experimentation, the participants also improvised during group songs by inserting extra choruses or interludes, interjecting lyrically relevant commentary, and making jokes. Rather than striving to perform a song the same way every time, the group adopted a flexible performance style. This approach provided a space for individuals to express themselves within the group context. Furthermore, it allowed them to voice their own ideas of what constitutes musical excellence, often favoring demonstrations of emotional engagement and performativity over tonal and rhythmic accuracy. This highlights the distinction between music-making and *musicking*, a phenomenon defined by Christopher Small as "taking part, in any capacity, in a musical performance, whether by performing, by listening, by rehearsing, or practicing, by providing material for performance (what is called composing), or by dancing." (1998, 9). A primary example of this occurred as we began learning the song "Fall Down Billy O'Shea."

This morbidly lighthearted song is about a man who drunkenly falls asleep on the Rogerson's Quay in Dublin and wakes to find that he has been conscripted onto a ship. Unfortunately, he does not know how to sail and dies after falling from the topmast yard. The song's narrative is broken up by the phrases "fall down me Billy" and "fall down Billy O'Shea," which occur every other line. These repetitive stock phrases provided an ideal opportunity to incorporate brief call-and-response solos, in which one person sings the line of a verse and the group responds with "fall down me Billy" or "fall down Billy O'Shea."

Verse 6
Cowhey: We wrapped him up in the canvas sail
All: Fall down me Billy
Cowhey: And we lowered him gently over the rail
All: Fall down Billy O'Shea

In addition to being fun, upbeat, and lyrically accessible, the alternation between solo voice and group singing provided an opportunity for a flexible tempo. This was particularly important for some of the soloists, who required additional help remembering phrases. For instance, Diarmuid Cowhey, the resident "jokester" of the group, was incredibly expressive when singing his verse but had trouble recalling the order of the words. Therefore, I would stage whisper a line to him and he would repeat it immediately afterward. This lyric prompting became an intentionally comical part of the song as Cowhey disrupted the driving tempo in order to take his time acting out the phrase "We wrapped him up in the canvas sail . . . and lowered him gently over the rail." This quickly became a highlight for the rest of the group, who looked to Cowhey expectantly as he delivered his verses with gusto, each time adding greater drama to his gestures.

These performative instances within the group numbers aided us in forming what Thomas Turino calls a "cultural cohort," or "social grouping[s] that form along the lines of specific constellations of shared habit based in similarities of *parts* of the self." (2008, 111). While our shared habit of learning trad allowed us to create a community, it was essential to solidify this cohort by establishing equity among members of the group. Though I technically served as the project organizer/music instructor, I attempted to distance myself from the role of "teacher" over time. Utilizing the IL principle of peer-to-peer learning, I encouraged the Rovers to take turns leading warm ups and songs, choose the repertoire they wanted to sing, and experiment on a variety of instruments. This helped destabilize learning hierarchies and allowed me to transition from the role of "leader" to that of facilitator. By empowering my collaborators to make decisions, the group took ownership of the workshops and became more outspoken about demonstrating their progress.

This became evident during the eighth workshop when Isobel O' Sullivan suggested that the group perform "Fall Down Billy O'Shea" for the Roselawn staff. Though initially hesitant, the Rovers were proud of sharing what they had learned, as evidenced by Isobel pumping her fist in a triumphant gesture and exclaiming, "Yes!" while Annie Conway chimed in, "We did it!," and David McMan said, "Let's do this every week!" Thus, each week we concluded our workshops by performing for the Roselawn staff members. These presentations allowed the group to further build their confidence through brief, informal performances. Most significantly, these mini-concerts were group directed and initiated by my collaborators. This is yet another example of how the Rovers exercised their agency as a group. Ultimately, they decided what repertoire we would learn and perform, how the workshops would be structured, and how the songs should be arranged (see fig. 11.1). Through the tenets of informal learning we created an accessible, (relatively) egalitarian, and collaborative community that promoted individual and group decision-making.

Concurrent with these workshops, I joined the trad group Cruinniú and was quickly embraced as part of their community. While some members had played trad their entire lives, others were coming to the genre for the first time. This range in skill affected the group culture, which was welcoming and laid-back. Eamonn O'Connor, banjo player and ten-year member of Cruinniú, commented on this supportive ethos stating, "People kind of come in and out and there's no pressure. You can sit down and if you can only play a few notes, no one is going to give out to you. You know, people might not be able to play every tune, but they're enjoying listening to it and they are learning a little bit each week." As O'Connor demonstrates, the primary value of Cruinniú is not a product of the music making itself but rather the process of listening, learning, and joining together in musical fellowship. It became clear that the inclusive ethos of Cruinniú closely aligned with that of the Rovers. Thus, Cruinniú seemed an ideal group to recruit as neurotypical participants in the project. The members took an eager interest in my research and when I informed them that the Rovers would be hosting sessions, many people enthusiastically agreed to participate.

Fig. 11.1. Roselawn Rovers Return performing during a workshop, December 14, 2017. Photograph by author.

PHASE II: THE COLLABORATIVE SESSIONS

Phase II of this project was hosted at the Hurler's pub in Castletroy. These collaborative sessions between the Rovers and Cruinniú consisted of instrumental tunes, Irish traditional songs, and great *craic*: communal exchange typified by humor, storytelling, and social intimacy that is characteristic of sessions (Hast and Scott 2004). Musically, most sessions primarily feature instrumental tunes interspersed with the occasional song; however, our sessions were fairly song heavy. While originally I intended for Cruinniú to lead instrumental tunes and the Rovers to take charge of songs, over the course of each session these roles organically merged as we joined together in music and camaraderie.

The first session began with a jig set led by John Fitzgerald of Cruinniú. The rest of Cruinniú was quick to join, accompanied by The Rovers, who provided a variety of percussive textures to the melodic set in the form of bongos, shakers, hand drums, bucket, and bodhrán. Following this set, we took a customary pause to chat. Conversation was initially tentative but relaxed as we began singing familiar songs from "Óró, sé do bheatha 'bhaile," a rousing rebel song, to "How Much Is That Doggy in the Window?" Throughout the evening, participants from Cruinniú and the Rovers continued to offer impromptu suggestions for songs and tunes. Though I was technically the session "leader," the participants took control, only occasionally looking to me to start a song or set.

The collaborative ethos of the session reached its height when the Rovers proposed we teach the rest of the group "Fall Down Billy O'Shea." Unfortunately, several of the Rovers who sang solo verses were unable to attend. To my utter amazement, both Gráinne Joyce and Jane Hartley, who up until that point had never sung during group songs, volunteered to sing solos. After briefly teaching Cruinniú the chorus, we launched into the song. As expected, the Cruinniú members caught on quickly. When we reached Joyce's verse she called out "Well, we are no sailors Captain dear" to which we all responded, "Fall down me Billy!" Then squinting down at the lyric sheet continued, "And a bit unhappy to . . . what's that now . . . ?"

"To reef," I said.

"Ah! To REEF or steer. That's an odd one," she responded.

Everyone laughed while singing, "Fall down Billy O'Shea!"

We sang through the chorus and then paused again, reaching Hartley's verse. Hartley, who is very soft-spoken, got everyone's attention by tapping loudly on the orange bucket with her triangle beater. In a *sprechstimme* style, she yelled, "He sent him up to the topmast yard!" The rest of the group leaned in closer, straining to hear Hartley's voice over the noise coming from the main bar. She took a deep breath and using the triangle beater to articulate each word, she shouted, "When he hit the deck he took it too hard!"

In response to this painful plot twist, the group sang, "Ouch! Fall down Billy O'Shea!"

We concluded the song with three repetitions of the chorus before finishing with a loud "Hey!"

As everyone applauded, Bob Richardson of Cruinniú looked at Hartley and cheered her by thrusting his fist into the air while exclaiming, "Yeah!" Grinning, Hartley mirrored his movements. She then turned to Fiona O'Connor, who rarely played during workshops but had been engrossed with the bongos during the song, and clapped for her. O'Connor smiled.

I turned to Joyce and said, "That was great! You've never sung in our workshops."

"I do like to sing in the pub now," beamed Joyce.

Before beginning the next set, we paused to engage in conversation, during which many Cruinniú members complimented the soloists saying, "Well done!"

"I've never heard that one before. I'll have to remember that now," said Richardson.

This performance of "Fall Down Billy O'Shea" was significant for several reasons. Firstly, several of the Rovers who had previously abstained from solos during workshops volunteered to perform. This reflected the confidence they felt in exercising their agency in this musical setting. Moreover, their willingness to demonstrate vulnerability through impromptu singing indicated a sense of trust in the community. When asked about her session experience Joyce commented, "The session in the Hurlers was very good. It was my favorite thing I could do. It was my first time doing it with the whole group in the pub and I really enjoyed the people we had. They were brilliant." Secondly, the Rovers stepped into the role of musical experts by teaching the rest of the group a new song. Using the same principles of peer-to-peer and aural learning employed in the workshops, the Rovers solidified their identities as fellow musicians. This allowed us to transition from two separate groups of musicians into a cohesive musical community united by the communal expression of Irish musical heritage. Turino explains this phenomenon in his book *Music as Social Life: The Politics of Participation*, stating, "The performing arts are frequently fulcrums of identity, allowing people to intimately feel themselves as part of the community through the realization of shared cultural knowledge and style and through the very act of participating together in performance" (2008, 2). Seen through this lens, the session reinforced cultural traditions while simultaneously forming a new community.

In postsession interviews, many Cruinniú members described the evening as "great craic." As previously stated, craic refers to the entertainment value of an event. Interestingly, the level of craic in a session is determined not by the musical virtuosity displayed but rather by the depth of emotional engagement one shares with others. Here craic is reminiscent of Victor Turner's concept of *communitas*, a brand of communal cohesion with great significance to the ritual realm (1969). As stated by sociologist Randall Collins, "ritual is a mechanism of mutually focused emotion and attention producing a momentarily shared reality, which thereby generates solidarity and symbols of group membership" (2004, 7). In this case, the session functioned as a ritual during which the craic generated through group musicking resulted in communitas, where "personal distinctions are stripped away allowing people to temporarily merge through their basic humanity" (Turino 2008, 18). This experience not only cemented feelings of group solidarity between two previously disparate groups but also recontextualized how many of the neurotypical musicians viewed disability.

Through my conversations with Cruinniú members, I learned that unless a person has a neurodivergent family member or works in the "care industry," they are unlikely to interact with neurodivergent individuals on a daily basis.¹ Thus, it is perhaps unsurprising that several Cruinniú members revealed that the time they spent with the Rovers altered their perception of disability. For many, this was tied to the Rovers's interest and ability to participate in the sessions, particularly as neurodivergent individuals are largely absent from most sessions. Catriona Aherne, a fiddler in Cruinniú, reinforced this sentiment, stating, "I was surprised, I must say. I thought they would be bored with it, but in actual fact they really participated, didn't they? I wouldn't have thought because I suppose in our group we don't have any people with intellectual disabilities, you know. I know they enjoy it when we go to play in Bawnmore.... They come to life with it. They love participating as well. So that's a nice part of it, but I wouldn't have associated those two [intellectual disability and traditional Irish music]."² Here Aherne speaks about her involvement in volunteering with the Brothers of Charity at their residential site, Bawnmore. While this experience has provided Aherne the opportunity to spend time with neurodivergent individuals, her interactions with the people at Bawnmore have been structured through a service user–service provider hierarchy.

In Ireland, "service users with intellectual disabilities" is the commonly accepted terminology and the way the Brothers of Charity referred to the neurodivergent individuals with whom I worked. Though I honor the linguistic preferences of my collaborators, several of my interlocutors stated that the term *service user* is problematic because it labels people with disabilities solely as beneficiaries. This linguistic marker is then manifested through daily interactions, one example being Aherne playing trad music at Bawnmore for a neurodivergent audience. By contrast, the collaborative sessions flipped this paradigm on its head by moving the Rovers from the role of receivers into the position of active participants in and cocontributors to a creative and cultural process. Aherne was making music *with* the Rovers rather than *for* them. This subtle but important shift not only altered Aherne's experience of interacting with neurodivergent musicians but also, as disability studies scholar Catherine Kudlick suggests, changed her perception of "what constitutes a capable citizen" (Kudlick 2013, 766). In the context of the session, the concept of a "citizen" differs greatly from neoliberal conceptualizations of citizenship, in which an individual's worth and access to membership in society is based on contributions to the market economy (McCluskey 2003, 785). By contrast, the criteria for citizenship in a session are based on one's engagement in the social and musical process. Capability is not determined by what one can produce (i.e., musical prowess) but, rather, by how a musician relates to and connects with other members of the community.

Eamonn and Mary O'Connor of Cruinniú elaborated on this concept, commenting that the session provided an environment for different groups to connect on a musical and human level:

> Eamonn: It's brilliant actually because you can be young or old; it doesn't matter. It doesn't matter who you are, if you're rich or poor or whatever. Music kind of transcends.... It opens up your eyes. Maybe originally you thought people with intellectual disabilities wouldn't be interested in music or wouldn't be part of it. But they obviously do.... They're just there part of the group and there's no one really judging them. They're just enjoying.
>
> Mary: They're normal people like everyone else.[3]

This final statement—"they're normal people like everyone else"—may seem self-evident. Sadly, this is not the case in society at large, which often views disability as defect. However, the collaborative sessions helped construct an alternative narrative, in which disability was seen as a difference of identity rather than a deficit of mind or body. This reinforces disability studies scholar and advocate Tobin Siebers's assertion that disability "is not a biological or natural property but an elastic social category both subject to social control and capable of effecting social change" (2008, 4). Within the scope of this project the sessions served as a site for integrating diverse identity categories and facilitating opportunities for social change by creating an inclusive environment.

In a personal interview, David McMan spoke about "fighting for disabilities" through advocacy projects at Roselawn. Though the Rovers regularly meet to discuss issues surrounding disability rights, this project represented a different opportunity for activism. When asked if he thought our sessions served as a form of advocacy, McMan replied, "Yeah. It was great to show everyone what we could do and to sing in the pub and meet new people."[4] Time and again, the Rovers expressed that the most valuable aspects of the sessions were (1) being in the public setting of the pub and interacting with new people, and (2) having the opportunity to demonstrate "what we could do." This highlights the importance of having a community forum for neurotypical and neurodivergent individuals to engage socially. Such interaction is essential to breaking down stereotypes that exist about people with intellectual disabilities.

Susan Wendell echoes this sentiment in her book *The Rejected Body*: "the exclusion of people with disabilities from many aspects of life in a society prevents non-disabled people from getting to know them, and also prevents people with disabilities from making their mark on culture, both of which contribute to their remaining the symbolic 'Other' to non-disabled people"

(1996, 64). Beyond being unable to form relationships with the neuromajority, such exclusion from community events leads to the permanent marginalization of neurodivergent people and their voices. According to Iris Marion Young, such marginalization "is perhaps the most dangerous form of oppression. A whole category of people is expelled from useful participation in social life and thus potentially subjected to severe material deprivation and even extermination" (1990, 53). However, this dire consequence can be counteracted through concerted efforts to overthrow these systems of exclusion. In the case of this project, our collaborative events served as a space for the Rovers to reverse the process of marginalization by replacing stigmatized images of intellectual disability with the faces of real people and musicians. Moreover, the sessions provided an environment for the Rovers to articulate their narratives in a traditionally neurotypical setting. This is powerful, not only for neurotypical musicians, who were presented with an opportunity to hear and *listen* to voices that are often absent from these musical gatherings, but also for the neurodivergent musicians, who are often silenced by disabling narratives. Such an experience demonstrates how community music programs can further social justice initiatives by cultivating an appreciation for neurodiversity that can then translate to greater integration and inclusion in society at large.

THE LIMITS OF INCLUSIVITY

Though most Cruinniú members viewed the Rovers as fellow musicians rather than "service users," this was not always the case. When asked about his perception of the sessions and the overall efficacy of trad music in facilitating interaction between the groups one neurotypical musician commented,

> Oh, certainly it worked. There's no question about that.... And I suppose, you know, for the kids, obviously it's fun for them. It's interaction with people. It's a day out.... And for someone like myself, it's fun, and you kind of feel you are contributing and helping somebody, which is nice too ... maybe they're even more open to [trad] than other people. They just want to be banging their drums and participating in whatever way they could. I'm not sure the genre was important for them. I think any kind of music ... and it wasn't so much the genre of Irish music ... that they could participate in is the important part.[5]

While well-meaning and spot-on with his assessment about the importance of participation, this individual's comments highlight several problematic conceptions about disability and the Rovers' contribution to the session. First, he suggests that the session solely served as an outing for the Rovers rather than as an event in which they could contribute to the creation of Irish musical culture. Secondly, he implies that the genre of trad was unimportant to the Rovers despite the fact that they had been learning this music for the past six months. Indeed, the music *did* matter to the Rovers, but their engagement with the trad genre was likely overshadowed by the manner in which they participated in musicking. It is important to note that while some sessions cater to virtuoso players, as previously mentioned, the vast majority of these gatherings are judged by the level of craic: "Enjoyment of the process of playing is as, if not more important than the quality of the musical interaction between individuals involved" (Fairbairn 1993, 30). Thus, this individual's subtle critique revealed that he was utilizing a value system that not only diverged significantly from that of the Rovers-Cruinniú conglomerate but also from that of many trad sessions. Furthermore, his interpretation suggests that he still viewed the Rovers as "service users" and perceived their musicking as deviating from standard session players. Though unintentional, this musician's comments dismiss the Rovers' connection to trad primarily because they did not display normative musical talent.

As William Cheng observed in *Just Vibrations*, "Sounding good grabs attention. It gets people to care" (2016, 8). This cultural trope of "sounding good" is pervasive in spreadable media that relies on images, videos, and audio recordings of "remarkable" musical performances by neurodivergent individuals to create "inspiration porn," "where images of people with disability are constructed as inspirational in order to make the non-disabled feel better about themselves" (Ellis 2015, 150). This not only reinforces damning narratives of "overcoming" disability through musical talent but also touts virtuosity as a legitimate bargaining chip for citizenship. These tropes fortify the insidious yet widely held belief that musical talent is a marker of humanity, and conversely, that its absence justifies the dismissal of neurodivergent people.

While some of the Rovers displayed what many would consider musical aptitude, the workshops and sessions were not intended to reinforce the politics of "sounding good." On the contrary, this project was meant to build community by questioning musical and social conventions. Musically, the Rovers accomplished this by "kripping" the soundscape through the unconventional performance of trad via auxiliary percussion, tonal exploration, rhythmic improvisation, and timbral creativity.[6] This neurodivergent soundscape encouraged new ways of listening to and understanding disability through nonnormative aural exchange. Socially, these sessions provided an opportunity for neurodivergent and neurotypical musicians to form relationships in an informal setting shaped by musical and social interaction rather than a formalized environment governed by institutional oversight. Though subtle, the distinction between formal and informal settings is essential: the former often seeks to promote the visibility of neurodivergent individuals in society, while the latter focuses on integration in the community.

CONCLUSION: BECOMING A PART

It is important to make the distinction between neurodivergent individuals being *in* the community and people with disabilities being accepted as *part* of the community. Despite the important work being done, many service organizations host programs that create pockets of neurodiversity in which neurodivergent individuals are transplanted into society but continue to interact primarily with other neurodivergent people rather than intermingling with the community. In this way, segregation still exists; it is just masked under the guise of community living. Ita Richardson of Cruinniú reflected on this phenomenon, stating that Ireland still has a long way to go in terms of fostering true integration and acceptance. According to Richardson, this project marks a departure from previous initiatives by providing opportunities for different populations to engage *with* rather than *alongside* one another:

> Where I come from we have a center ... way back then [childhood] it was residential. They [neurodivergent individuals] were living in dormitories. And recently the shift has been to get them out into houses, which at one level is great. And then getting people involved in community activities. But the big problem is they are involved in community activities in their own group rather than being involved with the general population. So that's the next shift that has to happen and it's starting to happen, but it hasn't really happened. And I came away from that Thursday night ... saying, "That's the first time I've really seen it working." ... This is the first time I've ever seen that interaction in a real way.[7]

As Richardson points out, facilitating opportunities for interaction, exchange, and relationship building between diverse populations is the next step to creating an inclusive community. It is only through individual exchange between neurodivergent and neurotypical people that we can truly begin to overturn stereotypes and foster meaningful relationships between diverse populations. I believe that musicological projects such as this have the power to build these relationships through inclusive and community-based musical practices.

This work is one of the many recent projects focused on social justice coming from applied ethnomusicology. Though applied research takes a variety of forms and spans myriad musical genres and geographic locations, these projects share an emphasis on serving communities through musical means. According to Jeff Todd Titon, "Applied ethnomusicology is best regarded a [sic] music-centered intervention in a particular community, whose purpose is to benefit that community.... It is music-centered, but above all the intervention is people-centered, for the understanding that drives it toward reciprocity is based in the collaborative partnerships that arise from ethnomusicological fieldwork" (Pettan and Titon 2015, 4). This project contributes to these parameters while simultaneously expanding them in two important ways. Firstly, while many applied projects examine preexisting communities, the Rovers-Cruinniú partnership was the result of a newly created project. This activist-oriented research is by no means the first intervention undertaken by an ethnomusicologist to fill a gap or serve a particular population. In fact, Michael Bakan's creation of the ARTISM ensemble, which was designed to provide a musical and creative outlet for neurodivergent children on the autism spectrum, serves as a model for establishing programs for neurodiverse populations (Bakan 2015a, 2015b). However, such projects are in the minority, and it is my hope that this research will contribute to the growing number of applied interventions that meet community needs through newly created programming.

Secondly, this project was specifically designed to benefit two separate populations by bringing them together to form one cohesive musical community. This required that I embed myself in Cruinniú as a participant while acting as a musical facilitator and program designer for the Rovers. My multifaceted role meant I also functioned as the initial locus of interaction between these two communities. While this complicated my positionality, it also allowed me to avoid traditional researcher-informant hierarchies by working collaboratively with my interlocutors to build a program that reflected their needs and identities. Through this reciprocal relationship, my collaborators have now taken ownership of the program, which continues in my absence. I served as the initial project creator and point of connection between the Rovers and Cruinniú. However, through their musical efforts and exchange, they have succeeded in creating a program that is all their own.

For me, this is what it means to be an applied ethnomusicologist: taking an active role in my research communities and employing my skills as a scholar and musician to help build bridges between diverse populations through collaborative partnerships. In the case of this project, this meant creating opportunities for musical and social exchange through program design and community networking. Though my work is specifically focused on facilitating exchange across neurotypical-neurodivergent boundaries through Irish traditional music, the infrastructural design of this project could be utilized to create programs designed to unite additional diverse populations through other community-based music genres. The landscape of ethnomusicology is indeed changing, as evidenced by the increasing number of musicologists pursuing research projects that foster reciprocity through the formation of on-the-ground partnerships with community collaborators. It is my hope that this pilot project will contribute to this trend by providing a blueprint for conducting innovative ethnomusicological research aimed at furthering social justice.

NOTES

1. It is important to note that neurodivergence and disability in general is not always readily apparent. Many people have invisible disabilities and "pass" as nondisabled. Therefore, it is likely that most of my seemingly neurotypical collaborators do in fact interact with neurodivergent individuals on a regular basis.

2. Catriona Aherne, personal communications with author, Limerick, Ireland, March 14, 2018.

3. Eamonn O'Connor and Mary O'Connor, personal communications with author, Limerick, Ireland, March 21, 2018.

4. David McMan, interview by author, Limerick, Ireland, April 16, 2018.

5. Anonymous, personal communications with author, Limerick, Ireland, May 2, 2018.

6. Regarding "kripping": Historically, the term *cripple* has been used pejoratively to describe people who identify as being disabled, often depicting these individuals as being incapable or weak. Recently, activists have transformed the term to *kripping* or *cripping* as a way to claim social power and control. Kripping or cripping resonates with the term *queering*, as both are employed to challenge and disrupt oppressive power structures. According to Hutcheon and Wolbring (2013), "much like the term 'queer' has taken on new meaning in those communities, 'cripple' is no longer just used by disability-identified people to reshape injurious words and to describe themselves using language of their choice: indeed, it has accumulated additional political and analytical power."

7. Ita Richardson, personal communications with author, Limerick, Ireland, March 13, 2018.

BIBLIOGRAPHY

Bakan, Michael B. 2015a. "Being Applied in the Ethnomusicology of Autism." In *The Oxford Handbook of Applied Ethnomusicology*, edited by Svanibor Pettan and Jeff Todd Titon, 278–316. New York: Oxford University Press.

———. 2015b. "'Don't Go Changing to Try and Please Me': Combating Essentialism through Ethnography in the Ethnomusicology of Autism." *Ethnomusicology* 59 (1): 116–44.

Bernini, Leah O'Brien. 2016. "The Neoliberalisation of Cultural Production: An Ethnography of Professional Irish Traditional Music." PhD diss., University of Limerick.

Cheng, William. 2016. *Just Vibrations: The Purpose of Sounding Good*. Ann Arbor: University of Michigan Press.

Collins, Randall. 2004. *Interaction Ritual Chains*. Princeton, NJ: Princeton University Press.

Ellis, Katie. 2015. "Disability and Spreadable Media: Access, Representation and Inspiration Porn." In *Disability and Popular Culture: Focusing Passion, Creating Community and Expressing Defiance*, 139–58. Farnham, UK: Routledge.

Fairbairn, Hazel. 1993. "Group Playing in Traditional Irish Music: Interaction and Heterophony in the Session." PhD diss., University of Cambridge.

Garland-Thomson, Rosemarie. 1997. *Extraordinary Bodies: Figuring Physical Disability in American Culture and Literature*. New York: Columbia University Press.

Harrison, Klisala. 2012. "Epistemologies of Applied Ethnomusicology." *Ethnomusicology* 565 (3): 505–29.

Hast, Dorothea E., and Stanley Scott. 2004. *Music in Ireland: Experiencing Music, Expressing Culture*. New York: Oxford University Press.

Hutcheon, Emily, and Gregor Wolbring. 2013. "'Cripping' Resilience: Contributions from Disability Studies to Resilience Theory." *Media/Culture Journal* 16 (5). https://doi.org/10.5204/mcj.697.

Johnston, Thomas J. 2013. "The Bloom of Youth: Conceptualising a Theory of Educative Experience for Irish Traditional Music in Post-Primary Music Education in Ireland." PhD diss., University of Limerick.

Kudlick, Catherine J. 2003. "Disability History: Why We Need Another 'Other.'" *American Historical Review* 108 (3): 763–93. Accessed March 11, 2013. http://www.jstor.org/stable/10.1086/529597.

McCluskey, Martha T. 2003. "Efficiency and Social Citizenship: Challenging the Neoliberal Attack on the Welfare State." *Indiana Law Journal* 78 (2): 799–876.

Pettan, Svanibor, and Jeff Todd Titon, eds. 2015. *The Oxford Handbook of Applied Ethnomusicology*. New York: Oxford University Press.

Shakespeare, Tom. 2013. "The Social Model of Disability." In *The Disability Studies Reader*, 4th ed., edited by Lennard J. Davis, 214–21. New York: Routledge.

Siebers, Tobin. 2008. *Disability Theory*. Ann Arbor, MI: University of Michigan Press.

Small, Christopher. 1998. *Musicking: The Meanings of Performing and Listening*. Middletown, CT: Wesleyan University Press.

Turino, Thomas. 2008. *Music as Social Life: The Politics of Participation*. Chicago: University of Chicago Press.

Turner, Victor. 1969. *The Ritual Process: Structure and Anti-Structure*. Chicago: Aldine Publishing.

Walker, Nick. 2022. "Neurodiversity: Some Basic Terms & Definitions." *Neuroqueer: The Writings of Dr. Nick Walker* (blog), 2022. Accessed May 19, 2022. https://neuroqueer.com/neurodiversity-terms-and-definitions/.

Wendell, Susan. 1996. *The Rejected Body: Feminist Philosophical Reflections on Disability*. New York: Routledge.

Young, Iris Marion. 1990. "Five Faces of Oppression." In *Justice and the Politics of Difference*, 39–65. Princeton, NJ: Princeton University Press.

TWELVE

THE SONIC POLITICS OF INTERRACIAL COALITIONS

SUSAN M. ASAI

YOU MIGHT ASK WHAT A journey entailing self-discovery, a love of music, and an affinity toward African American music and culture might elicit in the life of an ethnomusicologist.[1] As a third-generation Japanese American, my journey prompted choosing music and culture of Japan and that of African America, two areas of expertise required in my doctoral degree program at the University of California, Los Angeles (UCLA). Selected for their contrasts in aesthetics and performance styles, the two specializations developed along circuitous routes that remarkably converged as I turned my attention to the study of Afro Asian musicking and a perceived need for justice-oriented research. This account narrates my evolution as an ethnomusicologist and increased attention to the crossroads of Asian American and African American musicking sparked by the historical marginalization both groups share in the United States, and the adversities each currently faces—growing anti-Asian hate and police brutality. My answer to opposing these threats and other discriminatory pressures facing BIPOC populations is to build solidarity and form coalitions.

Within the past decade, the mass imprisonment of immigrants has steadily proliferated, leading to coalitions working to change federal anti-immigration policies. On March 30, 2019, the beating of *taiko* drums sounded a spirit of resistance at a protest rally in front of the Dilley migrant detention center in Texas. Organized by Tsuru for Solidarity (TFS), a national Japanese American political advocacy organization, protesters demanded an end to detaining asylum seekers forced to live in crowded and unsanitary conditions (Nakagawa 2020). A leader and drummer from the Native American Carrizo Comecrudo community, Juan Mancias, joined the TFS protest to add his voice and drumming.

Fig. 12.1. Graphic poster designed by Kalaya'an Mendoza. #WeKeepUsSafe. Twitter. Courtesy of artist. Used with permission.

During a two-day virtual conference on June 6–7, 2020, held in lieu of their national protest rally in Washington, DC (which was canceled due to COVID-19), TFS added the demands of thousands rallying in support of the Black Lives Matter (BLM) movement across the United States to protest police brutality following the wrongful death of George Floyd. TSF's interracial agenda has its roots in coalitions such as the Third World Strike, whose influential coalitional politics in 1969–70 San Francisco propelled the rise of mainly non-White students in their demands to have their histories and contributions added to university curricula (see fig. 12.1).

The national reckoning of racial injustice transpiring in the United States exposes the awkward position of Asian Americans, like myself, in a struggle with anti-Black bias in our communities. Those of us who support the Black Lives Matter (BLM) movement challenge anti-Black bias in our families and communities, endeavoring to promote interracial collaboration.[2] Many Asian Americans recognize the debt we owe Blacks for their civil rights gains that benefit us. We seek to subvert our status as the "model minority," which conservative pundits use to tout our advances as proof of "American fairness," effectively pitting us against other racial and ethnic groups and glossing over systemic inequities (Pan 2020, A1). The destruction of many Korean-owned businesses in the 1992 Los Angeles riots following the acquittal of police officers in the beating of Rodney King has exasperated relations between Blacks and Asians. Support for and participation in BLM offers us a chance to counter accusations of leaning toward Whiteness and its privileges and abetting the systemic oppression of African Americans.

In pressing for interracial alliances, I offer a narrative of past coalitional concord between Blacks and Asians that rewrites a history of racial tensions between our two demographic groups. There is a historical basis for the affinity between Asian Americans and African Americans. Historian Gary Okihiro writes, "We do share a history of migration, interaction, and cultural sharing, and commerce and trade. We share a history of European colonization, decolonization, and independence under neocolonization and dependency. We share a history of oppression in the U.S., successively serving as slave and cheap labor, as peoples excluded and absorbed, as victims of mob rule and Jim Crow. We share a history of struggle for freedom and the democratization of America, of demands for equality and human dignity, of insistence on making real the promise that all men are created equal" (1994, 34).

Hyejin Shim, a queer Korean and prison abolitionist also writes historically about Asian American allyship and activism, outlining social and political movements in which Asian Americans have struggled side by side with African Americans: prison abolition, antiwar, racial justice, disability justice, queer/trans feminists, immigrant rights, housing justice, rape and domestic violence, and labor. A shared history of systemic oppression underscores the fact that our liberations are entwined.[3]

The political dialectic between Asian Americans and African Americans in the 1960s set a vital precedent during a period of social and political turmoil and reconfiguration on both coasts spurred by Black nationalism and the Third World Liberation Front (TWLF). These forces catalyzed not only political interactions among people of color but artistic interchanges as well.

Two renowned Asian American activists—Grace Lee Boggs and Yuri Kochiyama—actively participated in the Black Power movement for two decades starting in the 1960s. The political affiliation of the two women helped set the stage for Asian, Black, Chicano, and Native American collaborators of the Third World Strike at San Francisco State University organized by the TWLF. Thus, the broader context for the political interaction between African Americans and Asian Americans was the Third World Liberation Front and its anti-imperialist politics and consciousness that united people of color globally in their struggle against US economic imperialism (Ho 2006). The Third World Strikes that took place at San Francisco State University (1968–69) and the University of California at Berkeley (January–March 1969) were a microcosm of the Third World movement's struggle over cultural and economic hegemony (Umemoto 1989, 15). Asian American, African American, Chicano, and Native American college students united to form one force in the TWLF. Together they strove for self-determinism in eliminating individual and institutional racism for themselves and their communities. Their cultural nationalist agenda was the impetus for the Third World Strikes; students at both campuses demanded ethnic study programs be put in place with student input in hiring faculty and designing the curriculum. These demands countered the Eurocentric curricula that either did not represent or distorted the histories of BIPOC (Black, Indigenous, people of color) in the United States. The TWLF's cultural nationalist agenda and concept of "self-determination" reveal the ideological influence of the Black Power movement, formed from the left wing of the civil rights movement in the 1960s. The anti-imperialist stance reflected events occurring internationally, including anti-imperialist wars raging in Asia, Africa, and Latin America. The writings of revolutionary intellectuals such as Frantz Fanon, Amilcar Cabral (Guinea), Ernesto "Che" Guevara, and Mao Zedong likewise influenced student activist thinking (Umemoto 1989, 10).

Drawing on the coalitional political success of TWLF, Asian American students united with community and cultural workers to forge the Asian American Movement (AAM), itself a coalition of Americans of Japanese, Chinese, and Filipino descent. The TWLF affiliate Asian American Political Alliance (AAPA) was a driving force of the AAM as it skillfully managed to link Asian American activists in different parts of the United States by organizing AAPA chapters that kept members informed of political goals and activities. Anti–Vietnam War activism among Asian Americans boosted the impetus for forming the AAM, which mobilized high school youth, tenants, small business owners, workers, senior citizens, and new immigrants to build an extensive network of grassroots organizations, providing community social services and spaces for emerging Asian American artists and cultural workers.

To strengthen its ability to act politically, the Asian American movement advocated constructing one's cultural identity and its concomitant culture as a foundation for empowering this demographic's ability to be heard in the US social, economic, and political landscape (Wei 1993, 20). Groundbreaking in the AAM's process of constructing an Asian American identity was the "multi-ethnic racial formation" that "challenged preexisting ideas about their race and national belonging and articulated a new form of Asian American identity"

(Maeda 1993, 2). This newly emergent identity clamored for Asian American cultural forms, incentivizing the ascent of Asian American musicking.

The creative force of Black Arts movement artists challenged Asian American literary and visual artists to form their own collectives in San Francisco and New York, spawning a base for Asian American musicking in the 1970s and 1980s. The Basement Workshop located in New York City's Chinatown was an Asian American political and arts organization that was active from 1970 to 1986.[4] The Black Arts movement offered a site of resistance, a subversive potential, and a strategy for Asian American artists as they sought new subjectivities to express an emboldened sociopolitical identity. It was the artistic credo and Afrocentric aesthetic of Black cultural nationalists in the 1960s that prompted Asian Americans to reimagine our identities and reclaim our heritage. Black cultural nationalists embodied the idea of culture as a form of resistance, a concept advanced by the African revolutionary Amilcar Cabral, who prescribed a "return to the source"—one's ethnic, ancestral roots—as a fundamental principle of national liberation (Maeda 1993, 24). Artists and activists embraced these ideas, fueling the newly envisaged political identity of being "Asian" American and not "Oriental."[5]

In rearticulating our heritage through music, we Sansei, third-generation Japanese Americans, turned to a number of sources from which to evoke a Japanese sensibility and aesthetic. Exposure to Japanese music took place in numerous contexts: at home, through recordings, radio, or live performances by a family member, and in community concerts, Buddhist services, and celebrations such as the Japanese Obon Festival. Japanese folk songs (*minyō*); Buddhist chanting (*shōmyō*); chamber music of the *koto, shamisen,* and *shakuhachi; shigin* (sung poetry); and music of the kabuki theater were all part of the soundscape in Japanese American homes and communities (primarily in San Francisco, Los Angeles, and New York, where I was born and raised). As musicians and composers, we developed our aesthetic palette through listening or direct instruction in the musical traditions of *gagaku* (ancient court music), koto, shamisen, shakuhachi, and taiko. Immersion in these genres introduced us to instrumental and vocal techniques and repertoire, pentatonic scales and traditional melodies, musical phrasing and form, rhythmic timing, aesthetic concepts, and timbres inherent in traditional Japanese music. Japanese American musician-composers drew from this musical vocabulary when they embarked on another musical journey in the medium of jazz.

My own musical pursuits through the lens of my Japanese heritage took me to Japan, where I studied koto for one and a half years from 1975 to 1976. Learning from a master koto musician-composer, Tamura Michiko, instilled my appreciation for the artistry and aesthetic sensibility of an instrument that traditionally is considered to be an attribute of a cultivated Japanese woman. Upon returning to the United States, I continued my koto instruction in New York City and then at UCLA while pursuing my doctorate in ethnomusicology. My stay in Los Angeles from the late 1970s through the 1980s coincided with an active period of innovative Asian American musicking. The Los Angeles jazz/pop/fusion band Hiroshima was highly popular with the support of the Japanese American community and local radio stations. The koto mastery of June Kuramoto, Hiroshima's star performer, inspired me and other koto players to experiment and learn to improvise, using the idiomatic sound and techniques of this thirteen-stringed board zither. My own explorations included a collaboration with jazz pianist-composer George Candreva on his unpublished jazz fusion composition, "Salutations to the Sea," featuring a koto solo improvisation.[6] In 1982, pop singer-songwriter James Robert Poggensee invited me to perform in his piece "Friends and Lonely Lovers." I discovered that the medium of jazz fusion enabled me to meld my ardor for jazz, an African American art form, with my musical sensibility informed by my Japanese heritage and study. This "musical coalescence" continued to evolve when I chose African American music as a second area of study along with my main concentration in Asian music. Years later, the two musicultures naturally merged in my focus on studying Afro Asian connections and affinities in music. In the current sociopolitical crisis in the United States, these connections and inclinations compel me to write about racial coalitions and music as a means to encourage cooperation and creative collaboration.

Remarkably, the sonic vocabulary of highly structured traditional Japanese music genres afforded Japanese American musician-composers immersed in the medium of jazz, especially free jazz, an alternative and deeply personal musical palette. Musicians sought freedom in jazz by moving away from Eurocentric parameters and harmonic structures and exploring improvisational ideas gleaned from African American blues and gospel roots and other musics rooted in African American culture. A more introspective approach toward one's artistry is what first attracted Asian American musician-composers to this improvisational music. In musician Paul Yamazaki's words, "what inspired many Asian American musicians was that in African American improvisational music, to really become a good improviser you have to explore the self. For the Asian American, part of that self is . . . taking a deeper look into Asian American culture and what informed that" (Auerbach 1985, 37).

The importance of improvisation as a vehicle for cross-cultural and intercultural communication and expression of one's humanity is widely accepted among musicians. Trombonist-composer-teacher George Lewis, a guiding figure for many Asian American jazz makers, instilled the idea among his mentees. Lewis's influence as a musician-composer stemmed from his innovative approaches to composition and improvisation shaped by his training with Muhal Richard Abrams of the Association for the Advancement of Creative Music (AACM) school. One of the performing groups that emerged from the AACM was the Art Ensemble of Chicago, whose Afrocentric, multimedia, and experimental performances particularly inspired musicians from San Francisco's AsianImprov collective. Several members of the AACM and Art Ensemble of Chicago, along with Bay Area affiliate musician Gerald Oshita, directly mentored Asian American neophyte improvisors. A protegé of George Lewis, saxophonist-composer-violinist-activist Francis Wong speaks about Lewis's view of improvisation as an effective means to interact with other musicians. Because improvisation is not defined by an a priori musical structure, it allows dialogue between musicians, a space in which artists can speak their own language yet communicate with one another. Improvisational exchanges constitute a form of interracial discourse, creating meaning for those making music together. Asian American musicians find the shared experience exciting.

In her book *Resounding Afro Asia: Interracial Music and the Politics of Collaboration*, ethnomusicologist Tamara Roberts presses for sustained engagements between racial and cultural groups in her analyses of the interracial and intercultural collaborations between Asian American and African American musicians. Her study of Afro Asian music ensembles reveals that "through mixing of racialized sounds, and, sometimes, explicit extra-musical politics, Afro Asian artists increase the opportunities for people of color to establish counterdominant formations" (Roberts 2016, 176). Roberts champions Afro Asian music alliances as an early force in cultivating relationships across racial and cultural lines, exploring new aesthetic fields, and developing interracial rapport through sound. Her study of Afro Asian music groups reveals interracial collaborations akin to relations in communities in which members share aesthetic pleasure, oppressions, and affinities. A model in coalitional work, collaborating musicians build relationships, strengthen interracial solidarity, develop interracial audiences, and "interpret texts in non-hegemonic ways" (8, 9). Such a model promotes diverse practices that embolden artists of color to increasingly work across racial and cultural borders. Roberts's seminal work on Afro Asian musicking draws increased attention to interracial artists as they collectively open insurgent spaces to represent themselves in dominant sites.

The 1979 band United Front exemplifies an early Afro Asian partnership comprised of Mark Izu (bassist), Lewis Jordan (saxophonist), Anthony Brown (drums), and George Sams (trumpet). I had the pleasure of interviewing Mark Izu several times over a period of thirty years to inquire about the groundbreaking role he played in the rise of the Asian American creative music scene in San Francisco and his subsequent musical direction that skillfully weaves his compositions with storytelling, theater, and dance. I learned that United Front—a pioneering group in the 1970s and early 1980s—coalesced when Izu and Jordan recruited trumpeter George Sams from the Black Artists Group (BAG) in St. Louis and Bay Area drummer Anthony Brown (Yanow 1994, 28).[7] United Front musically, racially, and politically mirrored the alliances and coalitions among people of color brought together by the Third World Strike in the 1970s. Members included two African Americans, Jordan and Sams; one Japanese American, Izu; and Brown, a biracial American of Japanese and African descent in an ensemble that relied heavily on collectively composing pieces that gave the band its signature sound. The quartet composed music with "a sense of empowerment and self-sufficiency" (Brown 2010). One perceives this empowered and determined sensibility in the piece "I Will Be Free," a track from their *Ohm: Unit of Resistance* album (RPM Records 1981). The piece crackles with energy as it heralds a call to stand and declare one's freedom, socially, politically, and artistically. The collective improvisation in the middle of the composition typified the group's free jazz–inspired approach. Use of the pentatonic scale C–E♭–F–G–B–C (the Japanese *kumoi-joshi* scale) as the melodic basis for the piece promotes an Asian sensibility. A second track, "Nothing Is More Precious Than Independence and Freedom," highlights spoken word performed by Lewis Jordan, alternating with the band's free-form sections that sonically narrate the text. The remainder of the composition is a series of either collectively improvised segments, jazz vamping, or free-flowing passages that allow players to explore musical ideas, giving the music a fresh and liberatory feel. United Front toured Europe on a yearly basis and recorded several albums. Regretfully, with not enough engagements in the United States to sustain the members, the group disbanded in 1985 (see fig. 12.2).

It is imperative to include in this discussion the late Fred Wei-han Ho (1957–2014), the fiercest politically ideological Asian American professional musician, composer-arranger, bandleader, writer, activist, and producer who played a critical role in the rise of Asian American jazz, blazing a new musical aesthetic.[8] His self-styled mohawk haircut and self-sewn Asian-inflected clothing design made him cut a striking figure. Fred Ho is one of the first musicians I interviewed in my search for an Afro Asian sound. I inquired about his strongly held political views and his innovative approach to crafting an Asian American sonic palette. His energy and commitment definitively moved Asian American music

Fig. 12.2. United Front band members: George Sams, Mark Izu, Lewis Jordan, and Anthony Brown. Photo credit: Jim Dong. Used with permission.

into a whole new realm. Ho came of age in the 1970s fully embracing the Black Power and Black Arts movements: "I was profoundly drawn to and inspired by African American music as the expression of an oppressed nationality due to its social role as protest and resistance to national oppression, and for its musical energy and revolutionary aesthetic qualities" (Ho 1995, 284). This artist's militant and radical stance resulted not only from his immersion in the Black Power movement but also from his participation in third-world radicalism and the Asian American movement (Fujino 2009, 8). Ho's political identity as a "revolutionary yellow nationalist" merged the Black Arts movement's cultural nationalist approach, the Third World Liberation's anti-imperialist view that targeted capitalism as the source of third-world peoples' oppression and exploitation by White people, and the Asian American movement's goal of empowering Asian Americans to raise their political visibility and reconfigure their representation in US national culture. Ho's Marxist-Leninist leanings intensified after he joined I Wor Kuen (IWK), an Asian American revolutionary group, at age nineteen and the League of Revolutionary Struggle (LRS), primarily a Chicano organization of the New Left that had coalesced with IWK. Raising the level of political and aesthetic standards for cultural and artistic output in addition to creating a broad base for innovative, oppositional, transgressive radical work were central to Ho in uniting radical politics and the arts. An intellectual, Ho's compositions and writings outlined a framework for revolutionary practice: "Every feature of the music is an expression of revolutionary dialectics. Demarcations are dissolved between soloist and ensemble; among the elements of melody, time, and harmony; between composition and improvisation; between 'tradition' and 'avant-garde'; between 'artist' and 'audience'; between 'art' and 'politics'; between 'Western' and 'Eastern'; . . . the continual exploding of time and pitch in quest of greater human expressiveness and a deeper spiritualizing of the music that is fundamentally rooted in the struggle to end all forms of exploitation and oppression and to seek a basic 'oneness' with life and nature" (Ho 1995, 286). His articles and books from 1984 to 2006 elucidate his conceptions about "political theory and activist transformation" that encouraged the use of art and music in unconventional and experimental ways that integrate activism and artistry (Fujino 2009, 29).

Ho was at the forefront of Afro Asian cultural politics. "My traditions are African and Asian American in artistic forms. My philosophy is internationalist and revolutionary socialist" (Ho 2009c, 220). *Afro/Asia: Revolutionary Political and Cultural Connections between African and Asians in the Americas*, which he coedited with Bill Mullen, is the culmination of Ho's view on Afro Asian unity. He advanced Afro Asian unity in performances of his Afro Asian Music Ensemble and Afro Asian Arts Dialogue with poet Kalamu Yu Salaam, a Pan-African cultural nationalist. One year after moving to New York City to pursue music as a profession in 1981, Ho founded Afro-Asian Music Ensemble (AAME) comprised of three saxophones and a standard rhythm section of piano, drums, and bass. He named the ensemble based on the historic Afro-Asian Unity conference that took place in April 1955 in Bandung, Indonesia. At the conference, newly independent countries and national liberation movements in Africa, Asia, and Central and South America and the Caribbean inaugurated the Non-Aligned movement of newly independent countries and national liberation movements. Sponsoring a benefit for the League of Revolutionary Struggle's *Black Nation* magazine is evidence of Ho's commitment to Afro Asian unity. The benefit featured the AAME opening the show and playing during intermission and a performance by drummer Max Roach and saxophonist Archie Shepp, accompanying poet Amiri Baraka. For more than twenty years, AAME served as Ho's primary band to accompany his large-scale operas, martial arts ballets, and music/theater epics (Ho 2009a, 168–69). The Afro Asian partnership with Salaam, blending music and poetry prompted Ho to expand his work to multimedia performances. Ideologically, Ho's Afro Asian musical syntheses served to promote his internationalist vision.

The cofounding of the Asian American Resource Workshop, Boston's first pan-Asian organization, initiated as an educational and cultural group for this demographic in 1979, points to Ho's early coalitional work. When he joined the LRS and IWK, he engaged in uniting diverse Asian/Pacific nationalities in the United States, forming a Pan-Asian core (Ho 2009b, 48). The very variety of musical styles and genres Ho incorporated into compositions is coalitional by nature; he included "West African, Latin, reggae rhythms, Chinese, Korean, and Filipino instruments, as well as Arabic and Japanese modes" (Fujino 2009, 26). Ho enumerates what he considers essential to coalitional work, asserting that it requires an ideological foundation, "a framework in which you analyze things, strive to be on the same page ideologically, and be able to critique and solve problems together creatively, yet with unity." Ho outlines three steps to form coalitions: (1) recruit scholars and intellectuals to target national cultural forms and traditions, foster standards of excellence based on a commitment to community, and shepherd coalition members in its liberation from White supremacy; (2) focus on institution building and cultural empowerment in lieu of government and corporate grants to support and disseminate work; and (3) forge a "base of support, direction, clarity, and vision" for activists, artists, and intellectuals in their collective efforts to overcome national oppression and solidify artistic and financial success (Ho 2009c, 221–23). Although Ho shifted to working solo from the late 1980s until his untimely passing in 2014, his hardline revolutionary politics and musicking advanced Asian American political empowerment and musical expression.

An example of sustained musical activism is pianist-composer Jon Jang's 2019 album, *The Pledge of Black Asian Allegiance*, consisting of an eleven-song cycle recorded with the Jon Jangtet and guests. Reenergized by the Black Lives Matter movement, Jang commemorates heroes of the Black and Asian communities while mourning the deaths of more recent victims of racial violence earmarked by the color of their skin. The album's first tune, "Yuri Kochiyama, Malcolm X!," honors two champions of the Black Liberation movement, featuring a reggae-influenced beat. Since the 1980s, Jang has been an unceasing advocate in connecting African American and Asian American communities through the force of music and more widely strives "to be in solidarity with all peoples of color." He asserts, "We didn't have Asian-American mentors in our search for creative music and freedom. All our mentors were Black, and Black music is a form of resistance." The pianist-composer firmly links Asian American experiences to Black freedom struggles (Ouellette 2020). As an early member of San Francisco's creative movement scene, Jang's uncompromising politics have always stood out. A prolific performer, composer, and activist whom I have interviewed and followed for many years, I am always struck by Jang's dedication and brio in his unceasing musical endeavors that continue to reinforce Afro Asian ties. This artist contributes greatly to the struggle of Asian Americans for increased political and artistic recognition.

The joining of creative forces between artists of various subaltern groups is one answer to forging coalitions that unify rather than divide us in the ideological struggle to gain political power and effective political representation. Affecting change depends on bold, creative visionaries such as multifaceted artist Nobuko Miyamoto. Miyamoto's legacy as an artivist[9] and cultural worker is well-known within Asian American circles. Her Afro Asian connections, which I've traced for three decades, have been strong throughout her career. My interviews with her have always been about pursuing creative ventures that address ongoing social and political challenges for Asian Americans and other people of color and their communities. Originally an activist singer-songwriter, Miyamoto diversified her socially and politically conscious art over the years, combining music with dance, movement, and spectacle. Her cross-cultural and interdisciplinary work conjoins the Japanese American community with other racial and cultural communities in Los Angeles in an array of pursuits that extend to educational programming about gardening and recycling waste intended to raise awareness of environmental stewardship.

In 1978, Miyamoto founded the Los Angeles–based Great Leap, Inc., which stands as a model arts and political advocacy community organization. Great Leap sets the standard for how to effectively structure such partnerships. Miyamoto's educational approach to community projects along with the success of her intercommunity programs garners strong funding from local, state, and federal sources. Local Los Angeles partners include the Japanese American Cultural and Community Center, Los Angeles County Arts & Culture, East LA Community Corporation, Arts District Little Tokyo, Artivist Entertainment, and New Generation Fund (housing) and Department of Cultural Affairs, City of Los Angeles. Great Leap has received state-sponsored support from California Cultural District, Little Tokyo, Alliance for California Traditional Arts, and the California Endowment. Financial backing from national organizations such as the Mellon Foundation and the Kresge Foundation has also been crucial. Great Leap's local and national assistance points to a certain logic in building alliances and coalitions: the more communities involved in events and projects, the broader the base for financial support and advocacy.

What sets Great Leap's activities and Miyamoto's artistry apart are the lectures, workshops, and seminars that engage artists, teachers, community organizers, corporate administrators, and cultural and faith-based groups, providing them with the tools to organize short- and long-term projects that promote increased interracial and cross-cultural understanding. In these interactive sessions, Miyamoto builds collaborative possibilities among participants through breathing, movement, and the sharing of stories with hopes of developing individual creativity and positive group dynamics. One such project is "Collaboratory"—an artist mentorship program that guides emerging artists and community members in the process of creating theater works of their personal stories. Embedded in the philosophy of Great Leap is a sense of passing on cultural and spiritual practices and merging or juxtaposing them in cross-culturally inventive ways that build community, and in the process, broaden audiences for progressive creative work.[10]

As a prototype for interracial and intercultural projects, FandangObon (launched in 2013) is a remarkable intercommunity initiative. Great Leap collaborated with Quetzal, the Chicano rock band from East Los Angeles in creating cross-cultural music for this event.[11] Mixing "rhythmic footwork, the strumming of *jarana*s (plucked lutes), and *fandango son jarocho* folk song verses" with *bon-odori* music and dance is a fresh example of bridging musical cultures.[12] Bon-odori folk songs, traditionally, accompany dancing for Obon festivals. From the intertwining of bon-odori and fandango songs emerges infectious music to accompany dancing and to celebrate the building of communities through the fusion of cultures.[13]

The Black Lives Matter movement is very personal for Miyamoto, whose African American husband and biracial son are at risk in a climate of ongoing racial injustices and police brutality faced by African Americans in the United States today. The murder of George Floyd on May 25, 2020, became the tipping point for many, igniting nationwide protests that came to be known as the Black Lives Matter movement. Miyamoto composed and produced the protest song "Black Lives Matter," adding her cry to the voice of millions in the United States and across the globe. The somber, jazz-inflected composition builds momentum with a weighty piano ostinato bassline and lyrics, outlining the history of injustice for Black lives, the sanctity of these lives, and, by association, all lives. The song climaxes with a chorus of "Black lives matter!" and ends quietly with a simple, repeated pentatonic melodic motif.

This moment calls for Asian American and African American musicians to bolster the legacy of interracial artivism, and coalesce with activist groups such as Tsuru for Solidarity, Asians 4 Black Lives (A4BL), NAACP, Black Lives Matter, and local organizations. A4BL is the most recently formed Asian American organization founded in response to a call from the umbrella organization Black Lives Matter Bay Area, comprised of the BlackOut Collective, Black Brunch Organizers, Onyx Organizing Committee, and others, following

George Floyd's death. A4BL acknowledges past tensions with African American communities created by White supremacist efforts to racially divide Black and Asian. A4BL is committed to the struggle to end all forms of violence against Black people and charges Asian Americans to rebuff the model minority myth historically constituted to nullify Black resistance and vindicate systemic racism. The A4BL agenda continues the legacy of activists Yuri Kochiyama, Grace Lee Boggs, and Kartar Dhillon of the Black Buffalo soldiers, who defected from the US army in support of Philippine independence. A4BL detail their strategy accordingly: "organizing our communities in solidarity and protesting, using a diversity of tactics including shutting down business as usual to ensure that each life wrongfully taken by the police does not go in vain. Deep, intentional relationship building is central to laying the foundations that make change possible; at the same time, it is not just a means to an end. Trust and interdependence are ends in themselves."[14] Musician-composers engage in building relationships and solidarity by intertwining music that promotes affinities among fellow activists and provides spirited support at rallies and gatherings.

Interdisciplinary artist and scholar Coco Fusco insists that artists' cultural border crossings and participation in multiple communities reflect contemporary American life in all its cultural variety. She contends that artists are moving beyond solely reconstructing their own cultural past, and are traversing other worlds, crosscutting different languages, aesthetic ideas, genres, and images into their work (Fusco 1999, 70, 71). Recontextualizing dominant cultural tropes promoted by the mainstream media and governmental institutions is a way for artists to resist and reshape them.

The political and musical affinities Asian American musician-composers share with their African American counterparts speak to the potential for interracial political coalitions to foster a future that reaches for equality and human dignity for all. Musical exchanges between cultural groups model and plant seeds for intercoalitional cross talk in the broader social and political realm. Inventive musicking builds communal and empathic consciousness and richly imbues the cultural landscape of the United States with the potential to promote a more inclusive political terrain and, ultimately, a more equitable society.

NOTES

1. I would like to acknowledge the continuing collaborative efforts of Asian American and African American musicians, propelling them toward relationships that promote greater dialogue and understanding. Acknowledgment is also due to my husband, Tezei, who guided me toward increased clarity in my writing for my two chapters in this anthology.

2. A Pew Research Center survey in June 2020 tabulated 75 percent of Asian Americans support the Black Lives Matter movement, compared with 60 percent of whites, 77 percent of Latinx, and 86 percent of Black respondents.

3. Shim 2020.

4. I was living in New York City from 1977 to 1978, attending Columbia University for my master's degree, but was unaware of the Basement Workshop's efforts to combine artistic expression with politics and community activism.

5. "Oriental" is a Eurocentric, outdated term used to categorize people of Asian descent, and it carries a pejorative designation of being exotic or Other.

6. "Salutations to the Sea" was never studio recorded. Also, I am not sure whether the studio recording of "Friends and Lonely Lovers" ever sold commercially.

7. The Bay Area attracted jazz musicians from cities as far flung as Chicago and St. Louis; many of them members of either Chicago's AACM or an analogous organization in St. Louis, BAG.

8. For a more in-depth study of Fred Ho's music and activism, I recommend *Wicked Theory, Naked Practice: A Fred Ho Reader*, edited by Diane C. Fujino (Minneapolis: Minnesota University Press, 2009), which is a compilation of Ho's writings that chronicle his evolution as a musician-composer, his political foundation, theories and analyses, and a framework for uniting music and radical politics. A second, more recent publication I suggest is *Yellow Power, Yellow Soul: The Radical Art of Fred Ho*, edited by Roger N. Buckley and Tamara Roberts (Urbana: University of Illinois Press, 2013), illuminating the contributions of this artist through the lens of scholars, artists, and friends.

9. An artivist is an artist who is also an activist. It is a term that has gained currency in the growing need for artistic expression as a form of resistance and protest.

10. Great Leap n.d.
11. View Great Leap 2014a and 2014b.
12. Great Leap n.d.
13. See Great Leap 2018.
14. Asians 4 Black Lives 2020. This article also gives a full listing of Asians 4 Black Lives' ten-point agenda for building back Black communities. See also Asians 4 Black Lives. n.d. Asians 4 Black Lives represents diverse Asian voices that include Filipinos, Vietnamese, South Asian, Chinese, Pakistani, Korean, Burmese, Japanese, and others.

BIBLIOGRAPHY

Asians 4 Black Lives. 2020. "Asians4BlackLives: Uplift Black Resistance, Help Build Black Power." Medium, June 1, 2020. Accessed November 4, 2020. https://medium.com/@asians4blacklives/asians-4-black-lives-uplift-black-resistance-help-build-black-power-b01ef091ccoc/.

Auerbach, Brian. 1985. "Asian American Jazz: An Oral History with Paul Yamazaki." *Options* (March–April): 37.

Brown, Anthony. 2010. "Asian American Jazz." Lecture, September 16, 2010. Asian American Center. Northeastern University, Boston, MA.

Fujino, Diane C. "Introduction." In *Wicked Theory, Naked Practice: A Fred Ho Reader,* edited by Diane Fujino, 7–38. Minneapolis: University of Minnesota Press.

Fusco, Coco. 1999. "Passionate Irreverence: The Cultural Politics of Identity." In *Art Matters: How the Culture Wars Changed America*, edited by Brian Wallis, Marianne Weems, and Philip Yenawine, 63–73. New York: New York University Press.

Ho, Fred Wei-han. 1995. "What Makes 'Jazz' the Revolutionary Music of the 20th Century, and Will It Be Revolutionary for the 21st Century?" *African American Review* 29 (2) (Summer): 283–90.

———. 2006. "Fred Ho's Tribute to the Black Arts Movement: Personal and Political Impact and Analysis." *Critical Studies in Improvisation* 1 (6). Accessed October 10, 2020. https://www.criticalimprov.com/index.php/csieci/article/download/57/100?inline=1/.

———. 2009a. "An Asian American Tribute to the Black Arts Movement." In *Wicked Theory, Naked Practice: A Fred Ho Reader*, edited by Diane C. Fujino, 161–210. Minneapolis: University of Minnesota Press.

———. 2009b. "Beyond Asian American Jazz: My Musical and Political Changes in the Asian American Movement." In *Wicked Theory, Naked Practice: A Fred Ho Reader*, edited by Diane C. Fujino, 46–63. Minneapolis: University of Minnesota Press.

———. 2009c. "Interview with Amy Ling." In *Wicked Theory, Naked Practice: A Fred Ho Reader*, edited by Diane C. Fujino, 218–28. Minneapolis: University of Minnesota Press.

Maeda, Daryl. 1993. *Chains of Babylon: The Rise of Asian America*. Philadelphia: Temple University Press.

Nakagawa, Martha. 2020. "Tsuru for Solidarity: A National Movement Shifts Online." *Rafu Shimpo (Los Angeles Japanese Daily News)*, July 4, 2020. Accessed August 20, 2020. http://www.rafu.com/2020/07/tsuru-for-solidarity-a-national-movement-shifts-online/.

Okihiro, Gary Y. 1994. "Is Yellow Black or White?" In *Margins and Mainstreams: Asians in American History and Culture*, 31–63. Seattle: University of Washington Press.

Ouellette, Dan. 2020. "Jon Jang Pledges the Black Asian Allegiance." *Jazz and beyond Intel*, November 2020. Accessed November 5, 2020. https://danouellette.net/j%26bi-oct-2020-dafnis/f/jazz-beyond-intel-november-20-jon-jang-mark-ruffin-elton-john/.

Pan, Deanna. 2020. "BLM Has Asian Americans Taking Painful Look at Own Racial Attitudes." *Boston Globe* 298 (22): A1, A7.

Roberts, Tamara. 2016. *Resounding Afro Asia: Interracial Music and the Politics of Collaboration*. New York: Oxford University Press.

Shim, Hyejin. 2020. "Asians 4 Black Lives: Structural Racism Is the Pandemic, Interdependence and Solidarity Is the Cure." *Medium*, July 9, 2020. Accessed November 2, 2020. https://medium.com/@asians4blacklives/asians-4-black-lives-structural-racism-is-the-pandemic-interdependence-and-solidarity-is-the-cure-9162167d92e1/.

Umemoto, Karen. 1989. "'On Strike!' San Francisco State College Strike, 1968–69." *Amerasia Journal* 15 (1): 3–41.

Wei, William. 1993. *The Asian American Movement*. Philadelphia: Temple University Press.

Yanow, Scott. 1994. "Enthusiasm." *Jazziz* 11 (2) (February–March): 28–34.

Yellow Power Yellow Soul. The Radical Art of Fred Ho. 2013. Edited by Roger N. Buckley and Tamara Roberts. Urbana, Chicago, and Springfield: University of Illinois Press.

DISCOGRAPHY

United Front. 1981. *Ohm: Unit of Resistance*. San Francisco: RPM Records. RPM-2.

VIDEOGRAPHY

Asians 4 Black Lives. n.d. Official Website. https://a4bl.wordpress.com/who-we-are/.

Great Leap. 2014a. "FandangObon Full Performance with Quetzal." YouTube. 7 min., 24 sec. Video. https://www.youtube.com/watch?v=ooNnphMIu6g/.

———. 2014b. "FandangObon Short Documentary." YouTube. 5 min., 15 sec. Video. https://www.youtube.com/watch?v=bPwaYvXH_gw/.

———. 2018. "FandangObon. 2017." YouTube. 4 min., 37 sec. Video. https://www.youtube.com/watch?v=xJb7ET7yyOY/.

———. n.d. Official Website. greatleap.org.

THIRTEEN

"¡VAMOS A PELEAR EN LA GUERRA!"

Musical Manifestations of Coalition Building in the South Texas Chicano Movement

ERIN E. BAUER

Desde Tejas a California From Texas to California
Campesinos están luchando. Farmworkers are struggling.
¡Los rancheros llore y llore The ranchers, crying and crying
De huelga ya están bien pandos! The strike has made them spineless!

—"EL PICKET SIGN" (*CONJUNTO AZTLÁN*)

The murder of Dr. Fred E. Logan Jr. in 1970 in the small town of Mathis, Texas, is a sickening example of the racist treatment of Mexican Americans in South Texas during most of the twentieth century. With his own testimony serving as the sole evidence in the case, the deputy sheriff who shot and killed Logan ostensibly acted in self-defense following an argument between the two men. No charges were filed. However, many believed the Anglo establishment targeted Logan for "his work among the city's poor, his political activism, and his incessant critique of police brutality in the region"; he was killed, in short, for his "work among Mexican Americans" (Hinojosa 2013, 437). The murder brought national attention to the power of Anglo-American landowners and politicians in South Texas during this time. Members of the Mexican American Youth Organization (MAYO), a Chicano rights organization from San Antonio, descended on Mathis to protest what historian Roberto Treviño referred to as "the tejano Jim Crow experience" (quoted in Hinojosa 2013, 438). Ideologically connected to the farm labor movement in California during the 1960s, although often overlooked within the historical narrative, social activists in South Texas during the 1970s fought against segregation in schools, deplorable living conditions for migrant farmworkers, and an absence of public health resources. Beyond the work of activist groups like MAYO, young musicians in South Texas used the arts to address social injustices amid new representations of cultural identity.

For example, Chicano student activists formed Conjunto Aztlán in 1977 as part of a renewed identification as ethnic Mexicans. In the 1970s, the two founding members of the group, Juan Tejeda and José Flores Peregrino, were students at the University of Texas at Austin and members of Chicano Artistas Sirviendo a Aztlán (CASA), a collective of Chicano artists in the area. The musicians connected their Mexican American heritage to its Indigenous roots. They linked instances of systemic racism in their community with concurrent struggles of the nationwide (but initially West Coast) Chicano movement. Accordingly, the name of the ensemble refers simultaneously to a Mexican American and Indigenous heritage, with *conjunto* indicating a Texas Mexican folk genre popular from the early years of the twentieth century and Aztlán referencing the mythical homeland of the Aztec people. In a recent conversation with me, Tejeda noted that the group "knew from the beginning" they "were going to be a different type of conjunto."[1] Inclusion within the conjunto genre implies a certain standardization of instrumentation, musical technique, structure, texture, repertory, language, and lyrical content. However, Conjunto Aztlán reinterpreted the genre through the use of vernacular, popular, and Indigenous musics; the Spanish, English, and Náhuatl languages; and socially conscious lyrics.

In doing so, the group forged connections with Chicano movement musicians across the United States and drew influence from the Latin American movement known as *nueva canción*. They thus altered generic assumptions, suggesting that the conjunto genre had shifted in local interpretation from its foundation in the early twentieth century to creating new forms of resistance among changing circumstances of Texas Mexican identity. Scholars like Manuel Peña (1985) have fundamentally connected conjunto music to a locally situated, working-class ethnic identity. However, translocal connections throughout the United States and Latin America challenge former understandings of sociocultural significance for audiences and participants alike. Conjunto Aztlán reproduced the ideological considerations, musical characteristics, and even certain repertories of activists in California and across Latin America.[2] In forging connections with the Chicano movement, the United Farm Workers, and nueva canción, the ensemble created modern associations with an urban community outside of the regional orientation. Similarly, as young, urban college students, these musicians were detached from the original identity of the conjunto community. Instead, they altered the folkloric genre to represent new types of Texas Mexican representation. In its modified form, conjunto forged connections with issues of social justice and brought meaning to the middle-class community removed from historical identities.

Negative constructions of Mexican American cultural identity by Anglo Americans in South Texas have persisted since the nineteenth century. During the Mexican American War (1846–48), Stephen F. Austin asserted that "a war of extermination is raging in Texas—a war of barbarism and of despotic principles, waged by the mongrel Spanish-Indian and Negro race, against civilization and the Anglo-American race" (García 2018). Leading a charge against the Mexican army, Sam Houston proclaimed that Whites would never "mix with the phlegm of the indolent Mexicans, no matter how long we live among them" (ibid.). Following the successful conclusion of the war, US secretary of state James Buchanan referred to the now-US American citizens living along the Texas-Mexico border as "an inferior, indolent, mongrel race" (ibid.). These ugly characterizations have continued into the twenty-first century. The United States government responded to the attacks on September 11, 2001, by expanding the border wall, despite no evidence of terrorism coming from Mexico. Campaigning for president in 2015, Donald Trump suggested that visiting Laredo, Texas, would put his life at risk: "I may never see you again, but we're going to do it" (Grieder 2019).[3] Attorney General Jeff Sessions later characterized El Paso, Texas, as "ground zero" and a "beachhead against the cartels" (Wilson 2018). These portrayals of the Texas-Mexico border community as poor, lazy, and violent have led to damaging policies, economic suppression, misinformed political rhetoric, and horrific events like the Walmart shooting in El Paso in 2019.

Scholarly interpretations of Texas Mexican music as inherently linked with negative stereotypes can exacerbate these consequences. Conjunto Aztlán's alterations to the regional art form break connections between "traditional" musical traits and what I view as "primitivist" understandings of culture, by which I mean harmful stereotypes of the musical community as simplistic and old-fashioned, uneducated and violent. The breadth of interpretive characteristics under the umbrella of conjunto suggests that historical limitations of culture are no more appropriate than strict sonic boundaries. In other words, if a variety of musical traits are accepted in a "conjunto" categorization, then Texas Mexican cultural identity must be equally broad. In this way, the activist impulses of musicians like Conjunto Aztlán during the 1970s influenced issues of social inequity beyond the artists' initial intent. Their activism addresses the struggle against social injustices associated with the Chicano rights movement but also suggests a new understanding of cultural categorization. It separates creative expressions from dangerous stereotypes of class, language, and ethnicity.

This chapter uses the music of Conjunto Aztlán and the artists' own interpretations of its regional significance to challenge homologous interpretations of genre as identity and to advance instead a fluid construct that accommodates new articulations of identity and sociocultural ideology.[4] Although scholars like Peña have consistently designated conjunto as a working-class representation, new musical traits suggest shifting interpretations of the genre across space and time. If we follow former connections between the music and sociocultural identification, these sonic alterations—of instrumentation, texture, structure, and so forth—indicate that cultural identity has also been altered or, at least, disconnected from its original musical representation. The music then becomes a musical style, subject to reinterpretations.[5] The activist impulses of ensembles like Conjunto Aztlán emulate nueva canción and the Chicano movement in confronting issues of social injustice. Yet they also address primitivist stereotypes between historical musical elements and perceptions of an old-fashioned and out-of-touch contemporary community. They tackle notions of the US-Mexico border population as a folkloric Other, accentuating more recent connections to communities in California, across the United States, and throughout Latin America.

HISTORICAL FRAMEWORK: TEXAS MEXICAN CONJUNTO, THE CHICANO MOVEMENT, AND NUEVA CANCIÓN

Starting in the early twentieth century, Texas Mexican conjunto music formed a sociocultural response to Anglo American and upward-aspiring Texas Mexican hegemony among the rural, working-class population in South Texas (see Peña 1985). The genre has historically served as a cultural representation of the rural, working-class community. Relatedly, the music frequently carries a stigma of low-class, "cantina music." Austin-based journalist Belinda Acosta describes conjunto as often "dismissed within the Latino community as working class, 'cantina trash' or '*borracho*' (drunk) music" (1998). The music most typically consists of a distinctive combination of button accordion with *bajo sexto*, a six-course, twelve-string Mexican bass guitar. In contemporary performances, electric bass and drums round out the standard four-person ensemble. However, the social identities of the performers and audience also lend an important defining feature to the music. For example, the instrumentation, repertory, structure, and sound of Mexican *norteño* music and so-called progressive conjunto ensembles closely correspond to the defining features of historical conjunto practices. However, the location and class typically associated with these two genres establish unique characterizations of the music.

In contrast, the continued categorization of groups like Conjunto Aztlán as "conjunto" suggests that musical characteristics alone do not define the genre. This is especially noticeable in the reluctance within the Texas Mexican community to admit related musics like norteño and progressive conjunto into a conjunto categorization. Conjunto Aztlán altered traditional musical traits to explicitly address issues of social justice, separating the genre from its historical identity. Over time, many members of the younger generation moved into the middle class. Instead of a counterhegemonic response by rural, working-class musicians *against* the urban, well-educated, and increasingly middle-class population, conjunto in the 1970s became an expression of an upwardly mobile population.

That said, although groups like Conjunto Aztlán represent a new class identity, working-class connections to the music endure. The genre gained new associations with the Chicano movement but also maintained former relationships to class, ethnicity, and location. Genre itself doesn't define an identity but can be harnessed to represent various sociocultural circumstances. Generic definition then comes through community-based notions of acceptance. Conjunto Aztlán manipulated the sonic footprint of conjunto but remained close enough to original expectations in both musical traits and cultural heritage to maintain acceptance within the community as "conjunto." In so doing, the group severed primitivist expectations of genre and identity in favor of contemporary connections between heritage and sociocultural identification.

That said, Texas Mexican conjunto has always existed as a form of social activism. From Mexican corridos documenting sociopolitical injustices during the nineteenth century to conjunto's nascence in response to Anglo-Texas hegemony, the genre has historically opposed discriminatory practices. As Tejeda emphasizes, "There's always been resistance [in Texas] . . . as the precursor to Chicano movement music . . . and the corridos were very important musical antecedent and resistance . . . to the injustices and the racism that Mexicans and indigenous people encountered here as part of Texas, of the US."[6] As such, Conjunto Aztlán used Mexican and other Latin American influences to expand historical elements of conjunto and better represent their contemporary cultural identities. They simultaneously addressed social inequities more commonly emphasized by the Chicano movement. Yet they also redefined what it meant to be Texas Mexican, beyond the limits of "old-fashioned" musical traits and corresponding perceptions of a fundamentally rural, working-class, and "traditional" community.

By using folkloric traditions to represent new cultural identities across issues of social justice, Conjunto Aztlán mirrored earlier strategies of the pan–Latin American nueva canción movement. Nueva canción (new song) practices originated with resurgent interest in traditional folkloric music in Argentina and Chile in the late 1950s. Musicians like Violeta Parra and Victor Jara in Chile gathered Indigenous music, promoted performances, and advocated for a new form of national identity rooted in folk tradition. Beginning in the 1960s (and after the 1959 Cuban Revolution), the movement spread throughout Latin America as a means to address social tensions in the region. Musical manifestations varied considerably with geography, depending on political particulars and local forms of expression. In general, however, the music can be defined as a combination of traditional, primarily Indigenous and Iberian-rooted musical instruments and forms with socially relevant lyrics.

Drawing from the collected folk traditions of various rural populations, nueva canción songs most typically employ uncomplicated melodies, accompaniments, and structures. Intense language conveys social significance with sparse, but often poetic lyrics. Yet complex lyrics form only one manifestation of social significance. Songs with seemingly innocuous texts also convey political dissidence through the use of folkloric elements and Indigenous instruments. Removed from their origins and repurposed to represent communities largely disconnected from corresponding sociocultural struggles, nueva canción songs display certain classist, albeit typically well-intentioned, usurpations of rural musics. Middle-class practitioners used the music of highland Andean villages, for example, to support leftist political positions linked to struggles for basic human rights amid revolutionary governments and oppressive right-wing regimes. These folkloric pursuits developed primarily in rejection of US cultural domination. For artists, local "authenticity" trumped global forms of commercialized expression. From a leftist perspective, folklore represented ordinary people but also provided a local alternative to the dominant popular culture tied to capitalist countries. In addition, these practices were viewed as "elevating" regional folk music for an inter/national concert audience.

In the United States during this time period, the Chicano movement paralleled the social activism of the preceding civil rights movement. Yet the Chicano movement also took cues from the leftist ideals of nueva canción. The start of the Chicano movement is often traced to 1965 with the Delano Grape Strike instigated by César Chávez and the National Farm Workers Association, later called the United Farm Workers (UFW). Chávez and other organizers encouraged workers to stop picking grapes and the public to stop buying grapes. In turn, they hoped that the loss in revenue would force growers to negotiate for improved working conditions, fewer hours, and better wages. Later, the movement expanded to include political rallies, protests, and marches throughout California, Colorado, New Mexico, and across the United States, advocating for better living conditions for Chicanx people. Finding resonance on college campuses, the movement became an affirmation of identity tied to Indigenous and mestizo heritages. However, Chicana feminists also confronted patriarchy within the movement.[7]

In addition to sociopolitical activism, the Chicano movement stimulated a rich expressive culture. Beyond issues of farmworkers' rights, better education, and ethnoracial unification, creative products like theater, visual art, and music promoted community solidarity. At the beginning of the grape strike, a recent college graduate and former migrant farmworker named Luis Valdez volunteered to develop a small theater organization called El Teatro Campesino (the farmworkers' theater). From 1965 to 1967, El Teatro Campesino produced a series of short, ten- to fifteen-minute, improvised one-act plays called *actos*. Much of the music associated with the Chicano movement came about through these productions.

In this regard, *movimiento* (movement) music drew from *carpa* (tent) theater, a subversive form of traveling entertainment popular in Mexico and the Southwest during the 1920s and 1930s.[8] Mirroring the folkloric elements of nueva canción but also taking influence from preceding Mexican practices, many of the so-called *huelga* (strike) songs associated with the early years of the Chicano movement then took the form of Mexican folk genres like *rancheras*, *corridos*, and *sones*. Drawing on established Mexican modes of musical parody and rhetoric and mimicking the socially relevant lyrics of nueva canción, the lyrics of these songs depicted the struggles of Mexican American farmworkers. They educated farmworkers about and persuaded them of the need for the union. Furthermore, the use of Mexican folk elements unified the diverse Mexican American constituency of the UFW. These songs were performed at picket lines, meetings, rallies, and other union demonstrations. The music was written and performed by amateurs, members of the UFW, rather than professional musicians. In line with the leftist sociopolitical impulses of nueva canción, anyone could contribute, regardless of background, education, or training.

In combining traditional musical forms with socially relevant lyrics, artists like Conjunto Aztlán followed the lead of Chicano movement musicians to address social tensions in South Texas through art. At the same time, these conjunto musicians shifted former working-class representations to support middle-class concerns. That being said, the separation of class considerations within this community is certainly not clear-cut. As in nueva canción practices, the political goals of middle-class activists often aligned with those of the working class. In addition, many Chicanx activists came from working-class backgrounds and moved into the middle class, relative to their parents, as they pursued college educations. Musicians like Conjunto Aztlán drew from working-class experiences to represent their own middle-class positionalities. They revised historical interpretations of the Texas Mexican art form to better represent modern realities, outside of the strict confines of location and class, demonstrating alterations to Texas Mexican identity in the middle of the twentieth century and to the generic definition of the music overall.

Texas Mexican conjunto is fundamentally a hybrid genre, emerging from a mixture of German polka music with Mexican rhythmic traits played on accordion and bajo sexto.[9] Over time, the genre also incorporated musical elements from the Mexican *huapango*, Cuban *bolero*, Colombian *cumbia*, and various US American popular styles. Closely linked with the Chicano movement and nueva canción, Conjunto Aztlán expanded this hybridity, incorporating original repertory and interpretive elements more closely associated with these activist movements. Subject matter shifted from declarations of love and loss and the historical narratives of corridos to statements of cultural injustice. That said, as mentioned above, corridos themselves frequently responded to cultural injustices. Groups like Conjunto Aztlán therefore took influence from older traditions to speak to contemporary circumstances. They drew from local traditions and global practices to represent their own cultural heritages.

Conjunto Aztlán emanates from the Austin region of Texas rather than locations like the Rio Grande Valley and San Antonio that are more closely associated with the conjunto tradition. These musicians were closely enough connected to a local musical context to achieve acceptance as "authentic" among the regional audience. Yet they remained far enough removed from more conservative practices to allow for sociocultural alterations to the historical genre. Situated in Austin, they also took advantage of the proximity of an accepting audience for such innovations. In this way, slightly disconnected from the principal historical location of conjunto but present within the primary sociocultural community, these artists pushed the boundaries of traditional interpretations to create a music simultaneously built on regional heritage but relevant among a new, urban generation. These innovations have subsequently opened the door for younger, San Antonio–based groups to push at the edges of the tradition from inside the traditional geography.

In contrast to former low-class associations, Texas Mexican conjunto music gained a new appreciation through its connection to the Chicano movement in the 1970s. As Peña explains, "Conjunto was sort of 'rehabbed,' if you will, by the Chicano movement in a romantic, nationalist thrust tied to discovering our roots. You have to remember that this was a time when any sort of behavior that smacked of middle-classism was scorned. Working class expressions were considered to be solidly Chicano (and) conjunto became a shibboleth for the movement" (quoted in Acosta 1998).

The adoption of a working-class representation among a socioeconomically broader community changed the contemporary performance, audience, and ultimate interpretation of the music. The younger generation of Texas Mexican musicians had once distanced themselves from the conjunto genre. Many identified with US American forms of popular music and genres like Tejano, relegating conjunto to a designated folkloric music. However, the music's use by groups like Conjunto Aztlán produced new cultural significance for the genre outside of historical boundaries of class, ethnicity, language, and location, as demonstrated by the music's increasing use by younger artists and in contemporary presentations like the Tejano Conjunto Festival (see Bauer 2019). In this regard, performances by Conjunto Aztlán demonstrate that Texas Mexican culture is not a fixed component of space and time but instead a fluid construct that changes to accommodate new articulations of identity and sociocultural ideology in the modern world. Despite fundamental connections to a particular class, ethnicity, language, and location, Conjunto Aztlán introduces new associations through the group's ties to the Chicano movement in the United States and nueva canción practices throughout Latin America. In following such connections, we can begin to understand new social identities across the Texas Mexican region.

MOVIMIENTO MUSIC IN SOUTH TEXAS: CONJUNTO AZTLÁN

Drawing from the earlier practices of both the nueva canción movement in Latin America and the Chicano movement in California, Conjunto Aztlán serves as an example of the musical manifestations of the Chicano movement (movimiento music) in South Texas during the 1970s and beyond. Throughout their existence, the group has been primarily performance-based, only recording their music in the 1990s. As Peregrino describes, "Just like a lot of folk groups or other movimiento groups, we placed more emphasis on performing and never really emphasized putting things in writing—keeping it in the oral tradition" (quoted in Acosta 1998). During the 1970s, the ensemble performed at clubs, festivals, and universities across Austin and the Southwest. They also performed at social/political events such as marches against police brutality, benefits for the Texas Farmworker's Union and the Brown Berets, fundraisers for community organizations like CASA and the League of United Chicano Artists (LUChA), conferences, and political rallies. Tejeda explains: "Where Chicano movement people gathered, *nuestra música* [our music] was there" (1999, 21; see fig. 13.1). Despite this performance-oriented identification, Conjunto Aztlán did record two albums (*Conjunto Aztlán* [1998] and *From Aztlán, With Love* [2004]) twenty-some years after their initial formation. As Peregrino notes, "As [John] Lennon and [Paul] McCartney said, we're not going to be able to be doing this when we're in our seventies.... It was time to get it down and record this bit of musical history" (quoted in Acosta 1998). In this regard, despite its provenance many years after the relevant time period of the Chicano movement, the group's first CD provides a quintessential representation of Conjunto Aztlán. Furthermore, many of the fundamental issues addressed by the Chicano movement in the 1970s have not yet reached resolution. Tejeda notes (in 1998, with the release of the ensemble's first CD): "The timing is right.... It's like the Chicano movement is coming back—the push for affirmative action, the push for bilingual education, immigrant bashing, all these issues are here again. It's like we're in a time warp. Those issues are relevant now" (quoted in Acosta 1998). As such, following the group's inception in the 1970s, their recorded release in the 1990s, and the persistence of similar sociocultural issues, analysis of this music remains stubbornly appropriate.

Conjunto Aztlan's first recording (*Conjunto Aztlán* [1998]) represents music associated with the Chicano movement from the 1970s.[10] The album is thus a "tribute" to earlier practices; a historical representation of the band's many years of social and political activism. As a recent rendition of older performances, the album was distributed across radio stations, record stores, and online platforms like iTunes and Apple Music. However, Peregrino emphasizes the fundamentally underground nature of movimiento music in line with nueva canción practices: "[Nueva canción music is] all almost underground, so how do they sell? When do you hear this music? Somehow people find out. Sometimes you visit someone and you hear a CD. You might begin to look for and listen to that kind of music because the regular stations don't play them. People get hungry for it and seek them out. That's where we fall, I think" (quoted in Acosta 1998).

The album mixes a standard Texas Mexican conjunto ensemble of button accordion, bajo sexto, bass, and drum set with additional guitars and percussion instruments (timbales, congas, and bongos, among others). It presents socially conscious lyrics in a combination of English and Spanish ("Spanglish"). It includes original songs and selections written by movimiento artists like Rumel Fuentes and Teatro Los Malqueridos from Texas, and Flor del

Fig. 13.1. José Flores Peregrino (bajo sexto) and Juan Tejeda (accordion) of Conjunto Aztlán perform in the mid-2000s. Photo credit: Juan Tejeda. Used with permission.

Pueblo and Teatro Campesino from California. Musically, the CD mixes the sounds of classic conjunto (polkas, waltzes, etc.) with Indigenous elements and characteristics of reggae, salsa, and rock. Of the sixteen songs on the album, comprising a variety of styles, "Vamos a pelear en la guerra" (Let's go fight in the war) and "Yo soy tu hermano, yo soy Chicano" (I am your brother, I am Chicano) serve as representative examples of typical regional characteristics with socially conscious lyrics. Beyond these conjunto-oriented examples, the album pushes the generic boundaries of the music even further from its historical roots. Yet despite the incorporation of unexpected musical characteristics, Conjunto Aztlán remain stubbornly characterized—for themselves, the local community, marketing professionals, scholars, and more widespread audiences—as "conjunto," demonstrating the persistence and also inappropriateness of homologous interpretations of genre and identity.

The lyrics of "Vamos a pelear en la guerra" present a battle against injustice and "los balazos de la policía" (the bullets of the police).[11] They trace an Indigenous and/or Mexican claim to the border with lines like "Vámonos a pelear en la guerra, / Que esta tierra es de nosotros" (Let's go fight in the war, / Because this land is ours). The refrain further emphasizes this relationship between the community and its land:

...No nos vamos a dejar....	We are not going to let them.
La semilla 'sta bien sembrada;	The seed is well sown;
No nos pueden desenraizar.	They cannot root us out.

A reference to the "Pistol of Aztlán" invokes the mythical homeland of the Aztec people.[12] The lyrics also portray a close, familial relationship among the Chicano community: "Y como hermanos y hermanas / por nuestros hijos lucharemos" (And like brothers and sisters / we will fight for our children). Lines indicating that "La madre campesina... [p]lanta semillas de revolución" (the peasant mother... [p]lants seeds of revolution) connect these struggles to the farmworkers and thus to the earlier Chicano movement in California. The song fits well within movimiento music with its folkloric genre and socially significant lyrics, its emphasis on the solidarity of the Chicanx people, and its connection to an Indigenous heritage. However, it is localized through the use of conjunto and its emphasis on the land, taken by the US government in relatively recent regional memory. Texas Mexican musicians, in particular, often express this notion of community-based unity (Chicano brotherhood or *carnalismo*) (Azcona 2008, 137). Furthermore, according to Chicago-based movimiento musician Jesus "Chuy" Negrete, these lyrics resonate better in Texas than in the Midwest: "Now, you sing that to a group of workers in Chicago and they say: 'But, what war?' It sounds almost like a historical song that somebody sang in 1849. Perhaps in Texas it still makes sense.... It is sung on the border and has that spirit of struggle" (quoted in Azcona 2008, 169). Although closely aligned with the Chicano movement, the music of Conjunto Aztlán thus speaks directly to Chicanx circumstances in Texas.

"Vamos a pelear en la guerra" uses a classic conjunto structure and sound with socially conscious lyrics to simultaneously speak to contemporary circumstances and Texas Mexican heritage. As such, it corresponds to nueva canción practices throughout Latin America that combine traditional genres and instruments with politically and socially charged lyrics. Conjunto Aztlán employ a variety of generic characteristics within their two recorded albums. However, "Vamos a pelear en la guerra" relies most heavily on elements of classic conjunto. The ensemble thus firmly establish the music they produce as "conjunto," despite new sociocultural identifications and interpretive characteristics. Conjunto music, then, shifts to represent modern realities.

In this song, the distinctive regional combination of button accordion with bajo sexto is sonically prominent, with electric bass and drum set carrying the rhythmic foundation. The recording employs a polka rhythm consisting of a bass drum on the beat (1 and 3) and snare drum off the beat (2 and 4). The song is in a traditional Mexican and Texas Mexican form comprising an instrumental introduction, verse and refrain, an instrumental interlude corresponding to material from the verse, a second verse and refrain, and a tag ending. As common to the conjunto tradition, the accordion plays a passage at the end of each vocal line. The instrument also frequently plays under the line, as more typically heard in modern conjunto renditions. The two vocal lines sing close harmonies in thirds, as is also common throughout the regional traditions. While the song is in Spanish throughout, Tejeda counts the group in with a combination of Spanish and English ("*uno, dos*, one, two, three . . . !"), indicating the bilingual and bicultural nature of the recording. Some contemporary conjunto artists demonstrate this biculturality by inserting elements of US American popular music into conjunto recordings. This recording instead maintains an earlier version of the tradition, using the musical style to conform to the local, sociocultural heritage and the lyrics to portray modern circumstances.

The song "Yo soy tu hermano, yo soy Chicano" also represents a distinctively Texas Mexican manifestation of the Chicano movement. The refrain emphasizes community-based unity as inherent to the construction of Chicano identity:

Yo soy tu hermano/a, yo soy Chicano/a.	I am your brother/sister, I am Chicano/a.
Dame tu mano, vamos a volar.	Give me your hand, let's fly.
Bien dice el dicho	The saying says it well:

si sangra mi hermano/a	if my brother/sister bleeds
Yo también sangro, la herida	I also bleed, the wound is the
es igual.	same.[13]

The depiction of social injustices again leads here to a call for militant action: fighting—violently, if necessary—for change: "Ya no me aguanto, yo quiero pelear" (I cannot stand it anymore, I want to fight). A pejorative reference to Texas Rangers (*rinches*) further localizes the song. As in the previous example, the Conjunto Aztlán recording of this song begins with a typical instrumental introduction, tag ending, and alternating sections of instrumental interludes with verse and refrain pairs. The rhythm and tempo of a polka, traditional conjunto instrumentation, close vocal harmonies, and accordion insertions at the end of each musical phrase and underlying the vocal lines connect the song to the Texas Mexican musical tradition. The use of these folkloric elements with socially charged lyrics then tie the song to the Chicano movement and, ultimately, to nueva canción.

Although Conjunto Aztlán were one of the most prominent groups to directly associate conjunto music with the Chicano movement, other musicians from South Texas have pursued comparable approaches during the intervening years. Ensembles like Little Joe Y La Familia, performing Tejano music during the 1970s, and Los Nahuatlatos, playing fusion music in the first decades of the twenty-first century, have responded to similar social impetuses. Conjunto Aztlán represent an oral tradition, corresponding to older techniques of the genre as a whole. Performance-based practices were recorded and programmed on the radio only some twenty years after the group's inception and only through financial support from the artists themselves. Alternatively, groups like Little Joe Y La Familia and Los Nahuatlatos rely on recordings for widespread dissemination of their music. This process alters the sociopolitical interpretation of the genre for performers, audiences, and external observers, since the recorded product—preconceived, practiced, and perfected—is inherently different from the physical sense of community created by live performance. Recent recordings of formerly oral practices facilitate links between local musicians and more geographically dispersed communities. However, as Light Carruyo asserts, these recordings simultaneously alter historically "tangible" communities created through "ties of kinship, daily interactions, and geographic proximity" in favor of the "imagined" communities associated with relocation to the studio (2005, 99).

In this regard, performance-based groups like Conjunto Aztlán spoke to a relatively small, physically present, and thus inherently limited audience.

In contrast, later instances of social activism in conjunto were influenced by movimiento practices but altered through expanded commercialization and distribution. Following the example of Conjunto Aztlán, these subsequent musicians used regional symbols like conjunto to reinterpret the construction of community across a range of socioeconomic and geographic circumstances. In connecting the conjunto tradition to the sociopolitical messages of the Chicano movement, Conjunto Aztlán made the regional music relevant among a younger and increasingly middle-class population. In disseminating their music through recordings and bringing additional generic characteristics into the regional art form, bands like Little Joe Y La Familia and Los Nahuatlatos have subsequently attracted a multiethnic and geographically diverse audience for the music. These two techniques of musical dissemination—live and recorded—create distinctive audiences far beyond the working-class community who are most closely connected to the musical genre.

As Thomas Turino argues, "cultural style and musical styles are integrally bound to definitions of social position and access to opportunities" (1993, 162). The reinterpretation of Texas Mexican conjunto by groups like Conjunto Aztlán brought a newfound appreciation for the music among younger audiences. The alteration of the genre to represent modern circumstances ultimately increased the social status and economic opportunities for associated musicians. With the advent of the Chicano movement, as Peña emphasizes, "No matter what your (class) status, the conjunto has become a symbol of *Mexican-American* heritage" (quoted in Acosta 1998, emphasis added). For Peña, a conjunto-influenced identification as Texas Mexican seems inherently connected to former working-class considerations. However, the use of the genre among a middle-class population breaks associations not only with class but also with culture. The separation of conjunto from its working-class roots severs associations between "traditional" musical elements, primitivist stereotypes, and Texas Mexican heritage. The embrace of conjunto among a middle-class, Mexican American (rather than Texas Mexican) community through its association with the Chicano movement removes its connotation as fundamentally working class. In turn, this process removes the characterization of the Texas Mexican population as similarly identified.

Sonically connected to a cultural community, protest songs can create communicative power for musical resistance. As observed throughout nueva canción practices, sociopolitical lyrics frequently add to meaningful interpretations. Since its inception as a form of cultural resistance during the early years of the twentieth century, conjunto music has served as a counterhegemonic response to mainstream discrimination. Although the circumstances for this discrimination have shifted in the last century, the music itself has adapted to absorb the fluidity of Texas Mexican culture across space and time. This reliance on the sonic capacity of protest music, in combination with politically suggestive lyrics, corresponds to Julius Carlson's assertion that the folkloric *sounds* of protest songs are "as central to their political connotations as their poetic texts" (2019, 2).

In Conjunto Aztlán's contributions to the Chicano movement, sociopolitical lyrics are important, but the evocative sound of button accordion with bajo sexto—historically representative of sociocultural struggle—is tied to regional resistance. The music, itself a cyclical fusing of transcultural elements, has, then, shifted to represent its community across multiple generations and continuing, but ever-changing injustices. As Carlson notes, "musical and lyrical content, and the significance of this content, is kaleidoscopic, changing from listener to listener and time period to time period" (2019, 18). Outside of narrative depictions of historical injustices in corridos and certain ties to subversive techniques in Mexico, the older conjunto tradition confronts sociocultural discrimination through sonic connotations. Seemingly innocuous lyrics cloak more meaningful social positionings in the symbolic correspondence between distinctive musical strains and the associated community. In traditional conjunto practices, the sounds of the music itself represent counterhegemonic expressions. This contrasts the use of parody in theater-based productions of the UFW or the use of double entendre in politically dangerous circumstances like that of Chile in the 1970s. Socially relevant lyrics in conjunto music signify a privilege among modern artists to explicitly articulate injustices.

CONCLUSIONS: NEW SOCIOCULTURAL INTERPRETATIONS OF TEXAS MEXICAN CONJUNTO

Through traditional genres and instruments combined with politically and socially charged lyrics, the music of the Chicano movement, or movimiento music, connected to nueva canción practices across Latin America. It affirmed a powerful sense of cultural identity and carved out a new musical space for ethnic Mexicans in the United States. Movimiento artists drew from Indigenous, Spanish, and mestizo heritages to root an art in Chicanx culture and society. These musicians contributed to Mexican American activism during the 1960s through the 1990s alongside Chávez and the general pursuit for bilingual education, integration in schooling and housing, and a more open job market. However, while the Chicano movement and its associated musics were commonly situated in California, Colorado, and New Mexico, Texas Mexican artists also participated in movimiento music. The activism of conjunto musicians in South Texas draws connections to the music and issues of social justice among today's Chicanx community in the United States and across Latin America.

In traditional interpretations, conjunto is fundamentally a local form of music connected to rural, working-class Texas Mexican identity. Yet it is also an explicit manifestation of cultural hybridity; the twentieth-century product of German polka music with Mexican instruments, rhythms, structures, and repertory. In combining conjunto with hybrid elements to represent new identities, groups like Conjunto Aztlán transfer traditional practices to their contemporary circumstances. Associations with the Chicano movement and nueva canción practices demonstrate new representations of location, class, urbanity, and education. As rural, class-based, and geographically insular identities shift, conjunto changes to accommodate new sociopolitical circumstances. It maintains its fundamental sense of cultural hybridity but expands to include additional sounds, structures, lyrics, and languages. The music retains its regional orientation but includes new connections outside of the original cultural community.

Tracing these alterations helps eliminate primitivist representations of Texas Mexican identity. Groups like Conjunto Aztlán reject strictly homologous notions of genre *as* identity to create new circumstances for the music in modern society. Instead of a notion that "old-fashioned" musical elements signify negative stereotypes of Texas Mexican communities, artists like Conjunto Aztlán demonstrate that adherence to folkloric genres can represent a variety of intentions. Music, by itself, does not determine identity.

NOTES

1. Juan Tejeda, interview with the author, July 12, 2018.
2. Conjunto-based connections in Chicano movement music remain most prominent between South Texas and California. Historically, many of the musical manifestations of the movement are situated in correspondence with the Farm Workers movement in California. Outside of its prevalence in Texas, conjunto itself has experienced a certain popularity in California. However, the Chicano movement did exist throughout the United States—particularly in Colorado and New Mexico—and examples of conjunto music are found in the Southwest, Midwest, Pacific Northwest, and elsewhere.
3. In fact, the rate of violent crime in the city at the time was "well below the state and national average" (Grieder 2019).
4. The so-called homology model of musical categorization refers to a one-to-one correspondence between genre and identification; a theorized and often imaginary association between categories of music and demographics of people. Historically, record

companies exploited such homologous relationships for marketing purposes. As David Brackett explains, "In this mode of identification, a race record finds an African American audience; an old-time record finds a rural, white, Southern audience; a mainstream record finds a white, bourgeois, Northern, urban audience; and a foreign record finds a foreigner" (Brackett 2016, 23).

5. Brenda M. Romero, personal communications with the author, October 2020.
6. Juan Tejeda, interview with the author, July 12, 2018.
7. Brenda M. Romero, personal communications with the author, October 2020.
8. Ibid.
9. German music arrived with German immigrants during the late nineteenth century, with business incentives from the Mexican government after they built a railroad to the north.
10. In contrast, the group's second recording, *From Aztlán, With Love* (2004), is a series of original love songs.
11. In "Vamos a Pelear en la Guerra," as performed and recorded by Conjunto Aztlán. From *Conjunto Aztlán* (1998). Used with permission.
12. "Pistolera de Aztlán." As Brenda M. Romero notes, this lyric conceivably references the Chicano scholarship of Americo Paredes's *With a Pistol in His Hand* (personal communications with the author, November 2020).
13. In "Yo Soy Tu Hermano, Yo Soy Chicano," as performed and recorded by Conjunto Aztlán. From *Conjunto Aztlán* (1998). Used with permission.

BIBLIOGRAPHY

Acosta, Belinda. 1998. "The Dialogue of Poets: Conjunto Aztlan's Movimiento Music." *Austin Chronicle*, April 17, 1998.

Azcona, Steven César. 2008. "Movement in Chicano Music: Performing Culture, Performing Politics, 1965–1979." PhD diss., University of Texas at Austin.

Bauer, Erin E. 2019. "Blurring Boundaries in Rosedale Park: The Importance of the Tejano Conjunto Festival on the Transnational Dissemination of Traditional Texas-Mexican Accordion Music." *Latino Studies* 17 (2): 164–86.

Brackett, David. 2016. *Categorizing Sound: Genre and Twentieth-Century Popular Music*. Berkeley: University of California Press.

Carlson, Julius Reder. 2019. "'Basta ya!': Aesthetic Calibanism and Cold War–Era Context in the Protest Songs of Atahualpa Yupanqui." *Music and Politics* 13 (2): 1–21.

Carruyo, Light. 2005. "La Gaita Zuliana: Music and the Politics of Protest in Venezuela." *Latin American Perspectives* 32 (3): 98–111.

García, Michelle. 2018. "The Border and the American Imagination." *Baffler*, July 2. https://thebaffler.com/latest/border-imagination-garcia/.

Grieder, Erica. 2019. "Trump Knows Nothing about Texas, and That's Hurting the Country." *Houston Chronicle*, January 22, 2019.

Hinojosa, Felipe. 2013. "¡Medicina Sí Muerte No!: Race, Public Health, and the 'Long War on Poverty' in Mathis, Texas, 1948–1971." *Western Historical Quarterly* 44 (4): 437–58.

Peña, Manuel. 1985. *The Texas-Mexican Conjunto: History of a Working-Class Music.* Austin: University of Texas Press.

Tejeda, Juan. 1999. "Música del Movimiento Chicano/Chicano Movement Music: An Overview." Unpublished manuscript.

Turino, Thomas. 1993. *Moving Away from Silence: Music of the Peruvian Altiplano and the Experience of Urban Migration.* Chicago: University of Chicago Press.

Wilson, Christopher. 2018. "5 Myths about US-Mexico Border." *Newsday* (New York), May 26. https://www.newsday.com/opinion/commentary/5-myths-about-u-s-mexico-border-1.18729832/.

DISCOGRAPHY

Conjunto Aztlán. 1998. *Conjunto Aztlán.* Pulsar Records: Los Angeles.

———. 2004. *From Aztlán, With Love.* Pulsar Records: Los Angeles.

PART IV

DIRECT ACTION

FOURTEEN

"MUSIC IS LIBERATION"

The Brass Liberation Orchestra and Direct Action

ANDREW G. SNYDER

"DIRECT ACTION IS ACTING AS if you're already free." A poster with these words hung in downtown Oakland's Unite Here union building, where the Brass Liberation Orchestra (BLO) used to hold weekly rehearsals across from the main city plaza, lovingly remembered by local activist communities as the site of Occupy Oakland in 2011. The BLO is a political brass band with a range of active participants from generally ten to twenty-five. The band was founded in 2002 to support leftist cultures in the San Francisco Bay Area. Sarah Norr, a former BLO drummer and union organizer with Unite Here (a national union that organizes hospitality workers), coordinated the band's use of the building. Norr is one of many BLO activists, professional and otherwise, who help the BLO network with leftist organizations and further the pursuit of its mission to use music to sustain and support direct actions, marches, and social justice organizations.[1]

In a *San Francisco Chronicle* article on the BLO, Megan Swoboda, former BLO trumpet player and comanager of the direct action training nonprofit Ruckus Society, claimed, "We're a political organization; we're not [just] a band.... I see the Brass Liberation Orchestra as our own direct action affinity group that focuses on using music as a tactical action element" (Kuperberg 2013). As a "direct action affinity group," the BLO works both autonomously as a band and together with many other action organizers in collective pursuit of common political goals, and it offers a range of creative interventions to activists and organizers. Since its inception, the band has participated in numerous major national and local campaigns, including antiwar, anti–corporate globalization, immigrant rights, LGBTQIA+ rights, antigentrification, Occupy, Black Lives Matter, and antifascist movements, among others.

In my conversations with participants in the Bay Area's activist communities, the band's presence at direct actions throughout the region has often been noted as a tangible contribution to social justice movements. In this chapter, I examine some of the ways that the BLO deploys music as a strategy of direct action. I explore two BLO direct actions in the LGBTQIA+ rights and Occupy movements to show how both presentational and participatory music making (Turino 2008) are used as effective action strategies. I refer to the process of "acting as if you're already free" as *the performance of freedom*, which I define as an affective strategy of protest and revolution. Through this performative lens, I consider the BLO both *in* and *as* direct action. I show that the BLO's actions serve as representative models of increasingly transnational forms of global protest cultures that use instrumental music to materially transform protest settings.

A GLOBALIZING NETWORK OF MUSIC AND ACTIVISM

I came to the BLO through engagement with the Bay Area Occupy Movement in late 2011. The group had been keeping the beat at the numerous protests, marches, and other actions of what became known as "American Fall" in solidarity with the Arab Spring. I became an active member on trumpet, leading, composing, improvising, arranging, and participating musically in at least one action per week until embarking on dissertation fieldwork in 2014, and I have remained a less active member until I left the Bay Area in 2020. My involvement with the BLO quickly introduced me to a larger transnational network of political brass bands that has grown increasingly connected in the United States, Europe, and Latin America in the past twenty years or so. This network has quickly consolidated since the founding of the HONK! Festival of Activist Street Bands in 2006 in Boston as the HONK! movement.

HONK! represents a network of brass bands with histories of participation in protest as far back as the 1960s, with roots in Vermont's Bread and Puppet Theater, which used brass bands in the Vietnam War protests. Part of the festival's original intent was to forge a space for connecting and networking for bands that defined themselves in some way as political. Many bands that have come to frequent the HONK! network do define themselves as explicitly political, but the festival's activist label has long been a subject of controversy as it is also a countercultural affair with limited activist manifestations. Subsequent versions of the HONK! Festival spread first to other cities in the United States—Seattle and Austin, among others—before later sprouting up in Australia, Brazil, Canada, Costa Rica, and the UK, with a current total of twenty-two HONK! festivals around the globe. In the face of the pandemic in 2020, the HONK! festivals held a HONK!United virtual festival, which showcased activist bands around the globe and further increased the growing self-consciousness of the movement as such.²

The BLO has been at the heart of the HONK! movement since its inception. Organizers of the original Boston HONK! have recounted to me that they knew the first edition of the festival would be successful once they had secured the BLO's participation, making the festival more than a regional northeastern affair. The band was founded by two sisters, Jamie and Alli Spector, who had been inspired by their experience with radical Italian brass bands that have since networked with American HONK! bands. An important American predecessor, of which early BLO members soon became aware, was Seattle's Infernal Noise Brigade, founded in 1999 to support the militant disruption of the World Trade Organization's meeting and combat corporate globalization (Whitney 2003). As the BLO's activities grew precipitously to support the anti–Iraq War protests in 2002, the group likewise inspired new bands, such as its "sister band," New York's Rude Mechanical Orchestra (RMO). The RMO's first major "gig" at the Republican National Convention in 2004 resulted in arrests of many musicians, including BLO musicians who had come to play in solidarity. The BLO has freely shared online its diverse repertoire—including New Orleans, Balkan, Latin American, Afrobeat music, and much more—helping promote an unofficial standard repertoire for HONK! festivals as many brass bands around the world have adapted BLO's arrangements.³

This is all to say that the BLO has been in active conversation for two decades with these and other bands from around the world who have appeared at HONK! festivals about the strategic effectiveness of instrumental music in social movements. Though this chapter focuses on the BLO's actions in its local Bay Area setting, my argument that the BLO's tactics reflect emergent translocal strategies of musical and political engagement should be understood in the context of the global connections I have briefly traced here. This musical networking correlates to the increasing translocalism of contemporary leftist activism (Castells 2012), and the BLO's actions reverberate far beyond their local settings. Indeed, Amelia Mason (2017) asserts that "the giant musical block party that is HONK! is a celebration of what is probably the most vibrant incarnation of the protest music tradition in America today."

DIRECT ACTION AND PREFIGURATIVE POLITICS

Movement organizers generally speak of the tactics of protest and direct action in relation to the achievement of a particular goal. For the BLO too, music is a goal-oriented activity—in some of the actions I have performed in, participants credited the BLO with "making" the action, that is, with determining its success. How can music be evaluated as successful, not in terms of popularity or aesthetic excellence, but in its capacity to affect tangible change in the act of protest?

While many studies have examined music in social movements, these are generally limited to analyzing lyrics, music industries, style, or the political work of musicians (for example, Rosenthal and Flacks 2011; Roy 2010; Eyerman and Jamison 1998). Lyrics especially are often studied as a window for understanding what Eyerman and Jamison (1998) call the "cognitive praxis" of a social movement, or how music diffuses interpretive frames and ideas to incite participation in social movements. These are essentially semiotic approaches; relatively little work has been done to understand how music is used as part of a direct action strategy and even less regarding how instrumental music expresses politics and interacts with protest and direct action, with exceptions (for example, Snyder 2020; Abe 2018; Manabe 2015; McKay 2007). In contrast to protest music based on critical lyrics, HONK! festival organizer Reebee Garofalo suggests that "we might think of HONK! bands as the ground game of progressive music" (forthcoming). Recent work in sound studies focusing on the transformative capacities of sound can lead us to more affective methods of interpreting musical activism.

When instrumental musicians use music strategically to achieve an explicit political change and confront hegemonic power to do so, they engage in what I call *instrumental protest*. I use this term not only to call attention to the particular musical efficacies of instrumental ensembles but also to evaluate their instrumentality in activating and pushing forward political struggles. Instrumental musicians deploy their musical and expressive repertoires to be effective in political struggles. Social movement scholar Charles Tilly (2010) has used the term *repertoire of contention* to refer to a given set of protest tools available to social movement actors. But despite the musical resonance of the term *repertoire*, the musical choices of protesters have rarely been interpreted as repertoires of contention. Here, I expand on Tilly's concept by examining the strategic musical choices of the BLO, what I call the band's *musical repertoires of contention* (see also Snyder 2020).

The term *direct action* commonly refers to political action that goes beyond sanctioned political processes to change policy, such as approved marches, electoral campaigns, and petitions of elected officials. It usually refers to nonviolent or violent protest actions in which protesters defy legal restrictions and take matters into their own hands. Examples include sit-ins, workplace occupations, property destruction, and putting one's body on the line, sometimes with the risk of great bodily harm. Even if an action's goal is to petition a target with the power of addressing demands, the mode of the action is "free" and direct if unmediated and undetermined by sanctioned channels of the political process. The popular guide *Organizing for Social Change* defines direct action as when "The people directly affected by the problem take action to solve it" in ways that alter power relationships and give them a sense of their own power defined on their own terms (Bobo 2003, 11). While members of the BLO are not always directly affected by the problem of a given action, the group acts as an affinity group to organizers and communities that plan such actions, and members let themselves be instruments for diverse social movements.

The BLO's reluctance to support political campaigns of any kind, for example, is indicative of the band's rejection of the mediated forum of electoral politics, which it believes involves a negotiation with status quo interests beyond redemption, at least as far as their project is concerned. BLO members themselves do not necessarily reject strategic participation in electoral politics or other conventional vehicles of political transformation, though some do. The BLO, as a band, can be understood as anarchist in its dismissal of working within institutional channels, which presumes a concession of freedom to the state. In his book *Direct Action: An Ethnography* (2009), on the global anarchist movements that emerged at the turn of the millennium and certainly influenced the BLO, David Graeber echoes Unite Here's poster mentioned previously in his definition of the term: "Direct action is the insistence, when faced with structures of unjust authority, on acting as if one is already free" (203). Further distinguishing protest from direct action, for Graeber, "Protest is like begging the powers that be to dig a well. Direct action is digging the well and daring them to stop you" (Trey 2014). Similarly, Bernard Harcourt (2013) notes that the politics of Occupy and other recent movements that have been influenced by contemporary anarchist thinking have promoted "political disobedience," as opposed to civil disobedience: "Civil disobedience aims not to displace the lawmaking institutions or the structure of legal governance, but rather to change the existing laws by demonstrating their injustice. Political disobedience, by contrast, resists the very way in which we are governed. It resists the structure of partisan politics, the demand for policy reforms, the call for party identification" (47). Linking this rejection of sanctioned channels of political expression to movement, performance, and freedom, André Lepecki suggests that direct action protesters embrace "choreopolitics," which invites "a redistribution and reinvention of bodies, affects, and senses through which one may learn how to move politically, how to invent, activate, seek, or experiment with a movement whose only sense (meaning and direction) is the experimental exercise of freedom" (2013, 20; quoted in Silverstein 2019, 4).

Building on these insights, I understand direct action to be a performance that actively counters hegemonic power by acting on the premise that the state has no legitimate authority to determine the mode of dissent.

Direct action is not only resistance, however; it also performatively offers positive, constructive alternatives through its enactment. Graeber writes that, ideally, direct action is "a way of actively engaging with the world to bring about change, in which the form of the action—or at least the organization of the action—is itself a model for the change one wishes to bring about" (2009, 206). For example, "the direct actionist does not just refuse to pay taxes to support a militarized school system, she combines with others to try to create a new school system" (203). In this sense, direct action is a form of "prefigurative politics," in which the action is a performative manifestation of new social and political relations as well as an explicit and targeted petitioning of power. The performance of freedom is not only the freedom *to* enact change on one's own terms but also freedom *from* conventional social and political relations that would inhibit such action. Building on Judith Butler's (2015) insight that action is performative and enacts new realities, I consider direct action to be the performative enactment of utopia (Dolan 2001), in which freedom from the state is experienced, if only temporarily, and can thereby be imagined and worked toward more completely.

For the BLO, the idea that musically supported direct action is tied in with an experience of freedom is clear from the very first point of unity in its mission statement: "Music is liberation." Indeed, instrumental music has a particular role to play in and as direct action, not in telling a story about injustice as much protest music does, but in working to directly enact utopia.

THE BLO AS DIRECT ACTION

The BLO's political values are operative not only in *what* the group supports but in *how* it operates and organizes itself. In a radio show made about the BLO and other political brass bands, "Marching for Change," the narrator suggests, "The BLO is itself a political project. What they play, how and when they play it, and how the group operates: it's all based on their desire for social justice" (Making Contact 2010).

The BLO's mission statement, written at the beginning of the group's formation and posted on its website, reveals the self-consciousness of its pursuits as a political project: "The Brass Liberation Orchestra makes loud on the streets to inspire, instigate, agitate, mourn, celebrate, and communicate. We stand in solidarity with groups and movements who are working for a more just and equitable world. We are a work in progress. We work to build a multigender/multiracial/multigenerational group that enhances and strengthens the culture of the Left" (Brass Liberation Orchestra 2013). The band organizes itself around five points of unity, published on the group's website and used to present a coherent political platform for members, prospective members, and political organizations interested in collaborating. Since they are crucial for understanding the band's project, I quote them in full:

1. Music is liberation: Culture is a celebration of life and human creativity. We use music as a response to oppressive society, to sustain and build our movements, and as expression of the world that we want to live in. BLO is a group of musicians (of all levels) and cultural workers who use culture to support causes of a broadly left nature.
2. Racial and social justice: We work to challenge and eliminate all forms of domination (racism, class oppression, sexism, hetero-sexism, ageism, ableism, etc.) both within our group and within the broader society. We pay particular attention to racism and White supremacy as we see these forms of oppression as a primary obstacle to building the just society that we all want to live in.
3. Diversity of political strategies: We agree that we will work together, making political art to contribute to leftist struggles without promoting any ideological tendency on the Left over another. We work in the spirit of left unity to overcome the fragmentation of the Left in the United States.
4. Respect for culture: We work for a society that respects all cultures and work to promote cross-cultural understanding, social justice, and human solidarity. We attempt to do this in a manner that avoids exploitation, stealing or ignorance of the world's cultures.
5. Respect for the earth: We work to reverse the trend of domination and misuse of the world's natural resources. Many of us are against capitalism because the destruction of the world's environment has reached the level of ecocide. (Ibid.)

Notwithstanding the often-overlooked fact that music can be just as much a vehicle for domination and division as for freedom and unity, the BLO's declaration that "music is liberation" expresses the belief that music is spiritually and politically emancipatory and embodies what I am calling the "performance of freedom." For this band, music provides a vehicle for political disobedience to oppressive regimes and helps musicians and protesters performatively act as though they are already free, hence allowing them to become more free. Animated by these goals, the BLO aims to operate differently from conventional bands and provide a resource and example to others. Bands formed afterward credit the BLO with inspiring its internal organization as well as what I call its musical repertoires of contention.

While the BLO's membership is diverse in terms of occupation—it counts union organizers, professors, the unemployed, students, activists, artists, tech workers, and teachers among its members—the group is majority White, its most active members are generally between the ages of twenty-five and forty, and membership generally shows a majority from relatively privileged backgrounds. The band addresses structural inequalities within the group by trying to maintain roughly equal gender balance and diversity in participation levels and leadership roles—important, if not entirely met, goals. Good faith attempts to broaden membership to include people of color, women, working class, and queer-identifying musicians have had varying success throughout the group's history, and the band has become notably more diverse in all respects in the decade I have been a part of it. The BLO actively rotates responsibilities—such as conducting, tactical organization, and rehearsal facilitation—in order to inhibit the solidification of firm roles and the emergence of hierarchy, though, in practice, differences in expertise and experience means members tend to maintain many roles.

The group operates as an ostensibly leaderless, horizontal collective, making decisions through a consensus model in which any proposal can be blocked by a single member. While I have seen the consensus method produce tension among members, my experience with the band has led me to conclude that consensus culture can promote a conciliatory decision process in which single-person blocks are highly discouraged but respected when they occur. According to members, the benefits of this horizontal model include active engagement in the decision-making process and rigorous critique of any proposal, while they also admit that the process can be slow and fraught with disagreement. In my experience, however, seniority, particular expertise, and entrenched social hierarchies do lead to certain members' opinions being given more weight than others.[4]

The BLO's consensus-based membership process weighs many factors discussed during a prospective member's interview, including experience in activism, experience in music and the arts, and ideological agreement with the points of unity. As point one makes clear, being a multilevel band is integral to the BLO's history and identity as a political project, and political experience, commitment, and savvy might count more than musical experience in some cases. The BLO has rejected musically solid White, male musicians due to perceptions of lack of political commitment and has imposed affirmative action strategies for membership, and members often argue that the band is "not a political education project." While the group has sometimes been perceived as exclusionary, members understand such sacrifices to be necessary for maintaining the ideological coherence of the band and its openness to musicians of color, as well as female, working-class, and queer-identifying musicians. Naomi Podber (2020), in her study of the Rude Mechanical Orchestra, refers to this dynamic as a tension between "wide inclusion," which seeks to build diverse, populist movements, and "provisional inclusion," which sets conditions on inclusion that can lead to demographic homogenization.

The result is a multilevel band in which participation of less experienced musicians and historically underrepresented populations is a priority. The meeting of differing musical skill levels can present challenges that other bands do not face, as musicians of all levels—professionals to beginners—seek common musical ground. The BLO prioritizes songs based on unchallenging melodies, simple chord structures, and repetitive grooves, though complexity varies widely. Within this context of simplicity, more musically advanced players fill in spaces with improvisation, polyrhythms, harmonies, countermelodies, and extended solo sections, while less experienced musicians are encouraged to learn these skills gradually. Still, more advanced musicians may have to check their authority on the way to the street, promoting the skills and leadership capacities of less experienced musicians rather than leading in a hierarchical manner, or risk complaints from other members of taking up space.

Beyond its participation in protest, the BLO sees itself as positively embodying direct action and enacting the performance of freedom in its organization. If leftist critique can broadly be understood as informing aspirations toward a society in which unequal power relationships are equalized through active engagement and attention, the BLO's attempts to promote diversity, equal powers of leadership, horizontal decision-making, and art as a vehicle of political and spiritual liberation can be understood as direct actions on the conventional notion of what a band is and what it is for—or music as direct action.

THE BLO IN DIRECT ACTION

A typical week in the BLO might include a nonprofit's fundraising party, an immigrant rights march, and a workplace occupation, as the band embraces a "diversity of tactics" that includes but is not limited to direct action. In these diverse performances, the band employs a range of musical repertoires of contention that members practice in weekly rehearsals to stay strategically flexible and effective in the varied and often unpredictable contexts in which it plays.

While songs with more complex forms are used on more presentational occasions and party settings, cyclical and simple forms allow the group to interact flexibly with protesters and spaces of contention. A system of hand cues indicating various sections of a song, drum breaks, solos, and solo bass line allows the group to respond musically to what is happening around it by rearranging the song in real time. The band might cut at times to just drum clicks over which the group will lead protesters in a topical chant or song. The mobility of a brass band enables the group to lead or follow activists and to engage with unknown spaces with little preparation.

BLO members often assert that deploying music in political actions makes possible the audibility and visibility of an action that might otherwise be easily ignored. By creating or strengthening the sense of being part of a community, music can provide an affective opening for participation in political action and for pushing all kinds of boundaries. Housing activist and BLO member Deepa Varma claims that the band can provide emotional and social support for protesters transgressing legal limits. The BLO can offer observers the sense that such inversions of the social order are not sporadic and irrational but intentional and thoughtful. Varma suggests, "A band occupying public space gives an action legitimacy because it projects organization."[5] Authorities have occasionally, if absurdly, noted the motivational power of marching bands in protests. In an article on the RMO, the *New York Times* claimed that "A police report prepared before the 2004 Republican National Convention in New York said that 'increases in beat are used to indicate an attack'" (Moynihan 2013).

The band receives gigs through its strong network within the Bay Area activist communities. Many band members are union organizers, food activists, direct action trainers, and social justice artists, and others are in frequent contact with other movement organizations that ask the BLO to perform. The band asks each organizer filling out a gig request to indicate whether the group has a permit, whether the event is arrestable, what the roles of people of color and relevant communities are, and what the BLO is expected to do during the action. Among the many parties and political events, direct actions tend to be unique performance experiences that are sometimes dangerous and arrestable but always adrenalin-producing and goal-directed.

The following two direct actions, a presentational intervention on a hotel with oppressive labor practices and the occupation of the Port of Oakland during the Occupy Movement in 2011, represent the more radical side of what the BLO engages. Drawing on Thomas Turino, I examine how the band strategically uses presentational and participatory forms of musical direct action. By presentational musical direct action, I mean that the transgression involved in musicians' performance is primarily an object of spectacle that is meant to change spectators' political opinions, priorities, and actions. By participatory musical direct action, I mean that strategically involving the audience in performance is the musical mode through which the direct action is enacted. While I find this duality helpful to understand the band's range of performance models, I recognize that often no clear lines exist between participatory and presentational modes of performances and that all "musicians" and "spectators" are always presenting, participating, and performing in myriad ways.[6]

A BAD HOTEL: PRESENTATIONAL INTERVENTION

Perhaps the BLO's highest-profile action in media terms has been its collaboration with Pride at Work in 2010. Pride at Work is a contingent of the AFL-CIO and promotes labor rights and awareness within the LGBTQIA+ movement. As the LGBTQIA+ movement had been gaining considerable mainstream acceptance, many worried that much of the movement's countercultural stance and resistant strategies may be lost in the process. The Pride parades, for example, are viewed by many of the more radical side to be commodified and commercialized spectacles, and some on the left actively avoid or protest them. In order to publicize labor issues within the LGBTQIA+ community, Pride at Work targeted certain hotels mired in labor disputes that many LGBTQIA+ tourists were known to stay in for Pride weekend. Workers in several hotels had already called for boycotts of the hotels for lack of fair contracts and health care. In preparation for an action supporting the worker campaign, Pride at Work and the BLO together rewrote Lady Gaga's "A Bad Romance" to "A Bad Hotel," arranged a brass band version, and created choreography.

In the video of the action, which received more than 400,000 YouTube hits, a lesbian couple, supposed tourists who are actually part of the action, are seen negotiating room rates at the front desk of the San Francisco Westin St. Francis. The next shot shows BLO and Pride at Work members quietly walking into the hotel with visible brass instruments. When one of the women sees the brass band, she loudly and theatrically exclaims, "Wait a second, honey! We can't check in here—this hotel's under boycott," at which point a flash mob of singers, dancers, and the BLO launch into the rewritten version of Lady Gaga's song. The band plays and sings with dancers performing elaborate choreography in the lobby.

> Oh no, don't get caught in a bad hotel (2x)
> Boycott, Boycott, Workers' rights are hot!

Boycott, Boycott, Boycott this hotel!
These workers need healthcare and a fair contract
This is a bad, bad hotel!
I want to party and let's do it in drag,
But not in a bad hotel
Want San Francisco and I want your gay ass
But not in a bad hotel!

During the performance, spectators look bewildered but entertained as activists pass out fliers about the campaign. A small child is seen snapping his fingers to the music. At the end, a member of Pride at Work explains to them the context and intent of the action. Then the group marches outside to parade in a picket line to a New Orleans second line tune.

In the *Huffington Post* article on the action and YouTube sensation, Paul Hogarth (2010) asked whether these viral revolutionary spectacles could be considered the "future of protest." While his insight may appear both prescient and dated with the proliferation of meme activism along with the explosive mass protests of 2020,[7] respectively, Hogarth argues that mass rallies and marches can be tired tactics that produce few results because of their low public visibility. In this early manifestation of meme-driven activism, he suggests that the flash mob captured on video, shared on social media, and reposted on LGBTQIA+ rights blogs, independent weeklies, and other fora perhaps enables a much stronger awareness of the issue through its entertaining and easily accessible format. Activists had hoped to get the message out especially to LGBTQIA+ tourists that they should not reserve these hotels. For Hogarth, the video got its "bang for the buck," considering that "they didn't have to mobilize a large number of people, the whole action took five minutes and nobody got arrested. How many times can you say that—and get that amount of media coverage?" Without social media, the action's impact would have been much smaller, as it's much harder to impress "apolitical tourists who have already paid for their hotel" (ibid.).

This BLO flash mob action embodied what I have called the performance of freedom of direct action, as musicians and dancers went beyond social conventions and laws to perform against unfair labor practices. Playfully transgressing the social expectations of behavior in a hotel lobby with a political message could be understood as an expression of prefigurative politics regarding the uses to which such spaces can and should be put. As an organized performance intended for viral sharing, this action would be closer to the presentational end of the spectrum, though the values of participation in the action were articulated in communal singing, dancing, and engagement with the audience. The BLO, acting as an action affinity group for Pride at Work and the hotel workers, used music to present the public with a political and moral choice.

OCCUPY OAKLAND PORT SHUTDOWN: PARTICIPATORY INTERVENTION

On November 2, 2011, Occupy Oakland staged a "general strike" day of actions, in reaction to state violence when police one week earlier had invaded the Occupy Oakland camp, one of a global proliferation of urban encampments in solidarity with the Occupy Wall Street Protests in New York. The major action of the day was to shut down the Port of Oakland in solidarity with the International Longshoreman and Warehouse Union (ILWU) in Longview, Washington, which represents port workers. Occupy Oakland achieved the shutdown with a mass convergence of tens of thousands of bodies at the entries of the port. Supporting the action and the entire day's events was the BLO, which played at Occupy Oakland's invitation. Though the band's participation was a small part of a much larger series of actions, the BLO imbued the volatile spaces with a sense of drama and carnivalesque transgression, as many protesters' exultation—expressed in dance, chant and song—took the edge off fears of arrest, violence and retaliation.[8] This was my first experience of the BLO, and I followed the band throughout the day as it supported the many actions of the general strike, prompting me to clean out my trumpet and initiate my own membership process.

The port is an institution of transnational capitalism and commerce that has a long history in Oakland residents' memory as an engine of displacement. West Oakland, once a vibrant immigrant and Black cultural center, has seen dramatic economic decline and high rates of poverty, urban violence, and food deserts. Recent gentrification, accelerated by the foreclosure crisis, has housing costs skyrocketing with long-term residents being pushed out of the community at alarming rates. The port has, in fact, been shut down many times since its massive expansion in the 1960s, including during the anti–Iraq War movement and many labor disputes. In shutting down the port, protesters enacted one of the central philosophies of the Occupy movement, the leftist view that communities should control the machinery that organizes their lives. Occupy Oakland's targeting of the port reflected a strategy that reached further back into Oakland's contested social histories and encouraged community members to assert their agency over institutions over which they have little control.

During the march to the port and its occupation, thousands of protesters were sonically saturated by the BLO as well as by sound trucks, drum groups, and overlapping chants scattered throughout the crowd. All these sounds contributed to the mobilization, heightening emotions among those involved and entraining participants to the rhythm of the march. The BLO helped enable the performance of collective ownership of the port through promoting musical participation. During the long hours of waiting to hear whether the port had been shut down, the band kept bodies on the site and buoyed the weariness of the protesters with syncopated beats and collective singing. Antiphonal chants such as "Whose port? Our port!" over BLO drumbeats rhetorically expressed the performance of collective ownership of the machinery of capitalism. Dancing at the port with exuberant transgression embodied the belief that the symbolic boundaries constructed by the state have no legitimate value. The entire general strike could be considered to be a performance of freedom, community, and the nonexistence of the state (see fig. 14.1).

At the port, the BLO kept protesters' moods festive, fearless, and high with a long rendition of the New Orleans second line "We Got That Fire," switching the refrain to "We shut the port down" and encouraging mass collective singing. The group created a mass dance party with Afrobeat classics, such as "No Agreement" and "JJD," and well-known Balkan tunes, including "Bubamara." The BLO actively engaged with the audience by encouraging other instrumentalists to join in, starting chants and songs and leading dances. Through instrumental protest, the band provided what George McKay (2007) calls "sonic territorialization," helping enable the occupation of the port, as the BLO countered fear and fatigue with mass exuberance. For drummer Josh Cohen, "the BLO can bring joy to intense situations and help create a participatory environment even while maintaining an unwavering political position."[9]

The BLO was well suited to support these actions because it rehearses music in order to be flexible and tactically effective. For example, in leading chants, the conductor of the BLO (a position that circulates song by song) will generally coordinate with organizers or others with megaphones. The conductor might cue the band so that horns drop out in order for a chant to be led under the drum section's 4/4 beat. After a bit of chanting, the conductor will cue the horns to come back in, often with the chanting continuing over it. By the time the song ends, the marchers have become participants in the sonic expression of protest, fully involved in its joint creation.

BLO saxophonist and professional union organizer Josh Sperry, pointing to an important inversion in the conventional band/audience relationship, observes that "the band can make people feel loud and important; as the music

Fig. 14.1. Occupy Oakland Port shutdown with BLO (BLO Facebook). Courtesy of author.

swells underneath, we make them feel like they are the speaker, the star. They are not there for the band—the band is there for them."[10] I have since seen and used these methods of musically involving protesters countless times to draw people into participating in political actions, and they never seem to fail to entrain the audience into the political goals of the action. Drawing people into musical activity is a mode through which they can musically perform political resistance as a community of protesters and "act as if they are already free."

As in the Pride at Work action, the BLO served as an action affinity group for Occupy Oakland, the ILWU, and the displaced peoples of West Oakland. In solidarity with ILWU, the shutdown represented a targeted action aimed at changing policy, specifically regarding labor contracts. But the day's events also embodied longer-standing tensions between organized labor and anarchist activists, for the latter of whom the shutdown might have represented a manifestation of a temporary autonomous zone (TAZ), a moment and place in which one might imagine that such institutional machinery would not have the dominant control over our lives that it currently does (Bey 1991). More broadly, the Occupy movement aimed to establish TAZs around the world that would prefigure a new kind of politics that might one day become permanent. Occupy, in its refusal to make demands of political administrations and argue for explicit policies, placed itself in a lineage of the broader growth in popularity of anarchist philosophy, values, and organizing since the anti–corporate globalization movement. The BLO acted in both capacities in this direct action as freedom *to* and *from*, in solidarity with the ILWU with the intent of changing policy, and as an anarchistic performance of uninhibited freedom not restrained by laws, conventions, and the state. The multiple solidarities expressed are indicative of the BLO's commitment to support unity on the left with a diversity of tactics, including music in direct action.

MUSIC AS LIBERATION

In performing the belief that "music is liberation," BLO promotes a prefigurative politics in which musical engagement is considered an enactment of freedom with calculated tactics and targets. The group's creative interventions of instrumental protest, many of which surpass legal limits, occur along a spectrum of presentation and participation, performance modes that for the BLO are not fundamentally opposed. Indeed, in most cases, it is through the catalytic presentation that the BLO ignites that political participation is magnified in a given action. Part of broader transnational networks, emblematized by but larger than the global HONK! network, the BLO's tactics and musical repertoires of contention shape and are shaped by protest movements around the world. In framing music as a tactic—a nimble source of musical support—rather than a performance that is the ultimate object of engagement, such bands offer innovative practical and theoretical modes of musicking rarely accounted for by scholars.

Though the question of efficacy is important to instrumental protest bands like the BLO that use music strategically to promote change, Kallman observes that "many [HONK!] bands reject a distinction between social process and social outcome. . . . This very specific focus on *process* is a way of both altering and re-constructing the world" (2020, 118). That is, BLO's engagements both *as* and *in* direct action constitute a means to an end and an end in itself, musically militating to enact utopia but not losing sight of realistic victories and strategic targets as well as the pursuit of a more just internal organization. Outside of "movement moments" when the tangible possibility of change is palpable, direct action and organizing remain part of a continuum of political engagement that makes larger flare-ups and progressive changes in the sociopolitical world possible. Music and other forms of play are a crucial part of what make these changes achievable, not only as chant-able slogans or lyrical critique, but also as performative and affective experiences that maintain enthusiasm and combat activist burnout through raucous celebration. Similarly, Rosenthal and Flacks argue that "music allows activists to carry their beliefs and loyalties with them in their everyday routines; it provides a bridge linking yesterday's demonstration with today's workday, between making history and making life. During times of movement inactivity, music serves as one way that the identities and ties essential to future movement activity are not lost in the press of daily routines" (2011, 127).

The BLO acts as if it is already free in order to become free. The band's intentions for its members and the communities it mobilizes are well summed up by Augusto Boal in his famous book *The Theater of the Oppressed*: "The spectator . . . assumes the protagonic role, changes the dramatic action, tries out solutions, discusses plans for change—in short, trains themself for real action. In this case perhaps the theater is not revolutionary in itself, but it is surely a rehearsal for the revolution" (1979, 122). After all, rehearsal is not for rehearsal's sake. Opening night is out there some day.

NOTES

1. Revised portions of this chapter appeared in French in a chapter by the author in *Politiques des musiques populaires au XXIe siècle* (2015).
2. See Garofalo (2020) for a more complete history of the growth of the HONK! network and Snyder, Allen, and Garofalo (2022) for an account of the virtual festival. Studies of diverse manifestations of this alternative brass band network, including on its development in Rio de Janeiro, Brazil (Snyder 2022) and a coedited volume on the global HONK! movement (Snyder, Allen, and Garofalo 2020), have occupied much of my academic and musical focus since my first chance encounter with the BLO.
3. See Brass Liberation Orchestra (2013).
4. See Kallman (2020) on the challenges of leaderless organization in HONK! bands.
5. Deepa Varma, interview by author, San Francisco, CA, January 18.
6. See Snyder (2019) for a critique of Turino's dichotomy.
7. See Andrew Snyder, "BLO and Pride at Work, 'Don't Get Caught in a Bad Hotel'," YouTube, May 19, 2022, https://www.youtube.com/watch?v=P-FnqI5D8Uc&ab_channel=AndrewSnyder/.

8. See utopiaparkfilms, "Brass Liberation Orchestra: Occupy Oakland General Strike 11.02.11," YouTube, December 29, 2011, http://www.youtube.com/watch?v=uJUBE8xpHVk, and Tripleshack, "Oakland General Strike—Brass Liberation Orchestra (Bubamara song)," YouTube, November 4, 2011, http://www.youtube.com/watch?v=OmbzwikZBgE/.

9. Josh Cohen, interview by author, San Francisco, CA, November 4, 2013.

10. Josh Sperry, interview by author, Oakland, CA, April 3, 2013.

BIBLIOGRAPHY

Abe, Marié. 2018. *Resonances of Chindon-Ya: Sounding Space and Sociality in Contemporary Japan*. Middletown, CT: Wesleyan University Press.

Bey, Hakim. 1991. *T.A.Z.: The Temporary Autonomous Zone, Ontological Anarchy, Poetic Terrorism*. Brooklyn: Automedia.

Boal, Augusto. 1979. *Theater of the Oppressed*. New York: Urizen Books.

Bobo, Kim, ed. 2003. *Organizing for Social Change: Midwest Academy Manual for Activists*. Minneapolis: Seven Locks Press.

Brass Liberation Orchestra. 2013. Brass Liberation Orchestra website. Accessed November 21, 2013. http://brassliberation.org/.

Butler, Judith. 2015. *Notes toward a Performative Theory of Assembly*. Cambridge, MA: Harvard University Press.

Castells, Manuel. 2012. *Networks of Outrage and Hope: Social Movements in the Internet Age*. Cambridge: Polity Press.

Dolan, Jill. 2001. "Performance, Utopia, and the 'Utopian Performative.'" *Theatre Journal* 53 (3): 455–79.

Eyerman, Ron, and Andrew Jamison. 1998. *Music and Social Movements: Mobilizing Traditions in the Twentieth Century*. Cambridge: Cambridge University Press.

Garofalo, Reebee. 2020. "The Many Roads to HONK! and the Power of Brass and Percussion." In *HONK! A Street Band Renaissance of Music and Activism*, edited by Andrew G. Snyder, Erin Allen, and Reebee Garofalo, 15–27. New York: Routledge.

———. Forthcoming. "HONK! Activism: Alternative Brass Bands as Political Projects." In *The Oxford Handbook of Protest Music*, edited by Noriko Manabe and Eric Drott. New York: Oxford University Press.

Graeber, David. 2009. *Direct Action: An Ethnography*. Oakland: AK Press.

Harcourt, Bernard. 2013. "Political Disobedience." In *Occupy: Three Inquiries in Disobedience*, edited by W. J. T. Mitchell, Bernard E. Harcourt, and Michael Taussig. Chicago: University of Chicago Press.

Hogarth, Peter. 2010. "'Caught in a Bad Hotel' = The Future of Political Protest." *HuffPost*, May 12, 2010. Accessed December 8, 2012. https://www.huffpost.com/entry/caught-in-a-bad-hotel-the_b_573407.

Kallman, Meghan. 2020. "Building Connections While Maintaining the Band: The Challenging Politics of Inclusion in Activist Work." In *HONK! A Street

Band Renaissance of Music and Activism*, edited by Andrew G. Snyder, Erin Allen, and Reebee Garofalo, 117–30. New York: Routledge.

Kuperberg, Jonathan. 2013. "Brass Liberation Orchestra Keeps Protest Beat." May 25, 2013. *San Francisco Chronicle*.

Lepecki, André. 2013. "Choreopolice and Choreopolitics: Or, the Task of the Dancer." *TDR: The Drama Review* 57 (4): 13–27.

Making Contact. 2010. "Marching for Change: Street Bands in the US." September 14, 2010. Accessed December 8, 2012. http://www.radioproject.org/2010/09/marching-for-change-street-bands-in-the-u-s/.

Manabe, Noriko. 2015. *The Revolution Will Not Be Televised: Protest Music after Fukushima*. Oxford: Oxford University Press.

Mason, Amelia. 2017. "In an Era of Protest, HONK! Fest's Activist Roots Come into Focus." *The Artery*, October 5, 2017. Accessed June 18, 2018. http://www.wbur.org/artery/2017/10/05/honk-fests-activist-roots/.

McKay, George. 2007. "'A Soundtrack to the Insurrection': Street Music, Marching Bands and Popular Protests." *Parallax* 13 (1): 20–31.

Moynihan, Colin. 2013. "The Revolution Will Have Live Music." *New York Times*, November 17, 2013. Accessed May 4, 2017. http://www.nytimes.com/2013/11/18/nyregion/the-revolution-will-have-live-music.html/.

Podber, Naomi. 2020. "Building Connections While Maintaining the Band: The Challenging Politics of Inclusion in Activist Work." In *HONK! A Street Band Renaissance of Music and Activism*, edited by Andrew G. Snyder, Erin Allen, and Reebee Garofalo, 131–44. New York: Routledge.

Rosenthal, Rob, and Richard Flacks. 2011. *Playing for Change: Music and Musicians in the Service of Social Movements*. Boulder, CO: Paradigm Publishers.

Roy, William. 2010. *Reds, Whites and Blues: Social Movements, Folk Music, and Race in America*. Princeton, NJ: Princeton University Press.

Silverstein, Shayna. 2019. "On Sirens and Lamp Posts: Sound, Space, and Affective Politics." *Music and Politics* 13 (1): 1–9.

Snyder, Andrew. 2015. "Cuivres critiques: La musique comme tactique d'action directe dans la baie de San Francisco." In *Politiques des musiques populaires au XXIe siècle*, edited by Jedediah Sklower, 211–32. Guichen: Éd. Mélanie Seteun.

———. 2019. "Playing the System: The Capitalist Industry of Participatory Music Education in Rio de Janeiro's *Oficinas*." *Journal of Popular Music Studies* 31 (3): 119–44.

———. 2020. "Politicizing Carnival Brass Bands in Olympic Rio de Janeiro: Instrumental Protest and Musical Repertoires of Contention." *Latin American Music Review* 41 (1): 27–58.

———. 2022. *Critical Brass: Street Carnival and Musical Activism in Olympic Rio de Janeiro*. Middletown, CT: Wesleyan University Press.

Snyder, Andrew, Erin Allen, and Reebee Garofalo, eds. 2020. *HONK! A Street Band Renaissance of Music and Activism*. New York: Routledge.

———. 2022. "HONK!United: A Virtual Global Festival of Activist Brass Bands during the COVID-19 Pandemic." *Music and Politics* 16 (1): 1–28.

Tilly, Charles. 2010. *Regimes and Repertoires*. Chicago: University of Chicago Press.

Trey. 2014. "Politics and Possibilities." *Occupy Central Series*. June 14, 2014. Accessed February 18, 2021. https://www.comparativist.org/2014/06/14/occupy-central-part-ii-politics-and-possibilities/.

Turino, Thomas. 2008. *Music as Social Life: The Politics of Participation*. Chicago: University of Chicago Press.

Whitney, Jennifer. 2003. "Infernal Noise: The Soundtrack to Insurrection." In *We Are Everywhere: The Irresistible Rise of Global Anti-Capitalism*, edited by Notes from Nowhere, 216–27. London: Verso.

FIFTEEN

ECOLOGICAL FRICTIONS AND BORDERLESS FUTURES

Art and Activism on a Sailing Ship

REBEKAH E. MOORE

Livestream from Benoa Bay, Bali, Indonesia, October 22, 2020

   As is customary for most public gatherings, the evening's performance opens with a welcome ritual of Balinese music, dance, and theater: tonight, a spectacular production of kecak. The polyrhythms of interlocking voices are complicated by body percussion, and synchronized fire dancers bring the performance to a dramatic climax of smoke, flame, and fireworks. The scene darkens, then glows blood red as a siren sounds, a speaker emits the SOS sequence in Morse code, and the waters radiate a bright green light, illuminating a scattering of unused life vests floating on the surface. A white spotlight searches the night, revealing the masts, sails, and deck of an old sailing ship. The spotlight finds its mark on the mainsail, casting a figure behind it in shadow, then outstretched arms reveal a cascade of fishing net serving as the figure's mantle. A strange composition of sampled and synthesized sounds provides an interlude of calm: nocturnal insects; the ketuk, the gamelan's timekeeper, and the kantilan, which carries its melody; a gentle tapping on an unseen surface; and the Morse code, fading now to the background. Another figure appears toward the ship's bow, shrouded in protective gear and a hood, crowned with a headlamp, and disguised behind a mask of shimmering gold coins. The figure raises a pair of drumsticks. The figure strikes. The entire ship seems to quake with the reverberation of a stretched-out, synthesized bassline and begs for the drop.

ECOLOGICAL FRICTIONS

> All that you can see
> beneath the sun
> what is made by humans
> now must be undone
>
> —"COLONY COLLAPSE," FILASTINE (2012)

In November 2021, following the twenty-sixth United Nations Conference on Climate Change (COP26) in Glasgow, environmental scientists, activists, and leaders of nations were disappointed to learn that renewed commitments to accelerate decarbonization had failed to plan for sufficient support for vulnerable nations or a phase-out of coal dependency to limit global temperature rise. The archipelagic Republic of Indonesia, the world's fourth-most-populous nation with the second-longest coastline and third-largest rainforest, went largely unmentioned in English-language news coverage of COP26 talks, even though Indonesia's most significant sources of carbon emissions, deforestation and coal production, are directly caused by the cheap fuel demands of the most populous and powerful signatory nations (see Nangoy and Suroyo 2021).[1]

Indonesia's vital role in decelerating global warming may not have garnered mainstream media attention during COP26, but the nation is well-known to students of ethnomusicology. The ostensible founders of the field, from the Dutch Jaap Kunst to the American Ki Mantle Hood, made specializations out of Javanese and Balinese gamelan music.[2] Dozens of English-language books and many more dissertations have been dedicated to the Indonesian music-dance-theater complex. Hundreds of college and community gamelan ensembles in the United States, Europe, and Australia have made an Indonesian art form a mainstay in the Western world's academic world music canon.[3] The ethnomusicologist's hunger for the Indonesian arts spans more than a century if we count our predecessors at the Berlin School of Comparative Musicology and is part of a long and complex history of cultural extractivism that bears critical reflection, as those who call ourselves "Indonesianists," present author included, witness how natural resource extractivism is threatening the people and places on which we have staked our academic careers.

Recent publications on music and environmental justice, particularly within ecomusicology, move beyond a general interest in the interrelationship of sound, culture, and the natural environment to an increasing concern about the consequences of human-caused ecological crisis.[4] As ethnomusicologist Timothy Cooley has noted, we are bearing witness to "the extinction of not only unprecedented numbers of biological organisms but also human traditions of ecological knowledge that are needed now more than ever" (Cooley et al. 2020, 302). While such threats have motivated some in music and sound studies to continue the work of cultural preservationism, under the new guise of cultural sustainability, it has led others to draw on ethnomusicology's long-established commitment to local and Indigenous perspectives to seek interdisciplinary conversations on what expressive culture and traditional ecological knowledge might offer us as truth, hope, or justice (Cooley et al. 2020; McDowell et al. 2021).

I offer this chapter as a contribution to these rich and exigent discourses on music and sound, nature and survival, a story unfolding about an old sailing ship of wood and steel, which has steered cross-cultural and cross-continental knowledge exchanges through music and spectacle for the sake of our species and all others. It is the story of *Arka Kinari*, a ship that sailed around the world and through a global pandemic, powered by the wind and the sun, and offered a floating, multisensory spectacle of music, video art, dance, and theater to coastal villagers on the remotest islands of Indonesia. *Arka Kinari* is a remarkable ship. It is also a radical reimagining of the band tour, the concert setting, and climate activism that recollects and activates old knowledge of the sea.

I first met the artists behind *Arka Kinari*, US-born Grey Filastine and Indonesia-born Nova Ruth, ten years ago, when I was living in Bali. I was working as a production manager for an international yoga and performing arts festival at the time, and I booked them to perform on our main stage. We have remained friends since. As an ethnomusicologist trained in the rich ethnographic traditions of folklore and ethnomusicology at Indiana University, whose theoretical orientation inclines toward participatory action, I initially hoped to weave this story by combining the threads of a years-long friendship with fieldwork involving participatory observation and long conversations. I planned to become a working member of *Arka Kinari*'s crew as we sailed through Indonesian waters in the summers of 2020 and 2021. But like all other fieldworkers of the COVID era, I was forced to change plans and rely instead on the sparse threads of news media coverage, truncated text message exchanges, rare phone conversations, and a scant twenty-four hours in Grey's good company when I invited him to my home in Boston for a speaking engagement at my institution. Regrettably, Nova could not join us: US visas, though always difficult to procure for citizens of Muslim nations, were nearly unattainable in 2021. Thus, there are missing threads to this story, and I hope that I, or someone else, can take them up in the future when border crossing is feasible once again.

THIS IS *ARKA KINARI*

The prefix *arka-* is borrowed from the Latin verb *arcere*, meaning vessel or repository, or "to hold off or defend." *Kinari* is a Sanskrit word, taken up in Hindu and Buddhist mythology as Kinnara and Kinnari, the half-human, half-bird lovers and guardians of humans during dangerous times. *Arka Kinari* set forth on its first voyage in 2019, but the artists who steered it have been planning this journey for decades.

Filastine, Grey's nom de plume, is a US-born percussionist, electronic music producer, and video artist who has divided much of his adult life between Barcelona and Indonesia. He is well-known for sonic interventions on the Anthropocene: his marching band, Infernal Noise Brigade, accompanied the 1999 WTO protests in Seattle, and during the 2015 COP21 Climate Change Summit in Paris, his "sound swarm" blasted a cacophony of melting glaciers, endangered animals, the SOS sequence, and crude oil propaganda through the city streets. His first public conjuring of what he describes as "a network of floating outlaw republics for a flooded near-future" took the form of material culture associated with the launch of his 2012 album, *LOOT* (Filastine 2012). He designed, printed, and widely disseminated an exchange currency called £ooT, which featured a braided and bandanaed woman rebel on one side and, on the other, a sailing ship with a satellite on its deck. The currency also garnered him attention from the FBI and a near-miss on a currency counterfeiting charge.

Java-born Nova Ruth possesses a reputation exceeding Grey's across the Indonesian archipelago. She is a social and environmental activist, founding member of award-winning rap and spoken word duo Twin Sista, and the daughter of famed electric guitarist Totok Tewel. In performance, Nova moves easily between rap and the vocal traditions of her childhood: Pentecostal hymnody, Islamic recitation, and *sindhèn* for the Javanese gamelan. In activism, she has epitomized a generation of Indonesian artivists[5] by mobilizing through intellectual and creative gatherings at her café and cultural space, Legipait in Malang, East Java, and staging critical interventions on social and environmental injustice through old and new music, art, and theater.

Nova and Grey describe *Arka Kinari* as their necessary response to the genuine threat of ecological collapse. As Grey explained in a 2021 lecture in Boston, "We felt for years that talking about this problem or even making music about this problem isn't really a proportionate response to the kind of existential crisis that we're facing. It almost feels like we're sleepwalking through a mass extinction event" (Filastine, 2021). So together, they started planning their wake-up call. They aimed to replace the convenience and fossil fuel dependence of international air travel, which they had depended on as international touring artists, with an unhurried journey by the ocean. They aimed to meet and exchange culture, ideas, food, and coffee, not with the rich, primarily city-dwelling audiences of the music festivals they were used to frequenting but, instead, with people dismissed or overlooked in global climate talks and by the live entertainment industries, people located on the remotest islands of the Indian and Pacific Oceans. "It [was] a plan that leveraged every shekel and every resource and every contact, and every skill that we have. And the idea [was] to build a platform where message and method meet, and to start operating as if fossil capitalism has already ended" (ibid.).

For years, Nova and Grey searched for what Grey describes as "a ship big enough to hold this dream." They needed a seaworthy vessel that could accommodate a stage for performances, subwoofers and speakers, solar panels, and a crew of up to eight people who would live on board for months. They initially hoped to build their ship from scratch, using the tools and technologies of Nova's sailing ancestors in Sulawesi. After learning they would have to depend on wood from poached logging, they scratched Plan A and created a database of every suitable and salvageable ship worldwide. They traveled to Australia, the United States, and Spain before finally finding the right ship, idling in a canal in the Netherlands, Indonesia's colonizer for 350 years.

Grey, Nova, and a team of supporters from New York, Indonesia, Brazil, Berlin, and Catalonia set to work to transform this veritable rust bucket into a vessel that could safely carry its crew of performers and novice sailors from the colonizer's waters to the formerly colonized republic. They had only three months and $30,000 to carry off this feat before the changing seasons would force them to delay their departure by a year. In the middle of the night in August 2019, following a dress rehearsal for an audience of supporters at the dock, *Arka Kinari* embarked on its first slow tour, and its crew raised their sails and hopes to the will of the wind (see fig. 15.1).

As partners who do not share citizenship, Filastine and Nova's art, marriage, and mobility have been fraught with the challenges of national border crossing. But through the depth of their convictions and breadth of their network of like-minded artists, activists, and seafarers, they had finally found a way to move freely together across the borderless, open waters.

TO HOLD OFF AND DEFEND

> *The figure behind the mainsail has slipped down onto the deck, revealing her costume of batik-dyed fabric, a heavy leather waist belt and boots, and tumbling jewels, resembling a mythical pirate proudly displaying her spoils. She begins to sing in the style of the* pesindhèn, *women performers providing the gamelan's vocal accompaniment. The sails, which had given shape to her shadow, now light up with a video-mapping display: the parallels of latitude and meridians of longitude stretch and contract, settling on the center of a spinning vinyl record, now transformed into a compass. The compass, now a point on the horizon, unreachable by a deserted road. The viewer is propelled forward over desert terrain, then among the rubble of a deserted town, then careening through the networks of narrow urban alleyways lined with motorbikes.*

Fig. 15.1. *Arka Kinari* at anchor in Pulau Satonda, Indonesia. Photo credit: Julieta Feroz. Used with permission.

From Rotterdam, *Arka Kinari* traveled for six months and thousands of nautical miles past Europe, Africa, and across the Atlantic, en route to Indonesia, Nova's home and Grey's frequent refuge. Their quickest route, a four-month journey through the Suez Canal, would have required sailing within proximity of war-torn Yemen and past Somalia into pirate territory—the consequence of livelihoods lost to multinational fishing companies. Their next-best option, a trip around the Horn of Africa, would have meant facing the unpredictable and often deadly storms brewing at the Cape of Good Hope. Thus, they chose the most protracted and slowest path, crossing the North Sea and sailing south toward West Africa and then across the Atlantic, with stops in Portugal, Morocco, Capo Verde, the Canaries, and the autonomous Indigenous territory of San Blas, where they practiced and fine-tuned their performance for curious dockside onlookers.

On *Arka Kinari*'s crowdfunding platforms, Grey and Nova's primary means for financing this slow tour, traditional seafaring is described as a model for knowledge exchange and carbon-free travel: "Until seafaring was bypassed by shipping containerization and air travel, the maritime network was the original internet, how ideas were spread. *Arka Kinari* revives these disappearing trade routes with *culture* as the cargo."[6] Media and communications scholar Nicole Starosielski has pointed out that the modern internet also depends on the sea, transmitting its data, from emails and financial transactions to long-range weapons testing, *under*sea, along a near immeasurable network of fiber-optic cables (Starosielski 2015). As a vessel for a seafaring epistemology, *Arka Kinari* is a *holder* and *defender* of preinternet, precapitalistic, and even precolonial ways of knowing: of an idealized egalitarian exchange of food, language, and ideas— even as it must also report on its progress via fiber-optic cables to patrons, fans, and news media to ensure the funding to journey onward.

Arka Kinari's is a journey made in explicit defiance of fossil capitalism. It is also a journey made in unmistakable reverence to a seafaring chronicle older and beyond colonialist and imperialist agendas, one that Vicente M. Díaz describes as "indigenously-ordered, anti-colonial praxis" (2011, 21). The Dutch flag, under which the crew sails, belies this agenda: it is nothing more than a cloak of Dutch regulatory control that permits the international crew members a turn at the helm. The performance of *Arka Kinari* is a deliberate conjuring of Nova's seafaring ancestry through both the aesthetic invocations of Indonesian gamelan music, shadow puppetry, and dance and the technical execution of Indigenous sailing.

Nova's ancestors are the famed Bugis sailors of Sulawesi, who, for hundreds of years, steered their wooden *pinisi* schooners as far as northern Australia, where they traded with the Yolŋu people of Arnhem Land for *trepang*, a sea cucumber, which would be boiled down, dried, and traded with Chinese seafarers for use as food and medicine.[7] Karin Amimoto Ingersoll's concept of a "seascape epistemology" is applicable here: developed through her examination of Kānaka Maoli ways of knowing the ocean through surfing, fishing, and navigation, she identifies "ocean literacy" as critical to Indigenous Hawaiian identity and resistance to cultural colonization (2016). By invoking Bugis seafarers in sailing, navigation, and performance, *Arka Kinari* becomes a vessel for a Bugis seascape epistemology that predates and outlasts the western European powers that warred for centuries for trade monopolies in Sulawesi and across modern Indonesia.

Much like the Marshallese practice of sounding the sea for navigation, cultural maintenance, and self-determination documented by Jessica A. Schwartz (2019), *Arka Kinari* calls attention to the trade routes and cultural contacts that defined Indonesia's seafaring past and potential. By defending these old ways, the ship also communicates a means of *species survival* in a borderless future, after the carbon economy collapse, when the fast rise of the sea due to thermal expansion and glacial and ice sheet melt compel mass migrations. As Nova explains in their fundraising video, this is "art to inspire resistance to the carbon economy, resilience to climate change, and reengagement with the last great commons: the sea" (Filastine & Nova 2019). By commons, Nova means something greater than the sea's legal boundlessness—though neoliberalist nations continue to lay claim to the ocean as a blue economy, or "the new frontier of economic development" (Gamage 2016, 2), a definition that would inevitably result in the *tragedy* of the commons. She means something greater than the 1.3 billion cubic kilometers of water it is estimated to contain or all the plants, animals, and minerals that dwell beneath its surface and on which human survival has thus far depended. She means commons beyond the realms of maritime trade, commerce, and nation-states—and even beyond Elinor Ostrom's principles for commons governance, which are limited in scope to "local needs" and by clear group boundaries (1990). Just as no one nation can lay sovereign claim to these common-pool (or common-sea) resources, so no one nation, community, or mode of inquiry can fully imagine and activate the solution to avoid ecological collapse.[8] What is needed is a pooling of knowledge—not for the management of common-pool resources, but rather for the collective imagination to understand our interconnections, the collective harm of our resource enclosures and borderlines, and the restorative potential of our ongoing and accumulating act of *commoning*, of "being-in-common" with all humans and more-than-humans on land, at sea, in the sky, and even beyond our own atmosphere (García-López, Lang, and Singh 2021).

TO WATCH OVER DURING DANGEROUS TIMES

As the crossroads of Asian, European, African, and Oceanic trade and cultural exchange, a global warming hot spot (Fan et al. 2021), and Nova's ancestral home, Indonesia was always meant to be *Arka Kinari*'s destination. The Republic of Indonesia comprises seventeen thousand islands and more than 270 million inhabitants. With coastlines totaling thirty-four thousand miles, approximately 60 percent of Indonesians live in coastal areas or low-lying coastal cities. Compounding ecological crises caused by deforestation, biodiversity loss, road traffic, and air and ocean pollution (Van de Vuurst and Escobar 2020), global climate change—causing sea-level rise, unpredictable waves and winds, an increase in ocean temperature, and rising ocean acidity—threatens the homes, livelihoods, and food security of tens of millions. Jakarta, the nation's capital, is one of the fastest-sinking cities in the world. Its vulnerability to flooding, tsunamis, and coastal storms has led to the unprecedented decision to relocate the political capital to the island of Borneo, home to one of the largest remaining forested areas in Southeast Asia. The global pandemic has placed a significant economic strain on a country already struggling with economic and political instability and welfare inequality. As a result, President Joko Widodo rolled back plans to eliminate deforestation, lifted restrictions on dimethyl production, and extended mining permits to forested areas, citing economic recovery as an urgent priority (Nangoy and Suroyo 2021).

In February 2020 in Oaxaca, *Arka Kinari*'s crew began preparing for the most arduous leg of their journey, across the Pacific Ocean to Indonesia, where they planned to meet the people whose lives and livelihoods have been and will continue to be threatened with ecological collapse. Nova flew back home to prepare for the ship's arrival. Grey would remain with the ship and its crew. Then the COVID-19 virus spread.

Indonesia quickly joined nearly every nation and closed its borders to keep the virus out. *Arka Kinari* had no safe harbor. After a short refuge in Hawaii, Grey and the ship's remaining crew were forced out to sea and an uncertain world shut down by the pandemic. For six months of what Grey described as "alternating crisis and salvation," *Arka Kinari* aimed west. They had hoped to stop at small islands in the Pacific to restock on supplies and make necessary repairs to the ship, but island nations and territories lacked the medical infrastructure to take on the risk of foreign visitors, so they were repeatedly turned away.

The crew's only connection to their terrestrial homes was the SAT phone used to send 140-character messages. They were locked out of humanity and every sovereign territory, while the rest of us were locked in. Thus, they sought refuge in places humans would never go, places like the Johnston Atoll, a US-administered territory and dump site for chemical and biological weapons. After months at sea, with supplies critically low and the ship in desperate need of repairs, *Arka Kinari* was permitted to land in Guam before continuing its journey. Back at sea, the motor died. With the help of a passing Chinese supertanker, they were able to continue heading toward Indonesian waters but with no guarantee that they would be granted safe passage once they arrived.

In August 2020, salvation came: after traveling a total of thirty thousand nautical miles, *Arka Kinari* was warmly welcomed by a cluster of outrigger canoes, *jukung*, into the public waters of Sorong, West Papua. They were the island's first foreign visitors since the pandemic began, a welcome made possible by Nova's tireless negotiations with the Ministry of Culture and Ministry of Immigration and, in no small part, the substantial international media attention the desperate *Arka Kinari* crew stirred up through SAT phone interviews with the press.

As I followed their journey from Mexico to Guam and finally to Indonesia, trapped in my own home and desperate for more information than the sparse social media posts, text messages, and long-form reports published by BBC News (Henschke 2021) and *Pitchfork* (Scruggs 2020) provided, I worried deeply for the crew's welfare. I struggled to imagine the hardships they faced along the way. I also couldn't help but contrast the crew's relatively brief displacement and eventual rescue with the closed borders barring so many of the 80 million refugees worldwide from haven. With that number destined to skyrocket because of the climate crisis—the human toll that the *Arka Kinari* crew highlight explicitly in their performances—the privileges of race, wealth, and celebrity will most certainly protect some over others.

After arriving in Indonesia and as travel restrictions eased, *Arka Kinari* traced the trade routes of the Banda Islands, a cluster of volcanic islands in the Maluku Regency, popularly known in the West as the Spice Islands. This region was the center of violent trade wars between the Spanish, Portuguese, British, and Dutch, all of whom sought monopoly over the trade of nutmeg, mace, and clove—luxuries consumed by only the wealthiest of Europe. The Dutch East India Company, one of history's most profitable and brutal commercial shipping enterprises, ruled over this region for nearly two hundred years after expelling the Portuguese and British and massacring, enslaving, starving, or exiling almost the entire Indigenous population. Now, Filastine, Nova, and the rest of their crew navigated public waterfronts and contact and conversation with coastal villagers suffering through the ecological frictions that disrupt centuries-old fishing practices and drive up the frequency of deadly cyclones, floods, landslides, and sinking shorelines (see Kasim 2021).

Arka Kinari makes a common cause of Angela Impey's conception of "mobility as aesthetic practice" (2018, 25) and calls to mind so many other examples of sonic protest in motion. Noriko Manabe described the sound trucks in Japan mobilized against the wars in Afghanistan and Iraq (2015, 155) and Mark Pedelty documented the band of protesters on a little boat on the Salish Sea, sounding trombones, drums, saxophones, and a tuba to defy an oil rig (2016, 1). They occupied public space to block the vehicles of injustice—whether war or an oil rig. Motion, mobilizing, and movement have long been powerful signifiers of—*motivators* for—change. In spectacle, sound, and mobility, *Arka Kinari* resembles these; however, in function, it does not call an enemy to battle, not even the colonizers. Instead, it calls on strangers for conversation. Its performance is an offering, or *banten*, in the Indonesian language: a selfless action to make and give sustenance in the form of food and drink, incense, prayer, and entertainment to others—gods, ancestors, friends, and strangers. In turn, they are greeted with a fanfare of music, dance, and welcome rituals equaling the spectacle of their most unusual sailing vessel. As Nova explained in her opening words to villagers in Kampung Fiat, recorded by *Arka Kinari*'s resident documentarian, "We came here to exchange knowledge, to exchange culture, and to exchange history so that we can guard these things together. We are also here to learn from you."⁹

Nova is expressing curiosity about Indigenous ecological knowledge that echoes Kyle Whyte's call for settler environmentalists to pay attention to Indigenous communities, which have "long histories of having to be well-organized to adapt to seasonal and inter-annual environmental changes" (Whyte 2017, 153). She is not interested in extracting Indigenous ecological knowledge for the education and benefit of wealthy nations. Rather, she is acknowledging her own accountability to contribute to ecological knowledge. She again aligns with Whyte as she takes up the concept of traditional ecological knowledge or TEK, which has often been tokenized and exploited by both well-meaning environmentalists and self-serving governments. As Whyte defines it, it is a concept for collaboration that "serves to invite diverse populations to continually learn from one another about how each approaches the very question of 'knowledge' in the first place, and how these different approaches can work together to better steward and manage the environment and natural resources" (Whyte 2013, 2).

In the Banda Islands, an exchange of climate resilience knowledge is made: *Arka Kinari* shares knowledge about solar panels and learns about the changing migration patterns of fish. A conversation on gender and the division of labor also unfolds: women have historically been barred from sailing, and many of those who meet Nova at port express disbelief and delight that a woman has traveled and labored so well at sea. By offering *Arka Kinari*'s crew food and drink, prayer, and entertainment, Banda Islanders are not passive audiences for international touring artists: they are cocreators of a pooled, ever-expanding knowledge—musical, theatrical, ecological, and existential—about humans and more-than-humans meeting at sea and along coastlines. Their villages become a refuge for these strange travelers, who disembark and rest until they are rejuvenated and ready to move to the next friendly harbor. Such exchanges signify the effect and affect of *Arka Kinari*'s invocation of Indigenous seafaring knowledge, provoking pride in local epistemologies and igniting conversation about the impact of the climate crisis, locally and around the world (see fig. 15.2).

BORDERLESS FUTURES

Over the course of eighty minutes, the soundscape will transform again and again, as the pair of performers move skillfully between instrumental and vocal

Fig. 15.2. Filastine and Nova. Portrait of the artists practicing their emergency flare chops. Used with permission.

> *traditions from the East and West, from the Northern and Southern Hemispheres: snare drum and computer; guitar, mbira, and melodica; rap and Javanese song. Video-mapping on the sails will navigate a journey around the world and through ecological frictions: stages of civilization and stages of nature's transmutation. Images of oil rigs will collide with army tanks and factory explosions. Drone footage of icy landscapes will preclude the moment of collapse when a mammoth wedge of glacier crashes into the sea before cutting to a landscape of automobiles trapped in an urban flood. The camera will dip beneath the ocean's surface for a few moments of peace amid a constellation of Rhopilema Nomadica, a jellyfish indigenous to Indonesia—glowing and pulsating ghosts that lock into rhythm with a dancer dressed to mirror them, undulating on the deck of the ship.*

In October 2020, *Arka Kinari* arrived in Benoa Bay, Bali, where the ship and crew remained through the worst of the monsoon season. The crew staged a performance finale to their long journey for those gathered at Benoa and, for the first time, for audiences around the world—including me—who joined via a livestream on the YouTube channel for the sponsoring Indonesian National Board for Disaster Management.[10] Benoa is an important place of contestation for Bali's own social and environmental activists, including many musicians and artists who, for nearly a decade, have fiercely defended the bay against a proposed land reclamation project for tourism that would squeeze out small-scale businesses, deny local fishers and residents access to the area, and decimate the marine ecosystem (Moore 2022). For now, all development projects are on hold because of the pandemic. The harbor continues to gift neighboring villages with an abundance of fish, thus offering food security during a devastating and ongoing economic recession.

Shortly after the performance, I spoke with Grey by phone and asked him what, if anything, about *Arka Kinari*'s journey might be replicated by other artists. He said, for one, carbon-free global travel is possible and gaining momentum, as evidenced by Greta Thunberg's crossing of the Atlantic by boat in 2019. He also spoke nostalgically of a return to the punk rock touring model of the 1970s and '80s, when bandmates would squeeze their bodies and gear into a small van and play gigs at small venues within proximity to save money, gas, and time. Of course, regional touring bands that lack the celebrity or major label backing for air travel have always prioritized efficient, land-based tour routes. But then and now, the world's top touring acts are prone to fly between one-off performances. Even underground electronic artists like Filastine might travel from the United States to Japan for a one-day EDM festival, only to fly immediately home or onward to the next performance. For *Arka Kinari*'s carbon-free travel to be replicated on a much larger scale, the entire international touring industry would have to be completely transformed. International mega festivals would be replaced by clusters of geographically proximate, smaller-scale performances. The radius or exclusivity clause often included in performance contracts to prevent featured artists from playing nearby venues or festivals, in the interest of driving up ticket sales for the contracting event, would need to be eliminated so that artists could spend more time and expend less fuel in a single location.

To a limited degree, live entertainment and touring conglomerates are taking steps to reduce their carbon emissions. The change agent for much of these efforts is UK nonprofit Julie's Bicycles, which, since 2007, has conducted research, policy advocacy, and sustainability partnerships with more than two thousand entertainment and performing arts organizations operating in the UK and worldwide. Most recently, it released a call to action to nations at the COP26 for governments to "link culture policy to environmental policy" (Julie's Bicycle 2021). Its biggest client is Live Nation Entertainment, the world's largest touring and promotions company, which announced its "Green Nation Touring Program" to enhance the sustainability of concert tours through green venue selection, efficient routing, and other efforts (Live Nation Entertainment

2021). Only time will tell whether these efforts are measurable and significant enough to warrant the significant marketing boon Live Nation and other entertainment corporations enjoy by aligning their companies with artist and audience concerns about the fate of the planet. UK rock band Coldplay has famously pressed pause on international touring altogether until they can ensure net-zero carbon performances. But an end to touring is not feasible for independent acts who depend on live performance revenue for their survival, particularly in the streaming era. To this concern, Filastine responded, "I understand that this is hard." He continued: "But you have to kind of nudge it, one way or another."

And what might ethnomusicology and sound studies gain from modeling *Arka Kinari*'s voyage through this global pandemic and climate emergency? As more of our work becomes oriented toward social and environmental justice, and as many of us question our modes and motivations for travel, the settings and reasons for our gatherings,[11] and the reach and utility of our scholarship, we might ask ourselves what sacrifices we are personally and professionally willing to make to reduce our carbon footprints. *Arka Kinari*'s journey might inspire more publications drawn from a pooling of cocreated knowledge, mirroring Grey and Nova's deep creative and activist investments in Indonesia. We might occasionally take up music, dance, and theater over the written word, as superior mediums for problem-solving in certain contexts. *Arka Kinari* might encourage us to expand our efforts in cultural reparations and reconsider our primary audiences.

Arka Kinari might compel us to question why we gather up other people's stories, who among us has the privilege to tell those stories and to whom and for whom we tell them. As we reckon with the extractivism of ethnomusicology's past and present, wherein the cultures of Black, Brown, and Indigenous people are so often mined like nonrenewables for settler-scholar's professional gain, *Arka Kinari* might encourage our own radical reimagining of the aims and outcomes of our ethnographic labor. Yet we might also recognize Kwame Anthony Appiah's cosmopolitan ethos in our compulsion to travel and make music and conversation with strangers: we do it to learn more about humankind and, therefore, ourselves; and in doing so, we expand our scope of ethical responsibility (2006).

Steered by musicians, artists, and activists Grey Filastine and Nova Ruth, *Arka Kinari* has circumvented the neoliberalist drive of both modern seafaring and band touring, survived border lockdowns and a global pandemic, and charted a new course for ethical cultural contact, conversation, and artmaking on the ocean, our planet's largest commons. Philosopher and education reformer John Dewey theorized that an artwork is not an independent material object, it emerges from the exchange between its making and receiving (1934). It is always interrelational, and thus, it always manifests ethical responsibility. As we all increasingly probe the ethical issues attending our social, political, technological, and ecological futures, we might take up the study of music and sound, like the ocean to *Arka Kinari*, as a commons—not as a set of publications hoarded within key-entry libraries and behind digital paywalls and not only as the fair use of these resources, but rather, as an ongoing pooling of knowledge that could expand beyond measure as long as we keep learning with others. Such a commons would nourish our need to live by and up to our individual and collective responsibility, for the health and well-being of all others, and to the cosmos we share.

NOTES

1. Indonesia is the largest exporter of palm oil worldwide and exports three times the amount of coal necessary to meet its own energy needs.

2. See as primers, Kunst ([1937] 1987) and Hood (1954).

3. For a history and ethnography of gamelan in the United States, see Clendinning (2020).

4. English-language literature includes Allen and Dawe (2016), Cooley (2019), Impey (2018), Manabe (2015), Pedelty (2016), and Silvers (2018).

5. A portmanteau word combining *art* and *activism*, *artivism* is a term Nova and many other Indonesian artists have adopted over the last decade to describe their dual orientations toward creative and social or environmental justice work. Grey and Nova have also described the *Arka Kinari* project as "artivism at sea" (Filastine 2021).

6. *Arka Kinari* (n.d.), emphasis mine.

7. For a thorough account of Macassan history and early trade relations between modern-day Australia and eastern Indonesia, see Clark and May (2013).

8. See chapter 4 in Capra and Mattei (2015).

9. Ind.: "Kami datang ke seni untuk bertukar ilmu, bertukar budaya, dan juga bertukar sejarah, lalu Bersama-sama ingin menjaganya. Kami juga ingin belajar dari apa yang adanya di sini." Author's translation.

10. Ind.: Badan Nasional Penanggulangan Bencana.

11. The ethics of travel for scholarly activity has been frequently interrogated by Aaron S. Allen and members of the Ecomusicology Special Interest Group for the Society Ethnomusicology, and it was addressed head-on at the 2020 meeting's board-sponsored roundtable, "New Gatherings: Creative Mobilities and Ethnomusicology in a Changing World." Also in 2020, the roundtable "Pathways to Environmental Accountability: Artist, Activist, and Research Perspectives," for which I served as chair, addressed how ethnomusicological work is shaped by environmental crisis and continues with conversation about how we might work together—musicians, activists, researchers, and institutions—to chart pathways to environmental accountability.

BIBLIOGRAPHY

Allen, Aaron, and Kevin Dawe, eds. 2016. *Current Directions in Ecomusicology.* New York: Routledge.

Amimoto Ingersoll, Karin. 2016. *Waves of Knowing: A Seascape Epistemology.* Durham, NC: Duke University Press.

Appiah, Kwame Anthony. 2006. *Cosmopolitanism: Ethics in a World of Strangers.* New York: W. W. Norton & Company.

Arka Kinari. n.d. "About." Accessed October 15, 2020. https://www.arkakinari.org/about.

Capra, Fritjof, and Ugo Mattei. 2015. *The Ecology of Law.* San Francisco: Berrett-Koehler Publishers.

Clark, Marshall, and Sally K. May, eds. 2013. *Macassan History and Heritage: Journeys, Encounters and Influences.* Canberra: Australian National University Press.

Clendinning, Elizabeth A. 2020. *American Gamelan and the Ethnomusicological Imagination.* Urbana: University of Illinois Press.

Cooley, Timothy J., ed. 2019. *Cultural Sustainabilities: Music, Media, Language, Advocacy.* Foreword by Jeff Todd Titon. Urbana: University of Illinois Press.

Cooley, Timothy, Aaron S. Allen, Ruth Hellier, Mark Pedelty, Denise Von Glahn, Jeff Todd Titon, and Jennifer C. Post. 2020. "SEM President's Roundtable 2018, Humanities' Responses to the Anthropocene." *Ethnomusicology* 64 (2): 301–30.

Dewey, John. 1934. *Art as Experience.* New York: Penguin Group.

Díaz, Vicente M. 2011. "Voyaging for Anti-Colonial Recovery: Austronesian Seafaring, Archipelagic Rethinking, and the Re-mapping of Indigeneity." *Pacific Asia Inquiry* 2 (1): 21–32.

Fan, Xuewei, Chiyuan Miao, Qingyun Duan, Chenwei Shen, and Yi Wu. 2021. "Future Climate Change Hotspots under Different 21st Century Warming Scenarios." *Earth's Future* 9 (6). https://doi.org/10.1029/2021EF002027.

Filastine, Grey. 2021. "Artivism at Sea: The Voyage of Arka Kinari." Public lecture, October 28, 2021. Northeastern University, Boston, MA.

Gamage, Rajni Nayanthara. 2016. "Blue Economy in Southeast Asia; Oceans as the New Frontier of Economic Development." *Maritime Affairs: Journal of the National Maritime Foundation of India* 12 (2): 1–15.

García-López, Gustavo A., Ursula Lang, and Neera Singh. 2021. "Commons, Commoning and Co-Becoming: Nurturing Life-in-Common and Post-Capitalist Futures (An Introduction to the Theme Issue)." *Environment and Planning E: Nature and Space*, November 24, 2021. Accessed December 1, 2021. https://doi.org/10.1177/25148486211051081.

Henschke, Rebecca. 2020. "In Mid-Pacific with Nowhere to Land." BBC News, May 30, 2020. Accessed October 15, 2020. https://www.bbc.com/news/stories-52852377.

Hood, Mantle. 1954. *The Nuclear Theme as a Determinant of Patet in Javanese Music.* Groningan: J. B. Wolters.

Impey, Angela. 2018. *Song Walking: Women, Music, and Environmental Justice in an African Borderland.* Chicago: University of Chicago Press.

Julie's Bicycle. 2021. "Julie's Bicycle Releases COP26 Call to Action." November 5, 2021. Accessed December 1, 2021. https://juliesbicycle.com/news/julies-bicycle-releases-cop26-call-to-action/.

Kasim, Ma'ruf. 2021. "Measuring Vulnerability of Coastal Ecosystem and Identifying Adaptation Options of Indonesia's Coastal Communities to Climate Change: Case Study of Southeast Sulawesi, Indonesia." In *Climate Change Research, Policy and Actions in Indonesia: Science, Adaptation, Mitigation,* edited by Riyante Djalante, Joni Jupesta, and Edvin Aldrian, 121–48. Cham, Switzerland: Springer.

Kunst, Jaap. (1937) 1987. *Music in Java.* New York: Springer.

Live Nation Entertainment. 2021. "Live Nation Announces Green Nation Touring Program, Giving Artists Tools to Reduce the Environmental Impact of Tours." April 21, 2021. Accessed December 1, 2021. https://www.livenationentertainment.com/2021/04/live-nation-announces-green-nation-touring-program-giving-artists-tools-to-reduce-the-environmental-impact-of-tours/.

Manabe, Noriko. 2015. *The Revolution Will Not Be Televised: Protest Music after Fukushima.* New York: Oxford University Press.

McDowell, John Holmes, Katherine Borland, Rebecca Dirksen, and Suo Tuohy, eds. 2021. *Performing Environmentalisms: Expressive Culture and Ecological Change.* Urbana: University of Illinois Press.

Moore, Rebekah E. 2022. "The Vernacular Cosmopolitanism of an Indonesian Rock Band: Navicula's Creative and Activist Pathways." In *Sounding Out the State of Indonesian Music,* edited by Andy McGraw and Chris Miller. Ithaca, NY: Cornell University Press.

Nangoy, Fransiska, and Gayatri Suroyo. 2021. "Indonesia Clings to Coal despite Green Vision for Economy." *Reuters,* September 20, 2021. Accessed December 1, 2021. https://www.reuters.com/business/energy/indonesia-clings-coal-despite-green-vision-economy-2021-09-20/.

Ostrom, Elinor. 1990. *Governing the Commons: The Evolution of Institutions for Collective Action.* Cambridge: Cambridge University Press.

Pedelty, Mark. 2016. *A Song to Save the Salish Sea: Musical Performance as Environmental Activism.* Bloomington: Indiana University Press.

Schwartz, Jessica A. 2019. "How the Sea Is Sounded: Remapping Indigenous Soundings in the Marshallese Diaspora." In *Remapping Sound Studies,* edited by Gavin Steingo and Jim Sykes, 77–105. Durham, NC: Duke University Press.

Scruggs, Gregory. 2020. "How the Pandemic Left This Experimental Act Stranded on a Ship in the Middle of the Pacific Ocean." *Pitchfork,* July 13, 2020. Accessed

October 15, 2020. https://pitchfork.com/thepitch/filastine-and-nova-arka-kinari-ship-stranded-pacific-ocean-pandemic/.

Silvers, Michael B. 2018. *Voices of Drought: The Politics of Music and Environment in Northeastern Brazil*. Urbana: University of Illinois Press

Starosielski, Nicole. 2015. *The Undersea Network*. Durham, NC: Duke University Press.

Van de Vuurst, Paige, and Luis E. Escobar. 2020. "Perspective: Climate Change and the Relocation of Indonesia's Capital to Borneo." *Frontiers in Earth Science*, January 30, 2020. Accessed December 1, 2021. https://www.frontiersin.org/articles/10.3389/feart.2020.00005/full/.

Whyte, Kyle. 2013. "On the Role of Traditional Ecological Knowledge as a Collaborative Concept: A Philosophical Study." *Ecological Processes* 2 (7): 1–12.

———. 2017. "Indigenous Climate Change Studies: Indigenizing Futures, Decolonizing the Anthropocene." *English Language Notes* 55 (1–2): 153–62.

DISCOGRAPHY

Filastine. 2012. *LOOT*. Digital album. Self-release. https://filastine.bandcamp.com/album/loot/.

VIDEOGRAPHY

Filastine & Nova. 2019. "Arka Kinari Fundraiser." YouTube.com, July 4, 2019. Video. Accessed October 15, 2020. https://www.youtube.com/watch?v=012AvPTcXlY/.

SIXTEEN

RAISING THE IMPERATIVE FOR DIRECT ACTION

SUSAN M. ASAI

I TURN TO MUSIC AND human rights as a broad frame from which to consider the question, "What potential does music have in effecting social change?" In her article, "Music and the Myth of Universality: Sounding Human Rights and Capabilities" Nomi Dave advocates for the *"moral imperative to care*, and to explore how music can protect and promote human rights and human capabilities" (2015, 1, emphasis added). The notion of caring is an antidote to the "globalization of indifference," a phrase Pope Francis penned in 2013 in numerous speeches, and in a 2014 TED conference decrying the plight of thousands of undocumented migrants and asylum seekers being turned away by countries whose shores they had reached, a situation for which Pope Francis blames capitalist markets and the consequent cultures they shape. Caring stirs empathy and altruism, basic building blocks that equip societies to sustain a moral compass.

It is critical for researchers to move beyond the outdated notion of music's universalist appeal, in its assumed ability to accompany daily activities, soothe, heal, or transform. Ethnomusicologists must ask: What do people need to improve their conditions, and how or what does music contribute to this end? In our ethnographic work we must analyze music's effectiveness as a tool for social change by shifting our focus from "music's ontological traits to its real-world effects" (Dave 2015, 14). Research methodologies must account for complexities arising from intersecting music and social practices embedded in the history and culture of a particular people to analyze music's effectiveness. Such methodological aims would facilitate ascertaining the efficacy of music in improving the lives of people we are studying.

Music educators Randall Everett Allsup and Eric Shieh place "the moral imperative to care" at the center of teaching (2012, 48). Teaching students how injustice marginalizes people develops empathic consciousness, something our brain's right hemisphere is already hard-wired to elevate (Gupta, "Between Music and Medicine"). For Allsup and Shieh, caring is the first step in preparing students to respond to acts of injustice, emphasizing that the imperative to care is "a democratic project," a perspective with the goal of repairing and transforming. They urge educators to engage students in a curriculum that provides them opportunities to participate as agents of change (Allsup and Shieh 2012, 49, 50).

The 2020 SEM preconference, "Music and Social Agency: Contestations and Confluences," demonstrate ethnomusicology's growing focus on the intersection of music and social justice. Expansive were the constellation of themes and threads presented: food justice; environmental justice; climate justice; music and human rights; SEM's role in supporting work involving musical activism; recalibrating our listening building alliances; resisting racial, legal, and business practices in the music industry; redefining research in ethnomusicology; and more, all shining a light on the changing social and political landscape. On a global scale, Michael Frishkopf's initiative—Music for Global Human Development (M4GHD)—at the Canadian Centre for Ethnomusicology is a far-reaching model: music-centered projects connect global actors to socially, politically, and economically marginalized populations suffering from the impacts of coloniality, in partnership with local musicians and local cognoscente to re-weave the social fabric of communities fighting dehumanization while connecting them to others globally (Frishkopf, "Music for Global Human Development").

EDITING AS DIRECT ACTION

My comments promote the justice-oriented approach Professor Emerita Brenda M. Romero and I took in planning and preparing this volume. Setting benchmarks for a more egalitarian process to editing publications is a step toward greater inclusiveness. Eileen Hayes, former president of the College Music Society identified how "institutional racism is replicated particularly by the gate-keeping apparatuses of academia including publishing practices." As an editor, it was critical for me to reflect on my position as a senior BIPOC scholar as I aspired to create equal access for authors. When Romero and I actively sought to publish an anthology featuring several of the ethnographic papers submitted to the Music and Social Justice paper competition sponsored by Crossroads Section, part of our quest was for equitable access. Such access is key for junior, international, BIPOC, and other marginalized scholars in their efforts to build a publication record. The anthology is unique, however, in that it combines research ethnographies with autoethnographies by senior scholars. Authors were invited to autoethnographically illuminate the challenges and barriers to professional development, sense of worth, and participation in home institutions and SEM. Allowing people to tell their stories paves the way to restorative justice and transformation (see Romero's chapter 17 for details on the anthology's process). Decolonizing efforts in the editing process entail mentoring scholars, particularly those who face limited publishing prospects owing to still evolving theoretical, language, or writing skills and whose careers are unfolding as they create a niche within ethnomusicology. Moving away from jargon-filled texts democratizes the exchange of ideas and promotes innovative ways of thinking. Breaking down strict adherence to colonizing linguistic structures promotes an ethos of openness, advancing the confidence of authors at all levels while also promoting literary accessibility without sacrificing sophistication and depth of ideas and concepts. As Eileen Hayes purports, "We must continue to resist the notion that 'diversity' and high quality are mutually exclusive." Mentoring requires an increased time commitment by editors to guide authors in crafting papers through several drafts. Such commitment is a strain, but it is a necessary practice in advancing impartial publishing opportunities.

Published volumes are an effective vehicle for coalitional projects that provide equal access for studies involving intersections of music with disability, critical race, gender and sexuality studies, Indigenous studies, and other marginalized and new areas of research and writing. Coalitions represent "a gathering," a coming together of scholars from a constellation of backgrounds and orientations that have the potential to expand and enrich research within our discipline. Allowing for reflexivity in matters of representation based on race, age, background, gender, and myriad other identities, coalitional projects also advance nuanced perspectives that, in turn, could introduce new trajectories in research and writing.

Coalitional publications require closer collaboration between editors, aiming to disassemble hierarchical attitudes and structures in decision-making. This requires numerous emails and virtual meetings to arrive at resolutions satisfactory to all. The collaborative labor among all editors for *At the Crossroads of Music and Social Justice* heightened the justice-oriented intent of the publication.

Challenges to forming coalitions are many. Editors can play a role by exploring affinities instead of being overly fixated on goals and building on a strength that emphasizes working together to activate new directions in collectively addressing inequities.

Interracial and intercultural coalitional projects contribute to larger movements that cultivate a sense of agency for individuals in the promise of equality and inclusion. In his article, "Interrogating Systemic Racism and the White Academic Field," published by the Franz Fanon Foundation, Nelson Maldonado-Torres proposes a more radical direction.[1] He endorses replacing the terms "diversity and inclusion" with the more direct action of "desegregation, reparations, and decolonization." Maldonado-Torres claims "diversity and inclusion have become a powerful tool in advancing systemic racism and coloniality in service of the white academic field, while making it appear that it is the one and only adequate response to racism and discrimination" (2020, 3).

We as a field and an academic society must, in the words of Leslie Tilley, "Commit to forefronting BIPOC voices in our publications, conferences, awards, and governance. There is a need to require a standard for the number of people of color at all levels of structure and recognition." I argue that publications must serve as an insurgent space in calling for restructuring the White academic field and its concomitant institutions.[2]

NOTES

1. *White academic field* is a term originally coined by members of the antiracist organization "Parti des indigènes de la république." It refers to academic disciplines that systematically produce and reproduce White supremacy and privilege and promote a conception of racism meant to uphold that supremacy (Maldonado-Torres 2020).

2. The practice of capitalizing *B* in *Black* to refer to the history, culture, and identity of people of African ancestry is in common usage. There is not as much consensus on capitalizing *W* when using the grammatically parallel term *White*. The controversy surrounding the practice of capitalizing *W* requires us to offer our reasoning for following this application. One perspective is that within the politicized context of this anthology, we should use *White* to embed the racial identity and privilege of this demographic in a discourse of inequality and exclusion. We align ourselves with the National Association of Black Journalists' recommendation that whenever a color is used to ascribe race, the word should be capitalized. James Baldwin, at a talk at Wayne State University in 1980, declared "white to be a metaphor for power" (Painter, "Why White Should Be Capitalized, Too"). His assertion supports capitalizing the *W* to mark the unjust racial power imbalance Blacks and other marginalized populations suffer. Painter, author of the *New York Times* opinion piece, also advocates capitalizing *White* to firmly locate "Whiteness" in the American ideology of race to equalize the high visibility of *Black* as a group identity.

BIBLIOGRAPHY

Allsup, Everett Randall, and Eric Shieh. 2012. "Social Justice and Music Education: The Call for a Public Pedagogy." *Music Educators Journal*. Accessed August 10, 2020. https://journals.sagepub.com/doi/10.1177/0027432112442969.

Dave, Nomi. 2015. "Music and the Myth of Universality: Sounding Human Rights and Capabilities." *Journal of Human Rights Practice*, 7 (1): 1–17.

Frishkopf, Michael. 2007. "Music for Global Human Development." Centre for Ethnomusicology. Media Wiki. Accessed July 11, 2021. https://www.artsrn.ualberta.ca/fwa_mediawiki/index.php?title=Music_for_Global_Human_Development.

Maldonado-Torres, Nelson. 2020. "Interrogating Systemic Racism and the White Academic Field." Fondation Franz Fanon, June 16. Accessed September 15, 2020. https://fondation-frantzfanon.com/interrogating-systemic-racism-and-the-white-academic-field/.

Painter, Nell Irvin. 2020. "Why 'White' Should Be Capitalized, Too." *Washington Post*, July 22, 2020. Accessed November 4, 2021. https://www.washingtonpost.com/opinions/2020/07/22/why-white-should-be-capitalized/.

SEVENTEEN

CIRCLING BACK ON DIRECT ACTION

On Difference and Representation

BRENDA M. ROMERO

THIS ANTHOLOGY IS DESIGNED TO be a reading source for social justice–oriented courses and curricula and an introduction to research that has real-world impact.[1] As Chicana feminist Gloria E. Anzaldúa proposed, "May we do work that matters. *Vale la pena*. It's worth the pain" (Anzaldúa 2005, 102; see also Cantú 2018, 13). As project originators, Susan M. Asai and I coalesced activist conversations going back to 1986 when we met in graduate school. In 2007, Professor Asai invited me to participate at an international UNESCO meeting in Paris, where we gave talks to share our perspectives about the role of music in building a better world.[2]

The Society for Ethnomusicology (SEM) was always our (inter)disciplinary home and our close association again bore fruit when we served as SEM Crossroads Section cochairs from 2015 to 2019. Founded as the Crossroads Project by Kyra D. Gaunt in 2003, the standing committee eventually became a dues-paying cohort, or section, within the larger SEM but seemed to be obscured and lose focus when SEM leadership created new entities to address issues of diversity, equity, and inclusion (DEI) within the society. In the meantime, recent BIPOC critiques (see Asai's chapter 16) and a growing awareness of the psychology of the coloniality of power have challenged us to reconsider how we use language.[3] As Kofi Agawu (1992, 245) submits, "Of all the currents of change that have swept the humanities during the last half-century, the most far-reaching revolve around language." Chippewa scholar Gerald Robert Vizenor coined the term *survivance* and many also use *resilience* to emphasize the failure of White conquest, given that resistance to domination has taken many forms. In her 2009 open letter, Eve Tuck (2009, 413) writes: "In damage-centered research, one of the major activities is to document pain or loss in an individual, community, or tribe. Though connected to deficit models—frameworks that emphasize what a particular student, family or community is lacking to explain underachievement or failure—damage-centered research is distinct in being more socially and historically situated.... Common sense tells us this is a good thing, but the danger in damage-centered research is that it is a pathologizing approach in which the oppression singularly defines the community." In addition, new scholarship surrounding intersectionality trumps Agawu's (2003) critique of the discipline of ethnomusicology as an inventor of difference. Thus, in 2017 Asai and I led the decision to change the name to "Crossroads Section for Difference and Representation."

In 2017, growing concerns in the US political and social landscape prompted the few remaining Crossroads members to advance the section as a forum for offering prizes for the best SEM paper presentations on music and social justice over a two-year period, starting from 2017–18 (awarded in 2019) and on odd years following. Crossroads Section members Dr. Loneka Battiste and Dr. Stephanie Khoury and ethnomusicology graduate student Benjamin Cefkin assisted in vetting submissions received from eighteen authors for the 2017–18 inaugural cycle of the paper competition. As I read through the submissions early in 2019, the warm feelings I experienced quickly became an imperative to share by creating an anthology that would advance music and social justice research in ethnomusicology and allied disciplines. I thought to solicit authors who had submitted for the Crossroads prizes to further develop their presentations into chapters for an anthology to commemorate the Crossroads Section inaugural prize competition and to invite the prize-winning authors to join our editorial board. Asai agreed to collaborate and we subsequently worked in tandem at every phase of the project.

Fortuitously, the prize recipients—Katelyn E. Best, David A. McDonald, and Andrew G. Snyder—agreed to join the anthology's editorial board. Nine authors (including the three prizewinners) accepted the invitation to publish in the anthology; when one withdrew, the editors solicited Rebekah Moore's 2020 SEM presentation because of its critical statement on music ecoactivism. Both McDonald's and Snyder's original submissions have since been published (2020 and 2022, respectively); thus, their essays in this anthology are newly written. In recognition of attaining the Crossroads Section prize for the presentation with the greatest potential impact, it seemed appropriate to ask David A. McDonald to write the anthology's introduction. This he did with an insightful summary of the thematic strands identified throughout the anthology while advancing perspectives for future ethnomusicological research.

Recognizing that our SEM community of authors for the anthology was primarily White, we needed a balance between competition and community values and decided to lift up the voices of senior scholars, most of them BIPOC (including Asai and myself) who had supported the efforts of the SEM Crossroads Section through their leadership. To quote Martha Ellen Davis at the 2021 SEM Virtual Preconference, "Taking life histories is important. An entire community and place can be described through the history of a single family." It was in like spirit that we specifically asked invited scholars to self-reflect about their encounters with social justice in their work and their resulting positionalities within a community of ethnomusicologists. Crossroads Section founder Kyra D. Gaunt's powerful opening autoethnography in this volume reveals pitfalls (like receiving mean-spirited hate mail or worse) that, according to Professor Emerita Charlotte Heth, "come with the territory" of being BIPOC in academia.[4]

Although initially conceived as brief contributions, the invited essays vary in length, which necessitated making space for a variety of writing styles—a representation of difference. Five invited chapters begin the anthology and Asai's and Moore's invited chapters are included as ethnographies.

SYNERGY—THE WHOLE IS GREATER THAN THE SUM OF ITS PARTS

I first learned about the concept of synergy in dance performance from a graduate school mentor, dance ethnologist Allegra Fuller Snyder (1972), daughter of renowned architect Buckminster Fuller and professor emerita at UCLA, who theorized the dancer as a synergistic resultant. During my dissertation fieldwork and after completing the dissertation, I performed on the violin for the Pueblo of Jemez Matachina Danza in New Mexico for nine years. I heard stories of miraculous healings resulting from music-bound rituals and ceremonies, some involving ceremonial dance (danza). At the time I was learning about Snyder's concept of synergy in dance performance, I took a class in American Indian music with Charlotte Heth (Cherokee). Over the many years in which I observed and participated in the danza, I also taught courses in American Indian music using Heth's syllabus, which I had much enjoyed. I began to notice the concept of synergy not only in the danza but also as an operational structure of the class. Heth's syllabus required each student to work on a different tribe or topic for the semester, beginning with a focus on what creation narratives tell us about the meaning of music in any given Indigenous society. Applying particular thematic content led to synergistic sharing three times during the semester, when it became easy to perceive the whole as greater than the sum of its parts. At the end of the semester, students realized they had learned much more than they had imagined they would, inspiring me to adapt the syllabus format in other classes and seminars I offered. As I was also thinking about synergy with regard to Native American Dance, I began to consider synergy an aspect of cultural coherence—an underlying Native paradigm that informs music and dance as healing modalities and a way of being.

Having learned about the synergistic impact of the intersections of music, the dancer, dance, contexts, and cosmologies, I began to think of synergy in everyday life. I was moved by this concept as I read the SEM presentations and felt the impact of a collective form of social capital. According to management theorist Sharon Timberlake, social capital "refers to the collective value of all social networks . . . 'and the norms of reciprocity and trustworthiness that arise from them'" (Putnam 1995, 19, cited in Timberlake 2005, 35). As the project began to unfold, interesting side conversations revealed unexpected synergies among us. Most critically, David A. McDonald, our first-prize winner, solicited our manuscript for the Indiana University Activist Encounters in Ethnomusicology and Folklore Series—for which he is a series editor. Additionally, Andrew G. Snyder had just completed editing *HONK! A Street Band Renaissance of Music and Activism*, and he proved to be indispensable in the editing process. In conversations across chapters, Katelyn E. Best led us to a new term, dysconscious(ness), for the ways humans internalize oppression, from internalized colonialism to internalized patriarchy, to the Deaf buying into myths about deafness (see note 16 in chapter 3).

I had learned that in the Zuni Pueblo in western New Mexico, folks adhere to a belief that no one person needs to know everything. Adapting a collaborative model, in which no one person was expected to cover everything, and judgments and issues were collectively decided, each of five editors was responsible for assigned chapters of the anthology. Editors conducted close edits of three ethnographic chapters each while also functioning as collaborative editors for an additional three. As we worked closely with authors to enhance the impact of their work, mentoring—typically missing from the editorial process—became a shared core objective (see Asai's chapter 16). This mostly worked, although ultimately, everyone read everything because all of the chapters were so engaging, and this created a collective synergistic momentum.

THE SYNERGISTIC MODEL—OR "GRASPING THE PEARL OF FREEDOM FROM THE DRAGON TIME"[5]

Rooted in interdisciplinary and intersectional studies, I draw on both personal and scholarly sources of inspiration in my subjective interpretation of synergy. First and perhaps most profoundly, it is a result of my early explorations of the Bahá'í Faith. Although it is beyond the scope of this essay to talk in depth about the role of religion or faith in our work—something Steven Loza has called on us to do as reflexive writers in his chapter in the anthology—I must acknowledge the impact of learning about the Bahá'í faith in my teens. Bahá'ís believe in the unity of all religions and peoples—"one love." They consider their organization a faith, not a religion, and they do not believe in proselytizing. Highly persecuted since their proclamations of prophecy in the 1840s in Persia, Bahá'ís believe it is incumbent on followers to find themselves in the company of those different from themselves, accepting that there are multiple ways of being in the world. Bahá'ís also believe that change in the current age will come primarily from horizontal action—group or collective action. These two ideas have stuck, although I am not a card-carrying Bahá'í.

Elsewhere I have talked about the implicit synergistic basis of Alan P. Merriam's (1964) three-part model for ethnomusicological research, which highlights sound, musical and societal concepts, and musical and sociomusical behaviors as fundamental to ethnomusicological understanding. Allegra Snyder's idea of holistic, embodied synergy in dance events resonated strongly with my experiences performing the violin or guitar for the Matachines *danza* in New Mexico, and observing the ceremonial practices surrounding this dance. I offer the following eureka moment I gleaned as a result of theorizing synergy. My question was how does Native song and dance ceremony heal? Perhaps it is the synergistic "expansion" of the ceremony's common cause that is able to overcome unharmonious energies? I came to believe that the power to heal depends on the strongest synergistic connections that exponentially generate the healing energy. Nonetheless, human beings do not easily align without common cause. The common cause and reason for a majority of American Indian ceremonies and rituals was in the past and continues to be to heal and renew a community. This anthology is based in the common cause of renewal, especially in the Society of Ethnomusicology during a time of upheaval, but also during a time of new White supremacist movements and a pandemic that has exposed social inequities as never before.

Subsequent to theorizing synergy over a number of years, I offer a few ideas and terms to elucidate this particular interpretation of the concept.[6] Synergy does not mean or imply serendipity or randomness, although it may happen; careful planning allows for the momentum to gather and "Become." "Synergistic product" can be an energy that heals through exponential expansion. The whole is greater than the sum of its parts. Synergy is not necessarily bound to place or nation. Based on Timberlake's definitions of social capital, mentioned earlier, I have coined the term *synergistic capital* that explains when things potentially align in ways that create energy or momentum toward a common cause. In this project, a variety of intersecting synergies were at play: an established professional community of SEM and Crossroads Section members; a long-standing professional and collegial relationship between the two senior editors; a wealth of research on music and social justice in circulation, as evidenced in the submissions for the inaugural Crossroads Section prizes; and the work of faculty members who have rallied for social justice through the years. As an editorial board, we later discovered other synergies (some mentioned previously) among us simply due to our diverse perspectives in a shared US society and to our interdisciplinary methods as ethnomusicologists and mutual respect as scholars.

Culture is not a static property to be examined and prodded and held up for all to see; from what I have observed, culture is more like a kaleidoscope of ever-shifting patterns. I have long contemplated such kaleidoscopic patterning as I've tried to piece together how the Matachines Danza—subject of my ethnographic fieldwork—could have survived in so many places, in so many versions. Suddenly, while reading the varied SEM presentations submitted for the Crossroads Section for Difference and Representation inaugural prize competition, I began to feel the synergistic potential inherent in the connections that had brought us, as a professional society, this far on the path of music and its intersections with social justice; the anthology is the result. In the face of recent organizational turmoil, I note the relative youth of our discipline: To coin a phrase from the young Black poet Amanda Gorman (who spoke at the 2021 Presidential Inauguration) "[SEM] isn't broken, but simply unfinished."

The anthology models an organizational process designed to promote an egalitarian project based on a theoretical application of the concept of synergy. Essentially, this meant working not just jointly but collaboratively for the best possible synergistic outcome, where the whole would be greater than the sum of its parts. The synergistic outcome manifested as a force for addressing and healing the wounds of marginalization and systemic racism by applying ethnomusicological research.

The topics featured in *At the Crossroads of Music and Social Justice* boldly recount the music making of myriad individuals, communities, and social movements as tools for altering social and political conditions and experiences that diminish people. All the ethnographies advance the frontiers of scholarship in an effort to be more inclusive and creative in approaches to research and writing. Of particular rarity, Dr. Katelyn E. Best's innovative study presents terminology and constructs of Deaf "sonic" perceptions to fashion a pioneering theoretical framework designed to liberate Deaf music culture and musicians from the dominance of hearing-centrism.

The chapters in the volume represent a range of theoretical frameworks meant to interrogate the successes and limitations of music's efficacy in settling conflicts, easing tensions, reconciling groups, promoting unity, and empowering marginalized communities. The contributions foster decentered and culturally diverse counternarratives that support musical diversity and representation. To quote Kronos Quartet's David Harrington: "If we gather together and use our best thinking, our best ideas, and our most charitable and wide-ranging visions for making the world a better place—a safer place for our kids, and grandkids, and great grandkids—then we're doing something" (Vaclavik 2021).

A glaring omission in the quest for social justice has been to ignore interethnic conflict. Many of us understand how government policies continue to work to prevent coalitions and community empowerment. Until we can decolonize ourselves from pernicious colonialities of power, we will not be free to fully participate in social justice endeavors. Social justice requires constant vigilance.

NOTES

1. In recognition of their mentorship, I dedicate this chapter to Norma E. Cantú and to the memory of anthropologist Susan MacCulloch Stevens (1934–2003), whose research and scholarship was critical to the Passamaquoddy people of Maine.
2. United Nations Educational, Scientific and Cultural Organization, focused on global peace and security.
3. Aníbal Quijano, Peruvian sociologist (1930–2018) developed the concept of coloniality of power as patterns of domination that have survived in the Americas since the 1500s. See Salgado et al. 2021.
4. Charlotte W. Heth, personal communications with author, December 13, 2020.
5. Unknown author. A saying said to be from India.
6. Over the past few years, I have often used the term *theorizing synergy* and adapted Merriam's model to a broadening perspective of dynamic cultural processes that I eventually named the "Synergy Cube" (after Merriam 1964, Wilbert 1976, and Kaemmer 1993; see Romero 2015).

BIBLIOGRAPHY

Agawu, Kofi. 1992. "Representing African Music." *Critical Inquiry* 18 (2): 245–66. https://www.jstor.org/stable/1343783.

———. 2003. *Representing African Music: Postcolonial Notes, Queries, Positions.* New York: Routledge.

Anzaldúa, Gloria E. 2005. "Let Us Be the Healing of the Wound: The Coyolxauhqui Imperative—La Sombra y el Sueño." In *One Wound for Another/ Una herida por otra: Testimonios de Latin@s in the U.S. through Cyberspace (11 de septiembre de 2001 – 11 de marzo de 2002)*, edited by C. Joysmith and C. Lomas.

Mexico City: Centro de Investigaciones Sobre América del Norte, Universidad Autónoma de México, with Colorado College and Whittier College.

Cantú, Norma E. 2018. "Doing Work That Matters: An Introduction to the Special Issue on Gloria Evangelina Anzaldúa." *Camino Real* 10 (13): 13–23.

Gandarilla Salgado, José Guadalupe, María Heydeé García Bravo, and Danielle Benzi. 2021. "Two Decades of Alíbal Quijano's Coloniality of Power, Eurocentrism and Latin America." *Contexto Internacional* 43 (1) (Jan–Apr): 199–222. Accessed December 28, 2021. https://www.scielo.br/j/cint/a/9BxwGvYxjb6YWswTpddQ9Hm/?format=pdf&lang=en/.

Kaemmer, John P. 1993. *Music in Human Life*. Austin: University of Texas Press.

McDonald, David A. 2020. "Junction 48: Hip-Hop Activism, Gendered Violence, and Vulnerability in Palestine." *Journal of Popular Music Studies* 32 (1): 26–43.

Merriam, Alan P. 1964. *The Anthropology of Music*. Evanston, IL: Northwestern University Press.

Putnam, R. D. 1995. "Bowling Alone: America's Declining Social Capital." *Journal of Democracy* 6 (1): 65–78.

Romero, Brenda M. 2015. "A Theory of Infinite Variation." In *Discourses in African Musicology: J.H. Kwabena Nketia Festschrift*, edited by Kwasi Ampene and Godwin Kwafo Adje, 125–54. Ann Arbor: Maize Books, an imprint of University of Michigan Publishing.

Snyder, Allegra Fuller. 1972. "'The Dance Symbol,' New Dimensions in Dance Research: Anthropology and Dance—The American Indian." In *CORD Research Annual* 6, edited by Tamara Comstock, 213–23.

Snyder, Andrew G. 2022. *Critical Brass: Street Carnival and Musical Activism in Olympic Rio de Janeiro*. Middletown, CT: Wesleyan University Press.

Timberlake, Sharon. 2005. "Social Capital and Gender in the Workplace." *Journal of Management Development* 24 (1): 35–44.

Tuck, Eve. 2009. "Suspending Damage: A Letter to Communities." *Harvard Educational Review* 79 (3): 409–27.

Vaclavik, Becca. 2021. "Kronos Quartet: Music for Change: The 60s, The Years That Changed America." CU Presents website, December 7, 2021. Accessed March 6, 2020. https://cupresents.org/2020/01/28/kronos/?utm_source=wordfly&utm_medium=email&utm_campaign=AS20%20Kronos%20eblast%202&utm_content=version/.

Wilbert, Johannes, ed. 1976. *Enculturation in Latin America*. Los Angeles: UCLA Latin American Center Publications, University of California.

CONTRIBUTORS

SUSAN M. ASAI is Professor Emerita from the Music Department at Northeastern University in Boston. Her research encompasses Japanese folk performing arts and Asian American music and cultural politics. She has published numerous articles and encyclopedic entries on Japanese/Asian American music and identity. Asai's book projects include *Nōmai Dance Drama: A Surviving Spirit of Medieval Japan* and *Sounding Our Way Home: Japanese American Musicking and the Politics of Identity* (forthcoming).

KATELYN E. BEST is Teaching Assistant Professor in Musicology at West Virginia University and Codirector of the Society for Ethnomusicology Orchestra. Her research focuses on Deaf music, hip-hop, and cultural activism. Her current work traces the development of dip hop (sign language rap) in the United States and examines sociocultural mechanisms that have historically colonized deaf experiences of music.

DAVID A. MCDONALD is Associate Professor and Chair of the Department of Folklore and Ethnomusicology at Indiana University. Since 2002, he has worked closely with Palestinian refugee communities in Israel, Jordan, the West Bank, and North America researching the performative dynamics of trauma, violence, and masculinity. He is author and editor of two books, *My Voice Is My Weapon* and *Palestinian Music and Song*.

BRENDA M. ROMERO is Professor Emerita at the University of Colorado, Boulder, with a doctorate in ethnomusicology (University of California, Los Angeles) and bachelor and master of music in music theory and composition

(University of New Mexico). In addition to extensive research in New Mexico, she conducted fieldwork in Mexico, Colombia, and Peru, including as Fulbright Scholar in Mexico (2000–2001) and in Colombia (spring of 2011). Her monograph, *Matachines Transfronterizos, Warriors for Peace at the Borderlands*, is forthcoming.

ANDREW G. SNYDER is Integrated Researcher in the Instituto de Etnomusicologia at the Universidade Nova de Lisboa in Portugal. He has written about alternative brass band movements in Rio de Janeiro, New Orleans, and San Francisco in his forthcoming book, *Critical Brass: Street Carnival and Musical Activism in Olympic Rio de Janeiro*, his edited volume *HONK! A Street Band Renaissance of Music and Activism*, and in various articles.

PAUL AUSTERLITZ, Professor of Music and Africana Studies at Gettysburg College, combines his scholarship specializing in Afro-Caribbean music with creative work as a jazz composer and bass clarinetist. He has authored two books: *Merengue: Dominican Music and Dominican Identity* and *Jazz Consciousness: Music, Race, and Humanity*. Austerlitz's recent trilogy of recordings, *Marasa Twa*, presents original compositions and arrangements forged as creative collaborations among musicians in Haiti, the Dominican Republic, and the United States.

ERIN E. BAUER is Assistant Professor of Musicology at the University of Wisconsin–Whitewater. Her current book project examines the recent worldwide spread of Texas Mexican accordion music, called conjunto. Bauer has presented her research at numerous national and international conferences. Her writing appears in *Rock Music Studies*, a number of essay collections, the *Latin American Music Review*, and *Latino Studies*.

ALEXANDRIA CARRICO is Lecturer at the University of Tennessee, Knoxville, and has a doctorate in musicology from Florida State University. Her work on traditional Irish music and music and neurodiversity appears in *Voices: A World Forum for Music Therapy* and in *The Journal of Interdisciplinary Voice Studies*. In her 2018 article published in *Folk Life: Journal of Ethnology*, she explores the intersections of race, gender, and social justice in American opera.

KYRA D. GAUNT is Assistant Professor of Music at the University at Albany–SUNY. Her prizewinning book, *The Games Black Girls Play: Learning the Ropes from Double-Dutch to Hip-Hop*, contributed to the emergence of music studies in hip-hop, hip-hop feminism, and black girlhood. She has written for the *New York Times* and appeared in a viral TED talk, and her current project examines how music orchestrates violence against Black girls online.

CONTRIBUTORS

KATIE J. GRABER is Lecturer in musicology at The Ohio State University with research interests in race and ethnicity, Western opera, and Mennonite music. She has published articles in *Ethnomusicology* and *Ethnomusicology Forum* and created a multimedia gallery on Mennonite diversity for the American Religious Sounds Project website.

CHARLOTTE W. HETH, PHD, is Professor Emerita from UCLA in music, ethnomusicology, and American Indian studies. She received her bachelor of arts and master of music in music from the University of Tulsa in Oklahoma. After teaching in secondary schools for ten years (including two years in Ambo, Ethiopia, as a Peace Corps volunteer, 1962–64), she earned her doctorate at UCLA in 1975.

HO CHAK LAW was born and raised in British Hong Kong and received his doctorate from University of Michigan, with his dissertation titled *Cinematizing Chinese Opera, Performing Chinese Identities, 1945–1971*. His recent publications appear in *Music and the Moving Image* and *Drama Review* (forthcoming). His current research interests cover the music ecology of Sinosphere and the cultural analysis of film music.

STEVEN LOZA is Professor of Ethnomusicology at UCLA and has served as Chair of the Department of Ethnomusicology and of the Global Jazz Studies Interdepartmental Program and as Director of the UCLA Center for Latinx Arts. He has conducted extensive research in Mexico, the Chicano/Latino United States, and Cuba, among other areas, and he is an active musician and composer. Loza's publications include four books, numerous research journal articles, and four edited anthologies.

REBEKAH E. MOORE joined the faculty of Northeastern University's Music Department in 2017, after a ten-year international career in festival production, band management, and arts administration. She is Assistant Professor of Music and Graduate Program Coordinator in Arts Administration and Cultural Entrepreneurship and cofounder of the Indonesian nonprofit Bersama Project, which confronts gender-based violence through music and the arts.

DARCI SPRENGEL is Ethnomusicologist (PhD, UCLA) and Assistant Professor of Popular Music at the University of Groningen. Her current work examines the political economy and racial politics of music streaming in Southwest Asia and North Africa. She was previously Junior Research Fellow at the University of Oxford and has published on independent music, class politics, and activism in the 2011 Egyptian revolution.

INDEX

Abu-Lughod, Lila, 160–61, 162, 163–65
academia: BIPOC scholars, 6, 7, 29, 33, 34, 60–61, 64, 278–79; conflation of hearing-centric, 86, 94; damage-centered research, 37n2, 57, 282–83; diversity lip service, 7, 32, 33, 34, 35, 36–37, 42, 61; engaged scholarship, 76; entrance barriers, 61, 62–63; ethnocentrism in, 6, 44; gatekeeping, 28, 34, 61, 63; hip-hop in, 26, 161; institutional racism, 6, 62, 63, 278, 280, 287; intentional participation with respect to inclusivity, 10, 118–19; "Interrogating Systemic Racism and the White Academic Field" (Maldonado-Torres), 280; music therapy, 88, 93; publishing, 14, 25, 41, 278–80; scholarship on Deaf music, 88; scholarship on *genízaro* consciousness, 54. *See also* Gaunt, Kyra D.; music education; SEM (Society for Ethnomusicology)
accessibility: considerations for the neurodivergent, 184–85, 186, 187; limited by global inequity, 131; membership in society, 191; to music at boarding schools, 71; to music by Deaf people, 88, 92, 95, 96, 97; to opportunities and social position affect musical style, 231; provided by Whiteness, 132; provided by White privilege, 124, 129; to publishing opportunities, 14, 278–79; to royalties, 93
Aceves, Joseph, 43
Acosta, Belinda, 220
African American music, 126, 200, 205, 212
Africanness, as American notion, 124. *See also* racecraft
Afro Asian musicking. *See* interracial coalitions
Allsup, Randall Everett, 278
American Indian music, 69–74, 184; *Indian Blues: American Indians and the Politics of Music 1879–1934* (Troutman), 71; resettlement, 69–71
American Musicological Society (AMS), 29
anarchist movements, 15, 243, 254
anti-Black racism, 27, 28–29
anti-corporate globalization movement, 239, 254
anti-imperialism, 202–3, 208
anti–Iraq War movement, 241, 251, 268
Anzaldúa, Gloria, 53
Appiah, Kwame Anthony, 272
applied ethnomusicology, 183, 196
Arab Spring, 138n5, 240
Arka Kinari, 264; about, 261; Benoa Bay, Bali, 259, 270–71; mobility as aesthetic practice, 268–69; as response to ecological threat,

Arka Kinari (Cont.)
262–63, 265–66; route, 264, 265, 266, 267, 268, 270. *See also* Filastine, Grey; Nova Ruth
Asai, Susan M.: assembling the anthology, 3, 5, 282; Crossroads name change, 283; life in academia, 6, 7; positionality, 14, 200, 204–5, 214n4
Asian American musicking, 204, 205
"The Astonished Ethno-muse" (MacAllester), 76
audiences: Brass Liberation Orchestra (BLO), 252–53; co-creators in expanding knowledge base, 269; colonial gaze, 11; compassionate gaze, 162, 165, 171, 173; Conjunto Aztlán, 13, 230–31; of Deaf music, 97, 98; etymology, 92; hip-hop, 162, 170–71; homologous interpretations of genre, 233–34n4; international vs intended, 164; inversion of the band/audience relationship, 252–53; orientalist thinking, 161; presentational intervention, 249; reconsidering, 272; responding to intersectional positionality, 172; in revolutionary dialectics, 209; Tanya Tagaq, 11, 142–45, 147–48, 149, 150, 152–54. *See also* Dewey, John
audiocentrism, 86. *See also* hearing-centrism
audism, 86, 91, 92, 95–96; becoming Deaf (concept), 97. *See also* hearing-centrism
aural-centrism, 86, 93, 94–95. *See also* hearing-centrism
Austerlitz, Paul, 37n4, 76–77; on his motivation, 79–80; *Lapriyè Djò* (Prayer for the primal wind), 80; "Music and Ritual as Modes of Afro-Dominican Empowerment," 79; *The Vodou Horn*, 78, 80
authoritarianism, 127, 128
autoethnography, 5, 8, 14, 16, 279, 284. *See also* Asai, Susan M.; Austerlitz, Paul; Gaunt, Kyra D.; Heth, Charlotte; Loza, Steven; Romero, Brenda M.

Bakan, Michael, 196
Baraka, Amiri, 76–77, 209
Battiste, Loneka, 283

Bauer, Erin, 12
Becker, Judith, 26, 78, 144, 153–54
Beloved (Morrison), 23–24
Benjamin, Ruha, 27, 28–29, 32–33
Berlin School of Comparative Musicology, 260
Best, Katelyn E., 9–10, 87–88, 283, 285, 287
Black Arts movement, 204, 208
Black Lives Matter (BLM) movement, 201; "Black Lives Matter" (Nobuko Miyamoto) (song), 212; Brass Liberation Orchestra (BLO), 239; and interracial coalitions, 13, 201, 201–2, 210, 212–13; Pink Menno, 112; social domination, 21, 24–25. *See also* Floyd, George
Black nationalism, 202, 204
Blackness: in Egypt, 11, 123–24, 126, 133, 137; musical, 25, 26; racecraft, 11, 123, 124, 126, 132, 133, 137. *See also* colorism
Black Power movement, 202, 203, 208
Blues People (Baraka), 76–77
Boal, Augusto, 255
Boggs, Grace Lee, 202, 213
Bohmer, Susanne, 29–30
Bourdieu, Pierre, 89
Brass Liberation Orchestra (BLO): as anarchist, 15, 243; "A Bad Hotel," 249–51; as direct action, 239, 244–47, 251, 253, 254–55; in direct action, 247–49, 254–55; HONK! movement, 13, 240–41, 254; membership, 246–47; musical repertoires of contention, 242, 247–48, 254; Occupy movement, 239–40, 248, 251–54, 253. *See also* LGBTQIA+ movement
Briggs, Joyce L., 29–30
Brooks, Daphne A., 35
Brown, Danielle, 1–2, 31–32, 34, 36
Buddhism, 78, 204, 261
Butler, Judith, 244

Cabral, Amílcar, 203, 204
Cachia, Amanda, 88, 97
calls to action: to be vigilant about exclusion, 106; to build coalitions, 212; for COP26 for governments to link culture policy to environmental policy, 271; Dylan

Robinson on, 21–22; and globalization, 25–26, 126; "I Will Be Free" (United Front) (song), 207; in Mennonite hymns, 116; for music studies to include critical studies of Hearing, 96–97; "Open Letter on Racism in Music Studies" (Brown), 1, 6, 15–16, 31–32; to replace diversity and inclusion with direct action terms, 280; for settler environmentalists to pay attention to Indigenous communities, 269; *This Bridge Called My Back: Writings by Radical Women of Color* (Moraga and Anzaldúa), 53; to transform ethnomusicology, 3–4, 280
Canadian Centre for Ethnomusicology, 278
capitalism: Brass Liberation Orchestra (BLO), 245, 252; folklore as alternative, 222; fossil, 263, 265; intellectual, 44; neoliberal, 37; responsible for asylum seekers, 277; as source for oppression, 208; transnational, 251
careers in academia for BIPOC people: full-professorship and tenure challenges, 6, 28, 33–34, 41, 60, 61, 77–78; health concerns, 60–61, 64–65; importance of mentorship, 5, 14, 53, 61, 64, 279, 285
Carlson, Julius, 232
Carrico, Alexandria, 10, 13, 182, 183, 185, 196–97
Cefkin, Benjamin, 283
Cheng, William, 194
chicano, history of the term, 50–51
the Chicano movement: Chicano Artistas Sirviendo a Aztlán (CASA), 218; class, 12, 218–19, 221, 225; Conjunto Aztlán (band), 12–13, 223, 225, 228–29; movimiento (movement) music, 223, 225, 226–28, 232; Norma E. Cantú, 53; nueva canción, 218, 222, 225, 230, 232, 233; tejano Jim Crow experience, 217; Texas Mexican conjunto music, 13, 220–25; United Farm Workers (UFW), 218, 222–23, 232
class: the Chicano movement, 12, 218, 221, 225; colorism, 123, 130, 131–32, 137; Conjunto Aztlán (band), 218–19, 221, 223–24, 230; conjunto music, 13, 218–19, 220–22, 224–25, 231, 233; foreign expertise, 129–30; included in good faith, 246; *Nanook of the North* (Flaherty), 148–49; oppression, 30
coalition building, 217, 218, 279–80. See also interracial coalitions
collaboration: achieved through coalitions, 205; to address institutional racism, 287; applied ethnomusicology, 196; the Chicano movement, 13; cultural cohort, 186; interracial, 201, 206, 212; Irish traditional music project, 187, 188–93; knowledge exchange with Indigenous communities, 269; synergy, 284; as vehicle for reconciliation, 170. See also coalition building
College Music Society (CMS), 63, 278
Collins, Randall, 190
colonialism: gendered violence as third world pathology, 163; logic of elimination, 169–70, 173; racecraft, 124–25; survivance, 64, 282; Tanya Tagaq, 153
colonial logics: benefit to ethnomusicology, 1–2, 4; elimination, 162; gender, 8, 12, 173; global White privilege, 123–24, 125, 129–30, 134; orientalism, 161, 204, 214n5; romanticization of Palestine, 172–73; the subaltern, 2, 32, 148, 211; superiority of Western music, 26; White privilege, 6, 7, 8, 16, 63, 129–32, 202. See also the Other; Whiteness; White supremacy
colonization: division to sow mistrust, 72; Egypt and Sudan, 124, 133; ethical witness, 170; ethnomusicology as ear, 4; ethnomusicology as voice, 1, 2; interracial alliances, 202; ocean literacy, 265; as productive human endeavor, 28–29
"Colony Collapse" (Filastine) (song), 259
colorism: "Adiós Llano de San Juan" (Vásquez) (poem), 50, 53; and career advancement, 61; anti-Blackness, 11, 132; Blackness in Egypt, 11, 123–24, 126, 133, 137; Brenda M. Romero, 49, 54–55, 56, 58; global White privilege, 123–24, 125, 134;

colorism (*Cont.*)
  not always Euro-American conceptions, 123, 127; performing expertise, 130, 131; trigueño (dark skinned), 50, 52; violence in United States, 210; Whiteness in Egypt, 123, 126, 129–30, 133, 134, 135, 137; Whiteness in Ghana, 132. *See also* class; race
compassionate gaze, 169–74
Conjunto Aztlán (band), 227; audiences, 230–31; *From Aztlán With Love* (album), 226–28; class, 218–19, 221, 223–24, 230; lyrics, 218, 222, 223, 226, 228–30, 232; "Vamos a pelear en la guerra" (Let's go fight in the war) (song), 228–29; "Yo soy tu hermano, yo soy Chicano" (I am your brother, I am Chicano) (song), 228–30
conjunto music: bajo sexto (bass guitar), 227, 229; Little Joe Y La Familia, 230, 231; lyrics, 231–32; nueva canción movement, 222; primitivist stereotypes, 219–20, 221, 231, 233; Texas Mexican, 220–21, 224–25, 226–27. *See also* Conjunto Aztlán (band)
Cooley, Timothy, 260
COVID-19 pandemic, 21, 22, 24–25, 72–73, 261, 266, 267–68, 271
critical race theory, 26, 123
Crossroads Project on Diversity, Difference, and Under-Representation: Kyra D. Gaunt, 2, 22, 23, 31, 36, 77, 282; Paul Austerlitz, 77, 78; politics of care, 23; Steve Loza, 47; transition to section, 282
Crossroads Section for Difference and Representation: addressing White supremacy, 3; commitments, 4; Kyra D. Gaunt, 2, 7, 36, 284; mandate, 2–3; mission, 36; Music and Social Justice paper competition, 278–79, 283–84, 287; name change, 2, 22, 282–83; Paul Austerlitz, 78; racism, 2–3; values, 3
Cruinniú, 183, 187, 188–93, 195
cultural preservationism, 260

DAM: *Channels of Rage* (Halachmi) (documentary), 160; criticisms for selling out, 160–61, 171; *Dabke on the Moon* (album), 160, 171; *Dedication* (album), 160; "If I Could Go Back in Time" (Salloum) (video), 161, 163–65, 166, 174; intrafamily femicide, 161, 163, 164, 166–67; the occupation, 160, 161, 163, 164, 165, 171–72, 174; pseudo-representatives of Palestine, 162; rise to acclaim, 170–71; "Who's the Terrorist?" (song), 172. *See also* hip-hop; *Junction 48* (Aloni) (film); Nafar, Tamer
Darrow, Ann, 93, 94
Dave, Nomi, 277
Davis, Martha Ellen, 284
Deaf Activism, 85–86, 87
Deaf-centric, 86, 99. *See also* hearing-centrism
Deaf culture: becoming Deaf (concept), 97; dysconscious audism, 66n17, 95–96, 285; expert listening, 97; hearing-centric education, 9, 96; hearing deafly, 97; hear same, 95; musical expression, 87–88; "Music and Deaf Culture: Images from the Media and Their Interpretations by Deaf and Hearing Students" (Darrow and Loomis), 93; signed language, 89–90. *See also* Deaf musicking
Deaf musicking: Darius "Prinz-D the First Deaf Rapper" McCall, 92; dip hop, 87, 97–98; "Imagined Hearing: Music-Making in Deaf Culture" (Jones), 89; materials as conductors, 90–91, 91; musicians denied compensation, 96; not limited to the ear, 88–89; "see the music," 89, 90
Deaf studies, 86, 88
decolonization: academia, 6, 14, 279; affinity between Asian Americans and African Americans, 202; hearing-centrism, 97, 98; listening practices, 173; Palestine, 162; reparations, 272, 280; SEM (Society for Ethnomusicology), 63; structures that oppress Deaf people, 9, 98–99
desegregation, 280
Dewey, John, 272–73
Dhillon, Kartar, 213
direct action: academic publishing as, 278–80; anthology, 14; definitions,

242–44; *Direct Action: An Ethnography* (Graeber), 243; motivational power of music, 244, 248; "Music and the Myth of Universality: Sounding Human Rights and Capabilities" (Dave), 277; *Organizing for Social Change* (guide), 243; performance of freedom, 244, 245, 247; as prefigurative politics, 241–44; SEM (Society for Ethnomusicology), 15; social media, 250; *The Theater of the Oppressed* (Boal), 255; Unite Here, 239, 243. *See also* Brass Liberation Orchestra (BLO)

disability rights movement, 184

disability studies, 183, 191, 192

discrimination: audism, 86, 91, 95–96; coalitions to fight, 200; Ebonics, 26. *See also* colorism

diversity: gender, 118; initiatives lacking intentionality, 21–22, 29, 31–32, 34, 35, 36–37, 61–62; Mennonite Church USA (MCUSA), 105, 106, 107, 108–9; music education, 9; recognizing diversity, 106; use direct action terms, 280. *See also* academia; aural-centrism; Crossroads Project on Diversity, Difference, and Under-Representation; LGBTQIA+ movement; neurodivergence; SEM (Society for Ethnomusicology)

documentaries: Greenwood massacre, 68; LGBTQ+ issues, 106. *See also* DAM; *Nanook of the North* (Flaherty)

Dust Tracks in the Road (Hurston), 25

ecomusicology, 260

Egypt: as a Black civilization, 126, 137; Blackface in, 133–34; foreigners as "experts," 129–32; gendered violence, 161, 162–63, 165, 166–67, 174; High Dam (band), 134, *135*; music, 123, 125, 127, 132; Mustapha Mahmoud Park Massacre, 133; No Color Campaign, 136; racialized policing, 127–28, 129, 130, 132; Whiteness in, 123, 126, 129–30, 133, 134; White people enjoy rights due to race, 128, 130–31

Eisenstein, Sergei, 150–51

El-Rifae, Yasmin, 128–29

equity, 3, 4, 13, 30, 34, 36, 63

ethnocentrism: in academia, 6, 44; hearing-centrism as, 9–10, 85–87, 88–94, 98, 99; *Nanook of the North* (film), 145

ethnochoreology, 53

ethnography, 8, 43–44, 144–45, 150, 243

ethnomusicology: benefiting from colonial logics, 1–2, 4; Black women ethnomusicologists, 25–28, 34–35, 36; coalition building with other disciplines, 279; cultural informant, 35, 151, 196; epistemic violence, 1, 2, 7, 11, 16–17, 31–32, 35; extractivism of cultures for professional gain, 6–7, 260, 272; fascination with protest songs, 12; intellectual capital does not include ideas of the marginalized, 44; need for humanizing mundane experiences, 172–73; universals, 63, 89, 124, 277; and White privilege, 6, 7, 8, 16. *See also* applied ethnomusicology; ecomusicology; fieldwork; linguistics

etic view, 97, 98

Eyerman, Ron, 242

Fanon, Frantz, 203

feminism, 28, 35, 36, 92, 167, 202, 223, 282

fieldwork: collaborative partnerships, 53, 196, 285; Deaf music, 87; developing friendships, 261; Matachines/Matachina Danza, 53, 57, 64, 284, 287; new models needed, 183; Palestine, 162

Filastine, Grey, 259, 261, 262–63, 264, 267, 268, 270, 271, 272

Film Form: Essays in Film Theory (Eisenstein), 150–51

First Nations. *See* American Indian music

Flacks, Richard, 255

Flaherty, Robert J., 142, 143, 144, 145, 146, 148, 149, 151

Floyd, George, 21, 31, 40, 201, 211–12. *See also* Black Lives Matter (BLM) movement

Floyd, Samuel, 23

folk: Black, 26; Bon-odori, 212; the Chicano movement, 222, 223, 225; Japanese, 204; Mennonite music, 112; Mexican Arts Series at UCLA, 45; missing from scholastic music surveys, 6, 44; Native music, 69. *See also* conjunto music
Forbes, Sean, 97, 98
Francis, Pope, 277
Friedner, Michelle, 90
"Friends and Lonely Lovers" (Poggensee), 205
Frishkopf, Michael, 278
Fusco, Coco, 213

Garland-Thomson, Rosemarie, 89
Gaunt, Kyra D.: Alan Merriam Prize, 33, 34, 37n4; Crossroads Project on Diversity, Difference, and Under-Representation, 2, 22, 23, 31, 36, 77, 282; Crossroads Section for Difference and Representation, 2, 7, 36, 284; feeling marginalized, 26, 27, 31; *The Games Black Girls Play: Learning the Ropes from Double-Dutch to Hip-Hop*, 25, 33; hate mail received, 27–28, 284; listening lovingly, 4–5; SEM (Society for Ethnomusicology), 5, 7, 23, 30–31; teaching style, 26–27
gender: access to published volumes, 279; being queer, 110–11; Blackness, 133; Brass Liberation Orchestra (BLO), 245, 246; and class, 123, 132, 137; collaborations, 73; colonial logics, 8, 12, 173; countercultural norms, 115; creating diversity, 118; division of labor, 269; heteronormativity, 3, 28, 29, 30, 31; performing, 112, 116; SEM (Society for Ethnomusicology), 34, 35; sexism, 28; United Nations Entity for Gender Equality and the Empowerment of Women, 161
gendered violence, 161, 162–63, 165, 166–67, 174
Gertz, Genie, 95
Ghana, 124, 128, 132
Ghannam, Farha, 123
global military-industrial complex, 125

gospel, 13, 108, 112, 205
Graber, Katie, J., 10, 11, 106, 107, 112, 116
Graeber, David, 243, 244
Gray, Mary, 110
Guevara, Ernesto "Che," 203

Harcourt, Bernard, 243
Haualand, Hilde, 95, 99
Hayes, Eileen, 278, 279
hearing-centrism: based on dysconscious audism, 66n17, 95–96, 285; concept, 96–98; defined, 86–87; disconnects music from the body, 91; as ethnocentrism, 9–10, 85–87, 88–94, 98, 99; impact on Deaf culture, 94–96; media's role, 93–94; music uses mediums that are hearing-centric, 92–93. *See also* Deaf-centric
Helmreich, Stefan, 90
Herrera, Eduardo, 113–14
Hesford, Wendy, 170
Heth, Charlotte, 6, 43–44, 47, 60, 68–69, 284
High Dam (band), 134–35, 135
hip-hop: as academic study, 26, 161; activism, 162–63; audiences, 162, 170–71; dip hop, 87, 97–98; in Egypt, 125; engaging international audiences, 170–71; *The Games Black Girls Play: Learning the Ropes from Double-Dutch to Hip-Hop*, 25, 33; Holly Maniatty, 85; *Junction 48* (Aloni) (film), 165–69; Killer Mike, 85; masculinities, 166, 167, 169, 174; *Slingshot Hip-Hop* (Salloum) (documentary), 160; Steve Chávez, 58. *See also* DAM; Signmark
Ho, Fred Wei-han, 207–10
Holcomb, Thomas K., 96
Holmes, Jessica, 97
homophobia, 114
homosexuality. *See* LGBTQIA+ movement; Pink Menno
HONK! movement: Brass Liberation Orchestra (BLO), 13, 240–41, 254; direct action, 242; *HONK! A Street Band Renaissance of Music and Activism* (Snyder), 285; origins, 240–41; Rude

Mechanical Orchestra (RMO), 241, 247, 248
Hood, Ki Mantle, 45, 260
hooks, bell, 5, 28, 149
"How the Peace Church Helped Make a Lesbian Out of Me" (Stoner), 115
Humphries, Tom, 86

Idea of the Holy (Otto), *The*, 78
identity: Asian American, 203–4; becoming African American, 23; community-based unity, 12, 229–30; Egyptian and African, 135; fetishization, 152; *genizaro* consciousness, 54; Hawaiian, 265; homologous interpretations of genre, 220, 228, 233; Manito, 54; Mennonite, 110–11, 112, 115–16; neurodivergence as minority, 182–83; Palestinian, 171; performing arts as central, 190; queer, 106, 110–11, 114–15; stereotype threats, 26; Texas Mexican, 218, 224, 233; tied to direct action movements, 255
imperialism: American, 125, 203; *America Tropical* (Siqueiros), 46; "An Open Letter on Racism in Music Studies" (Brown), 1, 2; anthology conceived as direct action, 14; *Arka Kinari*, 265; gaze, 143, 148–50; and Manitos, 58; Third World Liberation Front, 202–3
Impey, Angela, 268
inclusivity: belonging, 10, 26, 110, 111, 113, 118, 182, 203; creating community through exclusivity, 113, 118; missing for Deaf people, 96; neurodivergent individuals, 182–83; queer Mennonites, 107, 109, 110–11, 112, 113–15, 119; singing, 10, 106, 108, 112, 113, 116, 118–19; song choice, 114, 116, 118; vigilance needed, 106, 118; wide vs provisional, 247
Indonesia: Banda Islands, 269; ecological crises, 266–67; gamelan, 259; gamelon, 260, 263; Indonesian National Board for Disaster Management, 270; Maluku Regency, 268; Nova's home, 264
Ingersoll, Karin Amimoto, 265

institutional racism, 3, 6, 62, 63, 218, 278, 280, 287
interracial coalitions: African Americans and Asian Americans, 201, 201–2; Afro-Asian Music Ensemble (AAME), 209; Afro Asian musicking, 200, 206–7; *Afro/Asia: Revolutionary Political and Cultural Connections between African and Asians in the Americas* (Ho and Mullen), 207; "Collaboratory" (mentorship program), 212; Jon Jang, 210–11; as means to encourage cooperation and collaboration, 205; Obon Festivals, 204, 212; *The Pledge of Black Asian Allegiance* (Jang), 210; *Resounding Afro Asia: Interracial Music and the Politics of Collaboration* (Roberts), 206; shared musical affinity, 7, 213; steps for forming, 210; Third World Liberation Front (TWLF), 108, 202–3; Third World Strike, 201, 202, 207; Tsuru for Solidarity (TFS), 200–201, 210; United Front (band), 206–7, 208. *See also* Black Lives Matter (BLM) movement; coalition building
intersectionality, 10, 32, 35, 112, 166, 173, 174, 283, 285
Inuit stereotypes: the happy Eskimo, 146; katajjaq (Inuit throat singing), 29; Nanookmania contributed to, 144–45; obstinacy vs performing woman, 147–48, 150, 152, 154–55; reshaping to align with Indigenous epistemologies, 11; timelessness, 143, 148
Irish traditional music project: Brothers of Charity, 183–84, 191; disability recontextualized by neurotypicals, 182, 190–91, 192, 193; "Fall Down Billy O'Shea," 186, 187, 189–90; the limits of inclusivity, 193–95; performativity, 185–86. *See also* neurodivergence; Roselawn Rovers Return
Itasaka, Mami, 62, 62
"I Will Be Free" (United Front) (song), 207

Jamison, Andrew, 242
Japanese music, 204, 205

jazz: Association for the Advancement of Creative Music (AACM) school, 206, 214n7; *Blues People* (Baraka), 76–77; the Ensemble Dominicano (ED), 79; Global Jazz Studies Program (UCLA), 42, 45; Hiroshima (band), 205; improvisation, 13, 205–7; *Jazz Consciousness: Music, Race, and Humanity* (Austerlitz), 77–78; *Marasa Twa* (Austerliz) (trilogy album), 80; Mennonite music, 112; "Salutations to the Sea" (Candreva) (song), 205. *See also* UCLA (University of California, Los Angeles)
Jim Crow, 6, 44, 202, 217
Johnston, Thomas, 184
Jones, Jeannette DiBernardo, 89, 97, 98
Judaism, 170
Juhnke, Austin McCabe, 108
Junction 48 (Aloni) (film), 165, 166–69, 170, 171–72, 174
Just Vibrations (Cheng), 194

Kallman, Meghan, 254
Kanagy, Conrad L., 111
Keister, Jay, 61, 62
Kheshti, Roshanak, 93
Khoury, Stephanie, 283
King, Joyce, 95
King, Rodney, 41, 202
Kochiyama, Yuri, 202, 210, 213
Koskoff, Ellen, 22, 31
Krehbiel, Stephanie, 109, 113–15
Kudlick, Catherine, 191
Kunst, Jaap, 260

Law, Ho Chak, 11
Lepecki, André, 243
Leppänen, Taru, 93, 96–97, 98
Lewis, John, 36, 40
LGBTQIA+ movement: Brass Liberation Orchestra (BLO), 239–40, 249–51, 253; Mennonite Church USA (MCUSA), 107, 109–11; queer identity, 106, 110–11, 114; queering, 197n6; queerness, 106, 112, 114–16, 117–18, 197n6; queer rights, 202. *See also* queer theory

linguistics: borders and visas, 127; Deaf culture, 89, 90, 92–93, 95, 96; decolonizing structures, 279; gendered syncopation, 25; lyrics as window to cognitive praxis, 242; Mennonite Church, 108; nonlinguistic singing, 148, 151
listening lovingly, 4–8; critical listening, 8; deep listening as a form of redress, 152–54; expert listening, 97; hungry listening, 144; participatory listening, 5, 7–8; politics of care, 23; practices, 173; visual listening, 89
Loeffler, Summer, 88, 99
Logan, Fred E., Jr, 217
Loomis, Diane, 93, 94
Loza, Steven: *America Tropical* (Siqueiros) (mural), 46, 46; *Barrio Rhythm: Mexican American Music in Los Angeles*, 41; California State Polytechnic University, 40; "Challenges to the Euroamericentric Ethnomusicological Canon: Alternatives for Graduate Readings, Theory, and Method," 44; as educator, 41–42, 45, 47; scholarship, 41, 42–44, 45

MacAllester, David, 76, 78
Maldonado-Torres, Nelson, 280
male chauvinism. *See* toxic masculinity
Maler, Anabel, 91
Manabe, Noriko, 268
Mao Zedong, 203
Mason, Amelia, 241
McDonald, David A., 173, 283, 285
McKay, George, 252
McNickle, D'Arcy, 71
MCUSA (Mennonite Church USA). *See* Mennonite Church USA (MCUSA)
meme-drive activism, 250
Mennonite Church USA (MCUSA): BMC (Brethern Mennonite Council for Lesbian, Gay, Bisexual and Transgender Interests), 112, 120; four-part singing, 108, 112, 114, 115–16, 118; LGBTQ members, 10, 105, 113; members leaving, 109–10, 111; national conventions, 105, 108, 111, 112, 113, 119. *See also* Pink Menno

Mikdashi, Maya, 160–61, 162, 163–65
Mills, Charles W., 125
misogyny, 49, 167
Miyamoto, Nobuko, 211–12
Mohamed, Maha, 135–36, *136*
Montoya, Celeste, 162–63
Moore, Rebekah E., 6–7, 261, 283, 284
Moraga, Cherríe, 53
musical transcendence, 76, 78, 143–44
Music as Social Life: The Politics of Participation (Turino), 190
music education: Black American music missing in public school, 25; Black and Brown Conservatory of Music avoiding Western bias, 47; denies diversity of music, 9; disciplinary gatekeeping, 63; dominated by aural-centrism, 92, 93, 94; embodiment vs pedagogy, 26; impact of hearing-centrism, 94, 98–99; jazz programs lack students of color, 42; Mexican culture, 45; the moral imperative to care, 278; objective testing, 64; racism in programs, 61; required world music classes, 77; teaching punk rock music considered inappropriate, 60; Third World Strike, 201; traditional Irish music, 184. *See also* academia; Brown, Danielle
music industry, 92–93, 96, 126–27, 271–72
musicking, defined, 185–86
myths, 1, 285

Nafar, Tamer, 162, 165, 166, 167–69, 171–72, 173, 174. *See also Junction 48* (Aloni) (film)
Nanook of the North (Flaherty): audiovisual realignment, 150–52; *Battleship Potemkin* (Eisenstein), 150–51; camera hunter, 146, 149, 151; *A Dash to the North Pole*, 144; *The Esquimaux Village* (Porter and White) (film), 144; imperial gaze, 143, 148–50; *Lost in the Arctic* (Selig), 144; *My Eskimos Friends* (Flaherty), 142; taxidermic display, 143, 149, 151; unknown to the Inuit community for decades, 145; *The Way of the Eskimo* (Selig), 144. *See also* Inuit stereotypes
nationalism. *See* social domination
nationality, 127, 128, 130, 133, 137, 208
Native American. *See* American Indian music
Native American Dance, 285
neoliberalism, 272
neurodivergence: becoming part of community, 195–97; importance of belonging, 182; marginalization, 192–93; as "service users," 191, 193, 194. *See also* Irish traditional music project; Roselawn Rovers Return
Nova Ruth, 261, 262–63, 264, 265, 266, 267, 268, 269, 270
Nubian music, 125

Occupy movement, 239–40, 243, 248, 251–54, 253
Okihiro, Gary, 202
oppression. *See* social domination
Ostrom, Elinor, 266
the Other: Africa as, 124; Deaf people as, 87, 99; erasure, 2; gendered violence, 163; oriental as term, 214n5; people with disabilities, 192–93; perspective of Israeli life, 170; the Sudanese, 134; US-Mexico border population as, 13, 220

Palestine: invisible to ethnomusicology, 172–73; nationalism, 162; the occupation, 160, 161, 163, 164, 171–74; and oppression, 160, 166, 167, 168, 170, 173. *See also* DAM
patriarchy: the Chicano movement, 223; colorism, 49; gendered violence, 174; *Junction 48* (Aloni) (film), 165, 166–67; learning how to undo, 35; as productive, 28; religious, 160, 161, 165; White supremacy, 29, 30–31, 35
Pedelty, Mark, 268
Peña, Manuel, 218, 220, 224–25, 231
Pettan, Svanibor, 183
Pierre, Jemima, 124, 125, 128, 131, 132, 138n11, 138n13

Pink Menno: activism, 109, 118; exclusion through singing style, 114; liberation/assimilation dichotomy, 10, 106, 115, 118, 119; overview, 105–6; songbooks, 106, 112, 113, 116–18, *117*, 118
Podber, Naomi, 247
Porter, Edwin S., 144
positionality, 4, 10, 12, 76–77, 167, 173, 284. *See also* individual authors; listening lovingly: critical listening
positivism, 1, 94
postcolonialism, 2, 124, 128
poverty, 50, 168, 251
primitivism, 145, 149, 151, 154, 220, 231, 233
privilege. *See* colonial logics; racism; vulnerability
punk music, 60, 142

queer theory, 106, 110, 114. *See also* LGBTQIA+ movement

race, 123, 124, 125, 127, 128, 132, 148–49. *See also* Blackness; critical race theory
racecraft: al-agnabī (foreigner) as a racialized concept, 125, 129–32; al-ʿunṣūrriyya (form of racism), 125, 134, 136; asmar/samra (dark or brown skinned) as racialized concept, 123, 125; Blackness, 11, 123, 124, 126, 132, 133, 137; security as racialized concept, 125, 126–29
race riots, 41, 68, 202
racial justice, 125–26, 133, 137, 202
racial profiling, 127
racism: al-ʿunṣūrriyya (form of racism), 125, 134, 136; Argentinian soccer fans, 113–14; color-blind, 50, 65n3; DAM, 165; definitions, 28–29, 30; *Emancipation from Strife* (Loza) (musical suite), 40–41; human rights and structural inequity, 77; individual, 100n6; Kyra D. Gaunt's experiences, 27, 31, 33–34; in music programs, 61; *Nanook of the North* (Flaherty), 145; oppression, 22, 30, 31, 245; Steven Loza, 44; Third World Liberation Front, 203; White academic field, 280n1.

See also Crossroads Section for Difference and Representation; institutional racism
radical inclusivity, 4, 8–12, 14, 15, 16
reggae, 125, 228
Regini, Giulio, 128–29
Rejected Body, The (Wendell), 192
Rice, Tom, 89
Roberts, Tamara, 206, 214n8
Robinson, Dylan, 8, 9, 21–22, 58, 144, 173
Romero, Brenda M.: anthology preparation, 3, 5, 278–79; culture loss, 57–58; David F. García, 49–50, 52, 57, 65n4; early life, 54–57; engagement with music, 58–60; fieldwork, 53, 57, 64, 287; great-grandparents Maria Ignacita (Rodriquez) and Juan Pedro Romero, 55; life in academia, 6, 7, 41–42, 49, 60–64; synergy model, 54, 60
Roselawn Rovers Return, 181, 182, 183–87, *186*, 188–93, 194. *See also* Irish traditional music project; neurodivergence
Rosenthal, Rob, 255

Schwartz, Jessica A., 265
segregation, 68, 217
SEM (Society for Ethnomusicology): BIPOC women in, 22, 30–31, 34, 36, 46–47; conservative undercurrent, 63; diversity initiatives, 22, 25, 282; diversity lacking, 6, 21–22, 29, 77; diversity of elected positions, 30–31, 46–47; envisioned as instrument of direct action, 15; ethics of travel, 273n11; habits that continue domination, 30–33; oppression in, 7, 22–23, 31, 35; role in supporting activism, 278; social domination, 21, 22, 24–25, 29, 35; structural domination, 23, 27–30, 36. *See also* Crossroads Project on Diversity, Difference, and Under-Representation; Crossroads Section for Difference and Representation
sexism. *See* social domination
Sherif, Abdel Rahman, 133
Shieh, Eric, 278

Shim, Hyejin, 202
Siebers, Tobin, 192
Signmark, 85–86, 90, 91, 93, 97, 98
Skin, A Natural History (Jablonski), 65n2
Small, Christopher, 186
Snyder, Andrew G., 13, 14–15, 240, 251, 283, 284, 285, 286
social capital, 285
social domination: "Anti-essentialism and Intersectionality: Tools to Dismantle the Master's House" (Grillo), 32; of Deaf perspectives, 9, 92, 95, 98–99; diversity initiatives lacking intentionality, 21–22, 29, 31–32, 34, 35, 36–37, 61–62; dysconsciousness, 61, 66n17, 95–96, 285; ethical witnesses, 170; exclusion from society, 193; heteronormativity, 3, 29, 30, 31; *Joyful Militancy: Building Thriving Resistance in Toxic Times* (Montgomery and Bergman), 23; kripping, 197n6; maintained through unexamined habits, 16, 21–22, 29–30, 32–33; maintaining domination, 30–33; nationalism, 133, 162, 165, 202, 204, 208, 209, 225; normalization of dehumanizing behaviour, 28; "Open Letter on Racism in Music Studies" (Brown), 31–32; oppression defined, 29–30; and Palestine, 160, 166, 167, 168, 170, 173; participatory listening, 5, 7–8; race, 202, 206, 208; racism, 22, 30, 31, 245; radical inclusivity, 16, 114; SEM (Society for Ethnomusicology), 7, 21, 22–23, 24–25, 29, 31, 35; sexism, 27, 28, 29, 31, 152, 164, 165, 245; "'Sister, Can You Line It Out?': Zora Neale Hurston and the Sound of Angular Black Womanhood" (Brooks), 35. *See also* Black Lives Matter (BLM) movement; class; gender; gendered violence; hearing-centrism; racism; White supremacy
social justice. *See* accessibility; Black Lives Matter (BLM) movement; diversity
Sordinas, Augustus, 43
Soviet montage theory, 143
Sprengel, Darci, 11, 126

Starosielski, Nicole, 265
stereotypes: Africans, 133–34; conjunto as working class, 12–13; intellectual disabilities, 182, 192, 195; Manitos, 58; music and deafness, 92, 96; queer people, 111; Texas Mexican music, 219–20, 231, 233. *See also* Inuit stereotypes
stereotype threats, 26
structural domination, 23, 27–30, 36
structural violence, 35–36, 161, 163, 164, 166–67. *See also* gendered violence
Stuckey, Sterling, 23
Sulawesi, 263, 265
synergy, 285
systemic racism. *See* institutional racism

Tagaq, Tanya, 147: *Animism* (album), 143; *Anuraaqtuq* (album), 143; deep listening as a form of redress, 152–54; first viewing of *Nanook of the North* (Flaherty), 145; hungry listening, 144; improvisation, 146, 147, 148, 150; Inuti Tapiriit Kanatami, 145; katajjaq (Inuit throat singing), 11, 142, 146–47, 152, 153; live score to *Nanook of the North* (Flaherty), 142, 143–44, 146–47, 148, 150, 151, 152; musical transcendence, 143–44; performing body, 146–48, 153; pre-screening talk, 142–43; primary emotions, 143, 152–53; Toronto International Film Festival (TIFF) commission, 143, 145–46. *See also* Inuit stereotypes
Tayeb, Leila, 134
Taylor, Breonna, 21
Tilley, Leslie, 280
Tilly, Charles, 242
Titon, Jeff Todd, 196
toxic masculinity, 66n17, 167, 174
Treviño, Roberto, 217–18
Trout Powell, Eve, 133–34
Trump, Donald, 44, 219
truth telling, 4–8, 14, 16
Tuck, Eve, 37n2, 57
Turino, Thomas, 186, 190, 230, 248
Turner, Victor, 190

UCLA (University of California, Los Angeles): Afro-Cuban ensemble residency, 46; Brenda M. Romero, 59, 60; Chicanx Studies Department, 41; Department of Ethnomusicology, 42; Global Jazz Studies Program, 42, 45; Herb Alpert School of Music, 40; Mexican Arts Series, 45; Special Opportunity Fellowship, 59; sponsoring SEM (Society for Ethnomusicology) conference, 47; Susan M. Asai, 200, 205; UCLA Chicano Studies Research Center, 41

United Nations Conference on Climate Change (COP26), 260, 271

United Nations Entity for Gender Equality and the Empowerment of Women, 161

Varela, Francisco, 78
Vietnam War activism, 203
vulnerability: of Canadian Indigenous women, 152; of neurodivergent individuals, 190; in Palestine, 161, 162, 165, 169, 174; as a privilege, 168, 173; required for justice-oriented ethnomusicology, 16, 22, 36

Weedon, Chris, 92, 94
Wendell, Susan, 192

White, James H., 144
White fragility, 31
Whiteness, 13, 123, 126, 129–30, 132, 133, 134, 202, 280n2
White supremacy: Black female spectatorship, 149; coalitional work, 210; created tensions between racial communities, 213; Crossroads Section for Difference and Representation, 3; in Egypt, 11, 125, 132, 137; logics, 27; *Nanook of the North* (Flaherty), 149; new movements, 286; as obstacle to a just society, 245; Pink Menno, 112, 118; as productive human endeavor, 28–29; at SEM (Society for Ethnomusicology), 30–31; supports an economy of dependence, 131; undoing, 8, 24–25, 35–36; White academic field, 280n1
Wolfe, Patrick, 169

X, Malcolm, 49, 77, 210
xenophobia, 3, 163

Young, Iris Marion, 193
"Yuri Kochiyama, Malcolm X!" (Jon Jangtet) (song), 210

www.ingramcontent.com/pod-product-compliance
Lightning Source LLC
Chambersburg PA
CBHW021833220426
43663CB00005B/227